GCSE Computer Science for AQA 8525

Kevin R Bond

Educational Computing Services Ltd

Structure of the book

The structure of this book follows closely the structure of AQA's 8525 GCSE Computer Science specification for first teaching from September 2020. The content of the book has been constructed with the aim of promoting good teaching and learning, so where relevant practical activities have been suggested and questions posed for the student to answer. The book includes stimulus material to promote discussion and deeper thinking about the subject. Additional material to support teaching and learning will be available from the publisher's website. Please note that this additional material has not been entered in an AQA approval process.

About the author

Dr Kevin R Bond is an experienced author with a proven track record of successful writing for AQA's Computing specifications. Kevin has 24 years of examining experience. He also has many more years of experience teaching Computing and Computer Science. Before becoming a computer science teacher, he worked in industry as a senior development engineer and systems analyst designing both hardware and software systems.

Published in 2020 by
Educational Computing Services Ltd
42 Mellstock Road
Aylesbury
Bucks
HP21 7NU
United Kingdom
Tel: 01296 433004
e-mail: mail@educational-computing.co.uk

Every effort has been made to trace copyright holders and to obtain their permission for the use of copyrighted material. We apologise if any have been overlooked. The authors and publishers will gladly receive information enabling them to rectify any reference or credit in future editions.

First published in 2020

ISBN 978-1-8381026-0-9

Text © Kevin R Bond 2020
Original illustrations © Kevin R Bond 2020
Cover photograph © Kevin R Bond 2020

The right of Kevin R Bond to be identified as author of this work has been asserted by them in accordance with the Copyright, Designs and Patents Act 1988.

All rights reserved. No part of this publication may be reproduced or transmitted in any form or by any means, electronic or mechanical, including photocopy, recording or any information storage retrieval system, without permission in writing from the publisher or under licence from the Copyright Licensing Agency Limited, of Saffron House, 6 -10 Kirby Street, London, EC1N 8TS.

Approval message from AQA

> The core content of this textbook has been approved by AQA for use with our qualification. This means that we have checked that it broadly covers the specification and that we are satisfied with the overall quality. We have also approved the digital version of this book. We do not however check or approve any links or any functionality. Full details of our approval process can be found on our website.
>
> We approve print and digital textbooks because we know how important it is for teachers and students to have the right resources to support their teaching and learning. However, the publisher is ultimately responsible for the editorial control and quality of this book.
>
> Please note that when teaching the GCSE (8525) course, you must refer to AQA's specification as your definitive source of information. While this book has been written to match the specification, it cannot provide complete coverage of every aspect of the course.
>
> A wide range of other useful resources can be found on the relevant subject pages of our website: aqa.org.uk.

Acknowledgements

The author and publisher are grateful to the following for permission to reproduce images, clipart and other copyright material in this book under licence or otherwise:

Chapter 1.1
- Figure 1.1.1 Ball of wool Shutterstock / 59259781.
- Figure 1.1.1 Woollen pullover Shutterstock / 85713035.
- Figure 1.1.1 Head silhouette Shutterstock / 152509136
- Table 1.1.1 Music stave Shutterstock / 85713035.
- Figure 1.1.9 London underground map Reg. User No 16/E/3021/P Pulse Creative Ltd.

Chapter 1.2
- Figure 1.2.1 Silhouette and flight of steps Shutterstock / 145794110.
- Figure 1.2.2 Several flights of stairs Shutterstock / 349238483.
- Figure 1.2.3 Lift Shutterstock / 63152726.

Chapter 2.3
- Figure 2.3.2 Capstan Shutterstock / 381034510.

Chapter 2.6
- Figure 2.6.1 Queue of people in silhouette Shutterstock / 253319245.

Chapter 2.7
- Figure 2.7.1 Computer Shutterstock / 1226401.
- Figure 2.7.1 Keyboard Shutterstock / 58335720.

Chapter 2.9
- Figure 2.9.1 Computer Shutterstock / 329817896.

Chapter 3.3
- Figure 3.3.1 Highway code signs are based on Highway code signs © Crown copyright 2007, and are reproduced under Open Government Licence v3.0.
- Figure 3.3.2 Communicating machines Shutterstock / 1226401.
- Page 48 Tree stump Shutterstock / 97674011

Chapter 3.6
- Figure 3.6.1 Digital camera Shutterstock / 107741804.
- Figure 3.6.2 Mixing colours Shutterstock / 466868669.

Chapter 3.7
- Page 68 Tuning fork Shutterstock / 216877381.
- Figure 3.7.1 Oscilloscope Alamy / A24350.

Chapter 3.8
- Page 73 Man on suitcase Shutterstock / 622465202.
- Figure 3.8.2 Tree Shutterstock / 554825683.

Chapter 4.5.1
- Figure 4.5.1.1 John von Neumann Los Alamos National Laboratory / http://www.lanl.gov/resources/web-policies/copyright-legal.php.
- Figure 4.5.1.3 Papertape Licensed under the Creative Commons Attribution-Share Alike 3.0 Unported license / User: Poil-commonswiki.
- Figure 4.5.1.4 ENIAC / U.S. Army photo, http://ftp.arl.army.mil/~mike/comphist/.

Chapter 4.5.2
- Magnetic core Licensed under the Creative Commons Attribution-Share Alike 3.0 Unported license / Konstantin Lanzet.

Chapter 4.5.3
- Figure 4.5.3.1 BIOS Shutterstock / 513290245.
- Figure 4.5.3.1 CPU Shutterstock / 222009121.
- Figure 4.5.3.5 Bottleneck Shutterstock / 275770565.
- Figure 4.5.3.9 3-D scene rendering © 1995 Kwok Cheung Yeung now Dr Kwok Cheung Yeung. Image from Kwok's A level project 1995.

Chapter 4.5.5
- Figure 4.5.5.5 Sony memory stick image by KB Alpha (Own work) [CC BY 3.0 (http://creativecommons.org/licenses/by/3.0)], via Wikimedia Commons.
- Figure 4.5.5.5 SanDisk CompactFlash image courtesy of Western Digital Corporation.
- Figure 4.5.5.8 Flash drive © D-Kuru/Wikimedia Commons
- Figure 4.5.5.10 Flash drive innards Image reproduced with kind permission of StorageReview.com
- Figure 4.5.5.11 Google data centre image reproduced with kind permission Google/Connie Zhou

Chapter 5
- Figure 5.5 Reproduced with kind of permission of Claes-Göran Andersson
- Figure 5.17 Server Shutterstock /53738941

Chapter 6.2.2
- Figure 6.2.2.6 Skull and crossbones road sign Shutterstock / 576781585
- Page 6.2.2.7 Prisoner behind bars Shutterstock / 360621752
- Page 6.2.2.7 Silhouette of a hacker Shutterstock / 515918593

Chapter 6.3
- Figure 6.3.1 Reproduced with kind of permission of Luis von Ahn, Carnegie Mellon University
- Figure 6.3.2 Reproduced with kind of permission of Google Inc.
- Figure 6.3.3 Reproduced with kind of permission of Google Inc.
- Figure 6.3.4 Reproduced with kind of permission of Computing At School

Chapter 8
- Figure 8.2 Nike+ running watch and App (www.flickr.com/ivyfield/4762376623 CC BY 2.0)

Contents

How to use this book	xi
Introduction	xiii
1.1 Representing algorithms	**1**
What is an algorithm?	1
Flowcharts	3
Pseudo-code	6
What is decomposition?	7
What is meant by abstraction?	8
Explaining simple algorithms in terms of their inputs, processing and outputs	13
Determining the purpose of simple algorithms	15
1.2 Efficiency of algorithms	**16**
More than one algorithm can be used to solve a problem	16
Comparing the efficiency of algorithms	16
1.3 Searching algorithms	**21**
Linear search	21
Binary search	23
Comparing linear and binary search algorithms	26
1.4 Sorting algorithms	**28**
Sorting	28
Bubble sort algorithm	28
Merge sort algorithm	33
Comparing and contrasting merge sort and bubble sort algorithms	35
2.1 Data types	**38**
Introduction to programming	38
2.2 Programming concepts	**43**
Variable declaration	43
Constant declaration	44
Assignment	45
Sequence	49
Selection	49
Subroutine	50
Procedures and functions	52
Function	54
Definite (count-controlled) and indefinite (condition-controlled) iteration	59
Nested selection statements	65
Nested iteration statements	66
Using meaningful identifier names	67
2.3 Arithmetic operations in a programming language	**70**
Addition/Subtraction/Multiplication	70
Real division	70
Integer division	71
2.4 Relational operators in a programming language	**74**
Relational operators	74
2.5 Boolean operations in a programming language	**76**
Boolean operators	76
2.6 Data structures	**79**
The concept of data structures	79
One-dimensional array	80
Multi-dimensional arrays	87
Use of records	91
2.7 Input/output and file handling	**92**
Input/output	92
2.8 String-handling operations	**101**
Strings	101
String operations	101
Position	110
Concatenation	110
Character → character code	110
Character code → character	111
String conversion operations	112

2.9 Random number generation in a programming language	**121**
Random number generation	121
Random number generators in programming languages	122
2.10a Subroutines (procedures/functions)	**124**
Concept of subroutines	124
Advantages of using subroutines in programs	125
Using parameters to pass data within programs	126
Using subroutines that return values to the calling routine	130
Declaring local variables	132
Using local variables	133
Why use local variables?	133
2.10b Structured programming	**135**
The structured approach to program design and construction	135
Hierarchy charts	140
Advantages of structured programming	143
2.11 Robust and secure programming	**145**
Be able to write simple data validation routines	145
Program errors - syntax and logic	155
3.1 Number bases	**157**
Meaning of number base	157
Decimal (base 10)	157
Binary (base 2)	157
Hexadecimal (base 16)	158
Binary is used to represent all data and instructions	159
3.2 Converting between number bases	**161**
Converting from decimal to binary	161
Method 1	161
Method 2 - the method of successive division	161
Converting from binary to decimal	162
Converting from decimal to hexadecimal	162
Converting from hexadecimal to decimal	162
Converting from hexadecimal to binary	162
Converting from binary to hexadecimal	163
Using binary to represent decimal whole numbers	163
Using hexadecimal to represent decimal whole numbers	164
3.3 Units of information	**165**
Information	165
Powers of 10	166
Quantities of bytes	166
Powers of 2	167
3.4 Binary arithmetic	**169**
Adding two binary integers	169
Adding three binary integers	171
Shifting bits in a binary number	172
Situations where binary shifts are used	173
3.5 Character encoding	**176**
ASCII	176
Unicode	178
Character form of a decimal digit	179
Grouping of character codes	179
3.6 Representing images	**181**
What is a pixel?	181
Displaying an image	182
Image size of a bitmap	182
Colour depth of a bitmap	183
How does a bitmap represent an image?	184
Bitmap image file sizes	184
Converting a bitmap image into a bitmap	185
Converting binary data into a bitmap image	186
3.7 Representing sound	**187**
Sound is analogue	187
Recording sound in digital form	188
Sampling rate	189

Sample resolution	190
Calculating sound file sizes	190

3.8 Data compression — 192
- What is data compression and why compress? — 192
- Huffman coding — 193
- Run length encoding (RLE) — 198

4.1 Hardware and software — 200
- What is hardware? — 200
- What is software? — 200

4.2 Boolean logic — 201
- Background to logic gates — 201
- Truth tables — 202
- Logic gates — 203
- Constructing truth tables for simple logic circuits — 206
- Creating logic gate circuits — 207
- Boolean variables — 210
- Boolean expressions — 211
- Examples — 212

4.3 Software classification — 215
- What is system software? — 215
- What is application software? — 215
- Understand the need for, and functions of, operating systems (OS) and utility programs — 216

4.4 Classification of programming languages and translation — 219
- Levels of programming language — 219
- Low-level programming languages — 219
- Advantages of programming in machine code and assembly language compared with HLL programming — 222
- Disadvantages of programming in machine code and assembly language compared with HLL programming — 223
- Types of program translator — 224
- Role of an assembler — 224
- Role of a compiler — 224
- Role of an interpreter — 225
- The differences between compilation and interpretation — 225
- Situations in which assemblers, compilers and interpreters would be appropriate — 226

4.5.1 Systems architecture — 228
- Von Neumann architecture — 228
- Characteristics of the von Neumann architecture — 230
- Von Neumann computer system as a collection of subsystems — 231

4.5.2 Systems architecture — 233
- Main memory — 233
- System bus — 237
- Arithmetic and Logic Unit (ALU) — 238
- Control Unit — 239
- Clock — 240

4.5.3 Systems architecture — 242
- Effect of clock speed on CPU performance — 242
- Effect of cache type and cache memory size on CPU performance (Cache type not in AQA specification 8525) — 245
- Effect of Number of processor cores on CPU performance — 247

4.5.4 Systems architecture — 250
- Fetch-Execute cycle — 250

4.5.5 Systems architecture — 251
- Different types of memory, what they are used for and why they are required — 251
- Differences between main memory and secondary storage — 251
- Differences between RAM and ROM — 251
- Why is secondary storage used? — 251
- Magnetic storage — 252
- Solid state storage — 255
- Flash-based solid-state disk (SSD) — 256
- Advantages and disadvantages of solid state, optical and magnetic storage — 258
- Cloud storage — 259

5a Computer networks — 263
- What is a computer network? — 263
- The main types of computer network — 264
- LAN ownership — 265

Wired and wireless networks	267
Star network topology	268
Bus network topology	268
Network protocol	269
5b Network protocols	**271**
What is a network protocol?	271
Common network protocols	271
Internet Message Access Protocol (IMAP)	280
5c Network security	**282**
The need for and importance of network security	282
Network security methods	282
5d Four layer TCP/IP model	**286**
The four layer TCP/IP model	286
Application layer	287
Transport layer	287
Internet or IP (Internet Protocol) layer	288
Link layer	289
6.1 Cyber security threats	**291**
What is cyber security?	291
6.2 Social engineering threats	**291**
Unpatched and/or outdated code	298
Penetration testing	299
6.2.1 Social engineering	**301**
What is social engineering?	301
How to protect against social engineering	303
Blagging (pretexting)	304
Shouldering (or shoulder surfing)	304
Scenario 1 - stealing credentials	305
Scenario 2 - exploiting security vulnerabilities in web browsers	305
Phishing	305
Scenario 3 - malicious attachments	306
Scenario 4 - pop-up ads	306
6.2.2 Malicious code	**309**
Malware	309
Virus	311
Trojan	313
Spyware	315
6.3 Methods to detect and prevent cyber security threats	**317**
Biometric measures	317
Password systems	318
Automatic software updates	322
7.1 Relational databases	**323**
What is a database?	323
What is a relational database?	323
Modelling a relationship between two tables	324
Entity relationship diagram	325
Primary and foreign keys	325
Shorthand way of representing the structure of a table	326
Link tables	327
Types of database	328
7.2 Structured Query Language	**330**
Querying a database	330
Structured Query Language (SQL)	330
Retrieving data from a single table	330
Retrieving data from multiple tables	331
Relational or comparison operators for search condition	333
Deleting data in a single table	334
Inserting data in a single table	334
Updating data in a single table	335
SQL Tutorials	335

8. Ethical impacts of digital technology — 338
- What is ethics? — 338
- The challenges facing legislators in the digital age — 338
- General Data Protection Regulation 2018 — 339
- Geolocation- tracking you and your location — 341
- Investigatory Powers Act 2016 — 342
- Computer based implants — 346
- Issues around copyright of algorithms **(not in AQA specification 8525)** — 347
- Theft of computer code **(not in AQA specification 8525)** — 348
- Cracking and hacking **(not in AQA specification 8525)** — 348
- Environmental impact — 348
- Cyber security — 350
- Cloud storage — 350
- Autonomous vehicles — 350

Index — 365

How to use this book

The structure and content of this textbook maps to sections 3.1 to 3.8 of AQA's GCSE Computer Science specification (8525). For example, the chapter number 1.1 corresponds to specification section 3.1.1. The chapter title is Representing algorithms. The chapters in the book do not use the leading 3 as this designates Subject content – GCSE in the specification.

Flipped classroom

This textbook has been written with the flipped classroom approach very much in mind. This approach reverses the conventional classroom lesson and homework model of teaching. Instead, chapters in this textbook should be used to prepare for a lesson so that classroom-time can be devoted to exercises, projects, and discussions.

The features in this book include:

Learning objectives

Learning objectives linked to the requirements of the specification are specified at the beginning of each chapter.

Key concept — Concepts that you will need to understand and to be able to define or explain are highlighted in blue and emboldened, e.g. **Integers**. The same concepts appear in the glossary for ease of reference.

Key principle — Principles that you will need to understand and to be able to define or explain are highlighted in blue and emboldened, e.g. **Abstraction**. The same principles appear in the glossary for ease of reference.

Key fact / **Key point** — Facts and points that are useful to know because they aid in understanding concepts and principles are highlighted in blue and emboldened, e.g. **Whole number:** Whole number is another name for an integer number.

Information / **Background** — References information that has the potential to assist and contribute to a student's learning, e.g. Read Section 4.4.2 for more background on the arithmetic and logic unit. Background knowledge that could also contribute to a student's learning.

Did you know? / **Extension Material** — "Did you know?" - interesting facts to enliven learning. "Extension Material" - content that lies beyond the specification.

Task — Activity to deepen understanding and reinforce learning.

Programming tasks — Practical activity involving the use of a programming language to deepen understanding and reinforce learning of concepts and principles.

Questions — Short questions that probe and develop your understanding of concepts and principles as well as creating opportunities to apply and reinforce your knowledge and skills.

Web links for this book

Resources, solutions to questions, errata and the URLs of all websites referenced in this book are recorded at www.educational-computing.co.uk/aqacs/gcsecs8525.html. Past papers and mark schemes are available from
https://www.aqa.org.uk/subjects/computer-science-and-it/gcse/computer-science-8525/assessment-resources
Educational Computing Services are not responsible for third party content online, there may be some changes to this content that are outside our control. If you find that a Web link doesn't work please email webadmin@educational-computing.co.uk with the details and we will endeavour to fix the problem or to provide an alternative. Please also note that these links are not AQA approved.

Introduction

If you are reading this book then you will already have chosen to be a part of an exciting future, for Computer Science is at the heart of an information processing revolution. This revolution applies not just to seeking patterns of meaning in data accumulated on an unprecedented scale by the huge growth in connected computing devices but also the realisation that all forms of life are controlled by genetic codes. Genetic codes are instructions in a procedural information sense which together with the environment that they inhabit control and guide the development of organisms.

Computer scientists concern themselves with
- representations of information in patterns of symbols, known as data or data representations,
- the most appropriate representation for this data
- the procedures in the form of instructions that can transform this data into new forms of information.

The procedures themselves are also a form of information of an instructional kind.

The key process in Computer Science is **abstraction** which means building models which represent aspects of behaviour in the real-world which are of interest. For example, if we wanted to build an automated recommendation system for an online book store, we might choose to record the types of book and number of each type purchased as well as details that identify the respective customer.

Computer Science is not alone in building abstractions, mathematics and the natural sciences also build abstractions but their models only serve to describe and explain whereas Computer Science must, in addition, perform actions on and with the data that has been modelled if it is to solve problems. These actions are described by **algorithms** or step-by-step instructions which form what is called the **automation** stage of problem solving. Whilst it is true that automation of tasks existed before Computer Science, their nature involved concrete, real-world objects, e.g. the Jacquard loom, not informational abstractions such as an online book recommendation system.

So far it has not been necessary to mention digital computers. Digital computers are just the current means by which algorithms can be implemented to execute on data. Both algorithms and the models on which they act need to be **implemented**: algorithms in the form of code or instructions that a digital computer can understand, i.e. a computer program; models in data structures in a programming language.

Section 1 is largely about the fundamentals of algorithms, their efficiency, and two types of algorithms: searching algorithms and sorting algorithms.
Section 2 is about programming.
Section 3 is about fundamentals of data representation.
Section 4 is about computer systems, in particular
- What is hardware and what is software
- Boolean logic and logic gates, the building bricks of hardware
- Software classification and translators
- Systems architecture.

Section 5 is about fundamentals of computer networks.
Section 6 is about fundamentals of cyber security, in particular
- Cyber security threats
- Social engineering
- Malicious code
- Methods to detect and prevent cyber security threats.

Section 7 is about relational databases and Structured Query Language (SQL).
Section 8 is about Ethical, legal and environmental impacts of digital technology on wider society, including issues of privacy.
This textbook covers Python (version 3), C# and VB.NET, the programming languages supported by AQA for examinations from 2022 onwards.
In addition, it also covers programming languages Java and Pascal/Delphi.

1 Fundamentals of algorithms

1 Fundamentals of algorithms

Learning objectives:

- *Understand and explain the term algorithm*
- *Understand and explain the term decomposition*
- *Understand and explain the term abstraction*
- *Use a systematic approach to problem solving and algorithm creation representing those algorithms using pseudo-code, program code and flowcharts*
- *Explain simple algorithms in terms of their inputs, processing and outputs*
- *Determine the purpose of simple algorithms.*

1.1 Representing algorithms

What is an algorithm?

An algorithm is a precise description of steps necessary to accomplish a certain task or solve a particular problem. We call the collection of steps a method or procedure.

The notion of an algorithm is not limited to computer science.

Table 1.1.1 shows some fields of human activity in which algorithms are used.

Process	Algorithm	Example steps
Knitting a cardigan	Knitting pattern	1st row: Pearl9, Knit2, ...
Putting together flat pack furniture	Assembly instructions	Screw side panel to front panel
Bisecting an angle with compass and ruler	Drawing instructions	Place the point of the compass on A, and swing an arc ED
Playing music	Musical score	🎵

Table 1.1.1 Some fields of human activity in which algorithms are used

In each case the process is carried out by a human being.

Figure 1.1.1 shows that the process of knitting a cardigan consists of

- an input - balls of wool of a particular colour and yarn
- an output - the finished cardigan
- a processor - a human
- a precise finite sequence of steps expressed in a code which the processor (in this case a human) can interpret

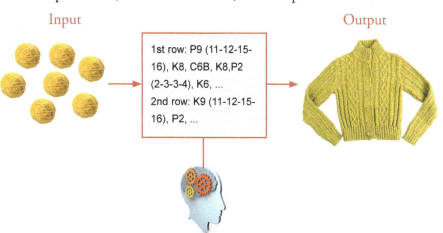

Figure 1.1.1 The process of knitting a cardigan

Key concept

Algorithm:
A description, independent of any programming language, of a procedure that solves a problem or task.
It consists of a precisely described sequence of steps for solving a problem or completing a task.
The algorithm must terminate and its action must be capable of completing in a finite amount of time.

Key concept

Sequence:
Consecutive steps or groups of steps processed one after another in the order that they arise.

1 Fundamentals of algorithms

An algorithm is a method for solving a problem (a task).
Interesting algorithms are ones which involve repeating instructions many times, something which a digital computer is capable of doing.

> All but the simplest of algorithms are challenging to design because:
> - The description of the algorithm has to be absolutely unambiguous in the sense that different interpretations are excluded
> - Each application of the algorithm for particular given inputs/problem instance has to reach the same result
> - An algorithm must be designed in a such a way that it works correctly for each of the possible inputs/problem instances and finishes in a finite time
> - An algorithm may have many problem instances as possible inputs, too many for it to be possible to test all of them.

Most cooking recipes are not algorithms. They are expressed too imprecisely and rely too much on the knowledge, experience and skill of the cook to be correctly interpreted. A less experienced cook may easily misinterpret the recipe's instructions or worse still not understand some. The range of input is also limited.

Tasks

1. This task illustrates the difficulty of writing an algorithm which is not open to misinterpretation.
   Using pen/pencil and paper execute the following instructions by hand:
   1. Draw a diagonal line
   2. Draw another diagonal line connected to the top of the first one
   3. Draw a straight line from the point where the diagonal lines meet
   4. Draw a horizontal line over the straight line
   5. At the bottom of the straight line, draw a curvy line
   6. Draw a diagonal line from the bottom of the first diagonal to the straight line
   7. Draw a diagonal line from the bottom of the second diagonal to the straight line

   What object have you drawn?
   Compare your result with a friend's.
   (CSInside, Algorithm Development, reproduced with kind permission of Professor Quintin Cutts, Glasgow university)

2. Write an algorithm to log into a school computer.

1.1 Representing algorithms

Flowcharts

A flowchart is a way of expressing an algorithm.

A flowchart expresses an algorithm in a diagram such as shown in *Figure 1.1.2*.

This flowchart is equivalent to the sequence of operations expressed in pseudo-code[1], a compact, informal language, as follows

>Turn on red light
>
>Wait 30 seconds
>
>Turn off red light

Just as a programmer might use pseudo-code to plan the sequence of operations in a program before writing it, so a programmer could instead use a flowchart.

A flowchart expresses the logic of an algorithm using flowchart symbols or basic elements shown in *Figure 1.1.3*.

A flowchart is interpreted by reading it from top to bottom, i.e. from Start to Stop.

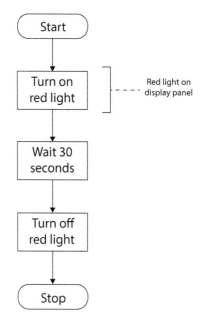

Figure 1.1.2 Sequential flowchart

There are seven basic elements or symbols commonly used in flowcharts:

- **Terminal symbol:** Indicates with Start and Stop the start and end of the algorithm
- **Operation:** Indicates any type of operation, e.g. Set variable x to the value 5
- **Input/Output:** Indicates any input or output, e.g. INPUT x, OUTPUT y
- **Decision:** Used to ask a question whose answer can be either TRUE or FALSE (YES or NO), e.g. "Is x = 5?". The flow path selected which exits the decision diamond depends on the answer
- **Connector:** Connectors are used to connect breaks in the flowchart, often used to split a large flowchart into smaller sections that can fit neatly onto a page
- **Control flow:** Used to show the direction of flow - can be down the page, up the page and across the page in either direction
- **Comment:** Is not part of the logic but is commonly used to describe and make clear what is happening at a particular place in the flowchart.

A flowchart can be drawn conveniently for simple problems only.

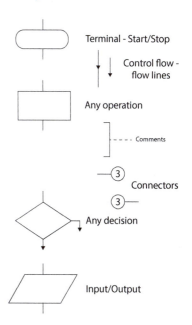

Figure 1.1.3 Flowchart symbols

Information

Download and install the RAPTOR flowchart-based programming environment from http://raptor.martincarlisle.com/.
Raptor enables the drawing of flowcharts (the symbols are slightly different in places from the standard flowchart symbols). These flowcharts can then be executed in Raptor in run mode or single-step mode. Behind the scenes, Raptor turns a flowchart into a form that can be executed, i.e. a program.
Watch the introductory tutorial at https://www.youtube.com/watch?v=ZcAALK3movs

---

1 See later in the chapter for an explanation of pseudo-code.

1 Fundamentals of algorithms

Figure 1.1.4 shows a branch (or jump) flowchart describing the sequence of operations in a human activity which consists of reading and reviewing a book.

This flowchart uses the decision flowchart element ◇ which has two possible outflows (branches) and one inflow.

In the example, if the answer is No to the question, "Want to review?", then the flow follows the branch labelled No.

If the answer is Yes then the flow follows the branch labelled Yes.

Taking the No branch avoids the Write review operation.

Figure 1.1.5 shows a loop flowchart.

The part of the flowchart "Read next page" and "End of book?", taken, together, is an example of a loop.

A loop represents a part of the flowchart which may be repeated a definite or indefinite number of times.

In this example, the loop repeats as many times as there are pages after the first page. This flowchart assumes that the book has at least two pages.

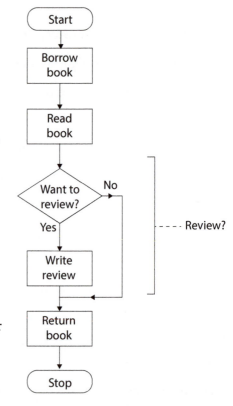

Figure 1.1.4 Branch flowchart

> **Did you know?**
>
> **When informal language fails to communicate:**
> In the next section you will explore pseudo-code. Pseudo-code is an informal language which you can make up, i.e. write the rules for. It is very important that your pseudo-code communicates what is to be done.
> AQA has specified a pseudo-code that seems to do its job of communicating very well but you don't have to stick to AQA's pseudo-code at
> http://filestore.aqa.org.uk/resources/computing/AQA-8525-TG-PC.PDF.
> You can invent your own. But take care. The following anecdote illustrates by analogy what can go wrong. The famous physicist Paul Dirac once was writing on a blackboard during a lecture and a student in the class raised his hand and said, "I don't understand that particular step you have just written down."
> Dirac stood silent for a long time until the student asked if Professor Dirac was going to answer the question. To which Dirac said, "There was no question."
> Another lecturer might have interpreted the student's informal way of asking a question and answered the student but not Dirac. Dirac was a stickler for the correct use of language.

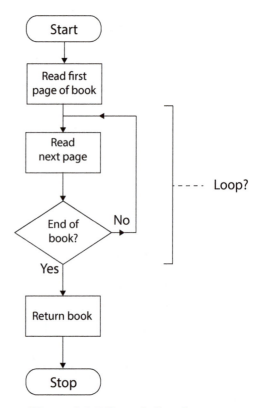

Figure 1.1.5 Branch flowchart

Tasks

❸ Redraw the flowchart in *Figure 1.1.5* so that it caters for a single-page book.

1.1 Representing algorithms

Figure 1.1.6 shows a simple problem which uses a loop, a loop counter, `i`, and an output operation, `OUTPUT i`.

The loop counter `i` is first initialised to 0 (`i ← 0`).

Its value is then increased by 1 from 0 to 1 (`i ← i + 1`).

Next, this value is outputted (the meaning of outputted could be: send the value to the computer monitor screen).

The value of `i` is checked next to see if it is 5 (Is `i = 5?`).

If it isn't, the No branch is followed returning the flow to the operation
$$i ← i + 1.$$
where the value of the loop counter `i` is increased by 1 from 1 to 2 (`i ← i + 1`) when `i = 1`.

This new value of `i` is then outputted.

Looping continues until `i = 5`.

The Yes branch is then followed and the flow stops.

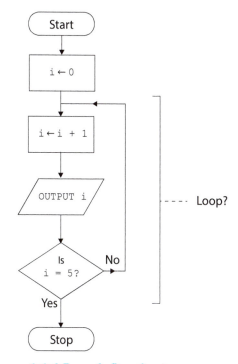

Figure 1.1.6 Branch flowchart

Tasks

4. Watch the following YouTube videos and then, using Raptor, create the flowcharts demonstrated in the videos.

    All these flowcharts using standard symbols are downloadable to study in pdf format from
    www.educational-computing.co.uk/GCSE/RaptorFlowchartExercises/TasksCh1.1.html.

    "Run" these flowcharts as described in the video (a program is executed which is generated in each case from the flowchart).

    These exercises are a good introduction to several important programming concepts.

    (a) https://www.youtube.com/watch?v=S9MimRICmKQ
    (b) https://www.youtube.com/watch?v=LQ76hbyE3gM
    (c) https://www.youtube.com/watch?v=lcVHOPou0UI
    (d) https://www.youtube.com/watch?v=GCNbWOh3iDM
    (e) https://www.youtube.com/watch?v=8BiWSXSMxyo
    (f) https://www.youtube.com/watch?v=zt5-qMgPJt8
    (g) https://www.youtube.com/watch?v=4b4aZ5GqAAM
    (h) https://www.youtube.com/watch?v=XVrOG7qaXgw
    (i) https://www.youtube.com/watch?v=5AP4EpLSwS8
    (j) https://www.youtube.com/watch?v=OnQ87Dw14U4
    (k) https://www.youtube.com/watch?v=kXxAGX0__Vo
    (l) https://www.youtube.com/watch?v=k0blfWj8M4M

1 Fundamentals of algorithms

Pseudo-code

Pseudo-code is a programming-like informal language which is employed to communicate a solution to a problem in a way that is independent of any particular programming language (programming languages are formal languages).

We can express an algorithm in pseudo-code before programming it in a particular programming language to create a program (a program is a sequence of instructions that can be interpreted either in text form or in 1s and 0s form by an electronic computer).

Figure 1.1.7 shows the steps (algorithm) expressed in a pseudo-code to swap the values in two variables, x and y before outputting the value of y.

> **The steps in a pseudo-code to swap the values in two variables x and y using a temporary variable temp before outputting the value of y**
>
> ```
> Temp ← x
> x ← y
> y ← Temp
> OUTPUT y
> ```

Figure 1.1.7 The steps expressed in pseudo-code to swap the values in two variables

There is no standard pseudo-code, that is why it is labelled informal.

This particular pseudo-code uses the symbol ← for an assignment operation, e.g. x ← 6 assigns the value 6 to the variable x.

Equally it could have used pseudo-code Set x to 6 for the assignment operation. You may invent your own pseudo-code. The most important thing to bear in mind is communication, i.e. "does your pseudo-code communicate steps that can be understood and easily followed?".

The pseudo-code that will be used in AQA's exam question papers can be downloaded from

http://filestore.aqa.org.uk/resources/computing/AQA-8525-TG-PC.PDF

The pseudo-code given in *Figure 1.1.7* is interpreted as follows:

If variable x contains 6 and variable y, 3, for example, then x will end up containing 3 and y, 6 after following (executing) these steps. The value 6 is then outputted.

Table 1.1.2 shows how the state of the variables x, y, and Temp changes, step-by-step.

> **Key concept**
>
> **Pseudo-code:**
> Pseudo-code is a programming-like language which is employed to communicate a solution to a problem in a way that is independent of any particular production programming language.

> **Key concept**
>
> **Variable:**
> A variable can be thought of as a container for a value, e.g. the integer 6.
> Like a physical container, a variable may be empty in which case we say that its value is undefined.

> **Key concept**
>
> **Assignment operation:**
> An operation which replaces the value contained by a variable with another value,
> e.g. if variable y contains 3 then the assignment operation y ← 6 replaces the 3 with 6.

> **Key concept**
>
> **Assignment operator:**
> The pseudo-code symbol ← is often used for the assignment operator.

Step		x	y	Temp
Temp ← x	Before	6	3	?
	After	6	3	6
x ← y	Before	6	3	6
	After	3	3	6
y ← Temp	Before	3	3	6
	After	3	6	6

Table 1.1.2 States of x, y and Temp whilst stepping through pseudo-code

Tasks

5 Write the pseudo-code equivalent of each of the flowcharts considered in tasks 4(a) to 4(g) inclusive.

What is decomposition?

Breaking big problems into smaller problems, or subproblems, is called decomposition.

It may be far easier to deal with a number of smaller problems each of which accomplishes a single identifiable task than one large problem.

If the subproblems can be solved directly then the decomposition is complete.

If not then subproblems are further divided and so on until small enough problems result which identify a single task and which can be directly coded, e.g. DrawCircle.

When decomposition is used to plan a solution it is called **top-down design**.

> The process of dividing the problem into smaller and smaller sub-problems is done until the sub-problems are
> - manageably small, and
> - solvable separately, i.e. relatively independent of one another.

Key principle

Decomposition:
Decomposition means breaking a problem into a number of subproblems, so that each subproblem accomplishes an identifiable task, which itself may be further subdivided. The process should continue until the subproblems are small enough to each identify a single task which can be directly coded in a subroutine.

Key principle

Subroutine:
A well-designed subroutine is one which contains only one function, e.g. to return the square of a given integer, or is one that performs a logically-related task, e.g. DrawCircle.

Example

Suppose the problem is calculating the area of a circle of a given radius.

Although this is a trivial example, it is intended to illustrate the process of decomposition in a simple way.

Figure 1.1.8 shows the breaking of this problem into three trivial subproblems.

```
Problem:
    Calculate the area of a circle of given radius r
Sub-problems:
    Get radius
    Calculate area
    Output area
```

Figure 1.1.8 Decomposition of a problem into sub-problems

Tasks

6 Decompose the problem of calculating the circumference of a circle of radius r.

7 Decompose the problem of calculating the area of a rectangle of width w, and height h.

8 Decompose the problem of finding and showing the average of four numbers.

1 Fundamentals of algorithms

What is meant by abstraction?

The human brain is an exceptional piece of biological machinery capable of recognising objects even when most of their detail has been removed.

This is illustrated in *Figure 1.1.9* which is an abstraction of an image of a child. The child depicted in the image is a real person and the image is a particular abstraction of the real child.

Figure 1.1.9 Silhouette image of a child

Humans deal with abstractions all the time, because they are useful in everyday problem solving.

For example, the solution to the problem of travelling from Marylebone to Russell Square by London Underground involves taking the Bakerloo line from Marylebone as far as Piccadilly Circus then changing to the Piccadilly line and travelling as far as Russell Square.

The map of the London underground shown in *Figure 1.1.10* is a useful abstraction. It is not the real thing but a useful depiction (abstraction) of it.

What makes it useful is that it does not include more details than needed to succeed in using it to reach the desired destination.

Figure 1.1.10 London underground map based on a design by Harry Beck

In this instance, the benefit of this kind of abstraction of the real world derives from the fact that **unnecessary details have been removed**.

Ease of use is a very good reason to work with an abstraction rather than the real thing.

What we end up with when unnecessary details are removed is an example of an **abstraction**, in particular **representational abstraction**.

> **Key principle**
>
> **Abstraction:**
> Abstraction is a process in which unnecessary details are removed from a problem to make the problem easier to solve.

Complexity is removed to make a problem easier to handle and solve.

The representation of the London Underground in Harry Beck's map design does not contain unnecessary detail such as roads and buildings above the underground rail system. The layout of the stations is also adjusted to make the map easy to use.

The London Underground map is said to be a **model** of the real underground system.

Models are used to understand the world by removing complexity and focussing on details relevant to the task in hand.

1.1 Representing algorithms

Example

Suppose we wish to calculate the sum of the first n natural numbers.

We have two choices of methods for calculating this sum $1 + 2 + 3 + 4 + ... + (n - 1) + n$ and $\dfrac{n \times (n + 1)}{2}$

Try both formulae for n = 6 and other values to convince yourself that the second formula produces the same result as the first.

Now we have two ways of decomposing the problem, Method 1 and Method 2.

Table 1.1.3 shows the two methods expressed in the pseudo-code defined by AQA pseudo-code.

Figure 1.1.11 shows Method 1 in equivalent flowchart form.

Figure 1.1.12 shows Method 2 in equivalent flowchart form.

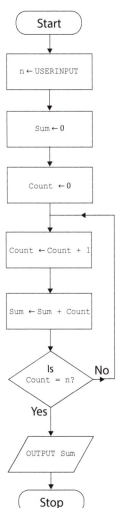

Method 1	Method 2

n ← USERINPUT
Sum ← 0
Count ← 0
REPEAT
  Count ← Count + 1
  Sum ← Sum + Count
UNTIL Count = n
OUTPUT Sum
	n ← USERINPUT
	Sum ← (n * (n + 1)) / 2
	OUTPUT Sum

Table 1.1.3 AQA Pseudo-code for Methods 1 and 2

Figure 1.1.12 Method 2 flowchart

Figure 1.1.11 Method 1 flowchart

The fact that the pseudo-code used in *Table 1.1.3* is slightly different from the pseudo-code used earlier in this chapter emphasises the fact that pseudo-code is an informal language, i.e. there are no hard and fast rules that must be obeyed.

This is not the case in a formal language, where in constructing statements with it the rules must be obeyed. Break a rule and the statement will be rejected because it is invalid.

Tasks

9. Download the Raptor flowchart **SumFirstNMethod1.rap** from
www.educational-computing.co.uk/GCSE/RaptorFlowchartPrograms/TasksCh1.1.html
Run this flowchart in single-step mode in Raptor for small values of n and observe how it works.

10. Download the Raptor flowchart **SumFirstNMethod2.rap** from
www.educational-computing.co.uk/GCSE/RaptorFlowchartPrograms/TasksCh1.1.html
Run this flowchart in single-step mode in Raptor for small values of n and observe how it works.

1 Fundamentals of algorithms

Process abstraction

When developing an algorithm that will be turned into a computer program for execution by computer, we write the steps of the algorithm in terms of what a computer can do.

These algorithm steps tend to be rather simple ones because a computer has a limited number of instructions it can execute, e.g. ADD, SUBTRACT, COMPARE, JUMP, etc.

This makes computer algorithms that do complex tasks long and intricate.

Hence computer algorithms can be

- hard to understand
- difficult to get correct
- tough to modify.

Is there a way to deal with this complexity?

There is, but only if the computer could be made "smarter" by performing complex operations in a single step.

To achieve this we must be able to **abstract away** the many simple steps of a specific task by hiding them behind a single name!

This is done by grouping a set of statements that accomplish a specific task into a "routine" and giving the "routine" a unique name. Then, whenever the specific task needs to be performed, the routine is **called** by name to execute the task conceptually as a single step.

The `CalculateSumTo` routine in *Figure 1.1.13* does many individual steps to calculate the sum, but it is not necessary to know the details (Note that this loop uses WHILE something true, i.e. Count ≠ n).

These details can be abstracted away inside a routine (formally a subroutine) and from thereon referred to by name only, i.e. `CalculateSumTo`.

To use this routine we call it by name as shown in *Figure 1.1.14*.

```
SUBROUTINE CalculateSumTo(n)
   Sum ← 0            NOT EQUAL TO
   Count ← 0             Raptor uses !=
   WHILE Count ≠ n
      Count ← Count + 1
      Sum ← Sum + Count
   ENDWHILE
   RETURN Sum
ENDSUBROUTINE
```

Figure 1.1.13 Subroutine CalculateSumTo

```
NatNum ← USERINPUT
Result ← CalculateSumTo(NatNum)
OUTPUT Result
```

Figure 1.1.14 Using CalculateSumTo subroutine

All that need concern us now is that the routine does what it is required to do, i.e. given a value for variable `NatNum`, calculate the sum of the natural numbers up to and including this value.

Figure 1.1.15 shows how subroutine `CalculateSumTo` is called in Raptor. The sum is returned in `Sum`.

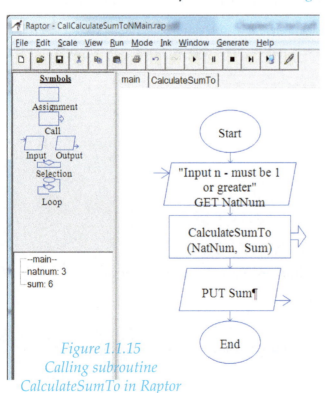

Figure 1.1.15 Calling subroutine CalculateSumTo in Raptor

Figure 1.1.16 shows subroutine `CalculateSumTo` flowchart in Raptor.

The power of abstraction in dealing with complexity means that the steps to calculate the sum of the first n natural numbers need writing just once.

Thereafter, all requirements to calculate this sum can be satisfied by simply calling this routine.

Subroutines allow different values to be "passed" and changed on each call to the subroutine.

These "passed" values are called parameters. `CalculateSumTo` has such parameters.

In Raptor they are `n` and `Sum` as shown in *Figure 1.1.16*. Parameter `n` can only be passed into the routine whilst parameter `Sum` can only be passed out.

Parameters make it easier to change the behaviour of the subroutine because each call to the subroutine can send a different initial value or set of initial values if there is more than one input parameter.

In Raptor, these values are passed in and out in `NatNum` and `Sum` respectively as shown in *Figure 1.1.15*.

In *Figure 1.1.14*, a value is passed in `NatNum` and `CalculateSumTo(NatNum)` evaluates to the calculated sum.

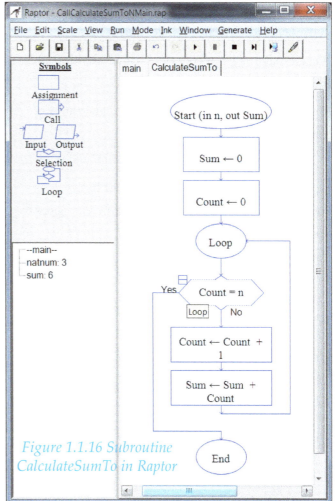

Figure 1.1.16 Subroutine CalculateSumTo in Raptor

To make this clearer we will use a subroutine that is already available in Raptor to draw circles of different sizes.

The subroutine is `Draw_Circle( x, y, radius, color, filled)`. The American spelling of `color` is used. It has five parameters, `x`, `y`, `radius`, `color`, `filled`. Their purpose is described in *Table 1.1.4*.

x	x coordinate of the centre of the circle
y	y coordinate of the centre of the circle
radius	radius of the circle
color	colour to be used for the outline of the circle and if the next parameter, filled is TRUE, the fill colour of the circle
filled	If TRUE the circle is filled, if FALSE it is not.

Table 1.1.4 The purpose of the parameters of Draw_Circle

The process of drawing a circle consist of many steps but this are hidden from the user.

This is called **process abstraction**.

1 Fundamentals of algorithms

Figure 1.1.17 shows *Draw_Circle* used four times to draw the filled concentric circles shown in *Figure 1.1.18*. We will call this set of concentric circles drawing a bull's eye.

We can then abstract to another level and create a subroutine for drawing a bull's eye :

```
BullsEye(x, y)
```

Figure 1.1.19 shows a Raptor flowchart in which `BullsEye` is called three times with different values for the parameters `x`, `y` each time:

> First time: `Firstx, Firsty`
> Second time: `Secondx, Secondy`
> Third time: `Thirdx, Thirdy`

Figure 1.1.20 shows the outcome. *Figure 1.1.21* shows the subroutine `BullsEye` Raptor flowchart.

Figure 1.1.18 Outcome of "executing" the flowchart

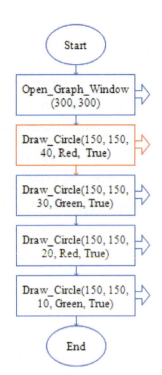

Figure 1.1.17 Flowchart describing the drawing of four filled concentric circles

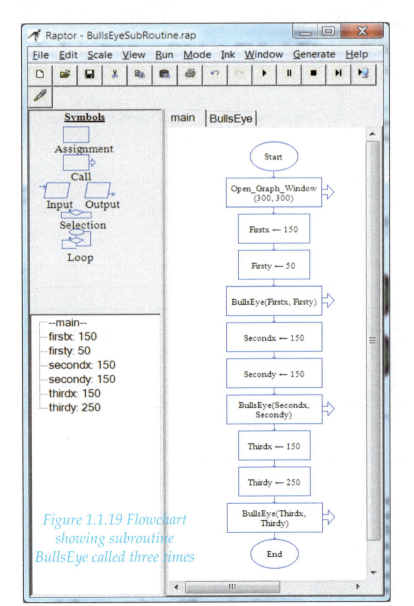

Figure 1.1.19 Flowchart showing subroutine BullsEye called three times

Figure 1.1.20 Outcome of calling BullsEye three time

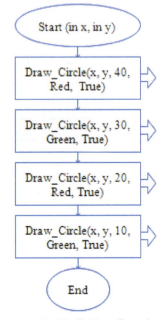

Figure 1.1.21 BullsEye flowchart

1.1 Representing algorithms

Tasks

11 Download the Raptor flowchart **BullsEye.rap** from
www.educational-computing.co.uk/GCSE/RaptorFlowchartPrograms/TasksCh1.1.html
Run this flowchart in single-step mode in Raptor and observe how it works.
Experiment with different x, y coordinate pairs, e.g. try x = 200, y = 200.

12 Download the Raptor flowchart **BullsEyeSubroutine.rap** from
www.educational-computing.co.uk/GCSE/RaptorFlowchartPrograms/TasksCh1.1.html
Run this flowchart in single-step mode in Raptor for small values of n and observe how it works.
Experiment with different coordinate pairs, e.g. try Firstx = 200, Firsty = 200.
How could you reduce the number of assignment boxes? Experiment.

Explaining simple algorithms in terms of their inputs, processing and outputs

Figure 1.1.22 shows

- a pseudo-code description of an algorithm for finding the largest integer amongst three given integers
- the inputs to this algorithm, x, y, z and the data type of the values that they store
- the output expected from the algorithm

The algorithm expresses the processing that should be applied to the inputs to produce the output.

Up until now, it was convenient to include input and output statements in our algorithms.

However, it is better to separate both input and output from the processing that the algorithm does as shown in *Figure 1.1.22*.

Input: x, y, z are three variables. Each stores an integer
Output: Largest is the largest integer
Algorithm:

```
Largest ← x
IF Largest < y THEN
    Largest ← y
ENDIF
IF Largest < z THEN
    Largest ← z
ENDIF
```

Figure 1.1.22 Input, Process, Output

In Raptor, we use a main flowchart "program" (*Figure 1.1.23*) which

- gets user input
- calls subroutine FindLargest (*Figure 1.1.24*)
  - FindLargest does the processing
  - FindLargest returns in Largest the largest integer
- The "program" then outputs the value of Largest to the user.

Here we have differentiated between user input and user output and the algorithm's input and output - *Figure 1.1.23*. The latter appear as an out parameter of subroutine FindLargest.

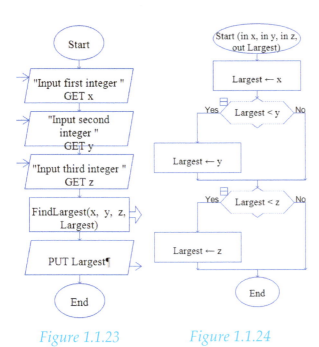

Figure 1.1.23 Calling flowchart

Figure 1.1.24 Called FindLargest subroutine

1 Fundamentals of algorithms

Questions

1 *Figure 1.1.25* shows the pseudo-code for a subroutine `FindLargest` that returns the larger of two integers.

(a) How many parameters does the subroutine `FindLargest` have?

(b) Subroutine `FindLargest` is called as follows

```
s ← USERINPUT
t ← USERINPUT
IF s ≠ t THEN
    Largest ← FindLargest(s,t)
    OUTPUT Largest
ELSE OUTPUT "Same"
ENDIF
```

In this pseudo-code ≠ means not equal to.

```
SUBROUTINE FindLargest(x,y)
    IF x > y THEN
        RETURN x
    ELSE
        RETURN y
    ENDIF
ENDSUBROUTINE
```

Figure 1.1.25

s	t	s ≠ t	x	y	x > y	Output message
5	5					
3	7					
8	2					

Table 1.1.5

The pseudo-code is designed to output a single message about the size of the two integers the user enters. Complete a copy of *Table 1.1.5* by hand tracing this pseudo-code for the given user inputs.

2 *Figure 1.1.26* shows pseudo-code which outputs a single message on the divisibility of an integer number entered by a user.

(a) Complete a copy of *Table 1.1.6* by hand tracing this pseudo-code for user input 7.

(b) Write a subroutine `IsNumberEven` which takes an integer and returns TRUE if the integer is divisible by two otherwise it returns FALSE.

(c) Write pseudo-code which uses `IsNumberEven` on user input stored in variable `n` and which outputs one of two possible messages

   "Number is even"
   or
   "Number is odd"

depending on what is returned from `IsNumberEven`.

```
n ← USERINPUT
REPEAT
    n ← n - 2         ← LESS THAN OR EQUAL TO
UNTIL n ≤ 0              Raptor uses <=
IF n = 0 THEN
    OUTPUT "Number divisible by 2"
ELSE
    OUTPUT "Number not divisible by 2"
ENDIF
```

Figure 1.1.26

n	n ≤ 0	Output message
7		

Table 1.1.6

1 Fundamentals of algorithms

Determining the purpose of simple algorithms

The purpose of simple algorithms may be discerned by hand tracing the steps of the algorithm and noting the values of any variables in a trace table.

Table 1.1.2 from earlier in the chapter is an example of a trace table.

Hand tracing is done by a human with pencil and paper and not by a computer.

A human reads each step in the algorithm starting from the beginning and simulates how the algorithm processes its input to produce output.

From this information, the human should be able to work out what the algorithm does if not known already, e.g. sorting a list of integers into ascending numerical order.

If the purpose of the algorithm is known then the purpose of hand tracing could be to check that the algorithm produces the expected output, i.e. that it performs as expected.

Sometimes, it is just enough to visually inspect the algorithm to work out what it does or what it will output for given inputs.

Questions

 What is the purpose of the algorithm shown in pseudo-code in *Figure 1.1.27*?

```
n ← USERINPUT
m ← USERINPUT
Count ← 0
p ← 1
IF m > 0 THEN
   REPEAT
      p = n * p
      Count ← Count + 1
   UNTIL Count = m
ENDIF
OUTPUT p
```

Figure 1.1.27

In this chapter you have covered:

- The meaning of the term algorithm
- The meaning of the term decomposition
- The meaning of the term abstraction
- Using a systematic approach to problem solving and algorithm creation representing those algorithms using pseudo-code, program code and flowcharts
- Explaining simple algorithms in terms of their inputs, processing and outputs
- Determining the purpose of simple algorithms.

1 Fundamentals of algorithms

1 Fundamentals of algorithms

Learning objectives:

- *Understand that more than one algorithm can be used to solve the same problem*

- *Compare the efficiency of algorithms explaining how some algorithms are more efficient than others in solving the same problem.*

Figure 1.2.1

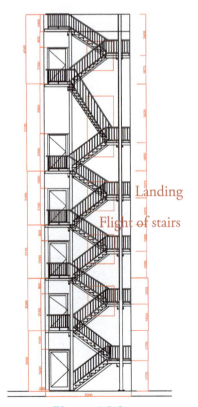

Figure 1.2.2

1.2 Efficiency of algorithms

More than one algorithm can be used to solve a problem

Two different algorithms for summing the first n natural numbers are shown in Table 1.1.3 in Chapter 1.1. Chapter 1.3 focuses on two different algorithms, linear search and binary search, for searching a list of items. Chapter 1.4 focuses on two different algorithms, bubble sort and merge sort, for sorting (placing in order) a list of items.

Why is it important to have more than one algorithm to solve a problem?

Reason: The programmed equivalents of algorithms do not all take the same time to execute or the same amount of space in memory.

One algorithm can take less time to complete a task or solve a problem than another or can take less space in memory than another.

Usually, if an algorithm takes less time it will do so at the expense of taking more space and vice versa.

Hence, computer scientists study and compare the efficiency of algorithms in time and space.

Comparing the efficiency of algorithms

An algorithm consists of a sequence of steps, step 1, step 2, etcetera, which we call computational steps.

An algorithm is turned into an equivalent computer program by replacing the steps, step 1, step 2 , etc, with their equivalent in some programming language.

Each programming language step will consume a certain amount of computer time when executed.

Suppose in some programming language each step takes on average StepTime seconds to execute on a particular computer.

And suppose the program coded algorithm performs a total number of steps, NoOfSteps, in completing the algorithm's task then the total time, TotalTime, for the execution of the program is given by

$$\text{TotalTime} = \text{NoOfSteps} \times \text{StepTime}$$

Figure 1.2.1 shows a person in silhouette climbing a flight of stairs of some five steps.

Figure 1.2.2 shows multiple flights of stairs.

1 Fundamentals of algorithms

Figure 1.2.3

Quite clearly, if the person in silhouette climbs to the very top in *Figure 1.2.2* at the same uniform rate as they climb to the top in *Figure 1.2.1* they will take longer because of the fact that there are more steps in *Figure 1.2.2*.

More steps means more time consumed.

Figure 1.2.3 shows a more direct way of reaching the top which relies on moving from floor to floor in one go.

If we consider each floor-to-floor movement as one step then this method to the top will take fewer steps to accomplish its task and consequently less time than climbing the stairs.

Figure 1.2.4 shows the output from a Python program running on an AMD® FX-6300 six-core processor.

This program times the execution of two different sorting algorithms, merge sort and bubble sort, respectively, applied to the same unsorted data set consisting of **50000** randomly chosen integers.

Note that the program code for the first sorting algorithm, merge sort, takes **0.64** seconds to complete its task whilst the program code for the second, bubble sort, takes **843** seconds or about **14** minutes to complete its task.

```
merge sort:    0.6415386604648237   seconds
bubble sort:   842.9913999518903    seconds


Process finished with exit code 0
```

Figure 1.2.4 Output from a Python program running on an AMD FX-6300 six-core processor. This program times the execution of two sorting algorithms merge sort and bubble sort on the same unsorted data set consisting of 50000 randomly chosen integers.

Information

Merge sort and bubble sort timing Python program may be downloaded from www.educational-computing.co.uk/GCSE/Ch1.2/MergeSortBubbleSortTiming.py.
To run this program download PyCharm Community edition from https://www.jetbrains.com/pycharm/

If a different computer had been chosen for this comparison exercise, the times would more than likely have been different but their ratio would have been very similar.

The reason for the difference in time taken is that the bubble sort algorithm takes many more steps than the merge sort algorithm to sort the same unordered list of integers.

This suggests that we can get a feel for how one algorithm compares time-wise with another by just comparing their number of steps.

For some algorithms the number of steps will be highly influenced by the size of the input. Size will be interpreted as the number of data items in the case of sorting algorithms.

1.2 Efficiency of algorithms

Figure 1.2.5 shows the comparison of execution times when the "size" of the input in each case is a list of 200 integers.

```
merge sort:   0.001364952947418879   seconds
bubble sort:  0.01024865033615643    seconds


Process finished with exit code 0
```

Figure 1.2.5 Output from a Python program running on an AMD FX-6300 six-core processor. This program times the execution of two sorting algorithms merge sort and bubble sort on the same unsorted data set consisting of 200 randomly chosen integers.

In *Figure 1.2.2* the landings between flights of stairs become less influential on the overall total number of steps (e.g. by counting walking across a landing as the equivalent of one step of a flight of stairs) as the number of flights of stairs increases.

The latter contributes much more than the former to the overall total.

This is also the case for algorithms.

Some types of steps dominate over other types simply because there are more of one type than another.

Table 1.2.1 shows in pseudo-code two algorithms, algorithm 1 and algorithm 2, for calculating the sum of the first n natural numbers,

i.e. $1 + 2 + 3 + \cdots + (n-1) + n$

The second algorithm involves the following 6 steps whatever the value of n:

1. 2 assignment steps ($\leftarrow$)
2. An input step (`USERINPUT`)
3. An output step (`OUTPUT Sum`)
4. An addition step (+)
5. A multiplication step (*)
6. A division step (/2)

The first algorithm involves a number of steps which varies with n as follows

1. 3 assignment steps ($\leftarrow$)
2. An input step (`USERINPUT`)
3. An output step (`OUTPUT`)
4. A comparison step (`Count < n`)
5. 2 assignment steps ($\leftarrow$) repeated n times (`WHILE` loop)
6. 2 addition steps (+) repeated n times (`WHILE` loop)

Algorithm 1	Algorithm 2

n ← USERINPUT
Sum ← 0
Count ← 0
WHILE Count < n
    Count ← Count + 1
    Sum ← Sum + Count
ENDWHILE
OUTPUT Sum
	n ← USERINPUT
	Sum ← (n * (n + 1))/2
	OUTPUT Sum

Table 1.2.1 AQA Pseudo-code for Methods 1 and 2

Setting aside whether or not each of the different type of steps (assignment, addition, etc) are "worth" different amounts of time, algorithm 1 takes more steps than algorithm 2 to do the same task.

1 Fundamentals of algorithms

Figure 1.2.6 shows the output from a python program running on an AMD FX-6300 six-core processor. This program times the execution of algorithms 1 and 2 for n = 10000000, 20000000, 30000000, 40000000 and 50000000.

```
Sum from 1 To   10000000
Total time taken by looping  3.390345964754102   seconds
Total time taken by formula  2.32976820546682e-06   seconds
Sum from 1 To   20000000
Total time taken by looping  6.8141607971068945   seconds
Total time taken by formula  2.3297682041345524e-06   seconds
Sum from 1 To   30000000
Total time taken by looping  10.12786437720345   seconds
Total time taken by formula  2.329768207687266e-06   seconds
Sum from 1 To   40000000
Total time taken by looping  13.594022164249822   seconds
Total time taken by formula  2.32976820005818388e-06   seconds
Sum from 1 To   50000000
Total time taken by looping  17.093877427400052   seconds
Total time taken by formula  2.329768207687266e-06   seconds

Process finished with exit code 0
```

Note that algorithm 1 (While loop) takes more and more time as n increases while algorithm 2 (formula) takes approximately the same time, 2.3 microseconds.

Figure 1.2.6 Output from a Python program running on an AMD FX-6300 six-core processor. This program times the execution of algorithms 1 and 2 for n = 10 00 0000, 20 000 000, 30 000 000, 40 000 000 and 50 000 000.

Algorithm 1 takes about 3.4 seconds to sum the first 10000000 natural numbers and 17 seconds to sum the first 50000000!

Comparing algorithm 1 with algorithm 2 by estimating and measuring how much time each takes to complete the same task is called comparing their time efficiencies.

In particular, comparing different algorithms by counting the number of steps each takes is known as comparing by time efficiency.

The comparisons are theoretical when they are done by hand and not by running the algorithms on a computer.

To "run" an algorithm we must turn it into a computer program and run the program on a computer. We can then take time measurements using a timer internal to the computer. However, we need to be careful when making comparisons because some computers are slower at executing programs than others.

Information

Sum of the first n natural numbers by both algorithms timing Python program may be downloaded from
www.educational-computing.co.uk/GCSE/Ch1.2/SumToNByLoopingAndByFormula.py.

Key point

Time efficiency of an algorithm:
The time efficiency of an algorithm is a theoretical time measured by hand in computational steps arrived at by counting the number of steps the algorithm makes to complete a task.
More steps means the algorithm will take longer than another algorithm requiring fewer steps to complete the same task.

Question

1. What is meant by the time efficiency of an algorithm?

2. Why do computer scientists study and compare the time efficiency of algorithms?

3. Is the following statement about comparing two different algorithms for solving the same problem generally true?
    "The one with the fewest number of lines of pseudo-code will take the least amount of time to solve the problem when the programmed equivalents of both are executed by computer, using the same programming language, the same input and the same computer for both."

1.2 Efficiency of algorithms

Question

4. Table 1.2.2 shows pseudo-code for two different algorithms each of which calculates the sum of the first m natural numbers where m is n, 2n, 3n, 4n, 5n, in turn. Table 1.2.3 shows an example for n = 5.

Table 1.2.4 shows the time in seconds taken by a programmed version of algorithm 1 for n = 1000000.

Table 1.2.5 shows the time in seconds taken by a programmed version of algorithm 2 for n = 1000000.

The same programming language and the same computer are used in each case.

(a) Which algorithm is more time efficient?

(b) How does this algorithm achieve its better time efficiency?

Algorithm 1	Algorithm 2

n ← USERINPUT
FOR i ← 1 TO 5
  Sum ← 0
  Count ← 0
  WHILE Count < i * n
    Count ← Count + 1
    Sum ← Sum + Count
  ENDWHILE
  OUTPUT Sum
ENDFOR
	n ← USERINPUT
	PreviousSum ← 0
	FOR i ← 1 TO 5
	  Sum ← PreviousSum
	  Count ← (i - 1) * n
	  WHILE Count < i * n
	    Count ← Count + 1
	    Sum ← Sum + Count
	  ENDWHILE
	  OUTPUT Sum
	  PreviousSum ← Sum
	ENDFOR

Table 1.2.2

n	m	Sum
5	5	15
	10	55
	15	120
	20	210
	25	325

Table 1.2.3

m	Time/s
1000000	0.44
2000000	0.85
3000000	1.28
4000000	1.70
5000000	2.12

Table 1.2.4

m	Time/s
1000000	0.45
2000000	0.42
3000000	0.43
4000000	0.42
5000000	0.43

Table 1.2.5

In this chapter you have covered:

- That more than one algorithm can be used to solve the same problem
- Comparing the efficiency of algorithms and how some algorithms are more efficient than others in solving the same problem.

Information

Comparing time efficiency Python program for question 4 may be downloaded from www.educational-computing.co.uk/GCSE/Ch1.2/MoreEfficientSumToNByLooping.py.

1 Fundamentals of algorithms

1 Fundamentals of algorithms

Learning objectives:

- *Understand and explain how the linear search algorithm works*

- *Understand and explain how the binary search algorithm works*

- *Compare and contrast linear and binary search algorithms.*

1.3 Searching algorithms

Linear search

Imagine a pile of animal name playing cards placed face down on a table in no particular order. The playing cards are labelled *ant*, *bee*, *cat*, *dog*, and *fox* and the pile is arranged as shown in Figure 1.3.1.

Searching for a particular card, say "cat", by turning over the cards in turn, starting from the card on top, is called a **linear search**. The red arrow in Figure 1.3.1 indicates the cards that have to be examined before the card labelled "cat" is found.

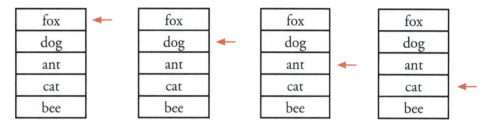

Figure 1.3.1 Linear search for the card labelled "cat"

Key point

Linear search:
Linear search scans each item or element in a collection of items, e.g. playing cards, in turn, starting from the beginning, until a match is found or the end of the collection is reached.

Linear search doesn't care whether the list is ordered or not.

Information

Linear search is often performed on lists of things, e.g. names

Questions

1. A pack of cards is shuffled to ensure that the cards are in no particular order and then placed face down on a table. Starting from the top of the pack, one playing card is turned over at a time until the Ace of Spades is found.

   (a) If the task was repeated many times, shuffling the pack of 52 cards before each new search, on average how many cards would need to be turned over to find the Ace of Spades?

   (b) What is the maximum number of cards that need turning over to find a match?

2. Approximately half of the pack is removed. Starting from the top of the pack, one playing card is turned over at a time until either the Ace of Spades is found or all the cards have been examined.
   What is the maximum number of cards that need turning over to find the Ace of Spades or to discover that the half-pack doesn't contain the Ace of Spades?

3. What is the maximum number of cards that have to be turned over in the pile of cards in Figure 1.3.1 to discover that "rat" is not amongst them?

1 Fundamentals of algorithms

> **Key concept**
>
> **Search length:**
> Search Length = no of elements of the vector which are examined before a match is found

Algorithm for linear search

Labelling the pile of animal name playing cards with the name, `Vector`, enables us to refer to the card on top as the card in location `Vector[1]`, the card below this card as the card in location in `Vector[2]`, and the jth card as the card in location in `Vector[j]`.

1	fox
2	dog
3	ant
4	cat
5	bee

Vector

Labelling the card that we are searching for, `ElementSought`, means that we can change this card to a different one and continue to refer to the card to search for by the label `ElementSought`. The number of elements, `NoOfElementsInVector`, is 5 in our example. The algorithm below performs a linear search on `Vector` assigning to `Result` the position in `Vector` of the element if found otherwise assigning it the value 0.

> **Key fact**
>
> **Average search length:**
> Average search length
> $\approx \dfrac{\text{NoOfElementsInVector}}{2}$
>
> $\approx$ means approximately

Linear Search Algorithm

```
j ← 0
Found ← False
REPEAT
   j ← j + 1
   IF Vector[j] = ElementSought THEN
      Found ← True
   ENDIF
UNTIL Found Or j = NoOfElementsInVector
IF Found THEN
   Result ← j
ELSE
   Result ← 0
ENDIF
```

> **Information**
>
> In assessment material, AQA will use array indexing which starts from 0 unless specifically stated otherwise.
> To test your understanding of the material in this chapter, it would be beneficial to work through the material again using for each array indexing that starts from 0.

Task

① Code the linear search algorithm in a programming language with which you are familiar. `Vector` can be implemented as a one-dimensional array of animal name strings or its equivalent. The animal name to search for should be entered at the keyboard and assigned to `ElementSought`. Your program should display the value assigned to `Result`.

Question

④ What is meant by linear search?

Binary search

If the elements have been ordered then a much shorter average search length can be achieved as follows:

Assuming elements in a list are stored in ascending order as shown in *Figure 1.3.2*, a search for an element with a particular value, e.g. "dog", resembles the way a telephone directory might be searched.

The approximate middle of the list is located (location labelled 5 in *Figure 1.3.2*) and its value examined.

If this value is too high (e.g. alphabetically) then the approximate position of the middle element of the first half is calculated and its value examined.

If the value is too low then the approximate position of the middle element of the second half is calculated and its value examined.

This process continues until the desired element is found or the search interval becomes empty.

> **Key point**
>
> **Search interval:**
> The range over which the search is conducted, e.g. from list elements 1 to 9 inclusive.

> **Key principle**
>
> **Binary search:**
> Searching for "pig" in the list in Figure 1.3.2 with elements labelled 1 to 9, the position of the middle element is calculated as follows
>
> middle position = (1 + 9) div 2
> = 10 div 2 = 5
>
> middle position = (6 + 9) div 2
> = 15 div 2 = 7
>
> middle position = (8 + 9) div 2
> = 17 div 2 = 8
>
> Generalising,
>
> middle position =
> (low + high) div 2
>
> where *low* is position no of lowest item and *high*, position no of highest item in list, e.g.
>
> low = 8, item = pig
> high = 9, item = red

Figure 1.3.2 Performing a binary search for the word "pig" on an ordered list of words

Figures 1.3.2 and 1.3.3 show an example of binary search on an ordered list of three-letter words. The elements in the list have been numbered, 1, 2, 3, ... 7, 8, 9, for convenience. The list is searched for the word "pig" which is located at position **8** in the list.

The middle element, "dog" is selected first and compared with "pig". It doesn't match.

As "pig" is alphabetically greater than "dog", the second half of the list "boy" to "red" is chosen to search next. This second half runs from "man" to "red".

Its middle lies between the word "pen" and the word "pig". We have to choose one or the other so the word that comes first, "pen", is chosen. It doesn't match the word "pig". As "pig" is alphabetically greater than "pen", the second half of the list "man" to "red" is chosen for the next search. This second half runs from "pig" to "red".

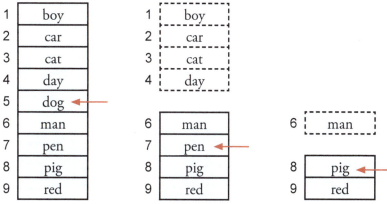

Figure 1.3.3 Performing a binary search for the word "pig" on an ordered list of words

Its middle lies between the word "pig" and the word "red". We have to choose one or the other so the word that comes first, "pig", is chosen. It matches. So "pig" is present in the list and is located at position 8 in this list.

> **Key principle**
>
> **Binary search:**
> Binary search uses a "divide and conquer" approach to searching a list by chopping the list into smaller and smaller lists to search until item found or list cannot be divided anymore.

Question

 What is meant by binary search?

Algorithm for binary search

Labelling the list to be binary searched as Vector, enables us to refer to the first element by its location Vector[1], the next element by its location Vector[2], and the jth element by its location Vector[j]. The range of the vector to be searched is stored in Low and High. For example, Low = 1, High = 9 means that the beginning of the range is location Vector[1] and the end of the range is Vector[9].

Labelling the element that we are searching for, ElementSought, means that we can change the value to a different one and continue to refer to the element to search for by the label ElementSought. The algorithm below performs a binary search on Vector assigning to Result the position in Vector of the element if found otherwise assigning it the value -1.

Binary Search Algorithm

```
Result ← -1
WHILE (Low <= High) And (Result = -1)
  Middle ← (Low + High) Div 2   {Find middle of list}
  IF ElementSought = Vector[Middle] THEN
    Result ← Middle      {Found}
  ELSE
    IF ElementSought < Vector[Middle] THEN
      High ← Middle - 1   {search lower half}
    ELSE
      IF ElementSought > Vector[Middle] THEN
        Low ← Middle + 1 {search upper half}
      ENDIF
    ENDIF
  ENDIF
ENDWHILE
```

1.3 Searching algorithms

Task

2. Using the list shown in *Figure 1.3.4*, hand trace the binary search algorithm given above for the value "red". Complete a copy of the table shown below.

Low	High	Middle
1	16	

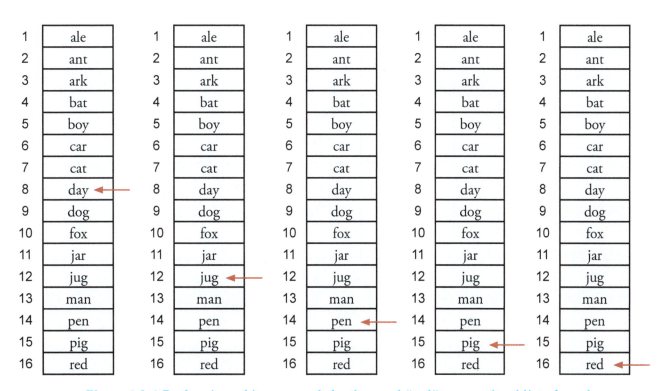

Figure 1.3.4 Performing a binary search for the word "red" on an ordered list of words

Task

3. How many elements of the list in *Figure 1.3.4* have to be examined when binary searching for the element "red"?

4. How many elements have to be examined when binary searching for
   (a) the element "day" in a list constructed from elements 1 to 8 of *Figure 1.3.4*?
   (b) the element "bat" in a list constructed from elements 1 to 4 of *Figure 1.3.4*?
   (c) the element "ant" in a list constructed from elements 1 to 2 of *Figure 1.3.4*?

25

1 Fundamentals of algorithms

Comparing linear and binary search algorithms

Table 1.3.1 summarises the outcomes of completing tasks 3 and 4. From *Table 1.3.1* we conclude that for binary search the maximum search length **increases linearly when the number of elements or items in a list doubles**. For example, if the number of items in the list is 8 (2^3), the maximum search length is 3 + 1, i.e. 4 items have to be examined at most to find a match or conclude that the sought item is not in the list.

If we have, say, 16777216 (2^{24}) in a list, the maximum search length is 24 + 1, i.e. 25 items have to be examined at most to find a match or conclude that the sought item is not in the list.

If we contrast this with linear search, then searching a list of 8 items requires 8 items to be examined if the sought item is the last item, i.e. maximum search length for this linear search = 8.

Similarly, searching a list of 16777216 items requires 16777216 items to be examined if the sought item is the last item, i.e. maximum search length for this linear search = 16777216.

Table 1.3.2 compares binary search with linear search for different lengths of list. This table shows clearly that **binary search is more efficient than linear search, timewise**. Each element or item of a list that has to be examined costs time. If, for argument's sake, it takes one microsecond to examine an item, then for a list of 16777216 items, binary search will take a maximum of 25 microseconds whilst linear search will take 16777216 microseconds or approximately 17 seconds.

We may draw a similar conclusion for the average search length.

Binary search can only be performed on ordered lists whereas **linear search can be performed on both ordered and unordered lists**. Sorting a list into order will take time but once ordered, binary search will perform searches on the list faster than linear search will on the unordered list with the speed advantage increasing with the size of the list.

No of items in list	No of items in list as a power of 2	Maximum search length
1	2^0	1
2	2^1	2
4	2^2	3
8	2^3	4
16	2^4	5

Table 1.3.1 Relationship between maximum search length and no of items in list for binary search

No of items in list	Maximum search length binary search	Maximum search length linear search
1	1	1
2	2	2
4	3	4
8	4	8
16	5	16
32768	16	32768
65536	17	65536
16777216	25	16777216

Table 1.3.2 Comparing maximum search length for binary and linear searches

Key fact
Binary search versus linear search:
Binary search is more efficient timewise than linear search.

Key fact
Binary search versus linear search:
Binary search can only be performed on ordered lists, linear search can be performed on both ordered and unordered lists.

1.3 Searching algorithms

Questions

6. State **two** requirements that a list must satisfy for an item to be found using binary search.

7. Explain why binary search is more efficient than linear search, timewise.

8. State whether it is possible to search an unordered list using
   (a) binary search
   (b) linear search.

In this chapter you have covered:

- linear search algorithm scans a list from the beginning until a match is found or the end of the list is reached.
- binary search algorithm uses a "divide and conquer" approach to searching a list by chopping the list into smaller and smaller lists to search until item found or list cannot be divided anymore.
- binary search is more efficient than linear search, timewise, because it examines fewer elements of a list
- binary search can only be performed on ordered lists
- linear search can be performed on both ordered and unordered lists

1 Fundamentals of algorithms

1 Fundamentals of algorithms

Learning objectives:

- *Understand and explain how the merge sort algorithm works*
- *Understand and explain how the bubble sort algorithm works*
- *Compare and contrast merge sort and bubble sort algorithms.*

1.4 Sorting algorithms

Sorting

In computer science sorting means arranging items into ascending or descending order, e.g. the following unsorted list of letters of the alphabet is sorted into ascending order when letter A is first, letter B second, and so on.

    Unsorted list: C F A E D B

    Sorted list (ascending): A B C D E F

The following unsorted list of letters of the alphabet are sorted into descending order when the letter F is first, the letter E second, and so on.

    Unsorted list: C F A E D B

    Sorted list (descending): F E D C B A

Bubble sort algorithm

Bubble sort is a simple sorting algorithm but not a very efficient one, stepwise.

It belongs to a family of sorting algorithms called "exchange" or "transposition" sorts.

In an exchange sort, **pairs of items that are out of order are interchanged until no more of these pairs exist**.

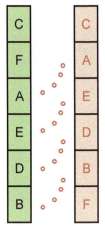

Figure 1.4.1 First pass

Figure 1.4.1 shows the "lighter" items bubbling up the list when out of order pairs are interchanged whilst the "heaviest" sinks to the bottom.

Clearly, more than one pass through the list is required before the items are sorted in ascending order with the lightest at the top and the heaviest at the bottom.

Figure 1.4.2 First pass showing comparisons and exchanges

The pairs that are compared on the first pass through the list in bubble sort C F A E D B are as follows:

    C & F - no exchange; F & A - exchange; F & E - exchange;

    F & D - exchange; B & F - exchange.

The first pass is shown in *Figure 1.4.2*.

The comparisons are pink squares ( ), the exchanges are red letters and no-exchanges are green letters.

As the list is not sorted by the end of the first pass, another pass is needed but we don't need to compare the last two items because the "heaviest", F, has sunk to the bottom.

The list to be sorted is now C A E D B F.

Task

Download python program from www.educational-computing.co.uk/GCSE/Ch1.4/MergesortBubbleSortTiming.py and run.

28

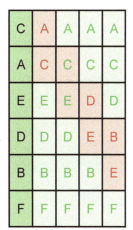

Figure 1.4.3 Second pass

> The pairs that are compared on the **second pass** through the list are as follows:
>
> C & A - exchange; C & E - no exchange; E & D - exchange;
>
> E & B - exchange.
>
> The second pass is shown in *Figure 1.4.3*.

As the list is not sorted by the end of the second pass, another pass is needed but we don't need to compare the last three items because the "heaviest", F, and the next "heaviest", E, have sunk to the bottom.

The list to be sorted is now A C D B E F.

> The pairs that are compared on the **third pass** through the list are as follows:
>
> A & C - no exchange; C & D - no exchange; D & B - exchange.
>
> The third pass is shown in *Figure 1.4.4*.

As the list is not sorted by the end of the third pass, another pass is needed but we don't need to compare the last four items because the "heaviest", F, the next "heaviest", E, and the next D have sunk to the bottom.

The list to be sorted is now A C B D E F.

Figure 1.4.4 Third pass

> The pairs that are compared on the **fourth pass** through the list are as follows:
>
> A & C - no exchange; C & B - exchange.
>
> The fourth pass is shown in *Figure 1.4.5*.

The list is now A B C D E F. It is sorted in ascending alphabetical order.

Unfortunately, the bubble sort algorithm makes one more pass.

> The pairs that are compared on the **fifth pass** through the list are as follows:
>
> A & B - no exchange.
>
> The fifth pass is shown in *Figure 1.4.6*.

Figure 1.4.5 Fourth pass

The items considered in each pass are shown in *Figure 1.4.7*.

The number of passes is one less than the number of items to be sorted.

Number of passes = NoOfItems - 1

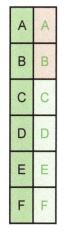

Figure 1.4.6 Fifth pass

List on 1st pass	C	F	A	E	D	B
List on 2nd pass	C	A	E	D	B	
List on 3rd pass	A	C	D	B		
List on 4th pass	A	C	B			
List on 5th pass	A	B				

Figure 1.4.7 Items that remain to be compared on each pass

1.4 Sorting algorithms

On the first pass, the number of comparisons is one less than the number of items to be sorted, i.e. 5 when number of items is 6. On the next pass, 4, then on the next 3, the next 2 and the last 1 as shown in *Figure 1.4.8*.

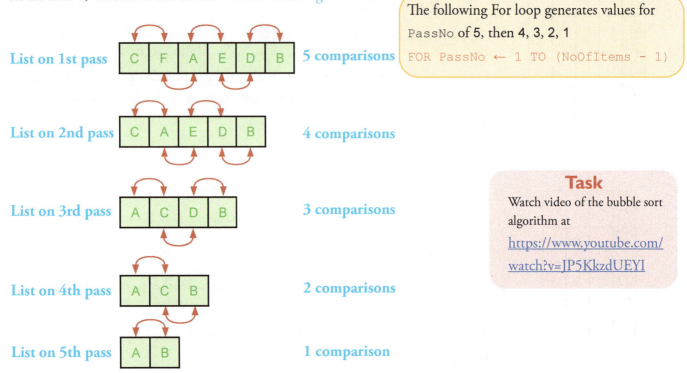

> The following For loop generates values for `PassNo` of 5, then 4, 3, 2, 1
>
> `FOR PassNo ← 1 TO (NoOfItems - 1)`

Task
Watch video of the bubble sort algorithm at
https://www.youtube.com/watch?v=JP5KkzdUEYI

Figure 1.4.8 Comparisons on each pass

Figure 1.4.9 shows the letters C, F, A, E, D, B stored in a structure consisting of six labelled storage cells.

The cells are labelled 0, 1, 2, 3, 4, 5, 6.

The cell labelling provides an index for selecting a particular cell of this structure just as the page number of a book is used to select a particular page.

Let the structure be referred to collectively by the name `ArrayOfItems`.

To address the contents of the cell labelled 0 we use the collective name for the whole structure and refer to the specific cell as follows

The contents of the next cell

and so on

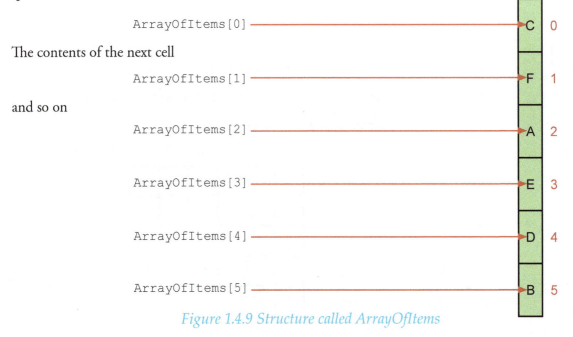

Figure 1.4.9 Structure called ArrayOfItems

30

1 Fundamentals of algorithms

To compare the letter in cell `0` with that in cell `1` we can use

```
IF ArrayOfItems[0] > ArrayOfItems[1]
```

To compare a pair of adjacent items at position `j` and `j+1` in `ArrayOfItems` (*Figure 1.4.9*) we can use

```
IF ArrayOfItems[j] > ArrayOfItems[j+1]
```

For example, if `j=0` then `j+1=1` and the example from the previous page:

`IF ArrayOfItems[0] > ArrayOfItems[1]` evaluates to False.

But if we set `j=1` then `j+1=2` and the following evaluates to True:

```
IF ArrayOfItems[1] > ArrayOfItems[2]
```

To swap or exchange a pair of items at position `j` and `j+1` we can use the following

```
Temp ← ArrayOfItems[j]
ArrayOfItems[j] ← ArrayOfItems[j+1]
ArrayOfItems[j + 1] ← Temp
```

Table 1.4.1 shows the values of `Temp`, `ArrayOfItems[j]` and `ArrayOfItems[j+1]` for `j = 1` during the swap.

j	Temp	ArrayOfItems[j]	ArrayOfItems[j+1]
1	F	F	A
1	F	A	A
1	F	A	F

Table 1.4.1 Trace table

To make 5 comparisions, then 4, 3, 2 and 1 we can use a For loop as follows

```
FOR j ← 0 TO (NoOfItems - (PassNo + 1))
```

Where `PassNo` is 1, then 2, 3, 4 and 5, `j` is `0 To 4`, then `0 To 3`, `0 To 2`, `0 To 1` and finally `0 To 0` as shown in *Table 1.4.2*.

PassNo	FOR j ← 0 TO NoOfItems-(PassNo+1)
1	FOR j ← 0 TO 4
2	FOR j ← 0 TO 3
3	FOR j ← 0 TO 2
4	FOR j ← 0 TO 1
5	FOR j ← 0 TO 0

Table 1.4.2

The bubble sort algorithm is given in *Figure 1.4.10*.

It consists of an outer loop

```
FOR PassNo ← 1 TO (NoOfItems - 1) ... ENDFOR
```

which controls an inner loop which is executed once for each value of `PassNo`

```
FOR j ← 0 TO (NoOfItems - (PassNo + 1)) ... ENDFOR
```

```
FOR PassNo ← 1 TO (NoOfItems - 1)
  FOR j ← 0 TO (NoOfItems - (PassNo + 1))
    IF ArrayOfItems[j] > ArrayOfItems[j + 1] THEN
      Temp ← ArrayOfItems[j]
      ArrayOfItems[j] ← ArrayOfItems[j + 1]
      ArrayOfItems[j + 1] ← Temp
    ENDIF
  ENDFOR
ENDFOR
```

Figure 1.4.10 Bubble sort algorithm

Information

Bubble sort is very inefficient. For example, if bubble sort is required to sort an ordered list of items into ascending order and the list is already in ascending order, it fails to notice this. Instead it ploughs on merrily through the outer and inner loops making unnecessary comparisons. Adding a flag `NoExchanges` can be used to stop the iterations. `NoExchanges` is set to True at the beginning of each pass and to False inside the inner loop if an exchange occurs. If `NoExchanges` is still True at the end of a pass, the list is ordered and the loop can be exited prematurely.

1.4 Sorting algorithms

Figure 1.4.11 shows how j varies on each pass.

Figure 1.4.12 shows this sequence for each pass.

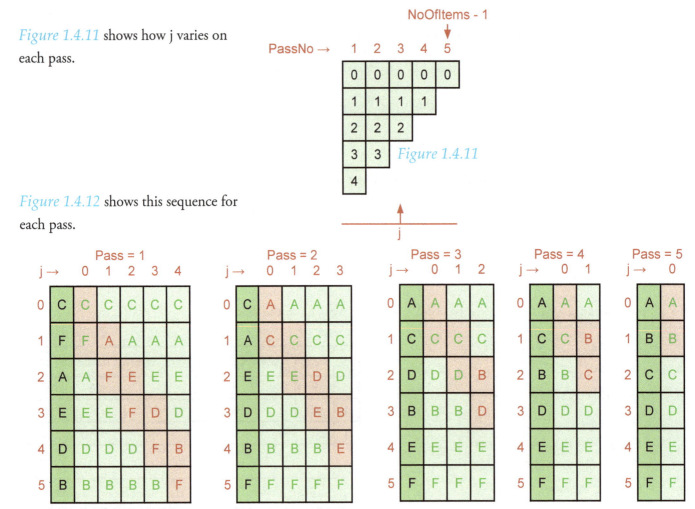

Figure 1.4.12 The range of values of loop counter j on each pass

Question

1. The following list of letters of the alphabet is to be sorted by bubble sort into ascending order with A first followed by B, and so on,

    F E D C B A

    Hand trace sorting this list into ascending order by completing a copy of the trace tables shown in *Figure 1.4.13*. The first pass has been done for you. The list of numbers to the left of each table is the index of `ArrayOfItems`.

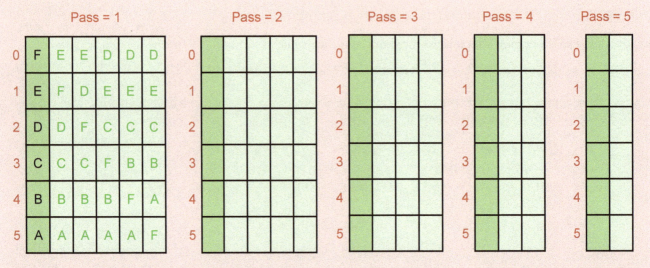

Figure 1.4.13 State of ArrayOfItems, during trace of bubble sort algorithm

1 Fundamentals of algorithms

Merge sort algorithm

Merge sort is an example of a **divide and conquer algorithm**, meaning that the problem of sorting an unsorted list of items is solved by dividing the problem into subproblems, solving the subproblems, and then merging the results to produce the sorted list.

- The divide and conquer approach divides the work into roughly equal parts.
- These equal parts are subdivided into roughly equal sub parts, and then each of these are divided equally, and so on until the work can be divided no further or until the problem is trivial to solve.

For example, suppose the task is to sort the following unsorted list of letters of the alphabet into ascending alphabetical order (A first, B second, and so on): Unsorted list: **G C H F A E D B**

We first divide the list into eight single-letter lists as shown in *Figure 1.4.14*.

Divide phase of merge sort

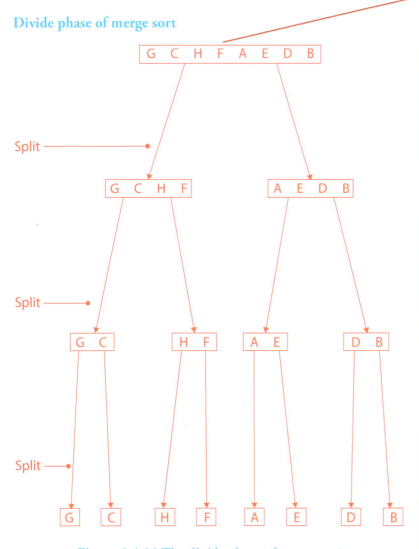

We divide (split in two) the list into two separate sub lists with each containing half the letters:

1. Unsorted sub list: **G C H F**
2. Unsorted sub list: **A E D B**

We then divide each sub list as follows

1. Unsorted sub list: **G C H F**
   1.1 Unsorted sub list: **G C**
   1.2 Unsorted sub list: **H F**
2. Unsorted sub list: **A E D B**
   2.1 Unsorted sub list: **A E**
   2.2 Unsorted sub list: **D B**

And again

1.1 Unsorted sub list: **G C**
   1.1.1 Sorted sub list: **G**
   1.1.2 Sorted sub list: **C**
1.2 Unsorted sub list: **H F**
   1.2.1 Sorted sub list: **H**
   1.2.2 Sorted sub list: **F**
2.1 Unsorted sub list: **A E**
   2.1.1 Sorted sub list: **A**
   2.1.2 Sorted sub list: **E**
2.2 Unsorted sub list: **D B**
   2.2.1 Sorted sub list: **D**
   2.2.2 Sorted sub list: **B**

Figure 1.4.14 The divide phase of merge sort

The final stage is a collection of single-letter sub lists.
Each single-letter sub list is by definition a sorted list of one.

1.4 Sorting algorithms

We now begin the next phase, the merge phase, the first stage of which merges the collection of eight single-letter sub lists into a collection of sorted two-letter sub lists as shown in *Figure 1.4.15*.

The next stage merges the collection of two-letter sub lists into a collection of sorted four-letter sub lists as shown in *Figure 1.4.15*.

The final merge occurs with the two sorted sub lists C F G H and A B D E as shown in *Figure 1.4.15* to produce the sorted list of letters A B C D E F G H.

Merge phase of merge sort

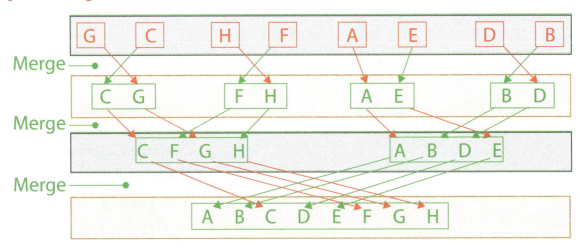

Figure 1.4.15 The merge phase of merge sort

Figure 1.4.16 shows the three merge stages for a set of cards labelled A, B, C, D, E, F, G, H respectively.

- The upper level of stage 1 is the collection of single-letter sorted lists.
- The lower level is the collection of two-letter sorted lists that results from moving the upper level to the lower level. The lower level is then moved to the upper level to produce the collection of four-letter sorted lists.
- Finally the upper level is moved to the lower level to produce the final sorted list.

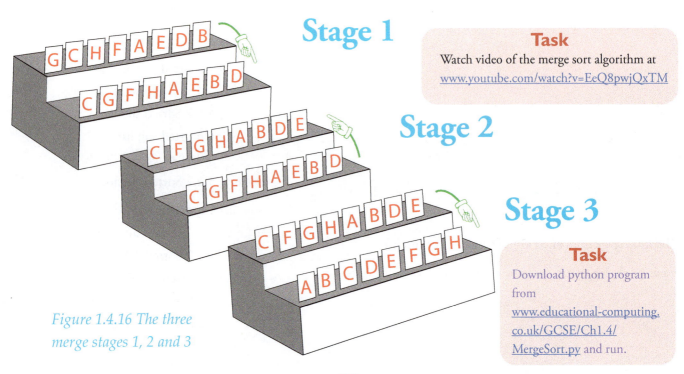

Figure 1.4.16 The three merge stages 1, 2 and 3

Task
Watch video of the merge sort algorithm at
www.youtube.com/watch?v=EeQ8pwjQxTM

Task
Download python program from
www.educational-computing.co.uk/GCSE/Ch1.4/MergeSort.py and run.

1 Fundamentals of algorithms

Question

2. The merge sort division of the following list of integers 8 5 7 1 9 4 2 3 into eight single-number lists is shown on the upper step in Figure 1.4.17 and in the upper set of boxes in Figure 1.4.18.

   This divided list 8 5 7 1 9 4 2 3 is to be merged into ascending order.

   (a) Copy Figure 1.4.18 and fill the blank boxes with the collection of two-number sorted lists that results from the first merge stage of merge sort.

   (b) Copy Figure 1.4.19 and fill the lower blank boxes with your answer to part (a). Fill the upper blank boxes with the collection of four-number sorted lists that results from the second merge stage of merge sort.

   (c) Copy Figure 1.4.20 and fill the upper blank boxes with your answer to part (b). Fill the lower blank boxes with the final sorted lists that results from the third merge stage of merge sort.

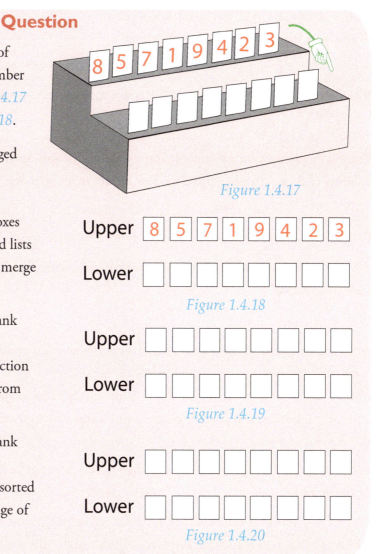

Figure 1.4.17

Figure 1.4.18

Figure 1.4.19

Figure 1.4.20

Comparing and contrasting merge sort and bubble sort algorithms

Merge sort can sort large volumes of data resident on magnetic disk

Merge sort is **well-suited to sorting really huge amounts of data that do not fit into main memory**.

Figure 1.4.21 shows a magnetic disk file, file A, containing a few integers in no particular order (although technically it could be many integers), and two other magnetic disk files, file B and file C, which have received the results of splitting the contents of file A as shown.

Only two integers at a time have to be read from file A into main memory.

The two integers are compared and then written out to disk file B or file C.

File A must then be emptied in preparation for receiving the partially ordered result of merging, in ascending numerical order, the contents of file B with the contents of file C.

The process is repeated until the contents of file A are sorted in ascending numerical order.

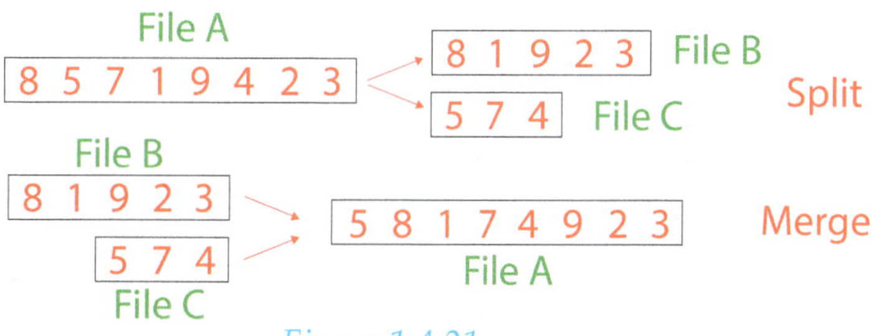

The use of magnetic disk files means that this particular form of merge sort is not limited by the capacity of main memory.

1.4 Sorting algorithms

Bubble sort is an in-memory sorting algorithm

Bubble sort is an in-memory sort algorithm.

All the data to be sorted has to fit into main memory otherwise bubble sort cannot do its job.

It is therefore **not suitable for sorting large volumes of data which could not fit into main memory**.

Bubble sort is slow to sort

There is another reason why bubble sort would not be appropriate for significant volumes of data even when this data does fit into main memory:

It is slow at sorting because it has to perform too many steps!

For example, for 1000 items, the total number of comparisons is **500500**.

Table 1.4.3 shows how the number of comparisons varies with the number of item to be sorted.

n	Total number of comparisons
1000	500500
10000	50005000
100000	500050000
1000000	500000500000
10000000	50000005000000

Table 1.4.3

Merge sort faster than bubble sort

An in-memory sort of an unsorted list of n items where n is greater than about 16 is faster with merge sort than with bubble sort - see *Table 1.4.4*.

The worst-case of a completely unsorted list is usually considered when making the comparison because it is possible to stop bubble sort when no exchanges have taken place on a pass.

For example, if the list is sorted already then bubble sort can be halted at the end of the first pass.

Table 1.4.4 shows how the number of operations for merge sort and bubble sort compare as the number of items n increases (technically, the parameter n in the bubble sort formula is one less than the number of items but it is acceptable to ignore this difference if we only want to get a feel for growth rate).

How much memory space is required?

Merge sort requires twice as much memory space as bubble sort to perform its sorting operation. In bubble sort, the rearrangement of items takes place within the data structure containing the list of items.

In merge sort, a second data structure is needed for the merge operation.

n	Merge sort No of steps	Bubble sort No of steps
2	4	3
4	16	10
8	48	36
16	128	136
32	320	528
64	1024	2080
128	1792	16512
256	4096	65792
512	9216	131328

Table 1.4.4

Information

The worst-case proves to be the most useful in practice when comparing algorithms.

For example, consider a safety-critical system such as a program that controls part of an aircraft.

The designer of the control needs to know, for example, "how long it will take from the pilot pressing the button that activates the control before the aircraft responds?".

If this time is too long another algorithm/mechanism will be needed that takes less time.

Note that it doesn't matter if the system works fast enough on average or even nearly every time.

It must work fast enough on every occasion!

1 Fundamentals of algorithms

> **Question**
>
> 3. You have a choice of two sorting algorithms, bubble sort and merge sort.
>
>   You are asked to choose which of the two sorting algorithms would be best or the only possible one to use for the following tasks:
>
>   (a) Sorting data stored on magnetic disk that does not fit into main memory.
>
>   (b) Sorting in ascending numerical order an unsorted list of 30 integers held in main memory.
>
>   (c) Sorting in ascending numerical order an unsorted list of 10000 integers held in main memory into ascending numerical order.

In this chapter you have covered:

- The merge sort algorithm which is an example of a **divide and conquer algorithm**, meaning that the problem of sorting an unsorted list of items is solved by dividing the problem into subproblems, solving the subproblems, and then merging the results to produce the sorted list.

- The bubble sort algorithm works by exchanging pairs of items that are out of order until no more of these pairs exist.

- Comparing and contrasting merge sort and bubble sort algorithms
  - Merge sort is well-suited to sorting huge amounts of data that do not fit into main memory.
  - Bubble sort can only sort data that fits into and is resident in main memory.
  - An in-memory sort of an unsorted list of n items where n is greater than about 16 is faster with merge sort than with bubble sort. The worst-case of a completely unsorted list is usually considered when making this comparison because it is possible to stop bubble sort when no exchanges have taken place on a pass.
  - Merge sort requires twice as much memory space as bubble sort to perform its sorting operation.

2 Programming

2 Programming

Learning objectives:

- *Understand the concept of a data type*

- *Understand and use the following appropriately*
    - *integer*
    - *real*
    - *Boolean*
    - *character*
    - *string.*

Information

This textbook covers Python (version 3), C# and VB.NET, the programming languages supported by AQA for examinations from 2022 onwards. In addition, it also covers programming languages Java and Pascal/Delphi.

Key term

Sequence:
A sequence is simply an ordered collection of things, e.g. a b c … or the sequence of digits in a telephone number, 433004.

Key term

Bit:
A bit is a binary digit which is either 0 or 1.

Key term

Bit pattern:
A bit pattern is a finite sequence of 0s and 1s, e.g. 0100100001101001.

2.1 Data types

Introduction to programming
The concept of a data type

The computer programs that you write in this course will control physical processes involving matter and energy at the level of atoms and electrons inside CPUs and memory but you will rely upon computing abstractions to hide much of this from you (until you hear the fan switch on that keeps a CPU cool).

Information is typically stored using just two levels of energy, one higher in energy than the other.

It is convenient to use a two symbol code consisting of 1 and 0 to represent these two levels.

The symbol 1 is usually chosen for the higher energy state and the symbol 0 for the lower energy state.

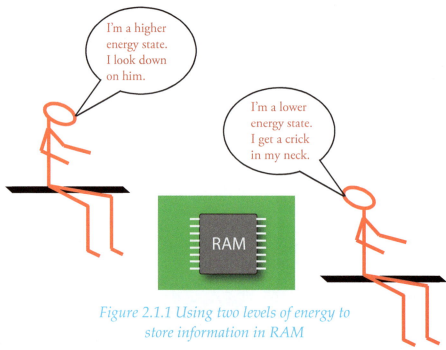

Figure 2.1.1 Using two levels of energy to store information in RAM

Computer memory, e.g. RAM, consists of a collection of individual storage cells, each capable of storing a single bit. A bit or binary digit encodes an energy state, i.e. 1 or 0.

Memory bits are typically grouped into blocks of 8, 16, 32, or 64 bits.
A 16-bit block might store the following bit pattern

0101110100000110

2 Programming

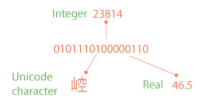

Figure 2.1.2 Different interpretations of the given bit pattern

> **Key point**
>
> **Meaning of datum:**
> A datum is a finite sequence of 0s and 1s, e.g. 0100100001101001.

> **Key term**
>
> **Integer data type:**
> A machine integer is a datum whose data type represents some finite subset of the mathematical integers.
> A fixed number of bits are allocated to the datum, e.g. 32 bits.
> Signed 32-bit (4-byte) integers range in value from
>   -2,147,483,648 through
>   2,147,483,647.
> The integer data type is free of rounding errors. Mathematical integers are represented exactly. However, this type has a limited range.

Computers process and store information, the question is:

> "What information do we want bit pattern 0101110100000110 to represent?"

Fortunately, we get to choose the interpretation when we write programs. Here are three choices of interpretation that we could make

1. integer - a positive or negative whole number
2. real - a positive or negative number with a fractional part
3. character - a unicode character representing a symbol in an alphabet.

The act of assigning an interpretation is what is meant by **data typing** and the specific interpretation, e.g. integer, is a **data type**.

Figure 2.1.2 shows what the three different interpretations of the bit pattern 0101110100000110 actually mean.

Until the bit pattern is interpreted, it is called a **datum**.

A datum is a finite sequence of 0s and 1s, e.g. 0101110100000110.

After interpretation it represents specific **information**, e.g. 23814 could be the attendance figure for a cricket match, 46.5 could be a cricketer's average batting score, and 崆 the lucky charm worn around the cricketer's neck (in Chinese it means Kongtong mountain).

We call a collection of bit patterns **data**. Data is the plural of datum.

Unless we know the meaning assigned to bit patterns, the only things that we see in a computer are data, i.e. uninterpreted bit patterns.

This is the **first role** performed by a **data type**: to establish what the bits/bit patterns mean.

The **second role** is to specify the number of bits allocated to each datum.

For example, characters might be represented in 8 bits (extended ASCII - see *Chapter 3.5*), integers in 32 bits, real numbers in 64 bits.

Table 2.1.1 shows some 8-bit patterns and their interpretation as ASCII characters.

Bit pattern	Character
01001000	H
01101001	i
01101111	o
00100000	space

Table 2.1.1 Some 8-bit patterns interpreted as ASCII characters

Characters are written surrounded by either single or double quotes, e.g. 'H', "H" depending on the programming language used.

If 8-bit patterns are "strung together", e.g. to form a 16-bit bit pattern, and each 8 bits of the 16-bit bit pattern is interpreted as a character then we have created another data type called **string**.

For example using *Table 2.1.1*, 0100100001101001 can be interpreted as meaning string "Hi" where 01001000 means "H" and 01101001 means "i".

2.1 Data types

The third role is to define the operations allowed on data.

For example, if the interpretation is data type *integer* then permitted operations should include at least addition, subtraction, and multiplication which produce a result of data type *integer*. For example 3 + 6 = 9.

If the interpretation is data type *real* then permitted operations should include at least addition, subtraction, multiplication and division which produce a result of data type *real*. For example 3.3 + 6.6 = 9.9.

What would not be allowed is any attempt to store the result of dividing one real by another if the destination of the result is storage reserved for an integer.

If the interpretation is data type *character* then a permitted operation could be to join two or more characters together to form a string (of characters).
For example, "H" + "i" = "Hi".

What would not be allowed is any attempt to join an integer to a character. For example, the operation "H" + 6 would not be allowed[1].

If the interpretation is data type *string* then a permitted operation could be to join two or more strings together to form a new string (of characters).
For example, "Hi" + " " + "Ho" = "Hi Ho". The space character is indicated by " ". It has bit pattern 00100000 in 8-bit ASCII. In this example, double quotes have been chosen for a string value and for a character value (different programming languages use different conventions).

Summarising, a data type

1. is a method of interpreting a bit pattern
2. specifies the number of bits allocated to each datum
3. defines which operations may be carried out on the bit pattern.

Programming languages provide abstractions to make life easier for you as a programmer. One such abstraction, is data typing.

Some programming languages include another data type, Boolean.

This data type has two possible values which are

True
False

It just remains to choose one bit pattern to represent True and a different bit pattern or bit patterns to represent False.

One 16-bit possibility is shown in *Table 2.1.2*. Other bit-pattern lengths may be used. Any bit pattern which isn't all 1s may be interpreted as representing False.

Bit pattern	Boolean value
1111111111111111	True
0000000000000000	False

Table 2.1.2 Some possible 16-bit patterns to represent the two Boolean values, True and False

Key concept

Data type:
A data type
1. is a method of interpreting a bit pattern
2. specifies the number of bits allocated to each datum.
3. defines which operations may be carried out on the bit pattern.

Did you know?

Real or floating point data type:
Computers store and manipulate real numbers such as 3.142 using the IEEE 754 floating point standard (knowledge of this is not required for GCSE Level). Real or floating-point numbers are little more than scientific notation encoded as bits. Real numbers can be very large or very small on a scale from the size of galaxies to the size of sub-atomic particles.
An alternative name for the data type real is float.

Key term

Boolean data type:
Two values only belong to the data type Boolean:
- the truth value True
- the truth value False.

Key point

Value:
Value means a datum together with its interpretation.

---

1 There are always exceptions to the rule: some programming languages impose no data type checking.

2 Programming

The Boolean data type values True and False are used where the answer to a question is Yes or No.

For example,

Question: Is it true that the sun rises in the East?
Answer: Yes

Rephrasing as a true or false statement

Statement: The sun rises in the East
Boolean value of statement: True

Another example,

Statement: The sun rises in the West
Boolean value of statement: False

Data types in some programming languages

Table 2.1.3 shows some of the integer, real, character, string and Boolean data types for the programming languages C#, Java, Pascal, Delphi, Python and VB.NET.

Language	Integer	Real	Boolean	Character	String
C#	**int**: 32-bit signed integer	**float**: 32-bit IEEE 754 floating point **double**: 64-bit IEEE 754 floating point	**bool**: true/false	**char**	**string**
Java	**int**: 32-bit signed integer	**float**: single-precision 32-bit IEEE 754 floating point **double**: 64-bit IEEE 754 floating point	**boolean**: true/false	**char**: single 16-bit Unicode character	**String**
Pascal	**Integer**	**Real**	**Boolean**: True/False	**Char**	**String**
Delphi	**Integer**: 32-bit two's complement integer -2147483648 to 2147483647	**Double**: 64-bit IEEE 754 floating point supporting approximately 15 decimal digits of precision in a range from 2.23×10^{-308} to 1.79×10^{308} (**Real** available as well)	**Boolean**: True/False	**Char**: holds a single character in 8 bits. **AnsiChar**: character type guaranteed to be 8 bits in size	**String**
Python	**int**: 32-bit signed integer	**float**: double-precision 64-bit IEEE 754 floating point	**bool**: True/False	**unicode**	**str**
VB.NET	**Integer**: 32-bit signed integer	**Double**	**Boolean**: True/False	**Char**: 2 bytes	**String**: 0 to approximately 2 billion Unicode characters (but depends on platform)

Table 2.1.3 Integer, Real/float, Boolean, Character, String data types for the given programming languages

2.1 Data types

Questions

1. Complete the table by assigning to each value the correct data type from the following list: integer, real, character, string, Boolean.

Value	Data type
"H"	
3.142	
"Hi"	
True	
18537	

2. Name **two** possible data type interpretations of the bit pattern 0100100001101001.

3. Would the following addition of two values be a valid operation in a programming language that enforced strict data typing: "two" + 3?

4. What is meant by data type?

5. Is $2^{2^{100}}$ in the integer range 0 to 2,147,483,647?

6. What is the data type of the result of evaluating the following expressions
   (a) 5 > 6   (b) 5 < 6   (c) 7 = 7?
   (Read 5 > 6 as the statement "5 is greater than 6", 5 < 6 as the statement "5 is less than 6")

7. A count is to be taken of the number of tickets sold for a school concert. The count will be incremented by one each time a ticket is sold.
   Select the most suitable data type for this count (tick **one** box only).

Count	Tick **one** box
String	
Real	
Integer	

8. Telephone numbers need to be stored in the following format ddddd dddddd where d is a digit.
   For example, 01296 433014 which consists of five digits followed by a space followed by six digits.
   Select the most suitable data type for a telephone number (tick **one** box only).

Count	Tick **one** box
String	
Real	
Integer	

9. The circumference of a circle of radius r is to be calculated to three decimal places. Select the most suitable data type for the circumference result (tick **one** box only).

Count	Tick **one** box
String	
Real	
Integer	

In this chapter you have covered:

- The concept of a data type
- The meaning and use of the following data types
  - integer
  - real
  - Boolean
  - character
  - string.

2 Programming

2 Programming

Learning objectives:

- *Use, understand and know how the following statement types can be combined in programs*
  - *variable declaration*
  - *constant declaration*
  - *assignment*
  - *iteration*
  - *selection*
  - *subroutine (procedure/ function)*

- *Use definite (count-controlled) and indefinite iteration (condition controlled), (including indefinite iteration with the condition(s) at the start or the end of the iterative structure)*

- *Use nested selection and nested iteration structures*

- *Use meaningful identifier names and know why it is important to use them.*

Key concept

Variable:
In programming, a variable can be thought of as a container for a value.
Like a physical container a variable may be empty, in which case we say that its value is undefined.

2.2 Programming concepts

Variable declaration

Variable

Data which are subject to change are modelled in a program by variables. A **variable** is simply a container in which a value may be stored for subsequent manipulation within a program - *Figure 2.2.1*.

The stored value may be changed by the program as it executes its instructions, hence the use of the term "variable" for the container.

Under the bonnet, the container is realised as one or more reserved memory locations in the RAM of the machine.

Variable declaration

A **variable declaration** is one way of causing a variable to be created.

For example, in Pascal/Delphi, an integer variable, x, may be declared as follows

```
Var
   x : Integer;
```

The amount of reserved memory allocated to a variable and what is allowed to be stored in this reserved memory depend upon its data type.

This declaration reserves a **named space** in memory (RAM) for a value of data type `Integer`. The space is named x and the amount of RAM is four bytes because that is what Pascal's `Integer` data type specifies[1].

By assigning different data types to each variable, *integers, numbers with a fractional part, characters, strings, arrays, records* and *other entities*, may be stored in these variables.

In some languages, e.g. Python, variables do not need an explicit declaration for memory space to be reserved. The declaration happens automatically when a value is assigned to a variable. Values in Python are strongly typed but variables are not.

Figure 2.2.1 shows the value 6 about to be stored in variable x represented by the yellow container

---

1   It is implementation dependent but four bytes is typical.

2 Programming

> **Key concept**
>
> **Variable declaration:**
> A variable declaration is one way of causing a variable to be created.

> **Key point**
>
> **Modelling data by variables:**
> Data which are subject to change are modelled by variables.

> **Key concept**
>
> **Constant:**
> In programming, data which never change are modelled in a program by constants. This means stating their values explicitly.
> To make a program easier to read, understand and maintain, a constant is given a symbolic name which can be used throughout the program whenever the value of the constant is required.

> **Questions**
>
> 1. What is a variable?
> 2. What is a variable declaration?
> 3. What is a constant declaration?

> **Information**
>
> This textbook covers Python (version 3), C# and VB.NET, the programming languages supported by AQA for examinations from 2022 onwards. In addition, it also covers programming languages Java and Pascal/Delphi.

Initialising variables

It is common practice to initialise a variable when it is declared.
For example, in Pascal/Delphi

```
Var
    x : Integer = 6;
```

In C#, an integer variable, x, may be declared and initialised as follows

```
int x = 6;
```

In Java, an integer variable, x, may be declared and initialised as follows

```
int x = 6;
```

In VB.NET, an integer variable, x, may be declared and initialised as follows

```
Dim x As Integer = 6
```

Constant declaration

Some of the data used in programs never change. For example, the ratio of the circumference of a circle to its diameter which is approximately 3.142.

Data which never change are modelled in a program by constants.

This means stating their values explicitly. To make a program easier to read, understand and change, a constant is given a **symbolic name** which can be used throughout the program whenever the value of the constant is required.

For example, in Pascal/Delphi a constant for the value 3.142 can be defined using the language keyword `Const` as follows

Language keyword → `Const`

```
Pi = 3.142;
```

Symbolic name for constant

In C# the symbolic name by convention is in uppercase and can use underscores for spaces, e.g. `NO_OF_DAYS_IN_WEEK`. The following is an example of a constant definition in C#

```
(public/private) const float PI = 3.142f;
```
or
```
(public/private) const double PI = 3.142;
```

The data type `double` is a double-precision 64-bit IEEE 754 floating point number. The data type `float` is a single-precision 32-bit IEEE 754 floating point number. In the case of `float` the letter `f` must be appended to the value.

In Java the symbolic name by convention is in uppercase and can use underscores for spaces. The following is an example of a constant definition in Java

```
(public/private)static final float PI = 3.142f;
```
or
```
(public/private) static final double PI = 3.142;
```

The data type `double` is a double-precision 64-bit IEEE 754 floating point number. The data type `float` is a single-precision 32-bit IEEE 754 floating point number. In the case of `float` the letter `f` must be appended to the value.

In VB.NET

```
Const pi As Double = 3.142
```

Python has no way to declare constants. Variables with symbolic names written in uppercase letters and with underscores for spaces signify that their values will be used as constants but the language cannot prevent the values from being changed. It is only a convention.

Questions

4. The calculation 2 x 3.141592654 x radius is made in several places in a program. Give **two** reasons why replacing 3.141592654 by the named constant `pi` could improve this program.

Assignment

An instruction which alters the value of a variable is called an **assignment statement** and the operation is called **assignment**. A value is copied into a variable when a computer executes an assignment statement. The action replaces the currently stored value in the variable as illustrated in *Figures 2.2.2* and *2.2.3* for a variable `x`.

For example, in Pascal/Delphi an assignment statement that **assigns** the value 6 to variable `x` is written as follows

```
x := 6;
```

The operand, `x`, to the left of the `:=` operator is the name of the variable and the operand, 6, to the right of the `:=` operator is the value that will be stored in the variable when assignment is carried out. The value in `x` before assignment occurs is overwritten by the assignment operation. This is shown by example in *Figure 2.2.3* where the value 4 is overwritten by the value 6.

The `:=` operator is called the **assignment operator**. In pseudo-code, a left-pointing arrow ← is used to represent the assignment operator.

The term "statement" is used universally for historical reasons. It would have been better to have adopted the term "command" or "instruction". Examples of assignment statements and assignment operators in other programming languages and in pseudo-code are shown below.

In C#,	`x = 6;`
In Java,	`x = 6;`
In Python,	`x = 6`
In VB.NET,	`x = 6`
In pseudo-code,	`x ← 6`

(See *Chapter 1.1* for an explanation of pseudo-code.)

Figure 2.2.2 shows the value 6 about to be stored in variable x which currently contains the value 4

Figure 2.2.3 shows that value 4 has been replaced by value 6

Key term

Assignment statement: An instruction which alters the value of a variable is called an assignment statement. The operation is known as assignment.

Questions

5. What is assignment?

2 Programming

Iteration

Suppose we are required to sum the first 10 natural numbers, i.e.

$$1 + 2 + 3 + 4 + 5 + 6 + 7 + 8 + 9 + 10$$

One way that this could be done is to **repeat** the addition of each natural number in turn to a running total, initialised to 0, **until** all 10 natural numbers have been added together.

In pseudo-code this might be expressed as shown in *Table 2.2.1*.

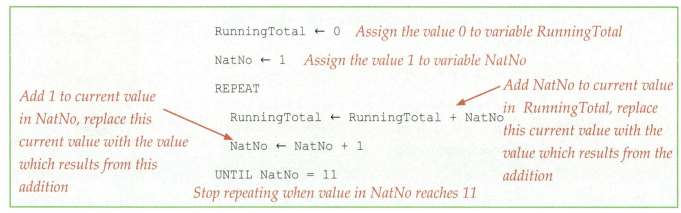

Table 2.2.1 Pseudo-code example which adds the first 10 natural numbers

Figures 2.2.4 and *2.2.5* show the execution of the assignment statement

```
NatNo ← NatNo + 1
```

split over two stages. `NatNo` contains the value 6 just before this statement is executed and afterwards it contains the value 7.

The pseudo-code in *Table 2.2.1* illustrates repetition or *iteration*. The general form of such iteration is

```
Repeat
    instructions
Until condition
```

which means that the instructions between the words `Repeat` and `Until` are executed repeatedly until the condition specified in `Until condition` is met.

The instructions between `Repeat` and `Until` are known as the **loop body**. The iteration performed by `Repeat Until` is called a **loop** because execution loops back and forth between `Repeat` and `Until`.

The condition occurring in `Until condition` is called the **terminating condition** of the loop.

Figure 2.2.4 shows the value 6 stored in variable NatNo, being copied then added to 1 and the result 7 about to be stored

Figure 2.2.5 shows the value 7 stored in variable NatNo

> **Key term**
>
> **Iteration statements:**
> Instructions are executed repeatedly until the terminating condition is met.

2.2 Programming concepts

Questions

6. Trace the execution of the pseudo-code shown in *Table 2.2.1*. Record in *Table 2.2.2* the value of `NatNo` and `RunningTotal` as they change during the execution. The first value of each variable has been recorded for you in the table.

NatNo	RunningTotal
1	0

Table 2.2.2 Trace table for NatNo and RunningTotal

The final value of `RunningTotal` should be **55**.

7. How would you change the pseudo-code in *Table 2.2.1* so that when executed, it adds the first **15** natural numbers?

   Check that your change is correct by hand-tracing the resulting pseudo-code. The final value of `RunningTotal` should be **120**.

Table 2.2.3 shows another way to add the first 10 natural numbers.

```
RunningTotal ← 0

NatNo ← 1

WHILE NatNo < 11      Stop repeating when value in NatNo reaches 11

    RunningTotal ← RunningTotal + NatNo

    NatNo ← NatNo + 1

ENDWHILE
```

Table 2.2.3 Pseudo-code example which adds the first 10 natural numbers

Questions

8 Trace the execution of the pseudo-code shown in *Table 2.2.3*. Record in *Table 2.2.4* the value of `NatNo` and `RunningTotal` as they change during the execution. The first value of each variable has been recorded for you in the table.

NatNo	RunningTotal
1	0

Table 2.2.4 Trace table for NatNo and RunningTotal

9 How would you change the pseudo-code in *Table 2.2.3* so that when executed it adds the first **15** natural numbers?

Check that your change is correct by hand-tracing the resulting pseudo-code. The final value of `RunningTotal` should be **120**.

10 What is the final value of `RunningTotal` when the following pseudo-code is executed by hand if x in `RunningTotal x Count` is the multiplication operator?

```
RunningTotal ← 1
Count ← 2
REPEAT
   RunningTotal ← RunningTotal x Count
   Count ← Count + 1
UNTIL Count = 11
```

Sequence

The following two instructions (assignment statements) of the pseudo-code in *Table 2.2.3* are executed one after the other

```
RunningTotal ← RunningTotal + NatNo

NatNo ← NatNo + 1
```

They form a *sequence* of steps governed by the following rules

1. The steps are executed one at a time
2. The order in which the steps are written is the order in which they are executed
3. Each step is executed exactly once.

We say that this part of the solution to the problem of adding the first 10 natural numbers is constructed using a program design principle called *sequence*.

Selection

If statement

If solutions to problems consist only of steps in sequence then there is no possibility of solving problems which need to deviate from the given sequence of execution if circumstances require this.

For example, suppose instead of summing the first 10 natural numbers we are required to sum only the even numbers amongst the first 10 natural numbers, using the pseudo-code in *Table 2.2.3*. The solution must test to see if the next natural number is even. Only if it is even will it then be added it to the running total.

The revised sequence section of the pseudo-code solution in *Table 2.2.3* will take the form

```
IF NatNo is even THEN            ── condition
    RunningTotal ← RunningTotal + NatNo  ── step
ENDIF
NatNo ← NatNo + 1
```

The conditional part of this pseudo-code fits the general form

```
IF condition THEN
    step
```

where *condition* specifies the circumstance under which the *step* is to be executed. If *condition* is true then *step* is executed; otherwise it is not.

`IF condition THEN step ENDIF` is a statement known as *selection*.

Suppose instead of summing the first 10 natural numbers we are required to sum the even numbers in one running total and the odd numbers in a different running total. We now have two alternative steps to be executed.

The revised sequence section of the pseudo-code solution in *Table 2.2.3* will take the form

```
IF NatNo is even THEN                            ── condition
    EvenRunningTotal ← EvenRunningTotal + NatNo  ── step 1
ELSE
    OddRunningTotal ← OddRunningTotal + NatNo    ── step 2
ENDIF
NatNo ← NatNo + 1
```

> **Key term**
>
> **Sequence statements:** Statements are executed one at a time, one after another in the order in which they are written with each executed exactly once.

> **Questions**
>
> 11. A variable x contains the value 7 and a variable y the value 3.
>
> Using only sequence, write assignment statements that swap the values contained in x and y. You may use Temp, a third variable.

2 Programming

The general form of selection in which selection is between one of two alternative steps is

```
IF condition THEN
    step 1
ELSE
    step 2
ENDIF
```

where `condition` determines whether `step 1` is executed or `step 2` is executed. We thus have two forms of `IF` selection statement:

```
IF condition THEN
    step
ENDIF
```

```
IF condition THEN
    step 1
ELSE
    step 2
ENDIF
```

> **Key term**
>
> **Selection:**
> A selection statement takes one of two possible forms:
> ```
> IF condition THEN
>     step
> ENDIF
> ```
> or
> ```
> IF condition THEN
>     step 1
> ELSE
>     step 2
> ENDIF
> ```
> The condition determines whether or not `step` is executed, `step1` or `step2` is executed.

> **Questions**
>
> 12. Rewrite the following IF statements as a single IF THEN ELSE ENDIF statement
> ```
> IF Age < 37 THEN AgeCategory ← 'A' ENDIF
> IF Age >=37 THEN AgeCategory ← 'B' ENDIF
> ```
>
> 13. The pseudo-code in *Table 2.2.5* finds the largest of two numbers, `No1`, `No2`.
> The value of the largest of the two numbers is stored in variable `Largest`.
> (a) If `No1` stores the value 6, `No2` the value 3 which branch of the selection statement is executed, THEN or ELSE? Explain your answer.
> (b) If `No1` stores the value 6, `No2` the value 7 which branch of the selection statement is executed, THEN or ELSE? Explain your answer.

> **Key fact**
>
> **Combining principles:**
> The three combining principles (sequence, iteration/repetition and selection/choice) are basic to all imperative programming languages.

```
IF No1 > No2 THEN
    Largest ← No1
ELSE
    Largest ← No2
ENDIF
```

Table 2.2.5 Pseudo-code to find the largest of two numbers

Subroutine

A subroutine is a **named self-contained block of instructions**, e.g. `drawsquare`.

By encapsulating and naming a block of instructions in a program it becomes possible to call the block from other parts of the program. This is very useful in situations where the same block of instructions or action or calculation needs to be repeated in multiple places in a program.

Suppose that we wish to draw the pattern containing six squares shown in *Figure 2.2.6*. The size (side-length) of the squares increases by the same fixed amount. One way of drawing a square with length of side, `size`, is to use a pen-carrying turtle moving under the guidance of the sequence of instructions or commands shown in *Figure 2.2.7*.

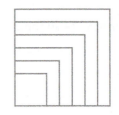

Figure 2.2.6 Pattern of squares

2.2 Programming concepts

```
turtle.forward(size)
turtle.left(90)
turtle.forward(size)
turtle.left(90)
turtle.forward(size)
turtle.left(90)
turtle.forward(size)
turtle.left(90)
```

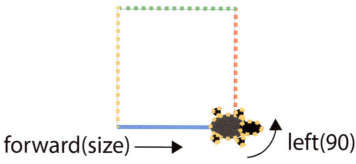

Figure 2.2.7 Path followed by a turtle obeying the sequence of commands shown opposite

It is good practice to use active verbs for subroutine names, e.g. Read, Write, Add, DoSomething.

If this sequence of instructions in *Figure 2.2.7* is named `drawsquare` then a program could call upon this subroutine to draw a square of a specific size, say, 25, as follows: `drawsquare(25)`

A program that calls upon the subroutine `drawsquare` is said to **call the subroutine** `drawsquare`.

To draw a differently-sized square of size, say, 35, `drawsquare` would need to be called upon as follows

`drawsquare(35)`

The square-drawing turtle subroutine itself could be written as shown in *Table 2.2.6*.

The variable `size` is called the **formal parameter of the subroutine**: it is used in the **body of the subroutine** to define how big the square will be.

When the subroutine is called, the **actual parameter** 25 or 35, for example, provides a specific value for `size`, and thus determines how big the square will be in each call.

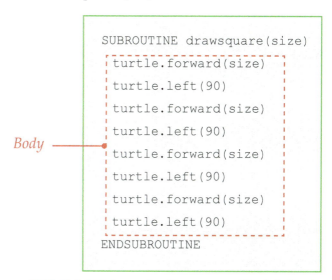

Table 2.2.6 Subroutine drawsquare(size) defined

The subroutine `drawsquare` itself calls subroutines `turtle.forward` and `turtle.left`.

To draw the pattern of squares in *Figure 2.2.6* we need the sequence of calls to subroutine `drawsquare` shown in *Table 2.2.7*.

Figure 2.2.7 shows how the `drawsquare` subroutine could be defined in Python 3.4 and how it would be called to produce the pattern of squares shown in *Figure 2.2.6*.

A subroutine may also contain its own *variable*, *type*, and *constant* declarations. In fact, it may also define other subroutines within its declaration section.

```
drawsquare(25)
drawsquare(35)
drawsquare(45)
drawsquare(55)
drawsquare(65)
drawsquare(75)
```

Table 2.2.7 Calling subroutine drawsquare(size) with different actual parameters

2 Programming

> **Key term**
>
> **Subroutine:**
> A subroutine is a named self-contained block of instructions, e.g. drawsquare, which may be called (i.e. executed) from anywhere within a program where its name appears.

> **Key term**
>
> **Procedure:**
> A procedure is a subroutine consisting of one or more statements or actions which may or may not return a result.

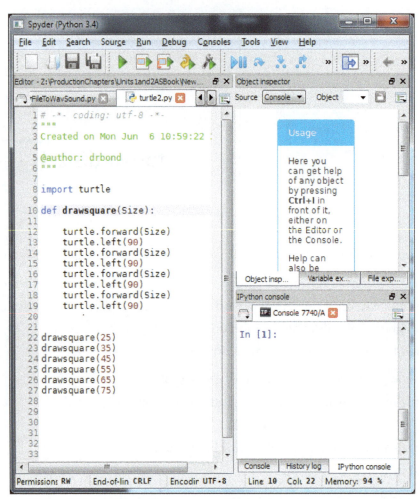

Figure 2.2.8 Python 3.4 program to draw a pattern of squares

Procedures and functions

There are two types of subroutines:

- Procedure
- Function

A procedure is a **subroutine consisting of one or more statements or actions which may or may not return a result**. If it returns a result it does so through output parameters in its interface - see page 126. The statements are referred to collectively by a name assigned to the procedure called the **procedure name**. The procedure must be declared/defined – its name must be stated and its statements listed. The procedure's statements are executed wherever its name is encountered in the executable part of a program - see *Figure 2.2.8*. This is called **calling a procedure**.

In Pascal, a procedure is declared and used as follows:

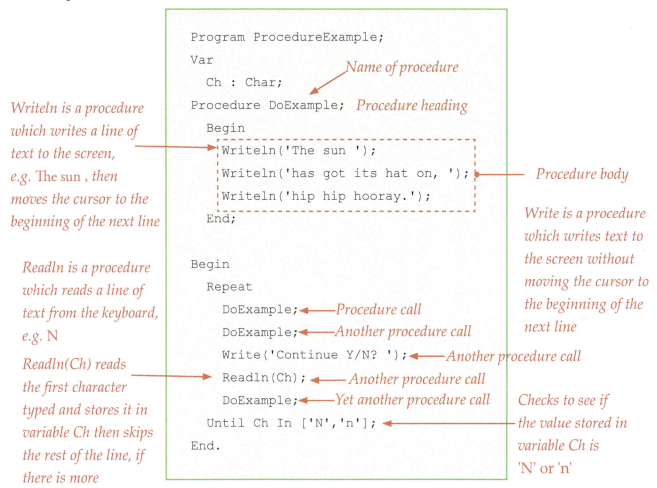

Writeln is a procedure which writes a line of text to the screen, e.g. The sun , then moves the cursor to the beginning of the next line

Readln is a procedure which reads a line of text from the keyboard, e.g. N

Readln(Ch) reads the first character typed and stores it in variable Ch then skips the rest of the line, if there is more

Write is a procedure which writes text to the screen without moving the cursor to the beginning of the next line

Checks to see if the value stored in variable Ch is 'N' or 'n'

Table 2.2.8 Pascal program containing calls to procedures DoExample, Writeln, Write, Readln

Table 2.2.9 shows a VB.NET program which declares a user-defined procedure called `DoExample`.

The procedure `DoExample` is called three times when the program executes. `Main()` is called to run the program.

In VB.NET, `Main()` is a standard procedure name found in every executable module (Visual Studio supplies a module template containing `Main()`).

VB.NET doesn't use the keyword `Procedure` but instead surrounds the body of the procedure with the keywords `Sub` and `End Sub`. Instead of the language keyword `Program` as in Pascal, VB.NET uses the keyword `Module`. It has a matching keyword `End Module` placed at the very end of the program.

```
Module ProcedureExample
    Sub DoExample()
        Console.WriteLine("The sun has ")
        Console.WriteLine("got its hat on,  ")
        Console.WriteLine("hip hip hooray.")
    End Sub
    Sub Main()
        DoExample()
        DoExample()
        DoExample()
        Console.ReadLine()
    End Sub
End Module
```

Table 2.2.9 VB.NET program containing calls to a procedure DoExample

2 Programming

Figure 2.2.9 shows one call to a Python 3.5 procedure with the name do_example which has been defined using Python's keyword `def`.

Procedure interface

A procedure interface is **a mechanism for passing data into and out of a procedure**.

In Pascal, for example, x is known as a **formal parameter** as shown in *Table 2.2.10*. This is a variable used in the body of the procedure and which appears in the interface. When the procedure is called an **actual parameter** is supplied through the procedure's interface, e.g. DoInterfaceExample(MyName) where the variable MyName is the **actual parameter**. The value in MyName is copied into the variable x when the procedure is called by DoInterfaceExample(MyName).

Suppose MyName stores the string 'Fred Bloggs', then the variable x in the body of the procedure will contain the string 'Fred Bloggs'.

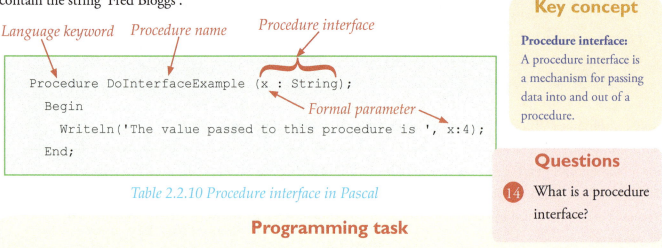

Figure 2.2.9 Shows one call to a Python 3.5 procedure with the name do_example which has been defined using Python's keyword `def`

```
Procedure DoInterfaceExample (x : String);
  Begin
    Writeln('The value passed to this procedure is ', x:4);
  End;
```

Language keyword — *Procedure name* — *Procedure interface* — *Formal parameter*

Table 2.2.10 Procedure interface in Pascal

Key concept

Procedure interface: A procedure interface is a mechanism for passing data into and out of a procedure.

Questions

14 What is a procedure interface?

Programming task

1 In a programming language with which you are familiar, write a program which defines a procedure that displays the message passed it through its interface.

Function

A function is a type of subroutine designed to **always return a single result**. The mechanism by which the result is returned is different from that used by a procedure.

Functions may appear in expressions such as 5 x cube(3) where cube is a mathematical function.
This is possible because a function **returns a value**.
So 5 x cube(3) evaluates to 5 x 27 which evaluates to 135.

In the first evaluation step, cube(3) is replaced by 27, the result returned from the execution of function cube(3). Any attempt to use a procedure in this manner would fail.

This is a key difference between a function and a procedure.

54

2.2 Programming concepts

Procedure calls do not support a mechanism by which a value is substituted for the procedure call when the latter completes and returns control. If the procedure did then it would be a function[2].

For example, the following does not make sense as an expression because drawsquare doesn't "evaluate" to a single value which can be multiplied by 5 to produce a numeric result, e.g. 127:

> 5 x drawsquare(3) where drawsquare is a procedure.

Because functions "evaluate" to a single value[3] they may appear on the right-hand side of an assignment statement.

For example,

> x ← cube(3)

After this statement is executed, the variable x contains/stores the value 27, because the result of calling cube(3) is 27.

Attempting the following would fail because Writeln is a procedure. It also would not make sense.

> x := Writeln('The sun has got its hat on');

In Pascal, the code Writeln('The sun has got its hat on') is a command which writes the string 'The sun has got its hat on' to the screen then moves the screen's cursor to the beginning of the next line.

Figure 2.2.10 shows a function cube(n) defined in Python 3.5, and then called with argument 3.

In function cube(n), n is called the formal parameter. When functions are called we use a slightly different terminology. The actual parameter is now called the **argument**.

For example, in the function call cube(3), 3 is the argument to the function.

Pascal makes a clear distinction between procedure and function by using different keywords for defining each. *Table 2.2.11* shows a function Cube being defined using the language keyword Function. As Pascal is a strongly typed language, the data type of the formal parameter and the data type of the returned value must be specified. It is Integer for both in this example.

> **Key term**
>
> **Function:**
> A function is a type of subroutine designed to always return a single result. It may appear in expressions and on the right hand-side of an assignment statement unlike a procedure.

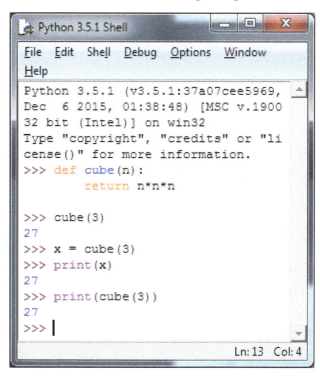

Figure 2.2.10 Function cube(n) defined and used in Python 3.5

Questions

15. State **one** key difference between a function and a procedure.

---

2 Impure functions in addition to returning a result, may have side effects which is the collective name for other things that the function may do as well.

3 In some programming languages functions are allowed to return a structured result i.e. a result with more than one value.

2 Programming

Pascal uses the name of the function to assign the value that is to be returned.

Alternatively, the keyword Result can be used in place of Cube.

```
Function Cube (n : Integer) : Integer;
  Begin
    Cube := n * n * n;
  End;
```

Table 2.2.11 Function Cube(n) defined in Pascal

C#

In C#, the approach to defining subroutines is different from Pascal. In C#, subroutines are called functions, whether in their behaviour they are procedures or functions. In C#, the subroutine heading takes the following form

<visibility> <modifier> <return type> <subroutine-name>(<parameters>)

The first part is the visibility, and is optional. If not specified then the function will be private.

The second part is the modifier, and is optional. If it is specified then the function belongs to the class otherwise it belongs to a specific object of the class[4]. The modifier is the keyword `static`.

The third part is the return type. If this is `void` then no result is returned via the function mechanism. In this case the subroutine behaves as a procedure. The term "`void`" is meant to indicate that the return value is empty or nonexistent.

If the return type is a valid data type, e.g. `int`, then a result is returned via the function mechanism. In this case the subroutine behaves as a function.

Figure 2.2.11 shows a Visual Studio 2015 C# program which defines a procedure `DoExample` which is called twice by `Main`. It is a procedure because the specified return type is `void`. The procedure belongs to the type `class Program` because the modifier is specified with the keyword `static`.

Figure 2.2.12 shows a Visual Studio 2015 C# program which defines a function `Add2Numbers` which is called by `Main`.

It is a function because the specified return type is `int`.

The function belongs to the class `Program` because the modifier of `Add2Numbers` is specified with the keyword `static`.

`Add2Numbers` is used as a function in `Main`. It appears on the right-hand side of an assignment statement as follows

```
int answer = Add2Numbers(4, 8);
```

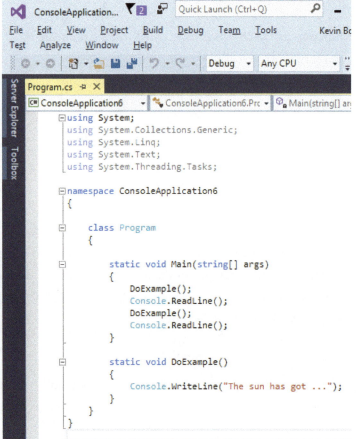

Figure 2.2.11 C# DoExample procedure

---

[4] Object-oriented programming not in GCSE

Function `Add2Numbers` makes it possible to add two numbers from various places in a program, simply by calling this function instead of having to write the calculation code each time.

Java

In Java, the approach to defining subroutines is similar to C#'s approach.

```
<visibility> <modifier> <return-type>
<subroutine-name > ( <parameters >) {
     statements
}
```

The statements between the braces, { and }, in a subroutine definition make up the body of the subroutine.

The first part is the visibility, and is optional. If it isn't specified then the function will be private.

The second part is the modifier, and is optional. If it is specified then the function belongs to the class otherwise it belongs to a specific object of the class[5]. The modifier is the keyword `static`.

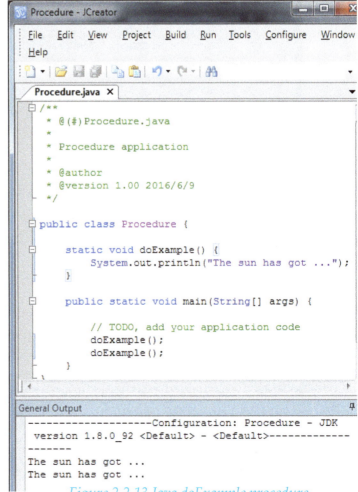

Figure 2.2.12 C# Add2Numbers function

The third part is the return type. If this is `void` then no result is returned via the function mechanism. In this case the subroutine behaves as a procedure. The term "`void`" is meant to indicate that the return value is empty or nonexistent.

Figure 2.2.13 shows a Java program which defines a procedure `doExample` which is called twice by `Main`. It is a procedure because the specified return type is `void`. The procedure belongs to the class `Procedure` because the modifier of `doExample` is specified with the keyword `static`.

Figure 2.2.14 shows a Java program which defines a function `add2Numbers` which is called by `Main`.

It is a function because the specified return type is `int`.

The function belongs to the class `JavaAdd2Numbers` because the modifier of `add2Numbers` is specified with the keyword `static`.

`add2Numbers` is used as a function in `Main`. It appears on the right-hand side of an assignment statement as follows

`int answer = add2Numbers(4, 8);`

Figure 2.2.13 Java doExample procedure

---

5   Object-oriented programming is not covered in GCSE

2 Programming

VB.NET

In VB.NET, the approach to defining a function is as follows

```
<visibility> <modifier> Function <FunctionName>
(<parameters>) As <return type>
        <Statements>
End Function
```

The first part is the visibility, and is optional. If it isn't specified then the function will be private.

The second part is the modifier, and is optional. The third part is the return type, e.g. Integer.

Figure 2.2.15 shows a VB.NET program which defines a function `Add2Numbers` which is called by `Main` from two different places in `Main`.

The return type of this function is `Integer`.

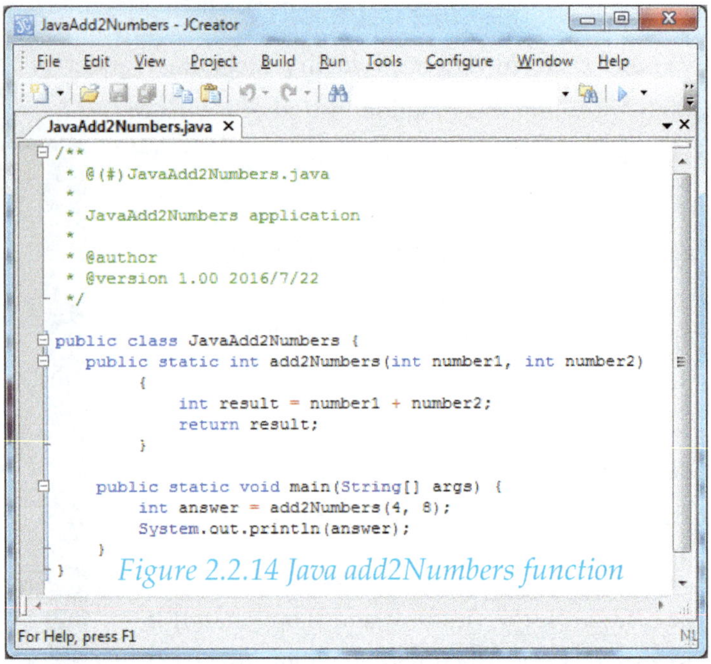

Figure 2.2.14 Java add2Numbers function

`Add2Numbers` is used as a function in `Main`. It appears on the right-hand side of an assignment statement as follows
`answer = Add2Numbers(4, 8)`

It also appears in a second call as an actual parameter to the procedure `WriteLine` as follows

`Console.WriteLine(Add2Numbers(6,9))`

```vb
Module FunctionAdd2Numbers
    Function Add2Numbers(number1 As Integer, number2 As Integer) As Integer
        Return number1 + number2
    End Function
    Sub Main()
        Dim answer As Integer
        answer = Add2Numbers(4, 8)
        Console.WriteLine(answer)
        Console.ReadLine()
        Console.WriteLine(Add2Numbers(6, 9))
        Console.ReadLine()
    End Sub
End Module
```

Figure 2.2.15 VB.NET Add2Numbers function

Programming task

2 In a programming language with which you are familiar:

(a) Write a program which defines a function that sums the first n natural numbers and returns this sum. The program should display this sum for a given n.

(b) Write a program which defines a function that sums the even numbers amongst the first n natural numbers and returns this sum. The program should display this sum for a given n.
(HINT: IF ((NatNo MOD 2) = 0) THEN Even ← True ELSE Even ← False)

(c) Write a program which defines a function that finds the largest of two given integers, x and y. The program should display the largest.

2.2 Programming concepts

Definite (count-controlled) and indefinite (condition-controlled) iteration

We introduced the concept of a loop in the section on iteration. In this section, we explore ways in which the number of iterations (i.e. repetitions of the body of the loop) is determined.

We have two cases to consider, definite and indefinite iteration:

- In **definite iteration**, the **number of iterations is known before the execution of the body of the loop is started**. For example, repeat 5 times writing the string "Hello World!" to the output device.
- In **indefinite iteration**, the **number of iterations is not known before the execution of the body of the loop starts**. The number of iterations depends on when **a specific condition is met** (and this depends on what happens in the body of the loop). For example, repeat printing the string "Hello World" until, when asked, the user declines to continue.

Definite (count-controlled) iteration

Suppose that we wanted to output the value of a variable i, first when it is 1, next when it is 2, and so on until it is 5. We could do this with a *repeat until* loop or a *while* loop as shown by the pseudo-code examples in *Table 2.2.12*. The number of iterations of each loop is known in advance, it is five, so these are examples of **definite iteration**.

Note that a

- *repeat until <condition>* loop executes at least once
- a *while <condition>* executes zero or more times

```
i ← 0
REPEAT
    i ← i + 1
    OUTPUT i
UNTIL i = 5
```

```
i ← 1
WHILE i ≤ 5
    OUTPUT i
    i ← i + 1
ENDWHILE
```

Table 2.2.12 Definite iteration with repeat and while loops

> **Key term**
>
> **Definite iteration:**
> In definite iteration the number of iterations is known before the execution of the body of the loop is started.

> **Key term**
>
> **Loop terminating condition:**
> The condition which causes execution of the loop body to terminate is known as the terminating condition.

Loop terminating condition

In both *repeat* and *while* loops quite a lot of work has to be done by the programmer.

In the example, the variable i has to be initialised, with 0 for the repeat loop and with 1 for the while loop.

It has to be incremented (i ← i + 1), and it has to be tested with the test condition i = 5 for the repeat loop and i ≤ 5 for the while loop.

The *repeat until* loop terminates when its test condition is true.

The *while loop* terminates when its test condition is false.

In each case, the condition which causes execution of the loop body to terminate is known as the **terminating condition**.

In definite iteration, this terminating condition is met after a known and predictable number of iterations.

2 Programming

For loop

There is an easier way for the programmer to program definite iteration called the **for loop**.

This pseudo-code for the *for loop* shown in Table 2.2.13 is executed as follows

Step 1: The initial value of variable `i` is set to 1, "`i ← 1`". This step happens only once, regardless of how many times the loop repeats.

Step 2: The "`To 5`" part evaluates the condition (`i ≤ 5`) by comparing the value of `i` with 5.

If `i` is less than or equal to 5, the condition evaluates to true, and the statement "`OUTPUT i`" is executed. This sends the value of i to the output device, e.g. the VDU.

If `i` is greater than 5, the condition evaluates to false, and **the loop is exited**. The instruction immediately following `ENDFOR` is then executed next.

Step 3: The value of `i` is incremented by 1.

Step 4: The loop returns to *step 2* to evaluate the condition again.

```
FOR i ← 1 TO 5
    OUTPUT i
ENDFOR
```

Table 2.2.13 Definite iteration with a for loop

Note that if the initial value of `i` is greater than the 5 as shown in Table 2.2.14 the body of the loop should not be executed.

Variable `i` in this example is called the **loop control variable**.

A loop control variable must be an ordinal data type. An ordinal data type is one that consists of an ORDERED set of things in which each member has a single value only,

e.g. an integer data type.

```
FOR i ← 6 TO 5
    OUTPUT i
ENDFOR
```

Table 2.2.14 Definite iteration with a for loop

Questions

16. What is the output of the following pseudo-code?
```
FOR i ← 1 TO 5
    j ← 2 * i
    OUTPUT j
ENDFOR
```

17. What is the output of the following pseudo-code?
```
FOR Ch ← 'A' TO 'C'
    OUTPUT Ch
ENDFOR
```

18. How many times is the pseudo-code loop executed in Table 2.2.14?

Figure 2.2.16 shows an example of a *for loop* in Delphi/Pascal.

Figure 2.2.17 shows an example of a *for loop* in VB.NET.

For loops in C# and Java take a different form from Delphi/Pascal and VB.NET. This form is as follows

```
for (initialiser; condition; iterator)
    body
```

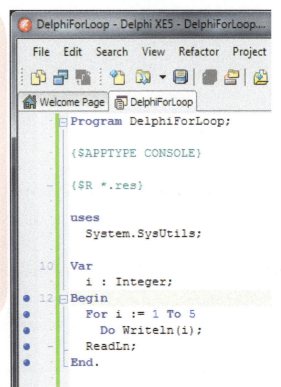

Figure 2.2.16 Delphi/Pascal For loop example

2.2 Programming concepts

Figure 2.2.18 shows a C# and *Figure 2.2.19* a Java *for loop* example.

The *iterator* `i++` means increment `i` by 1. The *initialiser* `int i = 1` means create a loop control variable `i` and give it an initial value of 1.

The condition `i <= 5` evaluates to true if `i` is less than or equal to 5; false if `i` is greater than 5. Python's *for loop* is different altogether from that of Delphi/Pascal, VB.NET, C# and Java.

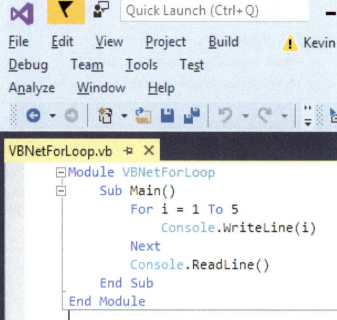

Figure 2.2.17 VB.NET For loop example

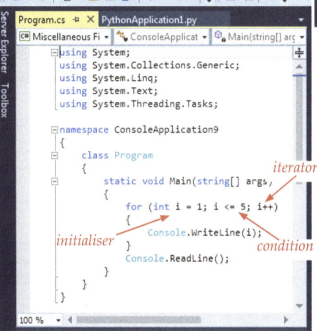

Figure 2.2.18 C# for loop example

Figure 2.2.20 shows a simple *for loop* example in Python 3.5.

The *range* function call `range(1,6)` generates the sequence of integers 1, 2, 3, 4, 5.

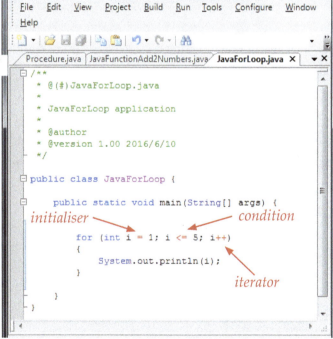

Figure 2.2.19 Java for loop example

The last value generated is always one less then the upper bound value for the range, e.g. the last value is 5 if upper bound is 6.

Step **1**: The loop control variable `i` is given the initial value **1**, the first value in the range.

Step **2**: The hidden condition (`i <= 5`) is evaluated by comparing the value of `i` with **5**.

If `i` is less than or equal to **5**, the condition evaluates to true, and the statement `print(i)` is executed.

If `i` is greater than **5**, the condition evaluates to false, and the loop is exited. The instruction immediately following the body of the loop is then executed next, if one exists.

Step **3**: The value of `i` is incremented by **1**.

Step **4**: The loop returns to the start of step 2 to evaluate the condition again.

2 Programming

> **Programming task**
>
> 3. In a programming language with which you are familiar, write a program that codes the pseudo-code shown in Question 16.

> **Key term**
>
> **Indefinite iteration:**
> In indefinite iteration, the number of iterations is not known before the execution of the body of the loop starts.

> **Key term**
>
> **Infinite loop:**
> If the terminating condition cannot ever be met for some reason then the execution remains within the repeat or the while loop indefinitely. We then have a situation called an infinite loop.

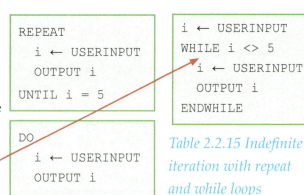

Figure 2.2.20 Python 3.5 For loop example in Visual Studio 2015

Indefinite (condition-controlled) iteration

The two cases of indefinite iteration to consider are *repeat* and *while* loops. "*For loops*" do not support indefinite iteration only definite iteration.

In *Table 2.2.15* the value of `i` in both pseudo-code examples is changed inside the loop in a way that cannot be predicted because it is obtained from the user through the input device, e.g. a keyboard, when `Input i` executes.

The value of `i` before the *while loop* executes is only known at the time of execution when `i ← USERINPUT` executes.

```
REPEAT
    i ← USERINPUT
    OUTPUT i
UNTIL i = 5
```

```
DO
    i ← USERINPUT
    OUTPUT i
WHILE i <> 5
```

```
i ← USERINPUT
WHILE i <> 5
    i ← USERINPUT
    OUTPUT i
ENDWHILE
```

Table 2.2.15 Indefinite iteration with repeat and while loops

It is therefore not possible to determine in advance the number of iterations of the body of each loop.

The number of iterations depends on when the terminating condition `i = 5` becomes true for the *repeat loop* and when the terminating condition `i <> 5` becomes false for the *while loop*.

If the terminating condition cannot ever be met for some reason then the execution remains within the *repeat* or the *while loop* indefinitely. We then have a situation called an **infinite loop**.

Table 2.2.16 shows how each loop could be written so that the iteration is infinite.

Sometimes an infinite loop condition was not the intention but the loop's programmer has got it wrong. Exiting the loop then becomes impossible by ordinary means because the loop terminating condition can never be met.

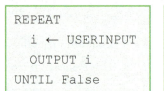
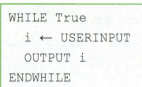

Table 2.2.16 Indefinite iteration with repeat and while loops showing a situation called an infinite loop

2.2 Programming concepts

Questions

19 What is the output of the following pseudo-code when the input is 1, 2, 3, 4, 0?

(a)
```
Sum ← 0
REPEAT
  n ← USERINPUT
  Sum ← Sum + n
UNTIL n = 0
OUTPUT Sum
```

(b)
```
Product ← 1
n ← USERINPUT
WHILE n > 0
  Product ← Product * n
  n ← USERINPUT
ENDWHILE
OUTPUT n
```

20 What is the output of the following pseudo-code?

(a)
```
j ← 4
REPEAT
  j ← j - 1
  OUTPUT j
UNTIL j < 1
```

(b)
```
j ← 4
REPEAT
  j ← j + 1
  OUTPUT j
UNTIL j > 6
```

(c)
```
j ← 4
WHILE j < 5
  j ← j + 1
  OUTPUT j
ENDWHILE
```

(d)
```
j ← 4
DO
  j ← j + 1
  OUTPUT j
WHILE j < 6
```

21 What is the essential difference between *definite* and *indefinite iteration*?

22 What is the essential difference between a *repeat until* loop and a *while* loop?

23 What is meant by an *infinite loop*?

24 Write a loop in pseudo-code which demonstrates an *infinite loop*.

Indefinite iteration in Pascal, Delphi, VB.NET, C#, Java, Python

Figure 2.2.21 shows two simple examples which illustrate how a *repeat* and a *while* loop can be constructed in Pascal/Delphi. The *while loop* is the only indefinite loop supported in Python. An example is shown in *Figure 2.2.22.*

Figure 2.2.23 shows a simple example which illustrates how a *repeat loop* can be constructed in VB.NET. The syntax of the construct is actually of the form *Do Loop Until <condition>*. *Figure 2.2.24* shows a simple example which illustrates how a *while loop* can be constructed in VB.NET using *Do While <condition> Loop*.

In C#, the *repeat loop* construct is implemented as a *do while loop* (*Figure 2.2.25*) and therefore the loop terminating condition is expressed as (`i != 5`), the inverse of what it would be if *repeat until* could be used. "`!=`" means not equal to.

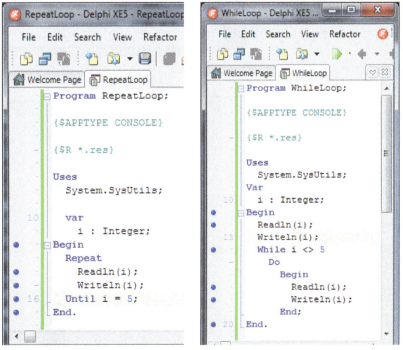

Figure 2.2.21 Repeat and while loops in Delphi
<> means not equal to in Pascal/Delphi

Figure 2.2.26 shows a simple example which illustrates how a *while loop* can be constructed in C#.

2 Programming

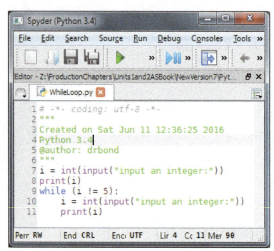

Figure 2.2.22 while loop in Python 3.4

!= means not equal to in Python

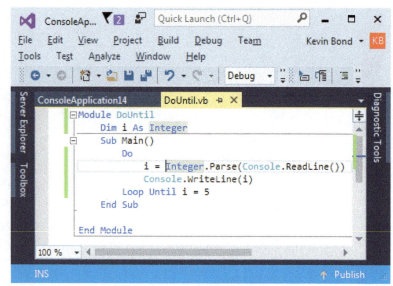

Figure 2.2.23 Repeat loop in VB.NET

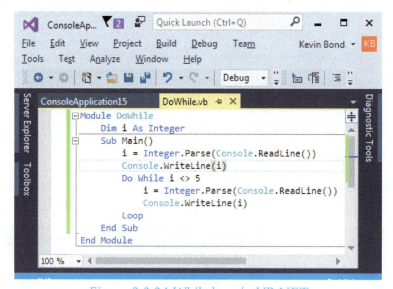

Figure 2.2.24 While loop in VB.NET

Figure 2.2.25 Repeat loop in C# is implemented as a do while loop

Figure 2.2.26 while loop in C#

2.2 Programming concepts

In Java, the *repeat loop* construct is implemented as a *do while loop* (Figure 2.2.27) and therefore the loop terminating condition is expressed as (i != 5), the inverse of what it would be if *repeat until* could be used. Figure 2.2.28 shows a simple example which illustrates how a *while loop* can be constructed in Java.

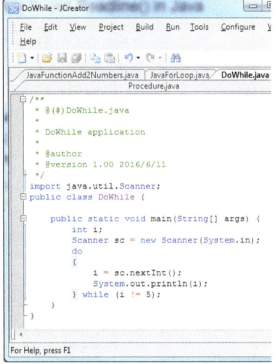

Figure 2.2.27 Repeat loop in Java is implemented as a Do While loop

Figure 2.2.28 While loop in Java

Programming task

 In a programming language with which you are familiar:
(a) Write programs that code the pseudo-code shown in Question 19(a) and 19(b).
(b) Write programs that code the pseudo-code shown in Question 20(a), 20(b), 20(c) and 20(d).

Nested selection statements

The pseudo-code in Table 2.2.17 contains three occurrences of *selection*, one marked in **black**, one in red and one in blue. The red-marked *selection* and the blue-marked *selection statements* are each nested inside the **black**-marked *selection statement*. This pseudo-code finds the largest of three numbers. The value of the first number is stored in variable No1. The value of the second number is stored in variable No2 and the third in No3.

The value of the largest of the three numbers is stored in variable Largest. If No1 stores the value 6, No2 the value 3 and No3 the value 8, the result of the comparison IF No1 > No2 is true because 6 is greater than 3.
The THEN block of the **black**-coloured *selection* is executed next.
This block contains another IF THEN ELSE statement, the one marked in red. The result of the comparison IF No1 > No3 is false because 6 is less than 8.
The ELSE coloured in red is executed next and the value stored in variable No3 is assigned to variable Largest.

```
IF No1 > No2 THEN
  IF No1 > No3 THEN
    Largest ← No1
  ELSE
    Largest ← No3
  ENDIF
ELSE
  IF No2 > No3 THEN
    Largest ← No2
  ELSE
    Largest ← No3
  ENDIF
ENDIF
```

Table 2.2.17 Pseudo-code to find the largest of three numbers

Questions

25 Using the pseudo-code in *Table 2.2.17*
   (a) If `No1` stores the value **6**, `No2` the value **7** and `No3` the value **5** which selection statements are executed? Explain your answer.
   (b) If `No1` stores the value **6**, `No2` the value **6** and `No3` the value **5** which selection statements are executed? Explain your answer.

Programming task

5 Write a program which defines a function that finds the largest of three integers, x, y, and z. The program should display the largest.

Nested iteration statements

We may place a *for loop* inside a *for loop* as shown in *Table 2.2.18*. The inner *for loop* executes for each value of the loop control variable `i` of the outer *for loop*. The trace table, *Table 2.2.19*, shows the output and the values of `i` and `j`, the outer loop and inner loop control variables, respectively, for the first few values of the trace. *While* and *Repeat* loops can also be nested.

```
FOR i ← 1 TO 5
   FOR j ← 1 TO 3
      OUTPUT i
   ENDFOR
ENDFOR
```

Table 2.2.18 Nested for loop

i	j	Output
1	1	1
1	2	1
1	3	1
2	1	2
2	2	2
2	3	2

Table 2.2.19 Trace table

Questions

26 What is the output of the following pseudo-code?

(a)
```
FOR i ← 1 TO 2
   FOR j ← 1 TO 3
      OUTPUT j
   ENDFOR
ENDFOR
```

(b)
```
For i ← 1 TO 3
   For j ← 1 TO i
      OUTPUT j
   ENDFOR
ENDFOR
```

27 What is the output of the following pseudo-code?

(a)
```
FOR Ch1 ← 'A' TO 'C'
   For Ch2 ← 'A' TO Ch1
      OUTPUT Ch2
   ENDFOR
ENDFOR
```

(b)
```
FOR Ch1 ← 'a' TO 'c'
   FOR Ch2 ← 'a' TO 'c'
      FOR Ch3 ← 'a' TO 'c'
         OUTPUT Ch1, Ch2, Ch3
      ENDFOR
   ENDFOR
ENDFOR
```

Programming tasks

6 In a programming language with which you are familiar,
   (a) Write a program that codes the pseudo-code shown in Question 26(a).
   (b) Write a program that codes the pseudo-code shown in Question 26(b).

2.2 Programming concepts

> **Questions**
>
> **28** Write the following nested *for loop* as a single *for loop*
> ```
> FOR i ← 1 TO 4
>   FOR j ← 3 TO 5
>     OUTPUT('*')
>   ENDFOR
> ENDFOR
> ```
>
> **29** Complete the trace table, *Table 2.2.20*, by hand tracing the following pseudo-code
> ```
> FOR i ← 0 TO 1
>   FOR j ← 0 TO 2
>     OUTPUT j
>   ENDFOR
> ENDFOR
> ```
>
> | i | j | Output |
> |---|---|--------|
> | 0 | 0 | |
> | | | |
> | | | |
> | | | |
> | | | |
> | | | |
> | | | |
>
> *Table 2.2.20 Trace table*

Using meaningful identifier names

The names that have been used for variables, constants, subroutines such as `RunningTotal`, `NO_OF_DAYS_IN_WEEK`, `drawsquare`, `Cube` are all examples of identifiers. These identifiers describe what they represent, e.g. `RunningTotal`. **When an identifier is descriptive of what it represents or of its purpose, we say that it has a meaningful name.**

The following points are relevant to why programmers should use meaningful identifier names:

- Meaningful identifier names make it easier for the programmer to understand the source code because meaningfully-named identifiers describe what they represent or do
- Programmers spend far longer reading their source code than writing it so it is important that the source code is as descriptive of what it does as possible
- Programmers spend a lot of time reading other programmers' source code as well as their own and so it is important that the source code is as descriptive of what it does as possible
- Program source code needs to make sense when it is read, i.e. it should be possible to understand what the source code has been written to do, otherwise its intention will be unclear
- A programmer may wish/has to use source code that someone else has written. To do this successfully they need at least to understand the source code
- A programmer may be tasked to debug a program because it contains runtime/logical errors, e.g. it doesn't do what it is expected to do. The programmer will need to understand the source code in order to debug it
- A programmer may also be tasked to modify a program because what it is required to do has changed. The programmer will need to understand the source code to change it successfully.

Table 2.2.21 shows pseudo-code which sums the first 10 natural numbers. Comments have been added to the pseudo-code which describe the purpose of each statement because the identifier names alone are not sufficient to make the purpose clear (this may be an oversimplified example but it is done to make a point).

```
x ← 0           // Initialise running total
y ← 1           // Initialise natural number
REPEAT
  x ← x + y     // add natural number to running total
  y ← y + 1     // Increment natural number
UNTIL y = 11    // Terminate loop when natural number is 11
```

Table 2.2.21 Pseudo-code to sum the first 10 natural numbers

2 Programming

Table 2.2.22 shows the pseudo-code rewritten with meaningful/self-describing identifier names.

> **Key term**
>
> **Meaningful identifier name:** When an identifier is descriptive of what it represents or of its purpose, we say that it has a meaningful name.

```
RunningTotal ← 0
NaturalNo ← 1
REPEAT
   RunningTotal ← RunningTotal + NaturalNo
   NaturalNo ← NaturalNo + 1
UNTIL NaturalNo = 11
```

Table 2.2.22 Pseudo-code to sum the first 10 natural numbers

The pseudo-code comments in Table 2.2.21 use **148** characters whilst the meaningful/self-describing identifiers in the pseudo-code in Table 2.2.22 use **61** characters.

We say that the pseudo-code in Table 2.2.22 is self-documenting and because of this comments are largely superfluous.

Questions

30 Why is it important to use meaningful identifier names?

Programming tasks

7 In a programming language with which you are familiar,
(a) Write a program to print a "4 times table" in the form
```
1 x 4 =  4
2 x 4 =  8
3 x 4 = 12
etc.
```
(b) Write a program to read in any integer, represented by the letter *n* say, and print an 'n times table'.

8 Write a program to print all the multiples of 3, starting at 3 and finishing at 90.

9 In a programming language with which you are familiar,
(a) Write a program to input 6 numbers and display how many of them are zero.
(b) Write a program to input 10 numbers and print the largest. (Hint: assume the first number is the largest, store it in Largest, compare each new number with Largest, store new number in Largest if new number is larger. Alternatively, set Largest to 0 at start of program, then compare each new number with Largest as before).

10 Write a program to determine if a given year is a leap year. A leap year is a year which is exactly divisible by 4 and not a century year unless the century year is exactly divisible by 400. (Hint: (Year MOD 4) = 0 tests for exact division by 4).

11 Write a program that will enable a user to input the day of the week on which a month begins and the number of days in the month. The program should produce as output a calendar for the given month in the format shown below

Sun	Mon	Tues	Wed	Thurs	Fri	Sat
		1	2	3	4	5
6	7	8	9	10	11	12
13	14	15	16	17	18	19
20	21	22	23	24	25	26
27	28	29	30	31		

The day on which the month begins should be entered as an integer where 1 corresponds to Sunday, 2 to Monday and so on.

Sequence, iteration and selection control constructs

The three combining principles (sequence, iteration/repetition and selection/choice) are basic to all high-level imperative programming languages.

These are the three basic control constructs necessary to build any program.

It can be shown that these three constructs are also sufficient to implement the control structure of any algorithm.

In this chapter you have covered:

- Using the following statement types as well as understanding and knowing how they can be combined in programs
  - variable declaration
  - constant declaration
  - assignment
  - iteration
  - selection
  - subroutine (procedure/function)
- Writing programs using the statement types above
- Interpreting and writing algorithms that make use of the statement types above
- Using definite (count controlled) and indefinite iteration (condition controlled), including indefinite iteration with the condition(s) at the start or the end of the iterative structure
- Using nested selection and nested iteration structures
- Using meaningful identifier names and why it is important to use them
- The three combining principles (sequence, iteration/repetition and selection/choice) which are
  - basic to all high-level imperative programming languages
  - the three necessary control constructs necessary to build any program
  - the three constructs sufficient to implement the control structure of any algorithm.

2 Fundamentals of programming

2 Programming

Learning objectives:

■ *Be familiar with and be able to use:*

- *addition*
- *subtraction*
- *multiplication*
- *real division*
- *integer division, including remainders.*

Information

This textbook covers Python (version 3), C# and VB.NET the programming languages supported by AQA for examinations from 2022 onwards. In addition, it also covers programming languages Java and Pascal/Delphi.

■ 2.3 Arithmetic operations in a programming language

Addition/Subtraction/Multiplication

Arithmetic expressions

$$5 + 2$$

is an example of an arithmetic expression.

This expression has two operands and one operator as shown in *Figure 2.3.1*.

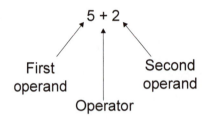

Figure 2.3.1 Arithmetic expression

Table 2.3.1 shows the arithmetic operators for the arithmetic operations addition, subtraction, multiplication and division in the programming languages C#, Java, Python, Pascal/Delphi and VB.NET.

		Arithmetic Operator				
C#	Java	Python	Pascal/ Delphi	VB.NET	Operation	Example
+	+	+	+	+	Addition	3 + 5 is 8 3.0 + 2.0 is 5.0
-	-	-	-	-	Subtraction	6 − 3 is 3 6.0 − 3.0 is 3.0
*	*	*	*	*	Multiplication	3 * 2 is 6 3.0 * 2.0 is 6.0
/	/	/	/	/	Division	5.0 / 2.0 is 2.5

Table 2.3.1 Arithmetic operations in C#, Java, Python, Pascal/Delphi and VB.NET

Care needs to be taken with division because two kinds of division exist:

- Real division
- Integer division.

Real division

In real division, the quotient is a number with a fractional part, e.g. if 3 is divided by 2 the quotient is 1.5 in real division

$$3 / 2 = 1.5 \quad \text{(Real division quotient)}$$

whereas in integer division the quotient is integer, e.g.

$$3 / 2 = 1 \quad \text{(Integer quotient)}$$

2 Fundamentals of programming

> ### Questions
>
> 1. Express the following mathematical formulae in programming language form using the arithmetic operators from *Table 2.3.1*.
>
>   (a) $b^2 - 4ac$ (b) $\dfrac{1}{1 + x^2}$ (c) $\dfrac{1}{u} + \dfrac{1}{v}$

Extension programming task

1. *Table 2.3.2* shows two simultaneous linear equations in two variables x and y. The coefficients are a, b, m, n. For example, if the two equations are

   5x + 4y = 22 and 3x + 8y = 30 then a = 5, b = 4, c = 22, m = 3, n = 8 and d = 30.

   To solve for x and y we can use the following

   $$x = \dfrac{(b*d - n*c)}{(m*b - a*n)} \qquad y = \dfrac{(a*d - m*c)}{(a*n - m*b)}$$

   | a.x + b.y = c |
   | m.x + n.y = d |

   Table 2.3.2

   Write a program to solve for x and y given the coefficients a, b, m, n of two simultaneous linear equations. Test your program with a = 5, b = 4, c = 22, m = 3, n = 8 and d = 30.

Programming languages differ in how they support the operations of real division and integer division. *Table 2.3.3* shows examples of both real and integer division in C#, Java, Python 2.x, Python 3.x, Pascal/Delphi and VB.NET.

Language	Example	Output
C#	`Console.WriteLine("Integer quotient: {0}", 3/2);` `Console.WriteLine("Real quotient: {0}", 3.0/2);`	`Integer quotient: 1` `Real quotient: 1.5`
Java	`System.out.println("Integer quotient: " + 3/2);` `System.out.println("Real quotient: " + 3.0/2);`	`Integer quotient: 1` `Real quotient: 1.5`
Python 3.x	`print("Integer quotient: ", 3//2)` `print("Real quotient: ", 3/2)`	`Integer quotient: 1` `Real quotient: 1.5`

Pascal/Delphi	`Writeln('Integer Quotient: ', 3 Div 2);`
	`Writeln('Real Quotient: ', 3/2);`
	`Writeln('Real Quotient: ', 3.0/2);`
		`Integer Quotient: 1`
		`Real Quotient: 1.5`
		`Real Quotient: 1.5`

VB.NET	`Console.WriteLine("Integer Quotient: {0}", 3\2)` `Console.WriteLine("Real Quotient: {0}", 3/2)`	`Integer Quotient: 1` `Real Quotient: 1.5`

Table 2.3.3 Comparison of real division and integer division in C#, Java, Python, Pascal/Delphi and VB.NET

Integer division

You may recall that at primary school you did integer division e.g. 10 divided by 3 is 3 remainder 1. The operation of integer division computes the integral part of the result of dividing the first operand by the second. The integral part is the whole number of times the second operand (the divisor) goes into the first operand (the dividend).

Figure 2.3.2 shows a length of rope of integer length L round a capstan of integer circumference C. The number of times that the rope can be wound on the circumference of the capstan is L DIV C where DIV is the **integer division operator** applied to an integer dividend and an integer divisor.

Figure 2.3.2 Rope wound round a capstan

2.3 Arithmetic operations in a programming language

The short length of rope left over is called the **remainder** because it is not long enough to fit the circumference. The remainder is given by *L* MOD *C* and is integral (a whole number).

Table 2.3.4 shows the integer division and integer remainder operators being used in C#, Java, Python, Pascal/Delphi and VB.NET.

Language	Example	Output
C#	`Console.WriteLine("Integer quotient: {0}", 5 / 2);` `Console.WriteLine("Integer remainder: {0}", 5 % 2);`	`Integer quotient: 2` `Integer remainder: 1`
Java	`System.out.println("Integer quotient: " + 5 / 2);` `System.out.println("Integer remainder: " + 5 % 2);`	`Integer quotient: 2` `Integer remainder: 1`
Python 3.x	`print("Integer quotient: ", 5 // 2)` `print("Integer remainder: ", 5 % 2)`	`Integer quotient: 2` `Integer remainder: 1`
Pascal/Delphi	`Writeln('Integer quotient: ', 5 Div 2);` `Writeln('Integer remainder: ', 5 Mod 2);`	`Integer quotient: 2` `Integer remainder: 1`
VB.NET	`Console.WriteLine("Integer quotient: {0}", 5 \ 2)` `Console.WriteLine("Integer remainder: {0}", 5 Mod 2)`	`Integer quotient: 2` `Integer remainder: 1`

Table 2.3.4 Integer division in C#, Java, Python, Pascal/Delphi and VB.NET

Questions

2 (a) How many times can a cotton thread of length **1655** cm be wound around a cotton reel of circumference **13** cm?
 (b) How much cotton thread is left over?

3 Convert **4589** minutes into hours and minutes.

4 Explain how DIV and MOD can be used to obtain the number of hundreds, tens and units of a 3-digit integer, N.

5 Dividing an integer x by an integer y using integer division, we obtain quotient q and the remainder r.
The relationship between x, y, q and r is expressed in the following formula   x = y * q + r
e.g. dividend x = 5, divisor y = 2, quotient q = 2, remainder r = 1, applying the formula 5 = 2 * 2 + 1.
Complete *Table 2.3.5*.

Dividend x	Divisor y	Quotient q	Remainder r
5	2	2	1
6	3	2	0
25	4	6	1
36	6		
121	7		
23	3		
1	3		
5	10		

Table 2.3.5

Programming task

2 Write a program to determine if a given year is a leap year.
A leap year is a year which is exactly divisible by **4** and not a century year unless the century year is exactly divisible by **400**.

3 Write a program to produce a display of the time of day in the form
   hours : mins : secs
given the time in seconds that have elapsed since 12:00 midnight.

4 Write a program to display the number of hundreds, tens and units of a 3-digit integer number, N.

5 Write a program to display the digits, one per line, of an integer, N.

2 Fundamentals of programming

Programming task

6 Write a program to work out the day of the week on which a given date falls using the formula shown below

DayCode = ((13 * Month – 1) DIV 5 + Decade DIV 4 + Century DIV 4 + Decade + Day – 2 * Century) Mod 7

This calculates the day of the week on which any date after 1 January 1583 will fall or has fallen.

In this formula, the year is considered as consisting of two parts neither of which have their usual meaning:
- a century represented by the first two digits of its integer representation, e.g. 20 in 2010, and
- a decade represented by the last two digits, e.g. 10 in 2010.

The date for which the corresponding day of the week is required must be coded in the following way:
- The day of the month an integer between 1 and 31 inclusive
- The year is an integer, e.g. 1996 represents the year 1996.
- The month must be coded as an integer as follows:
    - March is coded 1, April as 2 and so on until December, which is coded as 10
    - January and February are coded as 11 and 12 respectively of the **previous year**. So, for example, 15 February 1996 would be represented as day 15, month 12 of year 1995.

The result of applying this formula is an integer in the range 0 – 6 inclusive.
The integer 0 represents Sunday, 1 represents Monday and so on.
Your program should use the days of the week in its output, i.e. Sunday, Monday, etc.

Questions

6 The following pseudo-code calculates the quotient q and remainder r when an integer x is divided by an integer y using integer division

```
        r ← x
        q ← 0
        WHILE r ≥ y
            r ← r - y
            q ← q + 1
        ENDWHILE
```

Iteration	x	y	r	q	r ≥ y
0	7	2	7	0	True

Table 2.3.6 Trace table

Complete *Table 2.3.6* by tracing this pseudo-code by hand.

In this chapter you have covered:

- Using in a programming language and becoming familiar with:
    - addition
    - subtraction
    - multiplication
    - real division
    - integer division, including remainders.

2 Fundamentals of programming

2 Programming

2.4 Relational operators in a programming language

Learning objectives:
- *Be familiar with and be able to use:*
  - *equal to*
  - *not equal to*
  - *less than*
  - *greater than*
  - *less than or equal to*
  - *greater than or equal to.*

Relational operators

Expressions involving the relational operators shown in Table 2.4.1 produce Boolean results. For example,

$$2 < 3 \quad \text{True}$$
$$5 > 6 \quad \text{False}$$

Therefore, such Boolean expressions may be assigned to any Boolean variable, e.g. `FlagIsTrue`.

The following pseudo-code outputs the value True because 2 < 3 evaluates to True:

```
FlagIsTrue ← 2 < 3
OUTPUT FlagIsTrue
```

The following pseudo-code outputs the value False because 5 > 6 evaluates to False:

```
FlagIsTrue ← 5 > 6
OUTPUT FlagIsTrue
```

Information

This textbook covers Python (version 3), C# and VB.NET, the programming languages supported by AQA for examinations from 2022 onwards. In addition, it also covers programming languages Java and Pascal/Delphi.

Operator							Meaning	Example (Pascal)	Outcome
C#	Java	Python	Pascal/Delphi	VB.NET		AQA			
==	==	==	=	=		=	Equal To	6 = 6	True
<	<	<	<	<		<	Less Than	4 < 7	True
<=	<=	<=	<=	<=		≤	Less Than Or Equal To	7 <= 3	False
>	>	>	>	>		>	Greater Than	34 > 12	True
>=	>=	>=	>=	>=		≥	Greater Than Or Equal To	23 >= 23	True
!=	!=	!=	<>	<>		≠	Not Equal To	6 <> 6	False

Table 2.4.1 Relational operators in C#, Java, Python, Pascal/Delphi, VB.NET and in AQA assessments

Relational operators are more commonly used in selection statements and loops.

Information

In assessment material, AQA will use the following symbols:

$=, \neq, <, >, \leq, \geq$

For example,
```
IF x ≥ 6 THEN
   OUTPUT "x is greater than or equal to 6"
ELSE
   OUTPUT "x is not greater than or equal to 6"
ENDIF

WHILE x < 7
   x ← x + 2
   OUTPUT x
ENDWHILE
```

2 Fundamentals of programming

Questions

1. What is the outcome of evaluating each of the following expressions if `x` stores the value **5** and `y` the value **10**?
   (a)   x = y   (b) 2*x < y (c) 2*x ≤ y   (d)   x > y   (e) 2*x ≥ y (f) x ≠ y
   (g)   10*x ≠ 5*y

2. What value is output by the following pseudo-code if `Flag` is a Boolean variable?
   ```
   Flag ← 6 > 8
   OUTPUT Flag
   ```

3. What message is output by the following pseudo-code?
   ```
   IF  6 ≠ 6 THEN
      OUTPUT "Have a nice morning!"
   ELSE
      OUTPUT "Have a nice evening!"
   ENDIF
   ```

In this chapter you have covered:

- Using and becoming familiar with:
  - equal to
  - not equal to
  - less than
  - greater than
  - less than or equal to
  - greater than or equal to.

2 Fundamentals of programming

2 Programming

Learning objectives:

■ *Be familiar with and be able to use:*

- *NOT*
- *AND*
- *OR.*

2.5 Boolean operations in a programming language

Boolean operators

Operators which act on Boolean operands or Boolean values and evaluate or return a Boolean value are called **Boolean operators**.

Boolean operands or values are those that are either **True** or **False**.

Most programming languages support the Boolean operators NOT, AND, and OR so that a programming statement such as the following involving a Boolean operation can be written

```
IF (x > 5) AND (y < 3) THEN Output "A message"
```

Boolean operators are used to perform the **Boolean operations**

- x AND y
- x OR y
- NOT x

where x and y are Boolean variables or Boolean expressions.

For example if operand x is **True** and operand y is **False** then

- x AND y evaluates to **False**
- x OR y evaluates to **True**
- NOT x evaluates to **False**

Table 2.5.1 shows the symbols used for these Boolean operators in the programming languages, C#, Java, Python, Pascal/Delphi and VB.NET and their meaning. AQA's pseudo-code uses the same symbols as Pascal/Delphi.

> **Key term**
>
> **Boolean operators:**
> Operators which act on Boolean operands or Boolean values and evaluate or return a Boolean value are called Boolean operators.
>
> Most programming languages support the Boolean operators NOT, AND, and OR.

Boolean Operator					Meaning	Example (Pascal)	Outcome
C#	Java	Python	Pascal/Delphi	VB.NET			
!	!	not	NOT	Not	Evaluates to true, if operand false; Evaluates to false if operand is true	NOT True	False
&&	&	and	AND	And	Evaluates to true if both operands are true otherwise evaluates to false	True AND True	True
||	|	or	OR	Or	Evaluates to true if at least one operand is true otherwise false	True OR False	True

Table 2.5.1 Boolean or Logical operators operators in C#, Java, Python, Pascal/Delphi and VB.NET

> **Information**
>
> This textbook covers Python (version 3), C# and VB.NET, the programming languages supported by AQA for examinations from 2022 onwards. In addition, it also covers programming languages Java and Pascal/Delphi.

2 Fundamentals of programming

Operator precedence

Operator precedence refers to the order in which operators are applied to operands in an expression.

The **NOT** operator has the highest precedence, followed by the **AND** operator, then the **OR** operator.

Table 2.5.2 summarises operator precedence.

Operator precedence	Precedence
NOT	Highest (evaluated first)
AND	
OR	Lowest (evaluated last)

Table 2.5.2 Operator precedence of Boolean operators

For example, in the following logical expression `NOT y` is evaluated first because **NOT** has a higher precedence than **AND**.

```
x AND NOT y
```

If Boolean variable `y` stores the value **False**,

```
NOT False
```
evaluates to **True** because `y` is **False**.

Substituting **True** for `NOT y` in the expression

```
x AND NOT y
```
we obtain
```
x AND True
```

If Boolean variable `x` stores the value **True**, we obtain

```
True AND True
```

which evaluates to **True**.

If the expression is

```
NOT (x AND y)
```

then `x AND y` is evaluated first

The result of evaluating `x AND y` is **False** if `x` is False and `y` is **True**.

We now have

```
NOT (False)
```

which evaluates to **True**.

Now consider the logical expression with Boolean variables, x, y and z shown below

```
x AND y OR z
```

The operator precedence of **AND** is higher than **OR**.

If x and y store the value **False** and z the value **True** the expression evaluates in the following order

1. `x AND y` evaluates to **False**
2. `False OR z` evaluates to **True**

To change the order of evaluation we need to bracket the term `y OR z` in the expression `x AND y OR z` as follows

```
x AND (y OR z)
```

If x and y store the value **False** and z the value True the expression evaluates in the following order

1. `y OR z` evaluates to **True**
2. `x AND True` evaluates to **False**

2.5 Boolean operations in a programming language

Questions

1. What is the outcome of evaluating each of the following expressions if x stores the value **True** and y the value **False**
   (a) NOT x   (b) x AND y   (c) x AND NOT y   (d) x OR y   (e) NOT x OR y?

2. What is the outcome of evaluating each of the following expressions if x stores the value **True**, y the value **False** and z the value **False**
   (a) x AND y AND z
   (b) x AND y OR z
   (c) x OR y AND z
   (d) (x OR y) AND z
   (e) x AND NOT y AND z
   (f) x AND NOT (y AND z)?

3. Integer variable s stores the value 9 and integer variable t stores the value 8. What is the output of the following pseudo-code?

   ```
   IF (s > 3) AND (t < 6) THEN
      Output "Have a nice morning!"
   ELSE
      Output "Have a nice evening!"
   ENDIF
   ```

In this chapter you have covered:

- Becoming familiar with and using:
  - NOT
  - AND
  - OR.

2 Programming

2 Programming

Learning objectives:

- *Understand the concept of data structures*
- *Use arrays (or equivalent) in the design of solutions to simple problems*
- *Use records (or equivalent) in the design of solutions to simple problems.*

2.6 Data structures

The concept of data structures

Learning how to program is a process of developing the ability to model problems in such a way that a computer can solve them.

Array data structure

Suppose we needed to solve a problem which involved queueing. *Figure 2.6.1* shows an abstraction of a queue of people.

To represent this model in a computer programming language we use a data structure.

A data structure is a named collection of variables, possibly of different data types, which are connected in various ways. In the case of the queue, the person at the front of the queue is connected by relative position to the person next in the queue, this person is connected by relative position to the next and so on.

The cell is the basic building block of data structures. We can picture a cell as a box that is capable of holding a value drawn from some basic or composite data type. *Figure 2.6.2* shows a collection (aggregation) of cells representing a queue. This data structure is given a name, *Queue*, that refers to the collection of cells.

Each cell of *Queue* is designed to store a value of an integer data type.

The simplest data structure available in many programming languages is the array which is a sequence of cells of a given type.

Record data structure

Another common data structure in programming languages is the record data structure - *Figure 2.6.3.* A record is a cell that is made up of a collection of other cells, called fields, that may be of different data types. The record data structure can model a customer record from the real world and store values in its fields such as customer name, address, age, salary, job position.

Figure 2.6.1 Queue Abstract Data Type

> **Key concept**
>
> **Data structure:**
> A data structure is a named collection (aggregation) of variables, possibly of different data types, which are connected in various ways.
> The collection consists of cells representing some abstract data type, e.g. a queue which models a real world entity, e.g. a supermarket queue.
> The cell is the basic building block of data structures.

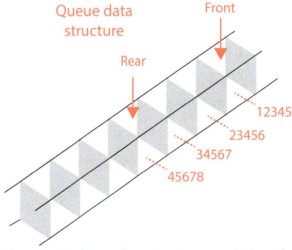

Figure 2.6.2 Queue data structure consisting of an aggregation of cells storing integers

Record data type

```
Record
    Surname : String
    Forename : String
    AddressLine1 : String
    AddressLine2 : String
    City: String
    Postcode : String
    Country : String
    Age : Real
    Salary: Integer
    JobPosition : String
End
```

Field

Figure 2.6.3 Record data structure

2 Programming

> **Questions**
>
> What is meant by a data structure?

One-dimensional array
The problem
Suppose you are tasked with writing a computer program to keep a set of one hundred temperature readings in memory so that calculations may be performed on these readings in a uniform manner. A sample of the first 8 readings is shown in *Figure 2.6.4*.

| 20.5 | 22.7 | 24.3 | 26.8 | 25.1 | 23.9 | 21.4 | 20.0 |

Figure 2.6.4 Sample of temperature readings

We could store the first of the readings in a variable, `Temperature1`, the second in a variable, `Temperature2`, and so on as shown in *Figure 2.6.5*. The data type chosen for `Temperature1` would be one that allows storage of a value possessing a fractional part, e.g. `float`. The same data type would be chosen for `Temperature2`, and each of the other 98 variables.
Using 100 separate variables, each of which is only able to store a single value, is not ideal.

The solution
What is needed is a *single variable* which can store many values.
For this we use an **array** variable, `Temperature`, as shown in *Figure 2.6.6*.

1. An array is a data structure which is capable of storing many values, e.g. 100 temperature readings: 20.5, 22.7, ..., 17.6

2. An array is also a single entity, referred to by a single name,
   e.g. `Temperature`.

3. The values stored in an array are all of the same data type, e.g. `float`.

4. The stored values are arranged in an order so that there is a first, a second, and so on.

Separate variables
In the separate variable approach, to extract, say, the value of the seventh temperature reading from among 100 separate variables, we need the name of the corresponding variable. We can construct this name by combining the name `Temperature` with the numeric name 7 to produce the name, `Temperature7`.

Variable	Value
Temperature1	20.5
Temperature2	22.7
Temperature3	24.3
Temperature4	26.8
Temperature5	25.1
Temperature6	23.9
Temperature7	21.4
Temperature8	20.0

Figure 2.6.5 Variables for first 8 readings

Variable	Value
Temperature	20.5
	22.7
	24.3
	26.8
	25.1
	23.9
	21.4
	20.0
	•
	•
	•
	17.6

Figure 2.6.6 Array variable with storage for 100 temperature readings

We then use this name to refer to the variable which contains the value of the seventh reading, i.e. 21.4 as shown in *Figure 2.6.5*. Perhaps we might want to output the value of this variable to the console.
Pseudo-code that does this is as follows

```
OUTPUT Temperature7
```

2.6 Data structures

Array index

Using an array to store 100 temperature readings, we retain the use of numeric naming 1, 2, 3, 4, ..., 100 and view the array as consisting of 100 elements with each element storing the value of a temperature reading.

To extract, say, the value of the seventh temperature reading, we construct a name by combining the name of the array, `Temperature`, with the numeric name 7 as follows `Temperature[7]` as shown in *Figure 2.6.7*.

We then use this name to refer to the **element** of the array which contains the seventh reading, i.e. 21.4 (see *Figure 2.6.7*).

Perhaps we might want to output the value of this variable to the console. Pseudo-code that does this is as follows

        OUTPUT Temperature[7]

Pseudo-code to output the first, second and third values of array `Temperature` is as follows

        OUTPUT Temperature[1]
        OUTPUT Temperature[2]
        OUTPUT Temperature[3]

The name that we use inside the square brackets is called the **array index**, e.g. 3 in `[3]`.

Pseudo-code to output all 100 values is as follows

        FOR i ← 1 TO 100
            OUTPUT Temperature[i]
        ENDFOR

Here the array index is a loop control variable `i` which ranges from 1 to 100.

We are not restricted to starting array indexing at 1. We can index from 0. In fact, many programming languages only offer array indexing from 0. Pascal and Delphi are exceptions. In fact, Pascal and Delphi allow indexing from any starting value of ordinal data type.

Variable	Index	Value
Temperature	[1]	20.5
	[2]	22.7
	[3]	24.3
	[4]	26.8
	[5]	25.1
	[6]	23.9
	[7]	21.4
	[8]	20.0
	⋮	⋮
	[100]	17.6

Figure 2.6.7 Use of an index in array variable Temperature

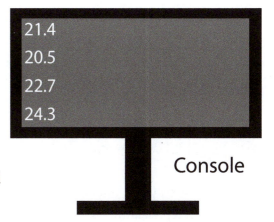

Console

Questions

2. A program is required to keep 10000 temperature readings in memory and to reference all the items in a uniform manner.
   Explain why it would be preferable to use a one-dimensional array to store the value of each reading instead of 10000 separate variables.

3. A one-dimensional array `Height` consists of 10 elements. Array indexing starts at 0 and ends at 9. The array stores the heights of 10 people. Write pseudo-code using a *for loop* to output all 10 heights in the same order that they are stored in the array.

Information

Square bracket notation:
AQA's pseudo-code uses square bracket notation [ ] to access values in an array as do many programming languages.

Information

In assessment material, AQA will use array indexing which starts from 0 unless specifically stated otherwise.

2 Programming

Basic operations that access arrays

The two basic operations that access the one-dimensional array `Temperature` are

- Extraction: this is achieved by evaluating `Temperature[i]` to identify a particular stored value in the array `Temperature`, e.g. if `i = 5`, then `Temperature[i]` evaluates to 25.1 - see *Figure 2.6.7*.

- Storing: this is achieved by executing the assignment `Temperature[i]` ← `x` which results in a copy of the value stored in `x` being assigned to the array `Temperature` at the location within this array identified by index `i`. Variable `x` holds the temperature reading to be stored in the array `Temperature`, e.g. if `i = 5` and `x = 25.1`, then `Temperature[5]` ← 25.1 results in 25.1 being stored in the array location with index 5.

Addresses

Numbers as names are also called **addresses**. We are familiar with numbers being assigned to houses: "Such and such lives at no 42".

We can therefore think of an array index as an address. Using an address also implies a location. For example, `Temperature[5]` is a **location** with address 5 within array `Temperature`.

Figure 2.6.8 shows storage bays for Russian doll objects. We can think of this structure as an array used for storing objects. Each bay within this array is a **location**. The structure is divided into cells, one above another. So we can also use the synonym **cell** for location.

Each location/cell is assigned an address. In this numbering scheme we have chosen to start the numbering from 0 and to label the lowermost cell 0. We could have started the numbering from 1 and we could have chosen the uppermost cell as the first cell. The choice is arbitrary. All that we need to ensure is that the numbering is ordered, i.e. 0, 1, 2, 3 or 1, 2, 3, 4, and each cell is assigned, in order, a unique number drawn from the range of numbers whether 0, 1, 2, 3 is chosen or 1, 2, 3, 4.

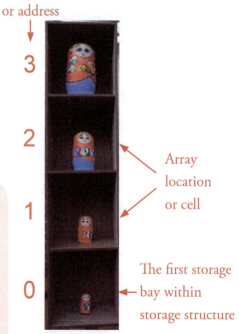

Figure 2.6.8 Location/cell view of an array with array index as a location address

> **Questions**
>
> 4 Explain why we can think of an array index as an address.
>
> 5 The first six prime numbers are stored in an array `primes`. We can represent this as follows: [2, 3, 5, 7, 11, 13]
> If array indexing starts from 0 what is stored in each of the following locations of array `prime`?
> (a) (i) `primes[1]` (ii) `primes[3]` (iii) `primes[5]`
>
> (b) If function `LEN(anArray)` returns the number of elements in an array, what is returned by the function call `LEN(primes)`?

2.6 Data structures

Questions

6 The following algorithm determines the average temperature of a set of temperature readings.

The temperature readings are stored in an array `temperature` as follows
[20.5, 22.7, 24.3, 26.8, 25.1, 23.9, 21.4]

Note: Array indexing starts at 1.

```
total ← 0.0
index ← 0
REPEAT
   index ← index + 1
   total ← total + temperature[index]
UNTIL index = LEN(temperature)
average ← total/LEN(temperature)
OUTPUT average
```

index	total
0	0.0
1	
2	
3	
4	
5	
6	
7	

Table 2.6.1

Complete the trace table *Table 2.6.1* for this algorithm and array `temperature`.

7 Array indexing starts at **0** for an array `Row` with **10** elements.
(a) What is the index of the last element?
(b) Write pseudo-code to output the value stored in the first cell of this array.

8 (a) Explain why the following pseudo-code will output the 10 values stored in the array `Row`.
```
i ← 0
WHILE i < 10
   OUTPUT Row[i]
   i ← i + 1
ENDWHILE
```
(b) What is the value stored in `i` when the loop terminates?

9 Rewrite the *While loop* pseudo-code in Question 8 so that it uses a *Repeat loop* with the terminating condition at the end of the loop.

Creating a one-dimensional array

Table 2.6.2 shows examples of how integer and real/floating point one-dimensional arrays may be created in C#, Java, Pascal, Delphi, Python[1] and VB.NET. For Python two approaches are used. The first uses Python lists and the second arrays from the NumPy library.

Python lacks native support for creating an array data structure within the language. The closest that Python gets to a native data structure that can be used like a one-dimensional array is a list (a list is actually a dynamic array). A list is just a sequence of values (think of a shopping list).

However, it is possible to create an array in Python with the `NumPy` package if this package is loaded with the command `import numpy`.

`NumPy` is short for Numeric Python.

With `numpy` installed we can use the `array` function to create an array.

Information

NumPy:
NumPy is the fundamental package for scientific computing with Python.

Anaconda:
Installing some of the larger Python libraries, particularly those such as NumPy which depend on complex low-level C and Fortran packages, is made easy with Anaconda. Anaconda will do all the dependency checking and binary installs required.
Anaconda is free to download and install from
https://www.anaconda.com/products/individual

---
[1] Spyder 4.1.4 the **S**cientific **PY**thon **D**evelopment **E**nvi**R**onment and Python 3.8

Language	Integer	Real/float
C#	int[] vector = new int[4]; int[] vector = {0,1,2,3};	float[] vector = new float[4]; float[] vector = {0.0,1.5,2.3,3.4};
Java	int[] vector = new int[4]; int[] vector = {0,1,2,3};	float[] vector= new float[4]; float[] vector = {0.0,1.5,2.3,3.4};
Pascal/ Delphi	Vector : Array[0..3] Of Integer; Vector : Array[0..3] Of Integer = (0,1,2,3);	Vector : Array[0..3] Of Real; Vector : Array[0..3] Of Real = (0.0,1.5,2.3,3.4);

Python	vector = [0,1,2,3,4] # list equivalent
	import numpy as np
	vector = np.array([0, 1, 2, 3])
	vector = np.empty([4],dtype=int)#empty array
	vector = np.zeros(4, dtype=int)
		vector = [0.0,1.5,2.3,3.4]
		import numpy as np
		vector = np.array([0, 1, 2, 3], dtype = float)
		vector = np.empty([4])#empty float array
		vector = np.zeros(4)

VB.Net	Dim vector(3) As Integer Dim vector = New Integer() {0,1,2,3}	Dim vector(3) As Double Dim vector = New Double() {0.0,1.5,2.3,3.4}

Table 2.6.2 Creating one-dimensional arrays of different array element data type

In Table 2.6.2, the Python list [0, 1, 2, 3] is supplied as argument to the function array to create array x as follows

$$x = np.array([0,1, 2, 3])$$

In Table 2.6.2, the program code x = np.zeros(4, dtype=int) uses the numpy function zeros to create a four-element array with each element initialised to 0. The default array element data type is float.

In IPython (ipython.org), %pylab will install numpy as well as matplotlib.pyplot, a plotting library for displaying data visually - see Table 2.6.3.

IPython is an interactive python useful for trying out ideas.

Python lists are unsatisfactory as proxies for arrays for the following reasons:

1. Elements of a list can be of different data types, e.g. [3, 4.5, 'hello', True, [34,56]]

2. Lists may grow or shrink, e.g. x = [0,1,2] x.append('a') x.pop()

3. Processing of Python lists is considerably slower than processing arrays from Numpy

Tables 2.6.3, 2.6.4, and 2.6.5 show examples of one-dimensional array creation in C#, Java, Pascal, Delphi, Python and VB.NET. The Python example uses IPython. IPython already has numpy in its namespace so use of the prefix np is unnecessary.

Language	Integer
Python 3.4 (IPython)	In [1]: %pylab In [2]: vector2 = array([0,1,2,3]), dtype=int) In [3]: vector4 = array([0.0,1.5,2.3,3.4], dtype=float) In [4]: print(vector2[0]) In [5]: print(vector4[3])
Python 3.4 (Scipy)	vector = [1,2,3,4] # list equivalent of an array print (vector[2]) import numpy as np vector2 = np.array([1,2,3,4]) print (vector2[2])

Table 2.6.3 Creating one-dimensional arrays of different array element data type

Information

This textbook covers Python (version 3), C# and VB.Net, the programming languages supported by AQA for examinations from 2022 onwards. In addition, it also covers programming languages Java and Pascal/Delphi.

2.6 Data structures

Language	Integer
| C# | ```
using System;
namespace Arrays
{
    class Program
    {
        static void Main(string[] args)
        {
            int[] vector1 = new int[4];
            int[] vector2 = { 0, 1, 2, 3 };
            float[] vector3 = new float[4];
            float[] vector4 = { 0.0f, 1.5f, 2.3f, 3.4f };
            double[] vector5 =  { 0.0, 1.5, 2.3, 3.4 };
            vector1[0] = 45;
            vector3[0] = 45.8f;
            Console.WriteLine(vector1[0]);
            Console.ReadLine();
        }
    }
}
``` |
| Java | ```
public class Arrays {
        public static void main(String[] args) {
            int[] vector1 = new int[4];
            int[] vector2 = {0,1,2,3};
            float[] vector3 = new float[4];
            float[] vector4 = { 0.0f, 1.5f, 2.3f, 3.4f };
            double[] vector5 = { 0.0, 1.5, 2.3, 3.4 };
            vector1[0] = 45;
            vector3[0] = 45.8f;
            System.out.println(vector1[0]);
        }
}
``` |
| Delphi | ```
Program ArrayVector;
{$APPTYPE CONSOLE}
{$R *.res}
Uses
  System.SysUtils;
Var
  Vector1 : Array[0..3] Of Integer;
  Vector2 : Array[0..3] Of Integer = (0,1,2,3);
  Vector3 : Array[0..3] Of Real;
  Vector4 : Array[0..3] Of Real = (0.0,1.5,2.3,3.4);
Begin
  Vector1[0] := 45;
  Vector3[0] := 45.8;
  Writeln(Vector1[0]);
  Writeln(Vector4[3] :6:1);
  Readln;
End.
``` |
| Pascal | ```
Program ArrayVector;
Var
  Vector1 : Array[0..3] Of Integer;
  Vector2 : Array[0..3] Of Integer = (0,1,2,3);
  Vector3 : Array[0..3] Of Real;
  Vector4 : Array[0..3] Of Real = (0.0,1.5,2.3,3.4);
Begin
  Vector1[0] := 45;
  Vector3[0] := 45.8;
  Writeln(Vector1[0]);
  Writeln(Vector4[3] :6:1);
  Readln;
End.
``` |

Table 2.6.4 Creating one-dimensional arrays of different array element data type

2 Programming

Language	Integer
| VB.NET | ```
Module Arrays
    Sub Main()
        Dim vector1(3) As Integer
        Dim vector2 = {0, 1, 2, 3}
        Dim vector3(3) As Single
        Dim vector4(3) As Double
        Dim vector5 = {0.0, 1.5, 2.3, 3.4}
        vector1(0) = 45
        vector3(0) = 45.8F
        vector4(3) = 45.8
        Console.WriteLine(vector1(0))
        Console.WriteLine(vector5(3))
        Console.ReadLine()
    End Sub
End Module
``` |

Table 2.6.5 Creating one-dimensional arrays of different array element data type

Iterating through the elements of a one-dimensional array

Iterating through the elements of an array is a common operation on arrays. *Figure 2.6.9* shows the use of a *For loop* to access each element of array `Vector` starting with the first element `Vector[0]`. The index used is `i`, the loop control variable. *Table 2.6.6* shows the value of `i` and the value of array `Vector[i]` in each iteration of the *For loop*.

The one-dimensional array `Vector` contains 4 elements with the following values 0.0, 1.5, 2.3, 3.4, respectively.

```
FOR i ← 0 TO 3
    OUTPUT Vector[i]
ENDFOR
```

Figure 2.6.9 Pseudo-code For loop

Table 2.6.7 shows the loop pseudo-code expressed in the programming languages C#, Java, Delphi/Pascal, Python and VB.NET.

Value of i	Element accessed	Value of element
0	Vector[0]	0.0
1	Vector[1]	1.5
2	Vector[2]	2.3
3	Vector[3]	3.4

Table 2.6.6 Value of loop control variable and element of array Vector on each iteration

Language	Integer
| C# | ```
int i;
for (i = 0; i < 4; i++)
{
    Console.WriteLine(vector[i]);
}
``` |
| Java | ```
int i;
for (i = 0; i < 4; i++)
{
    System.out.println(vector[i]);
}
``` |
| Delphi/ Pascal | ```
Var i : Integer;
.....
For i := 0 To 3
    Do Writeln(Vector[i]);
``` |
| Python | ```
for i in range(4):
    print(vector[i])
``` |
| VB.NET | ```
Dim i As Integer
For i = 0 To 3
    Console.WriteLine(vector(i))
Next
``` |

Table 2.6.7 Accessing the elements of a one-dimensional array by iteration with a For loop

Programming task

1. Write a program which iterates through `ArrayOneD` outputting each value in turn starting at the first value contained in this array. Assume the array is initialised as follows `ArrayOneD = [3,6,7,2]`.

2.6 Data structures

Computing a single value from the contents of a one-dimensional array

To sum all the elements of a one-dimensional array, Vector, we must access each element of this array in turn adding its value to a running total Sum. The variable Sum is initialised to contain zero. *Figure 2.6.10* shows pseudo-code that computes the sum of the elements of array Vector. Array Vector contains 4 elements with the following values 1, 3, 8, 9.

Table 2.6.8 shows the state of Sum before iteration begins and at the end of each iteration, e.g. after the first iteration variable Sum contains 1, after the second, 4.

```
Sum ← 0
FOR i ← 0 TO 3
    Sum ← Sum + Vector[i]
ENDFOR
OUTPUT Sum
```

Figure 2.6.10 For loop

Value of i	Element accessed	Value of element	Sum
			0
0	Vector[0]	1	1
1	Vector[1]	3	4
2	Vector[2]	8	12
3	Vector[3]	9	21

Table 2.6.8 Summing the elements of a one-dimensional array

Programming tasks

2. Write a program which iterates through ArrayOneD and sums the values contained in this array. Assume the array is initialised as follows ArrayOneD = [3,6,7,2].

3. Write a program which collects 6 integer values from the keyboard and stores them in an array called IntegerArray. The program is to display the contents of each cell of the array in turn, starting at the first cell, after all the values have been entered.

4. Using the same program structure, add code which calculates the average of the first three numbers stored in the array and the second three numbers.

5. Using the same program structure, add another array to the program of the same size and type as the first. Now add code to copy the contents of the first array to the second array so that the second array holds the contents of the first array in reverse order.

Multi-dimensional arrays

Two-dimensional arrays

We have so far considered how data may be stored in a one-dimensional array. A one-dimensional array has, of course, one dimension. We can visualise the items of data in a one-dimensional array arranged along a single axis as shown by the example in *Figure 2.6.11*.

Figure 2.6.11 Visualising items of numerical data in a one-dimensional array arranged along a single axis

If we have two dimensions for storing data then we can visualise the data stored in a grid-like fashion defined by two axes as shown in *Figure 2.6.12*.

The **structure** of 5 rows and 5 columns of data shown in *Figure 2.6.12* is called a **two-dimensional array** or **matrix.**
The matrix contains 5 x 5 = 25 numbers.

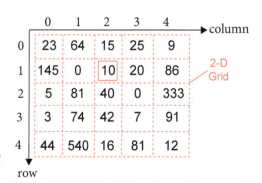

Figure 2.6.12 Visualising items of numerical data stored in a two-dimensional array laid out in two dimensions

2 Programming

In order to refer to a specific number, we need to specify both the **row** and **column** because the matrix has two dimensions. For example, the third value along in the second row in *Figure 2.6.12* is the number 10. This number has been marked by a red square in the figure.

The axes in *Figure 2.6.12* have been labelled, `row` and `column` so that the first row has value 0 and the first column has value 0. Therefore, the `row` and `column` values of the number 10 marked by a red square are 1 and 2, respectively.

Iterating through the elements of a two-dimensional array

Iterating through the elements of an array is a common operation on arrays. *Figure 2.6.13* shows the use of nested *For loops* to access each element of array `Array2D` starting with the first element `Array2D[0][0]`. The outer *For loop* uses the loop control variable, `i`. The inner *For loop* uses the loop control variable, `j`.

The two-dimensional array `Array2D` contains 3 x 3 = 9 elements with values as shown in *Table 2.6.9*.

```
FOR i ← 0 TO 2
    FOR j ← 0 TO 2
        OUTPUT Array2D[i][j]
    ENDFOR
ENDFOR
```

Figure 2.6.13 Pseudo-code that iterates through the elements of array Array2D

	0	1	2
0	12	45	6
1	9	23	65
2	2	18	33

Table 2.6.9 Array2D

The **trace table**, *Table 2.6.10*, shows the value of array `Array2D[i][j]` and the output for each value of `i` and `j`. A trace table is a table which shows the current values of variables used by the pseudo-code and its output whilst the pseudo-code is executed (traced) by hand. This execution by hand is called a **hand-trace**.

i	j	Array2D[i][j]	Output
0	0	12	12
0	1	45	45
0	2	6	6
1	0	9	9
1	1	23	23
1	2	65	65
2	0	2	2
2	1	18	18
2	2	33	33

Table 2.6.10 Trace table for pseudo-code

Questions

10 The following algorithm determines the average temperature of three sets of temperature readings each collected on a separate occasion.

The temperature readings are stored in a two dimensional array `temperature` as follows `[[5, 6, 6], [7, 9, 8], [2, 4, 5]]`

Each row corresponds to one set of readings.

Note: Array indexing starts at 1.

Complete the trace table *Table 2.6.11* for this algorithm.

```
total ← 0.0
row ← 0
column ← 0
noOfrows ← LEN(temperature)
REPEAT
    row ← row + 1
    noOfcolumns ← LEN(temperature[row])
    REPEAT
        column ← column + 1
        total ← total + temperature[row][column]
    UNTIL column = noOfcolumns
    column ← 0
UNTIL row = noOfrows
noOfreadings ← noOfrows * noOfcolumns
average ← total / noOfreadings
OUTPUT average
```

column	row	total
1	1	0.0
2	1	5.0
3	1	11.0
1	2	17.0
2	2	24.0
3	2	33.0
1	3	41.0
2	3	43.0
3	3	47.0

Table 2.6.11

2.6 Data structures

> **Questions**
>
> What is the output from the algorithm in question 10?

Creating two-dimensional arrays in some programming languages

Table 2.6.12 shows the creation of two-dimensional arrays in C#, Java, Pascal, Delphi, Python 3.4 and VB.NET.

Language	Integer	Real/float
C#	`int[,] array2D = new int[4,2];` `int[,] array2D = {{1,2},{3,4},{5,6},{7,8}};`	`float[,] array2D = new float[4,2];`
Java	`int[][] array2D = new int[4][2];` `int[][] array2D = {{1,2},{3,4},{5,6},{7,8}};`	`float[][] array2D=new float[4][2];`
Pascal	`Array2D : Array[0..3,0..1] Of Integer;` `Array2D : Array[0..3,0..1] Of Integer = ((1,2),(3,4),(5,6),(7,8));`	`Array2D: Array[0..3,0..1] Of Real;`
Delphi	`Array2D : Array[0..3,0..1] Of Integer;` `Array2D : Array[0..3,0..1] Of Integer = ((1,2),(3,4),(5,6),(7,8));`	`Array2D : Array[0..3,0..1] Of Real;`

Python	`array2D = []`
	`for row in range(4):`
	`    array2D.append([])`
	`    for column in range(2):`
	`        array2D[row].append(0)` #creating a 4 x 2 list equivalent
	`import numpy as np`
	`array2D = np.array([[1,2], [3,4], [5,6], [7,8]])`
	`array2D = np.empty([4,2],dtype=int)` # creates a 4 x 2 empty array
		`array2D = []`
		`for row in range(4):`
		`    array2D.append([])`
		`    for column in range(2):`
		`        array2D[row].append(0.0)`
		`import numpy as np`
		`array2D = np.empty([4,2],dtype=float)`

VB.NET	`Dim array2D(3, 1) As Integer` `Dim array2D = New Integer(3, 1) {{1, 2}, {3, 4}, {5, 6}, {7, 8}}`	`Dim array2D(3,1) As Double`

Table 2.6.12 Creating two-dimensional arrays of different array element data type

C#

The following creates a two-dimensional integer array of 4 rows and 2 columns

```
int[,] array2D = new int[4,2];
```

The following creates and initialises a two-dimensional integer array of 4 rows and 2 columns

```
int[,] array2D = {{1,2},{3,4},{5,6},{7,8}};
```

If the array is being initialised, `new int[4,2]` can be omitted. Array indexing is zero-based.

Java

The following creates a two-dimensional integer array of 4 rows and 2 columns

```
int[][] array2D = new int[4][2];
```

The following creates and initialises a two-dimensional integer array of 4 rows and 2 columns

```
int[][] array2D = {{1,2},{3,4},{5,6},{7,8}};
```

Array indexing is zero-based.

Pascal/Delphi

The following creates a two-dimensional integer array of 4 rows and 2 columns

```
Array2D : Array[0..3,0..1] Of Integer;
```

89

2 Programming

The following creates and initialises a two-dimensional integer array of 4 rows and 2 columns

```
Array2D : Array[0..3, 0..1] Of Integer = ((1,2),(3,4),(5,6),(7,8));
```
Array indexing is more flexible in Pascal and Delphi. It may begin at any value, e.g. -1, 1. Array is a keyword in Pascal and Delphi.

Python

The following creates an equivalent of a two-dimensional integer array of 4 rows and 2 columns by using lists within a list and initialises it with zeros

```
array2D = []
for row in range(4):
    array2D.append([])
    for column in range(2):
        array2D[row].append(0)
```

List indexing is zero-based.

The following creates an empty two-dimensional integer array of 4 rows and 2 columns by using the numpy library

```
import numpy as np
array2D = np.empty([4,2],dtype=int)
```

The following creates and initialises a two-dimensional integer array of 4 rows and 2 columns

```
array2D = np.array([[1,2], [3,4], [5,6], [7,8]])
```

VB.NET

The following creates a two-dimensional integer array of 4 rows and 2 columns

```
Dim array2D(3, 1) As Integer
```

Array indexing is zero-based. 3 and 1 are the upper bound index values.

The following creates and initialises a two-dimensional integer array of 4 rows and 2 columns

```
Dim array2D = New Integer(3, 1) {{1, 2}, {3, 4}, {5, 6}, {7, 8}}
```

Programming task

6. Write a program which creates a two-dimensional array `ArrayTwoD` and displays the values contained in the second row of this array. The array `ArrayTwoD` should be created with values arranged into rows and columns as follows

```
ArrayTwoD = [[3,6,7],
             [4,8,1],
             [9,3,8]]
```

2.6 Data structures

Use of records

Table 2.6.13 shows how to define a record data type in Pascal/Delphi, C#, Python, Java and VB.Net.

Figure 2.6.14 shows in pseudo-code how the fields of the record variable, `studentRecord` of data type `Exam` may be accessed using the dot notation, e.g. the name field is accessed with `studentRecord.name`.

```
RECORD Exam
    name : String
    examScore : Integer
    examGrade : Char
ENDRECORD
```

```
OUTPUT 'Input name: '
studentRecord.name  ←  USERINPUT
OUTPUT 'Input Mark Out Of 100: '
studentRecord.examScore  ←  USERINPUT
OUTPUT 'Input exam grade: '
studentRecord.examGrade  ←  USERINPUT
OUTPUT studentRecord.name
OUTPUT studentRecord.examScore
OUTPUT studentRecord.examGrade
```

Figure 2.6.14 Pseudo-code which shows how fields of a record can be accessed

Pascal/Delphi	C#

`TExam = Record`
`    Name : String;`
`    ExamScore : Integer;`
`    ExamGrade : Char;`
`End;`
	`struct Exam`
	`{`
	`    public string name;`
	`    public int ExamScore;`
	`    public char ExamGrade;`
	`};`

Python	**Java**

`class exam(object):`
`    def __init__(name,examscore,examgrade)`
`        self.name = name`
`        self.examscore = examscore`
`        self.examgrade = examgrade`
	`class Exam {`
	`    String name;`
	`    int examScore;`
	`    char examGrade;`
	`}`

VB.Net	

`Structure exam`
`    Public name As String`
`    Public examScore As Integer`
`    Public examGrade As Char`
`End Structure`	

Table 2.6.13 Defining the record data type in various programming languages

Programming task

7 Convert the pseudo-code in *Figure 2.6.14* into a program in a programming language with which you are familiar. You need to create a student record, `studentRecord` of data type `Exam`.

Change this program so that the exam grade is calculated on being input by the user.

Use the grade boundaries: grade A is 70 marks or greater, grade B is less than 70 but greater than 49 marks, grade C is less than 50 but greater than 39, grade U is less than 40.

In this chapter you have covered:

- The concept of data structures
- Using arrays (or equivalent) in the design of solutions to simple problems
- Using records (or equivalent) in the design of solutions to simple problems.

2 Programming

2 Programming

Learning objectives:
- *Be able to obtain user input from the keyboard*
- *Be able to output data and information from a program to the computer display*
- *Be able to read/write from/to a text file.*

2.7 Input/output and file handling

Input/output

Data is typically input into a computer by a user via a keyboard connected to the computer as shown in *Figure 2.7.1*. The data is processed by a program executing in the computer and information is produced.

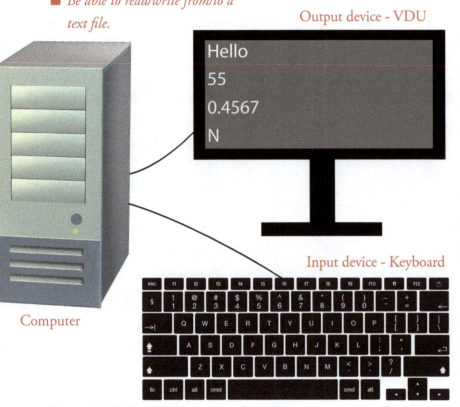

Figure 2.7.1 Computer connected to a VDU (output device) and a keyboard (input device)

This information is communicated to the user by being output to a computer display such as a visual display unit (VDU). The operating system in the computer usually echoes whatever is typed on the keyboard to the output device, i.e. the VDU.

For example, In *Figure 2.7.1* all of the text that appears on the VDU screen could just be data which has been typed at the keyboard. It appears on the screen of the VDU courtesy of the operating system.

Text is the operative word. It highlights the fact that a keyboard is a source of text, a sequence of characters. Each character corresponds in most ordinary situations to a key pressed on the keyboard, e.g. the key N.

Even when digit keys are pressed, e.g. to produce the sequence 55, it is still text.

"Under the hood", when the key labelled 5 is pressed, its ASCII code is generated and sent to the computer (actually a scan code is generated first). The operating system echoes this text to the screen as it is being typed.

> **Key term**
>
> **Text:**
> Text consists of sequences of characters, one sequence per line.

Obtaining user input from a keyboard

A program designed to process input data will usually access a line of input at a time from the user. In pseudo-code, the operation of obtaining user input from a keyboard is expressed as follows

```
aVariable ← USERINPUT
```

where `aVariable` is a variable of some data type (text input is automatically converted into a data type that matches the variable's data type, e.g. '55' ↦ 55).

2 Programming

The operator ← is the assignment operator which carries out the operation of assigning to variable, `aVariable`, the datum obtained from the keyboard (typed in by pressing keys).

Outputting data and information to a computer display

A program designed to produce output for a user to see immediately will send output to a visual device such as a VDU.

In pseudo-code, the operation of outputting a result stored in a variable `aResult` is expressed as follows

```
OUTPUT 'The result is: '
OUTPUT aResult
```

The program may have produced this output by processing input data. So that a user knows what input data to supply and when, a program will output a prompt to the user.

In pseudo-code, the operation of prompting a user for input is expressed as follows

```
OUTPUT 'Enter a number between 1 and 9: '
```

This is followed by an input statement such as

```
aNumber ← USERINPUT
```

Example

The following pseudo-code collects an integer from the keyboard, doubles it then outputs the result to the VDU

```
OUTPUT 'Enter a number between 1 and 9: '
anInteger ← USERINPUT
aResult ← anInteger * 2
OUTPUT 'The result is: '
OUTPUT aResult
```

> **Key term**
>
> **File:**
> A file is a data structure for storing data. The number of items of data stored in the file can vary in time and the amount of data is not limited in the way that other data structures are because files rely on secondary storage such as magnetic disk for their storage unlike arrays which rely on RAM storage.

Files (In specification 8520 but not in 8525)

A file is a data structure for storing data. The number of items of data stored in the file can vary in time and the amount of data is not limited in the way that other data structures are because files rely on secondary storage such as magnetic disk for their storage unlike arrays which rely on RAM storage.

By using secondary storage, files persist in time because secondary storage is non-volatile whereas RAM is volatile.

A file is assigned a name called its *filename* so that it can be referenced by name.

Files have structure which is either defined by the programmer at creation time, a file of some record type or is a commonly used structure such as text.

> **Extension Material**
>
> *Headings in red, e.g. Files, indicate that the following content was in specification 8520 - last examination summer 2021 - but is not in specification 8525 - first examination summer 2022)*

Questions

1. What is a file?

2.7 Input/output and file handling

Text files

Text files are files whose contents are sequences of characters organised on a line by line basis. For example, Shakespeare's Sonnet 116 shown in *Figure 2.7.2* consists of 14 lines as do almost all of Shakespeare's sonnets.

> Let me not to the marriage of true minds
> Admit impediments. Love is not love
> Which alters when it alteration finds,
> Or bends with the remover to remove:
> O, no! it is an ever-fixed mark,
> That looks on tempests and is never shaken;
> It is the star to every wandering bark,
> Whose worth's unknown, although his height be taken.
> Love's not Time's fool, though rosy lips and cheeks
> Within his bending sickle's compass come;
> Love alters not with his brief hours and weeks,
> But bears it out even to the edge of doom.
> If this be error and upon me prov'd,
> I never writ, nor no man ever lov'd.

Key term

Text file:
Text files are files whose contents are sequences of characters organised on a line by line basis.

Questions

2 What is a text file?

Figure 2.7.2 Shakespeare's Sonnet 116

Text files may be opened and read in a text editor such as Microsoft's WordPad. Text editors expect files to be organised on a line-by-line basis and to consist of characters that can read when displayed with the exception of some specific control characters.

Each line ends with a special control character called the end of line or *newline* character (character code 10 or character codes 10 and 13).

The only control characters that text editors are able to handle are characters called *whitespace* characters, i.e. characters with ASCII or UTF-8 character codes 32 (space), 10 (line feed), 13 (carriage return) and 9 (tab). Other control characters have an effect on a text editor which is unpredictable and usually render the display unreadable.

Non-text files do not display well in text editors because they often contain control character codes which text editors are unable to handle because they are not control character codes 32, 10, 13 or 9.

Not only can text files be read by text editors but they may also be created and edited in a text editor.

We turn to computer programs when we wish to manipulate text files in ways that text editors do not support.

Reading from a text file

Figure 2.7.3 shows a Python program which opens a text file with the filename 'sowpods.txt' for reading. The contents of this file is read one line at a time from the beginning of this file. Each line which is read is stored temporarily in the string variable `line`. The line of characters stored in this variable is displayed on the console by `print(line)`. Finally the file is closed.

```
f = open("sowpods.txt", "r")
for line in f:
    print(line)
f.close()
```

Figure 2.7.3 Python program which opens a text file 'sowpods.txt' for reading and displaying

aa
aah
aahed
aahing
aahs
aal
aalii
aaliis
aals
aardvark
aardvarks

Figure 2.7.4 The first few lines of the text file 'sowpods.txt'

2 Programming

The first thing that this Python program does is open the specified file in a particular mode, in this case, for reading.

The call to `open("sowpods.txt", "r")` returns a file handle which is assigned to file handle variable `f`. `"r"` specifies that the mode is reading.

The contents of file `"sowpods.txt"` are now accessed through file handle `f`.

Next, `for line in f` iterates through the file line-by-line. The file handle `f` is aware of the file structure, and is able to keep track of which line in the file is currently selected so that string variable `line` is able to receive the next line of the file.

The print statement `print(line)` outputs the line it currently stores followed by a newline character. A *newline* character is the line feed character (character code 10).

Unfortunately, this results in a blank line between lines appearing on the output because each line in `line` ends with a *newline* character as well.

```
>>>line = f.readline()
>>>line
'aa\n'
```

The solution is to delete the *newline* character ('\n') from the end of the string in variable `line` before `print(line)` is reached. *Figure 2.7.5* shows the revised Python program.

The action of strip() removes the *whitespace* at the end of the line, i.e. the *newline* character.

Summarising, reading from a text file takes the following form:

      open the text file for reading
      read the text file line-by-line
      do something with each line
      close the file

```
f = open("sowpods.txt", "r")
for line in f:
    line = line.strip()
    print(line)
f.close()
```

Figure 2.7.5 Python program which opens a text file 'sowpods.txt' for reading and displaying

We can also read from the file in the following ways:

`line = f.readline()` will read one line of the file into variable `line`.

`all_lines = f.read()` will read the entire contents of a file into variable `all_lines`.

Figure 2.7.6 and *Figure 2.7.7* show how to read from a text file in Pascal/Delphi, Java, VB.NET and C#.

Java requires try catch around the code because the methods which are called under the hood are designed to throw exceptions which have to be trapped (or caught).

Two ways of reading a file are shown for Java, VB.NET and C#.

2.7 Input/output and file handling

Pascal/Delphi

```
Program ReadingATextFile;
Var
  f : TextFile;
  Line : String;
Begin
  AssignFile(f, 'Sonnet116.txt');
  Reset(f);
  While Not Eof(f)
    Do
      Begin
        Readln(f, Line); {Read line of text from file into string variable Line}
        Writeln(Line); {Write line of text in string variable Line to output}
      End;
  CloseFile(f);
  Readln;
End.
```

Java

```java
import java.io.FileReader;
import java.io.BufferedReader;
public class ReadATextFile {
    public static void main(String[] args) {
      try{
              // Read the file and display it line by line.
              FileReader f = new FileReader("Sonnet116.txt");
              BufferedReader textReader = new BufferedReader(f);
              String line;
              while (( line = textReader.readLine()) != null ) {
                   System.out.println(line);
              }
          }
      catch (IOException e)
      {
            System.out.println(e);
      }

      FileReader inputStream = null;

      try {
              // Read the file and display it character by character.
              inputStream = new FileReader("Sonnet116.txt");
              int ch;
              System.in.read();
              while ((ch = inputStream.read()) != -1) {
                  System.out.print((char)ch);
              }
          }
      catch (IOException e)
      {
            System.out.println(e);
      }
    }
}
```

Figure 2.7.6 Reading from a text file "Sonnet116.txt" in Pascal/Delphi and Java

2 Programming

VB.NET

```vbnet
Imports System
Imports System.IO
Module Module1
    Sub Main()
        ' Reads the entire file at once
        ' Open the file using a stream reader.
        Using f As New StreamReader("Sonnet116.txt")
            Dim line As String
            ' Read the stream string variable line and write the string to the console.
            line = f.ReadToEnd() ' Reads to end of file
            Console.WriteLine(line)
        End Using ' Dispose of all the resources
        Console.ReadLine()
        ' Reads the file line-by-line.
        ' Open the file using a stream reader.
        Using f As New StreamReader("Sonnet116.txt")
            Dim line As String
            line = f.ReadLine()
            While Not (line Is Nothing)
                Console.WriteLine(line)
                line = f.ReadLine()
            End While
        End Using
        Console.ReadLine()
    End Sub
End Module
```

C#

```csharp
using System;
namespace ReadingATextFile
{
    class Program
    {
        static void Main(string[] args)
        {
         // Read the whole file into a string array lines.
            string[] lines = System.IO.File.ReadAllLines("Sonnet116.txt");
            foreach (string line in lines)
            {
                Console.WriteLine(line);
            }
            Console.ReadLine();
            string nextLine;
        // Read the file and display it line by line.
            System.IO.StreamReader f = new System.IO.StreamReader("Sonnet116.txt");
            while ((nextLine = f.ReadLine()) != null)
            {
                System.Console.WriteLine(nextLine);
            }
            f.Close();
            Console.ReadLine();
        }
    }
}
```

Figure 2.7.7 Reading from a text file "Sonnet116.txt" in VB.NET and C#

Writing to a text file

In Python, if we want to write to a file with filename `"studentresults.txt"`, we open this file in write mode (`"w"`) with

```
f = open("studentresults.txt", "w")
```

This will create a new file `"studentresults.txt"` or overwrite this file if it exists already.

The program in *Figure 2.7.8* collects a student name and the student's exam score typed at the keyboard and then using the file handle `f` to the opened file, writes student name then a comma then exam score on the same line to the opened text file

```
f.write(student_name + "," + exam_mark + "\n")
```

`"\n" is the` special control character called the end of line or *newline* character.

2.7 Input/output and file handling

This ensures that the file handle `f` is ready to write the next student name, comma, exam score combination on the next line.

Entering the student name "quit" causes the program to exit the *while loop* but not before printing "Quitting...". Finally the file is closed.

Figure 2.7.9 shows the contents of `"studentresults.txt"` produced by executing the program in *Figure 2.7.8*.

```
f = open("studentresults.txt", "w")
while True:
    student_name = input("Name: ")
    if student_name == "quit":
        print("Quitting...")
        break
    exam_mark = input("Exam score for " + student_name + " : ")
    f.write(student_name + "," + exam_mark + "\n")
f.close()
```

Figure 2.7.8 Python program which creates and writes lines of text to a text file 'studentresults.txt'

Bond K, 95
Cheadle P, 85
Gunawardena P, 90
Khan M, 88
De Silva S, 75
Smith E,55
Teng P, 85
Tipp S,30

Figure 2.7.9 Contents of "studentresults.txt" created by program in Figure 2.7.8

Appending to a text file

Changing the file mode to `"a"` allows new lines to be appended to the end of `"studentresults.txt"` if it exists or to an empty newly created `"studentresults.txt"` - *Figure 2.7.10*.

```
f = open("studentresults.txt", "a")
while True:
    student_name = input("Name: ")
    if student_name == "quit":
        print("Quitting...")
        break
    exam_mark = input("Exam score for " + student_name + " : ")
    f.write(student_name + "," + exam_mark + "\n")
f.close()
```

Figure 2.7.10 Python program which appends lines of text to an existing text file 'studentresults.txt'

Figure 2.7.11 shows two ways of writing to text files in Pascal/Delphi, Java and one way in VB.NET.

Pascal:

1. Line-by-line:
   ```
   For Line in Lines
       Do Writeln(f, Line);
   ```

2. Writing all the lines in one go
   ```
   Lines.LoadFromFile('Sonnet116.txt');
   Lines.SaveToFile('AnotherNewFile.txt');
   ```

Java:

1. Using `java.io.PrintWriter`
2. Using `java.io.PrintWriter` and `java.io.File`

VB.NET: Using `StreamWriter` and `WriteLine`.

Pascal/Delphi

```
Program WriteToATextFile;
Uses Classes;
Var
  f : TextFile;
  Lines : TStringList;
  Line : String;
Begin
  AssignFile(f, 'NewFile.txt');
  Rewrite(f);
  Lines := TStringList.Create;
  Lines.Add('Let me not to the marriage of true minds');
  Lines.Add('Admit impediments. Love is not love');
  Writeln(Lines.text);
  For Line in Lines
    Do Writeln(f, Line); {Write a line of text to text file}
  CloseFile(f);
  Lines.Clear;
  Lines.LoadFromFile('Sonnet116.txt');
  Lines.SaveToFile('AnotherNewFile.txt');
  Readln;
End.
```

Java

```
import java.io.IOException;
import java.io.PrintWriter;
import java.io.File;
public class WriteToATextFile {
  public static void main(String[] args) {
    try{
        PrintWriter printLine = new PrintWriter("Z:/NewFile.txt");
        String line = "Let me not to the marriage of true minds";
        printLine.println(line); // Write a line of text to the file
        printLine.close(); // Close the file
        File f = new File("Z:/AnotherNewFile.txt");
        if (!f.exists()) {
          if (f.createNewFile()) {
            PrintWriter newPrintLine = new PrintWriter(f);
            newPrintLine.println("Let me not to the marriage of true minds");
            newPrintLine.println("Admit impediments. Love is not love");
            newPrintLine.close();
          }
        }
    }
    catch (IOException e){
        System.out.println(e);
    }
  }
}
```

VB.NET

```
Imports System
Imports System.IO
Imports System.Text
Module Module1
    Sub Main()
        Try
            Dim w As StreamWriter = New StreamWriter("NewFile.txt")
            w.WriteLine("Let me not to the marriage of true minds")
            w.WriteLine("Admit impediments. Love is not love")
            w.Close()
        Catch e As Exception
            Console.WriteLine("The process failed: {0}", e.ToString())
        End Try
    End Sub
End Module
```

Figure 2.7.11 Writing to a text file in Pascal/Delphi, Java and VB.NET

2.7 Input/output and file handling

Figure 2.7.12 shows one way of writing to text files in C#.

```csharp
C#
using System;
using System.Text;
using System.IO;
namespace WriteToATextFile
{
    class Program
    {
        public static void Main()
        {
            try
            {
                using (StreamWriter w = new StreamWriter("NewFile.txt"))
                {
                    w.WriteLine("Let me not to the marriage of true minds");
                    w.WriteLine("Admit impediments. Love is not love");
                }
            }
            catch (Exception e)
            {
                Console.WriteLine("The process failed: {0}", e.ToString());
            }
        }
    }
}
```

Figure 2.7.12 Writing to a text file in C#

Programming tasks

1. Write a program which makes a copy of a text file. Your program should prompt the user to enter the names of the input and output text files.

2. Write a program that reads a text file and displays it with the corresponding line number at the beginning of each line. Start line numbering from 1.

3. The text file "**Dict5LetterWords.txt**" (download from www.educational-computing.co.uk/CS/Textfiles.html) contains 5 letter words. Write a program which finds all 5 letter words in this file which contain the substring 'oe'.

4. The text file "**sowpods.txt**" is an official Scrabble dictionary (download from www.educational-computing.co.uk/CS/Textfiles.html). Write a program to find all words containing a particular substring in the text file "**sowpods.txt**". The program should prompt the user to enter a substring to search for.

5. Write a program to create a Geography quiz which tests a user's knowledge of country capitals.
Use the text file "**countriescapitals.txt**" (download from www.educational-computing.co.uk/CS/Textfiles.html) which is a comma separated file of countries and their capitals.
The program should display the name of a country chosen at random from this text file and prompt the user to supply the name of the capital of this country. The program should then check the user's answer. If the user's answer is correct the program should respond "Well done, you got it right!". If the user's answer is incorrect the program should respond "Incorrect answer, the correct answer is ???????" where the correct answer is substituted for the string "???????" when the program executes.

In this chapter you have covered:

- Obtaining user input from the keyboard
- Outputting data and information from a program to the computer display
- Reading/writing from/to a text file.

2 Programming

2 Programming

Learning objectives:

■ *Understand and be able to use:*

- *length*
- *position*
- *substring*
- *concatenation*
- *convert character to character code*
- *convert character code to character*
- *string conversion operations.*

2.8 String-handling operations

Strings

A string is a sequence of zero or more characters.

The encoding used for each character in a string could be ASCII (7-bits), ANSI (8 bits = ASCII/OEM), or some version of Unicode, e.g. UTF-16.
UTF-16 is effectively how characters are maintained internally in .NET[1].
In versions of Delphi from Delphi 2009 onwards, string characters are encoded in UTF-16.

String operations

Strings are used to store human-readable text. The literal string, 'Hello World!', consists of twelve characters (10 letters, 1 punctuation mark and 1 space) placed between single quotes. Some programming languages use single quotes, some use double quotes and others allow the use of both, e.g. Python.

The literal string of twelve characters, 'Hello World!', is stored in a container with a capacity for more than twelve bytes because

- each character may need more than one byte, e.g. when UTF-16 is used
- some bytes must be used to store the count of characters or to indicate the end of the sequence of characters.

For this and other reasons programming languages provide a library of routines and string operators for programmers to use when working with strings.

String indexing

To access individual characters of a string an indexing scheme is required.

Figure 2.8.1 shows a scheme that starts numbering string elements (characters) at 0.

Figure 2.8.2 shows a Delphi XE5 program and its output.

The program creates a string container (variable) called `s` in a declaration.
The program assigns the string value 'Hello World!' to variable `s`.
It obtains the index number of the character 'H' when `s.IndexOf('H')` is evaluated.
This number is 0 which is written to the console by `Writeln`.
It then confirms that the index of 'H' is 0 with `Writeln(s[0])`.
The brackets `[]` are one mechanism by which individual characters of a string may be accessed. In this example, the index is treated as an offset. If the offset is 0 then we stay on 'H'.

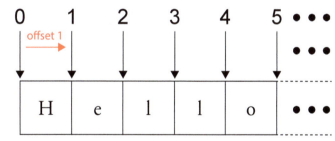

Figure 2.8.1 Zero-based numbering scheme for elements of a string

Information

Character:
The Unicode Glossary defines a character as:
The smallest component of written language that has semantic value.

---

1 .NET Framework is a software framework developed by Microsoft

2 Programming

```
Program StringIndexingExample1;
{$APPTYPE CONSOLE}
{$ZEROBASEDSTRINGS ON}
{$R *.res}
Uses
   System.SysUtils;
Var s : String;
Begin
   s := 'Hello World!';
   Writeln(s.IndexOf('H'));
   Writeln(s[0]);
   Readln;
End.
```

> **Key term**
>
> **Unicode:**
> Unicode is a computing industry standard for the consistent encoding, representation, and handling of text expressed in most of the world's writing systems. Unicode provides a unique number for every character: no matter what the platform; no matter what the program; no matter what the language.

Figure 2.8.2 String indexing illustrated by a Delphi XE5 program and its output

To test this, we try s[1] and s[4] - see Figure 2.8.3. The character one on from the beginning of the string is 'e', four on is 'o'.

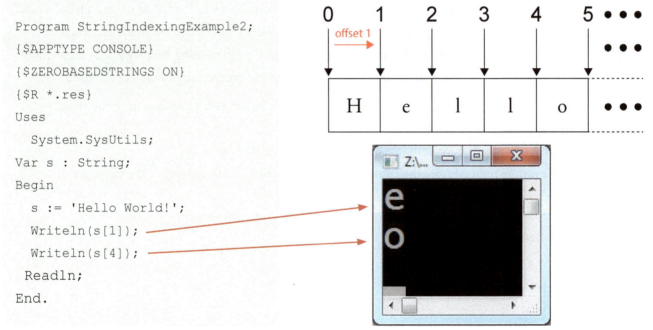

```
Program StringIndexingExample2;
{$APPTYPE CONSOLE}
{$ZEROBASEDSTRINGS ON}
{$R *.res}
Uses
   System.SysUtils;
Var s : String;
Begin
   s := 'Hello World!';
   Writeln(s[1]);
   Writeln(s[4]);
   Readln;
End.
```

Figure 2.8.3 String indexing illustrated by a Delphi XE5 program and its output, 'e' has index 1 because it is offset by 1 from beginning of string, 'o' has index 4 because it is offset by 4.

Figure 2.8.4 shows a VB.NET program which uses string indexing. In VB.NET the brackets () are used to access individual characters of a string. In this example, the index is treated as an **offset**.
If the offset is 0 then we stay on 'H'.

Figure 2.8.5 shows a C# program which uses string indexing. In C# the brackets [] are used to access individual characters of a string.

In this example, the index is treated as an **offset**. If the offset is 0 then we stay on 'H'.

2.8 String-handling operations

```
Module StringIndexing

    Sub Main()

        Dim s As String

        s = "Hello World!"

        Console.WriteLine(s)

        Console.WriteLine(s.IndexOf("H"))

        Console.WriteLine(s(0))

        Console.WriteLine(s(1))

        Console.WriteLine(s(4))

        Console.ReadLine()

    End Sub

End Module
```

Figure 2.8.4 String indexing illustrated by a Visual Basic 2015 program and its output, the index of 'H' is 0, 'e' has index 1 because it is offset by 1 from beginning of string, 'o' has index 4 because it is offset by 4.

```
using System;
namespace ConsoleStringIndexing
{
    class StringIndexing
    {
        static void Main(string[] args)
        {
            string s;
            s = "Hello World!";
            Console.WriteLine(s);
            Console.WriteLine(s.IndexOf('H'));
            Console.WriteLine(s[0]);
            Console.WriteLine(s[1]);
            Console.WriteLine(s[4]);
            Console.ReadLine();
        }
    }
}
```

Figure 2.8.5 String indexing illustrated by a Visual C# 2015 program and its output, the index of 'H' is 0, 'e' has index 1 because it is offset by 1 from beginning of string, 'o' has index 4 because it is offset by 4.

2 Programming

Figure 2.8.6 shows a Java program which uses string indexing.

```
public class StringIndexing {
    public static void main(String[] args) {
        String s;
        s = "Hello World";
        System.out.println("Hello World!");
        System.out.println(s.indexOf("H"));
        System.out.println(s.charAt(0));
        System.out.println(s.charAt(1));
        System.out.println(s.charAt(4));
    }
}
```

In Java, the function `charAt` is used to access individual characters of a string. In this example, the index is treated as an **offset**. If the offset is 0 then we stay on 'H'.

Figure 2.8.6 String indexing illustrated by a Java program and its output, the index of 'H' is 0, 'e' has index 1 because it is offset by 1 from beginning of string, 'o' has index 4 because it is offset by 4.

Figure 2.8.7 shows string indexing in Interactive Python 3.4.

The brackets `[ ]` are used to access individual characters of the string "Hello World!". In this example, the index is treated as an **offset**. If the offset is 0 then we stay on 'H'.

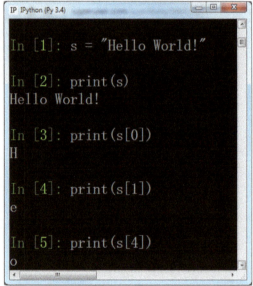

Figure 2.8.7 String indexing illustrated in Interactive Python 3.4 and its output, the index of 'H' is 0, 'e' has index 1 because it is offset by 1 from beginning of string, 'o' has index 4 because it is offset by 4.

Information

In Delphi prior to XE2 string indexing is one-based as shown in *Figure 2.8.8*. Indexing is treated as an ordinal number not an offset. Delphi XE3 onwards requires the directive ZEROBASEDSTRINGS OFF for one-based string indexing.

```
Program StringIndexingExampleOneBased;
{$APPTYPE CONSOLE}
{$R *.res}
Uses
   System.SysUtils;
Var s : String;
Begin
   s := 'Hello World!';
   Writeln(s);
   Writeln(s[1]);
   Writeln(s[2]);
   Writeln(s[5]);
   Readln;
End.
```

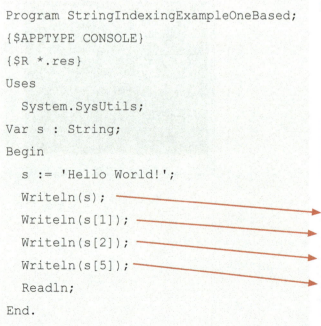

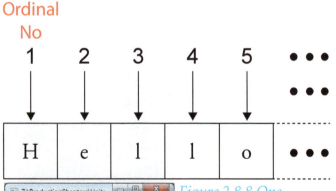

Figure 2.8.8 One-based string indexing illustrated by a Pascal/Delphi program and its output, the index of 'H' is 1, 'e' has index 2, 'o' has index 5.

2.8 String-handling operations

Length of a string

In Pascal and Delphi the **Length** function returns the number of characters in a string.

Figure 2.8.9 shows the `Length` function returning **12** for the length of string `s` which contains string value 'Hello World!'. The *For loop* iterates from **0** to **11** (`Length(s) - 1`) to access each character of this zero-based-indexed string and `Writeln(s[i])` then sends a copy of the selected character to the console where it is displayed.

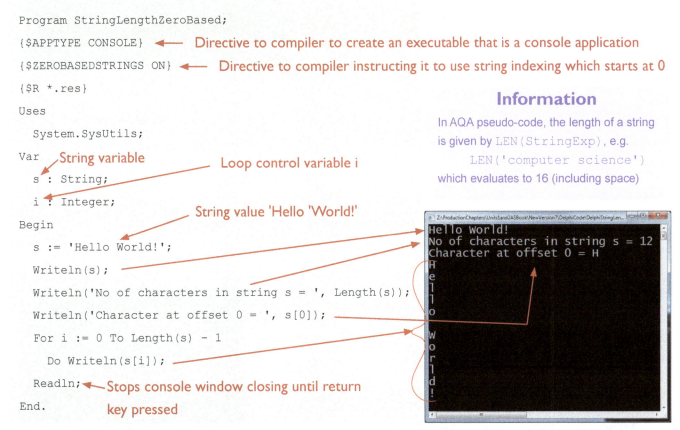

Figure 2.8.9 Using Pascal/Delphi's Length function to iterate through the characters of a zero-based string.

Figure 2.8.10 shows a C# program which uses the **Length** property of a C# string object. In C# a string is an object of type **String** whose value is a sequence of **Char** object characters. The **Length** property of a string represents the number of **Char** objects it contains. The alias **string** is used in place of the class type **String**. Letter case is significant in C#.

String objects are immutable: they cannot be changed after they have been created. All of the **String** methods and C# operators that appear to modify a string actually return the results in a new string object.

In the following source code, **string** is an alias for the **String** class in the .NET framework:

```
string s = "Hello World!"
```

In the source code

```
Console.WriteLine("No of characters in string s = {0}", s.Length);
```

The expression `s.Length` evaluates to the length of the string that `s` contains.

In the literal string value `"No of characters in string s = {0}", s.Length);`

`{0}` is a place holder for the returned string length value 12.

105

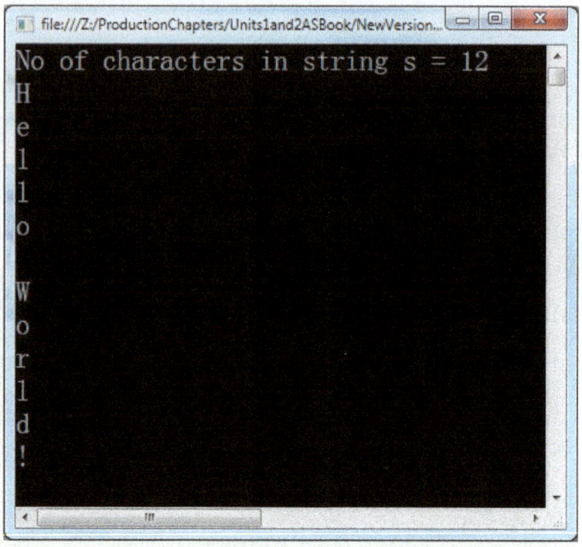

2 Programming

```
using System;
namespace ConsoleStringLength
{
    class Program
    {
        static void Main(string[] args)
        {
            string s = "Hello World!";
            Console.WriteLine("No of characters in string s = {0}", s.Length);
            for (int i = 0; i < s.Length; i++)
            {
                Console.WriteLine(s[i]);
            }
            Console.ReadLine();
        }
    }
}
```

Figure 2.8.10 Using C#'s Length property of a string object to iterate through the characters of a zero-based string.

Figure 2.8.11 shows a Java program which uses the **length** method of a Java string object. In Java, a string is an object of type **String** whose value is a sequence of characters of data type **char** - a single 16-bit Unicode character. The **length** method of a string object returns the number of characters it contains.

Enclosing a character string within double quotes automatically creates a new **String** object. String objects are immutable, which means that once created, their values cannot be changed.

```
public class StringLength {
    public static void main(String[] args) {
        String s;
        s = "Hello World!";
        System.out.println("No of characters in string s = " + s.length());
        for (int i = 0; i < s.length(); i++){
            System.out.println(s.charAt(i));
        }
    }
}
```

Figure 2.8.11 Using Java's Length property of a string object to iterate through the characters of a zero-based string.

Figure 2.8.12 shows a VB.NET program which uses the **Length** property of a VB.NET string object. In VB.NET, a string is an object of type **String** whose value is a sequence of characters of data type **char** - a single 16-bit Unicode character. The **Length** property of a string object returns the number of characters it contains.

2.8 String-handling operations

Enclosing a character string within double quotes automatically creates a new **String** object. **String** objects are immutable, which means that once created, their values cannot be changed.

```
Module StringLength
    Sub Main()
        Dim s As String = "Hello World!"
        Console.WriteLine("No of characters in string s = {0}", s.Length)
        For i As Integer = 0 To s.Length - 1
            Console.WriteLine(s(i))
        Next
        Console.ReadLine()
    End Sub
End Module
```

Figure 2.8.12 Using VB.NET's Length property of a string object to iterate through the characters of a zero-based string.

Figure 2.8.13 shows that the use of the Python `len` function applied to a string variable `s`, as follows: `len(s)`, returns the number of characters in the string value "Hello World!" which `s` contains.

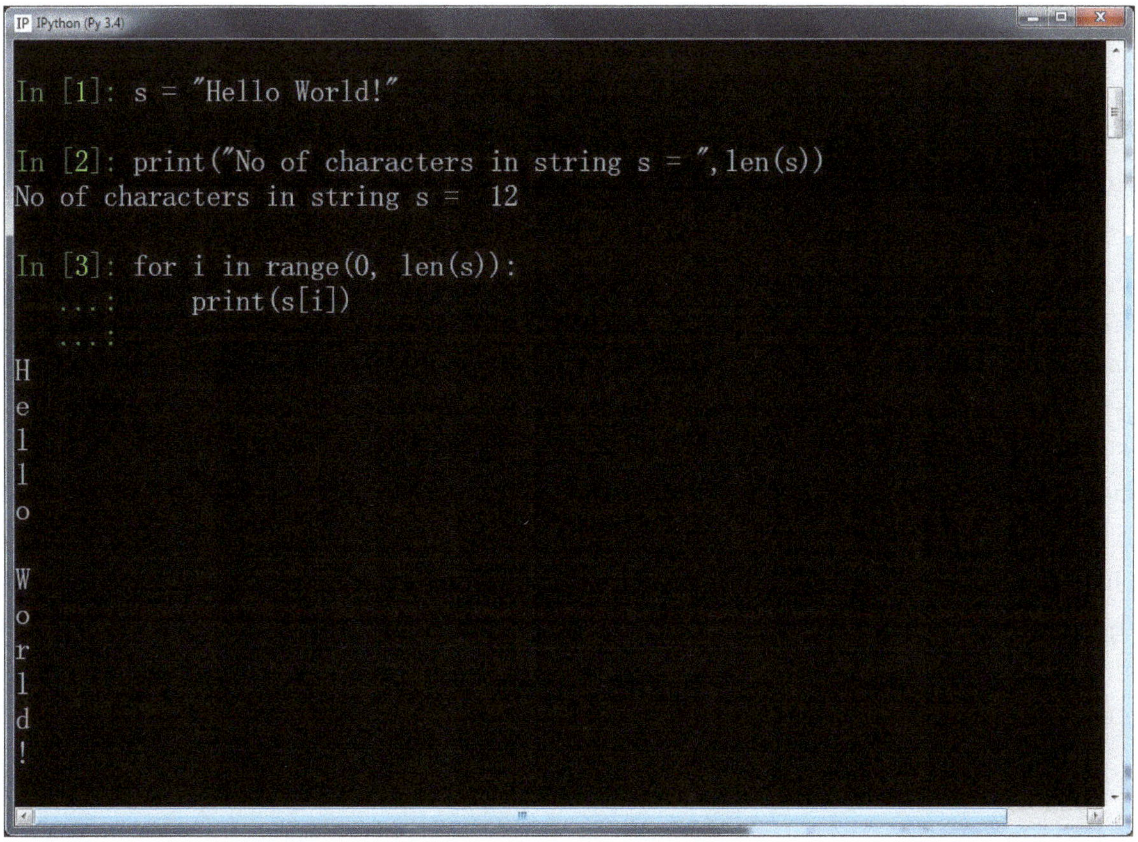

```
In [1]: s = "Hello World!"

In [2]: print("No of characters in string s = ", len(s))
No of characters in string s =  12

In [3]: for i in range(0, len(s)):
   ...:     print(s[i])
   ...:
H
e
l
l
o
 
W
o
r
l
d
!
```

Figure 2.8.13 Using Python's len function to obtain the length of a string, s, then iterate through the characters of this zero-based string.

Figure 2.8.14 shows that the use of the Pascal/Delphi `Length` function applied to a one-based string variable `s`, as follows: `Length(s)`, returns the number of characters in the string value "Hello World!" which variable `s` contains.

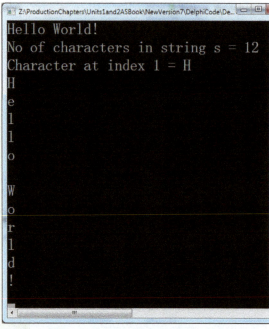

```
Program StringLengthOneBased;
{$APPTYPE CONSOLE}
{$R *.res}
Uses
   System.SysUtils;
Var
   s : String;
   i : Integer;
Begin
   s := 'Hello World!';
   Writeln(s);
   Writeln('No of characters in string s = ', Length(s));
   Writeln('Character at index 1 = ', s[1]);
   For i := 1 To Length(s)
     Do Writeln(s[i]);
   Readln;
End.
```

Figure 2.8.14 Using Pascal/Delphi's Length function to obtain the length of a string, s, then iterate through the characters of this one-based string.

Substring

A substring is a subset of a string, for example, the substring 'mit' is a subset of the string 'smith', located between one index, the `StartIndex = 1`, and another, the `EndIndex = 3` as shown in Figure 2.8.15.

Figure 2.8.15 shows two ways to identify a substring of the string by
- Index
- Offset

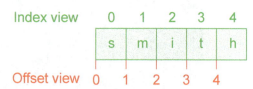

Figure 2.8.15 The string 'smith' and two ways to identify a substring of the string, by Index or by Offset

In the *index view* in Figure 2.8.15, if `StartIndex` is 1, then the index of the character 'm' is selected in the string s. In the *index view* in Figure 2.8.15, if the `EndIndex` is 3, then the index of the character 't' is selected in the string s. The substring returned is between index 1 and 3, inclusive, i.e. substring 'mit'.

Suppose a subroutine called `SUBSTRING` returns a substring of a given string, s. It is called with arguments s, `StartIndex` and `EndIndex` as shown in Table 2.8.1 and the substring returned is assigned to another string variable, `SubOfs`. In pseudo-code `SUBSTRING(1, 3, 'computer science')` evaluates to `'omp'` if indexing starts from 0. Therefore, the output of this pseudo-code is `'omp'`.

```
s ← 'smith'
StartIndex ← 1
EndIndex ← 3
SubOfs ← SUBSTRING(StartIndex, EndIndex, s)
OUTPUT SubOfs
```

Table 2.8.1 Pseudo-code showing a call to Substring

2.8 String-handling operations

In the *offset view*,

- the first character of the substring, 'm' is reached by an offset of one character from the beginning of the string s as shown in *Figure 2.8.16* - `StartOffset` is **1**.

- the last character of the substring, 't' is included by an offset of four characters from the beginning of the string s as shown in *Figure 2.8.16* (an offset of 0 is the first character 's' - `EndOffset` is **4**. A slice can then occur between 1 and 4 as shown in *Figure 2.8.16* to obtain the substring.

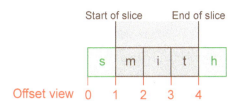

Figure 2.8.16 Taking a slice of the string 'smith' between StartOffset = 1 and EndOffset = 4

We can use `StartSlice` and `EndSlice` instead of `StartOffset` and `EndOffset`, to make it clearer that the selected substring is a slice through the string, i.e. `StartSlice = 1, EndSlice = 4`.

Table 2.8.2 shows examples of how a substring can be obtained in Pascal/Delphi, C#, Python, Java and VB.NET. Python has no substring subroutine. Instead, we use slice syntax to get parts of existing strings.

Pascal/Delphi	C#
``Program SubstringExample;
{String indexing starts at 1}
Var
s, SubOfs : String;
StartIndex, Count : Integer;
Begin
s := 'smith';
StartIndex := 2;
Count := 3;
SubOfs := Copy(s,StartIndex,Count);
Writeln(SubOfs);
Readln;
End.
{Copy treats zero-based strings as if
they are 1-based in Delphi with zero-
based compiler option ON}```	```using System;
namespace SubstringExample
{
class Program
{
static void Main(string[] args)
{
String s = "smith";
int startIndex = 1;
int endIndex = 3;
String subOfs = s.Substring(startIndex,endIndex);
Console.WriteLine("Substring is {0}",subOfs);
Console.ReadLine();
}
}
}```
Python	**Java**
``s = "smith"
start_slice = 1
end_slice = 4
sub_of_s = s[start_slice:end_slice]
print("Substring is ", sub_of_s)```	```public class SubstringExample {
public static void main(String[] args) {
String s = new String("smith");
int startSlice = 1;
int endSlice = 4;
String subOfs = s.substring(startSlice,endSlice);
System.out.println("Substring is " + subOfs);
}
}```
VB.Net	
``Module Module1
Sub Main()
Dim s As String = "smith"
Dim startIndex As Integer = 1
Dim endIndex As Integer = 3
Dim subOfs = s.Substring(startIndex, endIndex)
Console.WriteLine("Substring is {0}", subOfs)
Console.ReadLine()
End Sub
End Module``` ||

Table 2.8.2 Examples of how a substring can be obtained in Pascal/Delphi, C#, Python, Java and VB.NET

2 Programming

Position

Sometimes we may wish to discover if a given substring is present within a given string. For this we use a **position** function which returns the index within the given string of the first occurrence of the substring, e.g. in pseudo-code `POSITION('hello', 'e')` returns 1 because the index of `'e'` is 1 in `'hello'`, if indexing starts at 0. If the substring is not present in the given string then a value is returned outside the index range, e.g. -1. *Table 2.8.3* shows how this can be done in Pascal/Delphi, C#, Python, Java and VB.NET.

Pascal/ Delphi	`Position := AnsiPos('ello', 'Hello World!');`
	`If Not (Position = 0)`
	`  Then Writeln('String contains ello')`
	`  Else Writeln('Not found');`
		The AnsiPos function finds the position of one string 'ello' within another 'Hello World'.
		If the string is not found, 0 is returned.
		The search is case sensitive.

C#	`string s = "Hello World!";`
	`if (s.IndexOf("ello") != -1)`
	`{`
	`    Console.WriteLine("String contains ello");`
	`}`
		Function `IndexOf` returns the index of a substring. First it scans the String. And if the substring is not found, it returns -1.

VB.NET	`Dim s As String = "Hello World!"`
	`If Not s.IndexOf("ello") = -1 Then`
	`    Console.WriteLine("String contains ello")`
		Function `IndexOf` returns the index of a substring. First it scans the String. And if the substring is not found, it returns -1.

Java	`String s = "Hello World!";`
	`if (s.indexOf("ello") >= 0){`
	`    System.out.println(" String contains ello")`
	`}`
		Function indexOf returns the index within this string of the first occurrence of the specified substring. If it does not occur as a substring, -1 is returned.

Python	`str1 = "Hello World!"`
	`str2 = "ello"`
	`if (str1.find(str2) != -1):`
	`    print ("String contains ello")`
		Function find returns the index within this string of the first occurrence of the specified substring. If it does not occur as a substring, -1 is returned.

Table 2.8.3 Examples of searching for a substring within a given string in Pascal/Delphi, C#, Python, Java and VB.NET

Concatenation

The concatenation of strings is the operation of joining character strings end-to-end.

For example, the concatenation of "john" and "smith" is "johnsmith".
The concatenation of "john" and " " and "smith" is "john smith".
The most common way of concatenating strings is to use the '+' operator.

For example in Java:
```
String a = "Hello";
String b = " World!";
String c = a + b;
System.out.print(c);
```

The concatenation operator '+' is common to all the programming languages covered in this chapter.

```
Program CharacterExample;
{$APPTYPE CONSOLE}
{$R *.res}
Uses
  System.SysUtils;
Var
  Ch : Char;
Begin
  Ch := 'A';
  Writeln(Ch);
  Writeln(Ord(Ch));
  Readln;
End.
```

Figure 2.8.17 The Char data type and the Ord function in Pascal/Delphi which converts a character to its character code.

Character → character code

Sometimes an operation needs to be carried out on a single character value, e.g. 'A', or a variable of character data type, e.g. `Ch`. In pseudo-code `CHAR_TO_CODE('A')` evaluates to 65 using ASCII/Unicode.

In Pascal and Delphi, the `Char` data type is used to create a single character variable and the `Ord` function converts a character value to its character code as shown in *Figure 2.8.17*.

In VB.NET, a character variable is declared using the `Char` data type as shown in *Figure 2.8.18*. The `Asc` function returns the character code for a given character value.

In Java, a character variable is declared using the `char` data type and to convert a character value to its character code in Java, data type casting is used as shown in *Figure 2.8.19* where `(int) ch` casts the value contained in `ch` to a value of type `int`.

The `char` keyword is used in C# to declare an instance of the `System.Char` structure that the .NET Framework uses to represent a Unicode character. The value of a `Char` object is a 16-bit numeric (ordinal) value. To convert a character to its character code in C#, data type casting is used as shown in *Figure 2.8.20*.

Figure 2.8.21 shows the use of the `ord` function in Python 3.4 to convert a character to its character code.

```
Module CharacterExample
    Sub Main()
        Dim ch As Char = "A"
        Console.WriteLine(ch)
        Console.WriteLine(Asc(ch))
        Console.ReadLine()
    End Sub
End Module
```

Figure 2.8.18 The Char data type and the Asc function in VB.NET.

```
public class CharacterExample {
    public static void main(String[] args) {
        char ch = 'A';
        System.out.println(ch);
        System.out.println((int) ch);
    }
}
```
causes data type cast from char to int

Figure 2.8.19 The char data type in Java and the use of data type casting, (int) to convert a character to its character code.

```
using System;
namespace CharExample
{
    class Program
    {
        static void Main(string[] args)
        {
            char ch = 'A';
            Console.WriteLine(ch);
            Console.WriteLine((int) ch);
            Console.ReadLine();
        }
    }
}
```
causes data type cast from char to int

Figure 2.8.20 The char data type in C# and the use of data type casting, (int), to convert a character to its character code.

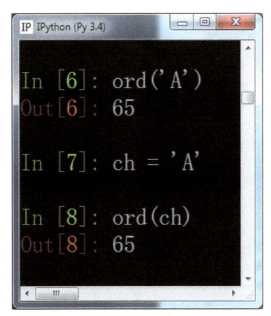

Figure 2.8.21 Using the ord function in Python 3.4 to convert a character to its character code.

Character code → character

In pseudo-code `CODE_TO_CHAR(97)` evaluates to `'a'` using ASCII/Unicode. *Table 2.8.4* shows how to convert from character code to character in C#, Java, Pascal/Delphi, Python and VB.NET and display the result in the console window. C# and Java use data type casting whilst Pascal/Delphi and VB.NET use a function, `Chr`, and Python a function `chr`.

Language	Code
C#	`Console.WriteLine((char)65);`
Java	`System.out.println((char)65);`
Pascal/Delphi	`Writeln(Chr(65));`
Python	`print(chr(65))`
VB.Net	`Console.WriteLine(Chr(65))`

Table 2.8.4 Code to convert character code to character in C#, Java, Pascal/Delphi, Python and VB.NET and display the result in the console window.

2 Programming

String conversion operations

String to integer

In pseudo-code `STRING_TO_INT('21')` evaluates to integer 21.

C#

A string can be converted to a number using methods in the `Convert` class or by using the `TryParse` method found on the various numeric types (int, long, float, etc). `Convert.ToInt32` converts an integer written in string form, e.g. "-125" to a 32-bit integer value, e.g. -125.

```
Console.WriteLine("String -125 has integer value {0}", Convert.ToInt32("-125"));
```

There are also other methods that may be used when converting a string representing a numeric value:

- `Parse`: If the string is not in a valid format, `Parse` throws an exception. `Int32.Parse("-125")` returns the 32-bit integer value -125. *Table 2.8.5* shows an example of this.
- `TryParse`: In the example in *Table 2.8.5*, `TryParse` returns **true** if the conversion succeeded, storing the result in `anotherNumber`, and **false** if it fails.

Both methods ignore *whitespace* at the beginning and at the end of the string, but all other characters must be characters that form the appropriate numeric type (int, long, ulong, float, decimal, etc). Any *whitespace* within the characters that form the number causes an error.

Java

The `Integer.parseInt(String s)` static method parses the string argument `s` as a signed decimal integer and returns an `int` value as shown in *Table 2.8.5*. The resulting value is not an instance of Java's **Integer** class but just a primitive `int` value.

The `Integer.valueOf(String s)` static method will return an `Integer` object holding the value of the specified `String s` argument.

VB.NET

A string can be converted to a number using methods in the `Convert` class or by using the `TryParse` method found on the various numeric types (int, long, float, etcetera). `Convert.ToInt32` converts an integer written in string form, e.g. "-125" to a 32-bit integer value, e.g. -125.

```
Console.WriteLine("String -125 has integer value {0}", Convert.ToInt32("-125"))
```

There are also other methods that may be used when converting a string representing a numeric value:

- `Parse`: If the string is not in a valid format, `Parse` throws an exception. `Int32.Parse("-125")` returns the 32-bit integer value -125. *Table 2.8.5* shows an example of this.
- `TryParse`: In the example in *Table 2.8.5*, `TryParse` returns **true** if the conversion succeeded, storing the result in `anotherNumber`, and **false** if it fails.

Python

The Python standard built-in function `int()` converts a string into an integer value. It is called with an argument which is the string form of an integer. It returns the integer that corresponds to the string form of the integer.

Table 2.8.5 shows an example of the use of `int()`.

Pascal

The `StrToInt` function converts an Integer string such as '-125' to an integer as shown in *Table 2.8.5*.

Delphi

The `StrToInt` function converts an Integer string such as '-125' to an integer.

2.8 String-handling operations

It is also possible to use `Parse` and `TryParse` as follows:

```
AnotherNumber := System.Int32.Parse('-125');
Writeln(AnotherNumber);
If System.Int32.TryParse('-125', YetAnotherNumber)
   Then Writeln(YetAnotherNumber)
   Else Writeln('String could not be parsed');
```

Table 2.8.5 shows examples of the use of each.

Language	Code

C#	`Console.WriteLine("String -125 has integer value {0}",`
	`                Convert.ToInt32("-125"));`
	`int number = Int32.Parse("-125");`
	`Console.WriteLine(number);`
	`int anotherNumber;`
	`if (Int32.TryParse("-125", out anotherNumber))`
	`    Console.WriteLine(anotherNumber);`
	`else Console.WriteLine("String could not be parsed.");`

Java	`int number = Integer.parseInt("-125");`
	`System.out.println("The number is: " + number);`
	`int anotherNumber = Integer.valueOf("-125");`
	`System.out.println("The number is: " + anotherNumber);`

Pascal	`Number := StrToInt('-125');` `Writeln(Number);`

Delphi	`Var Result, YetAnotherNumber : Integer;`
	`............`
	`Number := StrToInt('-125');`
	`Writeln(Number);`
	`AnotherNumber := System.Int32.Parse('-125');`
	`Writeln(AnotherNumber);`
	`If System.Int32.TryParse('-125', YetAnotherNumber)`
	`   Then Writeln(YetAnotherNumber)`
	`   Else Writeln('String could not be parsed');`

Python	`print(int("-125"))`

VB.NET	`Console.WriteLine("String -125 has integer value {0}",`
	`                Convert.ToInt32("-125"))`
	`Dim number As Integer = Int32.Parse("-125")`
	`Console.WriteLine(number)`
	`Dim anotherNumber As Integer`
	`If Int32.TryParse("-125", anotherNumber) Then`
	`    Console.WriteLine(anotherNumber)`
	`Else Console.WriteLine("String could not be parsed")`
	`End If`

Table 2.8.5 Code examples in C#, Java, Pascal, Delphi, Python and VB.NET which demonstrate how to convert an integer in string form to an integer value

2 Programming

String to real

In pseudo-code `STRING_TO_REAL('16.3')` evaluates to the real `16.3`.

C#

A string can be converted to a number using methods in the `Convert` class or by using the `TryParse` method found on the various numeric types (int, long, float, etc). `Convert.ToSingle` converts a number written in string form, e.g. "-125.5" to a single precision floating point value, e.g. -125.5. See below and *Table 2.8.6*.

```
Console.WriteLine("String -125.5 has float value {0}", Convert.ToSingle("-125.5"));
```

The precision of a single floating point number is 7 decimal digits.

There are also other methods that may be used when converting a string representing a numeric value:

- `Parse`: If the string is not in a valid format, `Parse` throws an exception.
  `float.Parse("-125.5")` returns a single precision floating point value -125.5. *Table 2.8.6* shows an example of this.
- `TryParse`: In the example in *Table 2.8.6*, `TryParse` returns **true** if the conversion succeeded, storing the result in `anotherNumber`, and **false** if it fails.

Both methods ignore *whitespace* at the beginning and at the end of the string, but all other characters must be characters that form the appropriate numeric type (int, long, ulong, float, decimal, etc). Any *whitespace* within the characters that form the number cause an error.

Java

The `Float.parseFloat(String s)` static method parses the string argument `s` as a signed number and returns a floating point value as shown in *Table 2.8.6*.

The `Float.valueOf(String s)` static method will return a `Float` object holding the float value represented by the argument string `s`.

VB.NET

A string can be converted to a number using methods in the `Convert` class or by using the `TryParse` method found on the various numeric types (int, long, float, etcetera). `Convert.ToSingle` converts a number written in string form, e.g. "-125.5" to a single precision floating point value, e.g. -125.5. See below and *Table 2.8.6*.

```
Console.WriteLine("String -125.5 has float value {0}", Convert.ToSingle("-125.5"))
```

The precision of a single floating point number is 7 decimal digits.

There are also other methods that may be used when converting a string representing a numeric value:

- `Parse`: If the string is not in a valid format, `Parse` throws an exception.
  `float.Parse("-125.5")` returns a single precision floating point value -125.5. *Table 2.8.6* shows an example of this.
- `TryParse`: In the example in *Table 2.8.6*, `TryParse` returns **true** if the conversion succeeded, storing the result in `anotherNumber`, and **false** if it fails.

Both methods ignore *whitespace* at the beginning and at the end of the string, but all other characters must be characters that form the appropriate numeric type (int, long, ulong, float, decimal, etc). Any *whitespace* within the characters that form the number causes an error.

Python

The Python standard built-in function `float()` converts a string into a floating point value. It is called with an argument which is the string form of a number. It returns the floating point value that corresponds to the string form of the number.

Table 2.8.6 shows an example of the use of `float()`.

2.8 String-handling operations

Pascal
The `StrToFloat` function converts a number string such as '-125.5' to a floating point value as shown in *Table 2.8.6*.

Delphi
The `StrToFloat` function converts a number string such as '-125.5' to a floating point value.
It is also possible to use `Parse` and `TryParse` as follows:

```
AnotherNumber := System.Single.Parse('-125.5');
Writeln(AnotherNumber);
If System.Single.TryParse('-125.5', YetAnotherNumber)
   Then Writeln(YetAnotherNumber)
   Else Writeln('String could not be parsed');
```

where `AnotherNumber` and `YetAnotherNumber` are single precision floating point variables declared as follows

```
Var
   AnotherNumber, YetAnotherNumber : Single;
```

Table 2.8.6 shows examples of the use of each. To use double precision substitute `Double` for `Single` in the code above.

Language	Code

C#	`Console.WriteLine("String -125.5 has float value {0}",`
	`            Convert.ToSingle("-125.5"));`
	`float number = float.Parse("-125.5");`
	`Console.WriteLine(number);`
	`float anotherNumber;`
	`if (float.TryParse("-125.5", out anotherNumber))`
	`    Console.WriteLine(anotherNumber);`
	`else Console.WriteLine("String could not be parsed.");`

Java	`float number = Float.parseFloat("-125.5");`
	`System.out.println("The number is: " + number);`
	`float anotherNumber = Float.valueOf("-125.5");`
	`System.out.println("The number is: " + anotherNumber);`

Pascal	`Writeln(StrToFloat('-125.5'):8:2);`

Delphi	`Var Result, YetAnotherNumber : Single;`
	`............`
	`Writeln(StrToFloat('-125.5'):8:2);`
	`AnotherNumber := System.Single.Parse('-125.5');`
	`Writeln(AnotherNumber:8:2);`
	`If System.Single.TryParse('-125.5', YetAnotherNumber)`
	`   Then Writeln(YetAnotherNumber:8:2)`
	`   Else Writeln('String could not be parsed');`

Python	`print(float("-125.5"))`

VB.NET	`Console.WriteLine("String -125.5 has float value {0}",`
	`            Convert.ToSingle("-125.5"))`
	`Dim Number As Single = Single.Parse("-125.5")`
	`Console.WriteLine(Number)`
	`Dim AnotherNumber As Single`
	`If (Single.TryParse("-125.5", AnotherNumber)) Then`
	`    Console.WriteLine(AnotherNumber)`
	`Else Console.WriteLine("String could not be parsed.")`
	`End If`

Table 2.8.6 Code examples in C#, Java, Pascal, Delphi, Python and VB.NET which demonstrate how to convert a number in string form to a floating point value

2 Programming

Integer to string

In pseudo-code `INT_TO_STRING(16)` evaluates to the string '16'.

C#

An integer can be converted to its equivalent string form using `Convert.ToString`, e.g. -125 to its string representation, e.g. "-125". See below and *Table 2.8.7*.

```
Console.WriteLine(Convert.ToString(-125));
```

Java

The **Integer** class has a static method that returns a `String` object representing the specified `int` parameter, e.g.

```
System.out.println(Integer.toString(-125));
```

as shown in *Table 2.8.7*.

VB.NET

An integer can be converted to its equivalent string form using `Convert.ToString`, e.g. -125 to " -125" as shown below and in *Table 2.8.7*.

```
Console.WriteLine(Convert.ToString(-125))
```

Python

The Python standard built-in function `str()` converts a number to its equivalent string form. It is called with a number argument, e.g. -125 and returns the equivalent string form "-125" as shown in *Table 2.8.7*.

Pascal/Delphi

The `IntToStr` function converts an integer such as -125. to its equivalent string form '-125' as shown in *Table 2.8.7*.

Language	Code
C#	`Console.WriteLine(Convert.ToString(-125));`

Java	`System.out.println(Integer.toString(-125));`
	`String numberString = String.valueOf(-125);`
	`System.out.println(numberString);`

Pascal/Delphi	`Var`
	`  NumberString : String;`
	`......................`
	`NumberString := IntToStr(-125);`
	`Writeln(NumberString);`

Python	`print(str(-125))`
VB.NET	`Console.WriteLine(Convert.ToString(-125))`

Table 2.8.7 Code examples in C#, Java, Pascal, Delphi, Python and VB.NET which demonstrate how to convert an integer to an equivalent string form

Real to string

In pseudo-code `REAL_TO_STRING(16.3)` evaluates to the string '16.3'.

C#

A number stored in floating point form can be converted to its equivalent string form using `Convert.ToString`, e.g. -125.5 to its string representation, e.g. "-125.5". See below and *Table 2.8.8*.

```
Console.WriteLine(Convert.ToString(-125.5));
```

Java

The `Float` and `Double` classes each have a static method that returns a `String` object representing the specified `Float` or `Double` parameter, e.g.

```
System.out.println(Float.toString(-125.5f));
System.out.println(Double.toString(-125.5));
```

as shown in *Table 2.8.8*.

2.8 String-handling operations

Java has IEEE 754 single and double precision types supported by keywords:

```
float f = -125.5f;   // 32 bit float, note f suffix
double d = -125.5d;  // 64 bit float, suffix d is optional
```

Alternatively, we may use `String.valueOf(float f)`. If a float value, e.g. -125.5, is passed to this method as an argument, then the string representation of -125.5 is returned, i.e. "-125.5".

```
float number = -125.5f;
String numberString = String.valueOf(number);
```

VB.NET

A number stored in floating point form can be converted to its equivalent string form using `Convert.ToString`, e.g. -125.5 to " -125.5" as shown below and in *Table 2.8.8*.

```
Console.WriteLine(Convert.ToString(-125.5))
```

Python

The Python standard built-in function `str()` converts a number with a fractional part to its equivalent string form. It is called with a number argument, e.g. -125.5 and it returns the equivalent string form "-125.5" as shown in *Table 2.8.8*.

Pascal/Delphi

The `FloatToStr` function converts a number stored in floating point form such as -125.5 to its equivalent string form '-125.5' as shown in *Table 2.8.8*.

Language	Code
C#	`Console.WriteLine(Convert.ToString(-125.5));`

Java	`System.out.println(Float.toString(-125.5f));`
	`System.out.println(Double.toString(-125.5));`
	`float number1 = -125.5f;`
	`String numberString1 = String.valueOf(number1);`
	`System.out.println(numberString1);`
	`double number2 = -125.5;`
	`String numberString2 = String.valueOf(number2);`
	`System.out.println(numberString2);`

Pascal/Delphi	`Var`
	`   NumberString : String;`
	`......................`
	`NumberString := FloatToStr(-125.5);`
	`Writeln(NumberString);`

Python	`print(str(-125.5))`
VB.NET	`Console.WriteLine(Convert.ToString(-125.5))`

Table 2.8.8 Code examples in C#, Java, Pascal, Delphi, Python and VB.NET which demonstrate how to convert a floating point value to an equivalent string form

Programming tasks

1. Write a program which takes as input a string and prints out the number of characters in it.

2. Write a program which takes as input a word and checks if the first and last letters of the word are the same. The program should print either "The first and last letters are the same" or "The first and last letters are different".

3. Write a program which takes as input 2 words and prints the word made from the last 3 letters of the first word and the first 3 letters of the second word.

Programming tasks

4. Write a program which takes as input a sentence and calculates how many words are in the sentence. The program should print this number (with appropriate message). Assume a word ends with a space unless it is the last word in the sentence, a sentence ends with a full stop.

5. Write a program which inputs two words, a master word and a test word. The program should check whether or not the test word appears anywhere in the master word and then print an appropriate message. For example "THE" appears inside the word "STRENGTHEN" but not inside "STEALTH". The program should first check that the test word is shorter than the master word; if not it should print the message "Test word too long" and request a new test word.

6. Write a program which takes as input a pair of words and prints a third word made from the letters at the end of the first word if they are the same as the letters at the beginning of the second word, e.g. IGNORANT and ANTLER are input, the output is ANT, otherwise the program should request another pair of words.

7. Write a program which takes as input a word and prints out a new word made from reversing the order of the letters in the input word, e.g. input word = "BEAR", output word = "RAEB".

8. Write a program which takes as input a pair of words and checks if one is an anagram of the other. The program should output the message "ANAGRAM" if it is and the message "NOT AN ANAGRAM" if it isn't.

9. Write a program which takes as input a word and determines whether or not the word is a palindrome. (A palindrome is a word that reads the same forwards and backwards. E.g. ROTOR.)
Test your program on the following palindromes DAD, NOON, MADAM, REDDER, ROTOVATOR.

10. Write a program which takes a single word containing only upper case letters of the alphabet as input, and outputs an encrypted version of the word using the following simple encryption algorithm:
Character code for "A" + (((Character code of letter to encrypt - character code for "A") + 13) MOD 26)

Questions

The variables r, s and t in *Figure 2.8.22* are assigned string values.

1. Tick **the** box which shows the concatenation of r and s.

Concatenation of r and s	Tick **one** box
rs	
goodness gracious	
goodnessgracious	

```
r  ←  'goodness'
s  ←  'gracious'
t  ←  'me'
```

Figure 2.8.22

2. The characters of a string may be accessed by index. Assuming indexing starts at 1, r[4] is the character 'd'. Tick the boxes which correspond to the **three** true statements in the table.

Statement	Tick **three** boxes
LENGTH(r) > LENGTH(s)	
POSITION('ness', r) returns 5	
r[7] = s[8]	
s[LENGTH(r) - LENGTH(t)] = 'i'	
r[LENGTH(r) - LENGTH(t) + 1] = 's'	

2.8 String-handling operations

Questions

3 Develop a subroutine called `Prefix`, using either pseudo-code or a flowchart, which takes two strings called `wordstr` and `prefixstr` as parameters and determines whether the string `prefixstr` matches the beginning of `wordstr`.

For example using the strings:

$$\text{wordstr} \leftarrow \text{'goodness'}$$
$$\text{prefixstr} \leftarrow \text{'good'}$$

The string `'good'` matches the beginning of string `wordstr` so `Prefix(wordstr, prefixstr)` should return `true`. The first character `'g'` of `'good'` matches the first character of `'goodness'`, the next character `'o'` of `'good'` matches the next character of `'goodness'` and so on.

The string `'food'` does not match the beginning of string `wordstr` so `Prefix(wordstr, prefixstr)` should return `false`. The first character `'f'` of `'food'` does not match the first character of `'goodness'`.

Your subroutine should:
- work for strings of all lengths greater than 0
- return `false` if the length of `prefixstr` is greater than the length of `wordstr`.

The start of your subroutine has been completed for you.

```
SUBROUTINE Prefix(wordstr, prefixstr)
```

4 Some programming languages support a string handling subroutine, `Substring`, (or its equivalent) which returns a substring of a given string.

`Substring` takes three parameters, `aString`, `startindex`, and `endindex` as follows:

```
Substring(aString, startindex, endindex)
```

For example, assuming indexing of strings starts from 0

`Substring('goodness', 0, 4)` returns `'good'`.

Alter the body of your pseudo-code answer in question 3 for subroutine `Prefix` so that it uses subroutine `Substring`.

5 The following string conversion functions are available:

`StrToInt(aString)` - converts a numeric string `aString` to its integer equivalent, e.g. `StrToInt('125')` returns `125`.

`IntToStr(n)` - converts an integer `n` to its string equivalent, e.g. `IntToStr(125)` returns `'125'`.

`RealToStr(n)` - converts a real number `n` to its string equivalent, e.g. `RealToStr(125.5)` returns `'125.5'`.

`StrToReal(aString)` - converts a numeric string `aString` to its real number equivalent, e.g. `StrToReal('125.5')` returns `125`.

Complete the table by filling each box with what is returned from each function call.

Function call	Returns
`IntToStr(-459)`	
`StrToInt('-563')`	
`RealToStr(0.561)`	
`StrToReal('34.998')`	
`IntToStr(StrToInt('78'))`	

2 Programming

Questions

6 A function `Position` is used to discover if a given substring is present within a given string.

`Position` returns the index within the given string of the first occurrence of the substring.

If the substring is not present in the given string then -1 is returned.

For example, the function call `Position('ello', 'Hello World!')` returns 1.

Revisit question 3 and rewrite the body of this subroutine so that it uses subroutine `Position`.

7 The function `Chr` converts a character to its equivalent character code.

The function `Ord` converts a character code to its equivalent character.

The character codes for the letter characters 'A', 'B', 'C', ... 'X', 'Y', 'Z' of the alphabet have corresponding character codes, 65, 66, 67, ...88, 89, 90.

Complete the table with the result returned by each function call.

Function call	Result
`Chr(65)`	
`Ord('B')`	
`Chr(Ord('C') - 1)`	
`Ord(Chr(89))`	
`Chr(Ord('A') + 23)`	

In this chapter you have covered:

- Using and becoming familiar with:
  - length
  - position
  - substring
  - concatenation
  - character → character code
  - character code → character
  - string conversion operations
    - string to integer
    - string to real
    - integer to string
    - real to string.

2 Fundamentals of programming

2.9 Programming

Learning objectives:

- *Be able to use random number generation.*

2.9 Random number generation in a programming language

Random number generation

Random numbers

An algorithm which generates a random, or apparently random, sequence of numbers is called a **random number generator**.

For example, suppose we require a method for selecting an integer at random from the set of integers 1, 2, 3, .., N.

For small values of N simple mechanisms exist.

For example:
- for N = 2 we can toss a coin
- for N = 6 we can roll a six-sided die - one of the die shown in *Figure 2.9.1*
- for N = 12 we can roll a 12-sided die
- for N = 36 we can use a roulette wheel (ignoring 0 on wheel).

Figure 2.9.1 Rolling dice

Every number in the chosen set of integers 1, 2, 3, .., N, is equally likely.

Statistically, each number from the set should appear on average the same number of times in a long sequence generated by coin tossing or dice rolling.

The sequence generated which satisfies these two conditions is called a **random sequence**.

Pseudorandom numbers

Most computer generated random numbers use pseudorandom number generators (PRNGs) which are algorithms that can automatically create long runs of numbers with good random properties but eventually the sequence repeats.

This kind of random number is adequate for many situations, e.g. computer simulations and cryptography.

However, pseudorandom generated number sequences are not as random as coin tosses and dice rolls or random sequences generated from physical phenomena such as electrical noise.

Pseudorandom number generator algorithms generate a random sequence which is completely determined by a shorter initial value known as a seed value or key.

As a result, the entire seemingly random sequence can be reproduced if the seed value is known.

Randomizing the seed

Although it is possible to set the seed manually, using the same seed will generate the same pseudorandom sequence of numbers.

However, the choice of seed can be randomized. One method relies upon sampling the computer's system clock another chooses from a small set of truly random numbers.

For example, in Python one would call the procedure `random.seed(None)` to use the system clock to generate a randomised seed. Next, function `random.random()` is called. It returns the next random floating point number in the interval [0.0, 1.0). "[" means 0.0 is included in the range. The symbol ")" means 1.0 is excluded.

For example, in one call to `random.seed(None)` followed by `random.random()`, 0.40488239522745517 was returned.

However, the pseudorandom number generated by the call `random.seed(1)` followed by `random.random()`, produced 0.13436424411240122 as the first number in the sequence every time and the same sequence of numbers on calling `random.random()` again and again.

2 Fundamentals of programming

Random number generators in programming languages

Table 2.9.1 shows pseudorandom number generator subroutines for Python, Java, Free Pascal, Delphi, C# and VB.NET.

Language	Pseudorandom number generator subroutine	Explanation

Python	`random.random()`
	
	`random.randint(a, b)`
	`random.randint(N)`
		Returns the next random floating point number in the interval [0.0, 1.0)
		Returns a random integer N such that
		a <= N <= b
		Returns `Random integer` in interval [0,N].

Java	```import java.util.Random```
	```public class PRSG {```
	``` public static void main(String[] args){```
	``` System.out.println(Math.random())```
	``` }```
	```}```
		`Math.random()`
		Returns the next pseudorandom, double value in the interval [0.0, 1.0).

Java	```public class PRSG {```
	``` public static void main(String[] args){```
	``` Random pRSG = new Random();```
	``` System.out.println(pRSG.nextInt(10));```
	``` }```
	```}```
		Returns the next pseudorandom, int value in the interval [0, 10)

Free Pascal	```Uses```
	``` SysUtils;```
	```Var```
	``` Hours, Mins, Secs, Millisecs : Word;```
	```Begin```
	``` Randomize;```
	``` Writeln(Random :20:18);```
	``` DecodeTime(Now, hours, mins, secs, milliSecs);```
	``` RandSeed := milliSecs;```
	``` Writeln(Random :20:18);```
	``` Writeln(Random(10));```
		`Randomize` changes the seed used to generate its range of pseudo random numbers.
		The `RandSeed LongInt` variable can be set directly.
		`Random` returns a random `real` number in the interval [0.0, 1.0)
		`Random(N)` returns a random number in `LongInt` integer interval [0, N).

Delphi	```Randomize;```
	```Writeln(Random :20:18);```
	```DecodeTime(Now, hours, mins, secs, milliSecs);```
	```RandSeed := milliSecs;```
	```Writeln(Random :20:18);```
	```Writeln(Random(10));```
		`Random` returns a random real number in range [0.0, 1.0)
		`Random(N)` returns a random number in `LongInt` integer interval [0, N).

C#	```Random n = new Random();```
	```Console.WriteLine("Randomly generated number in range [0.0, 1.0) : {0}", n.NextDouble());```
	```Console.WriteLine("Randomly generated number in range [0, 10) : {0}", n.Next(10));```
		`new Random()` initializes a new instance of the `Random` class, using a time-dependent default seed value.
		`NextDouble()` gets next `double` random no in interval [0.0, 1.0).
		`Next(N)` gets next integer random no in interval [0,N).

VB.NET	```Dim n As New Random()```
	```Console.WriteLine("Randomly generated number in range [0.0, 1.0) : {0}", n.NextDouble())```
	```Console.WriteLine("Randomly generated number in range [0, 10) : {0}", n.Next(10))```
		`new Random()` initializes a new instance of the `Random` class, using a time-dependent default seed value.
		`NextDouble()` gets next `double` random no.
		`Next(N)` gets next integer random no in interval [0,N).

Table 2.9.1 Shows pseudorandom number generator subroutines for the languages

2.9 Random number generation in a programming language

Table 2.9.2 shows how the seed value may be set in Python, Java, Free Pascal, Delphi, C# and VB.NET.

Language	Seed setting subroutines	Explanantion

Python	`import random`
	`random.seed(None)`
	`random.seed(seedvalue)`
		`random.seed(None)`, None means system clock sets `seed`.
		The seed is `seedvalue`, e.g. 1.

Free Pascal	`Randomize`	Initializes the random number generator by giving a value to `Randseed LongInt` variable, calculated with the system clock.

Delphi	`Randomize`
	`DecodeTime(now, hours, mins, secs, milliSecs);`
	`RandSeed := milliSecs;`
		`Randomize` changes the seed used to generate its range of 2^{32} pseudo random numbers.
		
		The `RandSeed LongInt` variable can be set directly.

C#	`Random(N)`	Initializes a new instance of the `Random` class, using the specified seed value `N` of type `Int32`.
VB.NET	`Random(N)`	Initializes a new instance of the `Random` class, using the specified seed value `N` of type `Int32`.

Table 2.9.2 Shows seed setting for Python, Free Pascal, Delphi, C# and VB.NET

Programming tasks

1. Write a program to generate and display 10 random floating point numbers in the interval [0.0, 1.0), i.e. 0.0 ≤ x < 1.0.

2. Write a program to generate and display 10 random integers in interval [0, 10), i.e. 0 ≤ x < 10.

Questions

1. What is the role of a seed in the generation of pseudorandom number sequences?

2. A certain online Poker site found that a group of players was winning every time against the computer-generated poker hands. On investigation, it was discovered that the group was familiar with the programming language used to program the poker game and had also worked out how to obtain the uptime of the server.
Explain one way this group could have accurately predicted the computer-generated poker hands.

Information

AQA pseudo-code:
RANDOM_INT(IntExp, IntExp)
For example, RANDOM_INT(3, 5) will randomly generate 3, 4 or 5.

In this chapter you have covered:

- Using random number generation in a programming language.

Did you know?

The history of pseudorandom number generator algorithms began during the Manhattan project in the Second World War when John von Neumann devised the middle-square method of generating pseudorandom number sequences - the method was marked Top Secret initially. A quick way of generating random numbers was needed for simulations for the nuclear bomb programme.

2 Programming

2 Programming

Learning objectives:

- *Understand the concept of subroutines*
- *Explain the advantages of using subroutines in programs*
- *Describe the use of parameters to pass data within programs*
- *Use subroutines that return values to the calling routine*
- *Know that subroutines may declare their own variables, called local variables, and that local variables usually:*
  - *only exist while the subroutine is executing*
  - *are only accessible within the subroutine.*
- *Use local variables and explain why it is good practice to do so.*

2.10a Subroutines (procedures/functions)

Concept of subroutines

A subroutine is a named self-contained block of instructions, e.g. `drawsquare`. By encapsulating and naming a block of instructions in a program it becomes possible to call the block from other parts of the program. This is very useful in situations where the same block of instructions or action or calculation needs to be repeated in multiple places in a program.

A program that references the subroutine `drawsquare` by name at a particular place in the program flow is said to **call the subroutine** `drawsquare`. It is sufficient to just use its name, `drawsquare`, to cause its block of instructions to execute.

Subroutines have been covered in depth in *Chapter 2.2*.

A subroutine may contain its own variable, type, label and constant declarations. A subroutine may also define subroutines which it may use and it may use subroutines defined elsewhere (usually library or language-defined subroutines).

A subroutine is a named 'out of line' block of code that may be executed (called) by simply writing its name in a program statement.

This is illustrated in *Figure 2.10a.1* which shows the control structure of a program block consisting of program statements **S1**, **S2**, **S3**, a selection statement (shown as **?**) controlling execution of two statements **S4** and **S5**. This selection statement is followed by a loop which controls a block of statements **S**.

A procedure **T** consists of program statements **S1**, **S2**, **S3** (different ones from the program block statements) and a loop controlling a block of statements **S** (also different from the program block **S**).

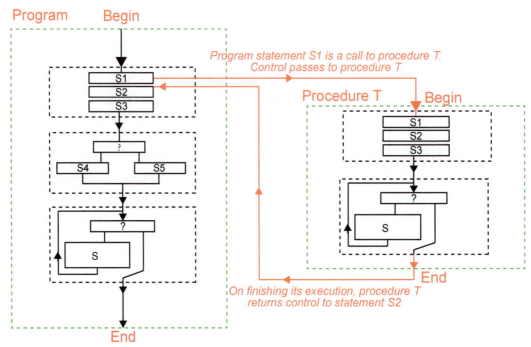

Figure 2.10a.1 In line flow of control to out of line flow of control to a named out of line block of code

2 Programming

The flow of control in the program block is *in line*, forwards from the beginning to the end, except when statement **S1** is encountered. This statement transfers control *'out of line'* to procedure **T**.

Flow of control in procedure **T** is from its beginning to its end.

On reaching the end of **T**, control is transferred back to the program block.

Execution is resumed in the program block at statement **S2**, the statement immediately following **S1**, where the call to **T** occurred. If **T** was a function then control would be returned to statement **S1** along with the function's result.

Procedure **T** is a subroutine.

In Pascal, statement **S1** which is a call to a procedure **T** which doesn't use parameters is simply `T;`

In VB.NET, the call to a procedure **T** which doesn't use parameters would be `T()`.

Questions

1. What is meant by "a subroutine is a named 'out of line' block of code that may be executed by simply writing its name in a program statement"?

Advantages of using subroutines in programs

Without programming language support for subroutines (procedures and functions), all programming would consist of blocks of program instructions all in a line with unnecessary repetition of instructions.
This would make even programs of modest size

- difficult to understand
- difficult to debug.

Removing blocks of instructions from the program block and placing these in 'out of line', named subroutine blocks (*Figure 2.10a.1*) separate from the control flow of the program block, reduces the intellectual demand needed to understand what the program does.

- The program block is reduced in length because where it relies on the instructions in subroutines these are referenced by a short and descriptive name (ideally).
- If subroutines are self-contained they can be worked on separately. This is useful when writing and debugging software.
- In software projects involving a team of developers, different subroutines can be given to different members of the team to write and debug.
- The more self-contained (independent) the subroutine, the easier it is to write and debug without having to understand the program block in which it is called.
- Subroutines written for one program may be reused in a different program. The more self-contained they are the easier it is to do this.
- If a subroutine is particularly useful, it may be added to a library of subroutines which can be imported into any program which needs them.

Questions

2. State and explain **three** advantages of using subroutines in programs.

2.10a Subroutines (procedures/functions)

Using parameters to pass data within programs

A subroutine parameter is one way of passing data into and out of a subroutine.

When a subroutine is called, any data passed to it via the subroutine parameter mechanism is copied into the memory area reserved for subroutine formal parameters as shown in the memory schematic in *Figure 2.10a.3*.

There are two ways that data may be passed via the subroutine parameter mechanism into a subroutine:

- Call by value
- Call by reference/Call by address

We illustrate both with data stored in two program variables, x and y.

The variable name x maps to value 25 and the variable name y maps to 17.

We can express this as follows where the symbol ↦ means 'maps to'

$$x \mapsto 25 \text{ and } y \mapsto 17$$

This mapping is set up at the point in time when statements

```
x ← 25
y ← 17
```

are executed in the program shown in *Figure 2.10a.2*. The subroutine memory area shows two variables, r and s, called **formal parameters** of the subroutine. *Figure 2.10a.3* shows these mapping to 25 and 5674.

$$r \mapsto 25 \text{ and } s \mapsto 5674$$

This mapping is set up at the point in time when

```
T(x, y)
```

is executed in the program shown in *Figure 2.10.2*. Close inspection of the memory map in *Figure 2.10a.3* indicates that the datum associated with x has been copied into the location in the subroutine memory area associated with r.

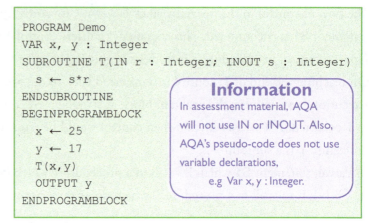

```
PROGRAM Demo
VAR x, y : Integer
SUBROUTINE T(IN r : Integer; INOUT s : Integer)
    s ← s*r
ENDSUBROUTINE
BEGINPROGRAMBLOCK
    x ← 25
    y ← 17
    T(x,y)
    OUTPUT y
ENDPROGRAMBLOCK
```

Information
In assessment material, AQA will not use IN or INOUT. Also, AQA's pseudo-code does not use variable declarations, e.g Var x, y : Integer.

Figure 2.10a.2 An example of a pseudo-code program with a subroutine call involving data associated with two program variables being passed to the subroutine

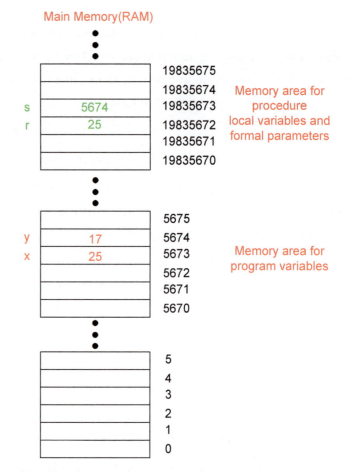

Figure 2.10a.3 Memory map showing an area reserved for program variables and an area reserved for subroutine variables

Similarly, close inspection shows that the program memory address **5674** of the location in program memory associated with y has been copied into the location in the subroutine memory area associated with s.

Now when we look at the subroutine header we see that the r parameter is labelled an IN parameter and the s parameter is labelled an INOUT parameter:

```
SUBROUTINE T(IN r : Integer; INOUT s : Integer)
```

The interpretation of `IN r : Integer` is as follows: a value is to be copied into the formal parameter r when the subroutine is called.

This is what is meant by **Call by Value**.

The interpretation of `INOUT s : Integer` is as follows: an address of where a value can be found in the program memory area is to be copied into the formal parameter s when the subroutine is called.

This is what is meant by **Call by Reference/Call by Address**.

This copying takes place when the subroutine is called with **actual parameters** x and y by the program statement

$$T(x, y)$$

If a subroutine has the address of a datum in the program memory area then the subroutine may change the value in this area. The subroutine in *Figure 2.10a.2* does this with an assignment statement

$$s \leftarrow s*r$$

Call by reference/address thus can have the **side-effect** of changing the value of a variable in another area of memory. This side-effect can be desirable and intended or undesirable.

Call by value cannot change the original value which has been copied.

Call by reference/address should be used as follows

- when a datum is too big to pass by value, i.e. it would take up a lot of space in subroutine memory or it would take too long (relatively speaking) to copy into subroutine memory, e.g. a large array
- when more than one result of executing the subroutine needs to be returned from the subroutine call and the language RETURN mechanism doesn't support this
- when the data type of the result to be returned is not supported by the mechanism used by a function to return a result. Function return uses a different mechanism from subroutine parameters to return a result.

If only a single result needs to be returned and the data type of the result is supported by the function mechanism for returning results then a function should normally be used.

When a subroutine calls a subroutine, the subroutine memory area is used for both the calling subroutine and the called subroutine parameters/variables.

Figure 2.10a.4 shows Call by Value and Call by Reference/Address support in the programming languages Python, Java, Pascal/Delphi, C# and VB.NET.

Figure 2.10a.5 shows an example in Java of Call by Value.

Figure 2.10a.6 shows an example in Java of Call by Reference/Address.

Figure 2.10a.7 shows an example in Pascal of Call by Value and Call by Address.

Figure 2.10a.8 shows an example in C# of Call by Value and Call by Reference/Address.

Figure 2.10a.9 shows an example in VB.NET of Call by Value and Call by Reference/Address.

> **Key term**
>
> **Subroutine parameter:** A subroutine parameter is a mechanism for passing data into and out of a subroutine.

> **Key term**
>
> **Call by value:** Formal parameter of subroutine gets a copy of the datum associated with the actual parameter used in call to subroutine.
>
> **Call by address:** Formal parameter of subroutine is assigned the address in memory of the datum associated with the actual parameter used in call to subroutine.

2.10a Subroutines (procedures/functions)

Language	Call by Value	Call by Reference/Address
Python	Python is neither "call by value" nor "call by reference". In Python a variable is not an alias for a location in memory. It is a binding to a Python object.	

Java	`void a(int r){`
	`    r = r +10;`
	`}`
		There is no call by reference/address only call by value but a reference may be passed by value:
		`class Test{`
		`    int x =5;`
		`    void c(Test r){`
		`        r.x = r.x+10; //object variable x is changed`
		`    }`
		`}`

Pascal/ Delphi	`Procedure A(r : Integer);`
	`  Begin`
	`    r := r + 10;`
	`  End;`
	`Function B(s : Integer) : Integer;`
	`  Begin`
	`    B := s + 10;`
	`  End;`
		`Procedure C(Var r : Integer);`
		`  Begin`
		`    r := r + 10;`
		`  End;`

C#	`static void a(int r)`
	`{`
	`    r = r + 10;`
	`}`
		`static void b(ref int s)`
		`{`
		`    s = s + 10;`
		`}`

VB.NET	`Sub A(ByVal r As Int)`
	`    r = r + 10`
	`End Sub`
		`Sub B(ByRef s As Int)`
		`    s = s + 10`
		`End Sub`

Figure 2.10a.4 Call by Value and Call by Reference/Address support in the programming languages Python, Java, Pascal/Delphi, C# and VB.NET

```
public class CallByValue {
  public static void main(String[] args) {
    int x = 5;
    System.out.println("Before call to c " + x);
    c(x);
    System.out.println("After call to c " + x);
  }
  static void c(int r){
    r = r + 10;
  }
}
```
Figure 2.10a.5 Java example of Call by Value

```
public class CallByReference {
   int x = 5;
   void c(CallByReference s){
     s.x = s.x+10;//object variable x is changed
   }
   public static void main(String[] args) {
    CallByReference exampleCByR = new CallByReference();
    System.out.println("Before Before call to c " + exampleCByR.x);
    exampleCByR.c(exampleCByR);
    System.out.println("After call to c " + exampleCByR.x);
   }
}
```
Figure 2.10a.6 Java example of Call by Reference

2 Programming

```
Program CallByValueAndCallByAddress;
Procedure A(r : Integer);
  Begin
    r := r + 10;
  End;
Function B(s : Integer) : Integer;
  Begin
    B := s + 10;
  End;
Procedure C(Var s : Integer);
  Begin
    s := s + 10;
  End;
Var
  x, y : Integer;
Begin
  x := 5;
  y := 5;
  A(x);
  Writeln(x);
  Writeln(B(y));
  C(y);
  Writeln(y);
  Readln;
End.
```

Figure 2.10a.7 Pascal example of Call by Value and Call by Reference

```
using System;
namespace CallByValueAndCallByReference
{
    class Program
    {
        static void Main(string[] args)
        {
            int x;
            x = 10;
            a(x);
            Console.WriteLine(x);
            b(ref x);
            Console.WriteLine(x);
            Console.ReadLine();
        }
        static void a(int r)
        {
            r = r + 10;
        }
        static void b(ref int s)
        {
            s = s + 10;
        }
    }
}
```

Figure 2.10a.8 C# example of Call by Value and Call by Reference

Questions

3 Explain the role of a subroutine parameter.

4 Explain

(a) Call by value

(b) Call by address

Using subroutines with interfaces

```
Subroutine T(IN r : Integer; INOUT s : Integer)
  s ← s*r
EndSubroutine
```

In the subroutine T, the part

```
        IN r : Integer; INOUT s : Integer
```

```
Module Module1
    Sub Main()
        Dim x As Integer = 5
        A(x)
        Console.WriteLine(x)
        B(x)
        Console.WriteLine(x)
        Console.ReadLine()
    End Sub
    Sub A(ByVal r As Integer)
        r = r + 10
    End Sub
    Sub B(ByRef s As Integer)
        s = s + 10
    End Sub
End Module
```

Figure 2.10a.9 VB.NET example of Call by Value and Call by Reference

is called the subroutine's **interface**. A subroutine interface is a mechanism by which data may be passed in and out of a subroutine via subroutine parameters.

2.10a Subroutines (procedures/functions)

Using subroutines that return values to the calling routine

Subroutines

After a subroutine is executed, control returns to the statement calling the subroutine. If the subroutine is a procedure then the calling statement's execution is complete. If the subroutine is a function, then the function returns a result to the calling statement which this statement may or may not deal with before it completes its execution.

For example, if the calling statement is as follows

$$x \leftarrow \text{SquareOf(2)}$$

the result 4 is returned by the call to function `SquareOf` and this result is then assigned to variable `x`.

Returning a result

If a result needs to be returned from an executing subroutine then a programmer may choose from two subroutine options:

- Procedure with the result returned via an INOUT or OUT parameter (call by address/reference)
- Function with the result returned via the function return mechanism

Procedure option

The procedure option has been covered in a previous section of this chapter. An OUT parameter is similar to an INOUT parameter but some programming languages differentiate between the two by requiring an INOUT parameter to be initialised with a value whereas an OUT parameter can be passed uninitialized or undefined (see C#).

> **Information**
>
> In C# a value must be assigned to an OUT parameter within the subroutine, whereas an INOUT parameter can be left unchanged.

Function option

In some programming languages, e.g. Pascal, a function specifies a return value within the body of the function by executing an assignment statement whose left-hand side is the name of the function - *Figure 2.10a.10*.

```
Function SquareOf (Number : Integer) : Integer;
  Begin
    SquareOf := Number * Number;
  End;
```

Figure 2.10a.10 Pascal function SquareOf which returns an integer result to the calling statement

> **Information**
>
> In Delphi, when a function is called, a variable is automatically created with the name Result of the same type as the return type of the function. It is available for the programmer to use to hold the result value to be returned by the function. Its value is passed back to the calling statement when the function returns.
>
> The implicitly declared variable Result can be seen as equivalent to an OUT type parameter - where the value upon entry to the function is undefined. It is still possible in Delphi to use the Pascal convention of using the name of the function to assign the result. In Pascal, assigning a value to be returned to the name of the function does not automatically cause the function to return. Similarly, in Delphi assigning a value to be returned to the name of the function or to the variable Result does not automatically cause the function to return. In both Pascal and Delphi, usual practice is to use a temporary local variable to hold the result to be returned and assign this to Result or the function name at the end of the function, which is the place where control passes back to the calling statement.
>
> In other programming languages, e.g. C#, functions use an explicit return statement
>
> `return expression`
>
> In addition to specifying a value, return causes the immediate termination of the function.

Figure 2.10a.11 shows a rather contrived C# function `Calculate` with three return expression statements.

The program executes when **Main** is called. The logic of the program selects

```
return number * number
```

because parameter **number** is **2**.

At this point control passes back to the calling statement

`Console.WriteLine(Calculate(2));`

This statement then outputs the value **4**.

If control did not pass back at this point then `return 6`, the last statement in `Calculate`, would be executed with the outcome that the return value would change to **6**.

The fact that the output is **4** and not **6** confirms that **return** causes the immediate termination of the function.

```
using System;
namespace FunctionReturn
{
    class Program
    {
        static void Main(string[] args)
        {
            Console.WriteLine(Calculate(2));
            Console.ReadLine();
        }
        static int Calculate(int number)
        {
            if (number == 2)
            {
                return number * number;
            }
            if (number == 4)
            {
                return number * number * number;
            }
            return 6;
        }
    }
}
```

Figure 2.10a.11 C# function Calculate which returns an integer result to the calling statement

Type of result returned

Many programming languages place restrictions on the type of the result returned by a function.

Figure 2.10a.12 shows a Pascal program which defines and uses a function whose result type is a **composite data type**.

A composite data type or compound data type is any data type which can be constructed in a program using the programming language's primitive data types and other composite types. It is sometimes called a **structured data type**, but this term is more commonly reserved for arrays and lists.

The act of constructing a composite type is known as composition.

When not to use a function to return a result

Although it is possible to return multiple separate results from a function, it is not normally considered good practice. For example, in *Figure 2.10a.13* the Pascal function returns one result in INOUT parameter **s** and another result via the function return mechanism:

Both results in this example return a value which is a scalar data type, in this case, an integer.

A scalar data type is a single value data type.

It would be better to use a procedure with two INOUT parameters instead of a function.

```
Program FunctionReturnType;
Type
  TArrayType = Array[1..10] Of Integer;
Function Test (x : TArrayType) : TArrayType;
  Var
    i : Integer;
  Begin
    For i := 1 To 10
      Do x[i] := 2 * x[i];
    Test := x;
  End;
Var
  y : TArrayType = (1,2,3,4,5,6,7,8,9,10);
  z : TArrayType;
Begin
  z := Test(y);
  Writeln(z[2]);
  Readln;
End.
```

Figure 2.10a.12 Pascal function test which returns a result of composite type to the calling statement

```
Function D(Var s:Integer) : Integer;
  Begin
    ...
  End;
```

Figure 2.10a.13 Pascal function D which returns two results

2.10a Subroutines (procedures/functions)

Programming tasks

1. Write and test a function which accepts a string as input and returns the string reversed.

2. Write and test a function which accepts a string as input and returns the number of words it contains, e.g. "Hello World" contains 2 words.

Declaring local variables

A subroutine may declare its own variables and use these within the body of the subroutine as shown in the subroutine `DoExample` in *Figure 2.10a.14*.

```
SUBROUTINE DoExample(IN x : Integer)
   Var
      s, t : Integer          ← Declaration of two local
                                 variables, s and t
      OUTPUT x
      s ← 6
      t ← 7                   ← Using local variables, s and t
      OUTPUT s + t               in body of subroutine

ENDSUBROUTINE
```

Figure 2.10a.14 Subroutine with local variables

> **Key term**
>
> **Local variable:**
> These are variables declared inside a subroutine and used within the body of the subroutine. The lifetime of a local variable is the lifetime of an execution of the subroutine in which the local variable is declared.
> The scope of a local variable is the scope of the subroutine in which it is declared – scope means where the local variable is visible and can be accessed.

The variables *s* and *t* are known as **local variables**.

They are only visible inside subroutine `DoExample`, i.e. they cannot be accessed from outside the subroutine. In fact, they do not exist until the subroutine starts executing.

They disappear when the subroutine stops executing. Thus any values that they hold are stored temporarily.

Lifetime

The lifetime of a local variable is the lifetime of an execution of the subroutine in which the local variable is declared.

Visibility

The scope of a local variable is the scope of the subroutine in which it is declared – scope means where the local variable is visible and can be used.

Programming tasks

3. Write and test a function which calculates x^n where $n \geq 1$.
   Use the following algorithm to calculate x^n

   ```
   Power ← x
   Count ← 1
   WHILE Count < n Do
      Power ← Power * x
      Count ← Count + 1
   ENDWHILE
   ```

   Your function should make use of local variables.

2 Programming

Using local variables

Figure 2.10a.15 shows the declaration and use of local variables (called `i` and `j`) in the programming languages Pascal/Delphi, C#, Python, Java and VB.NET.

Pascal/Delphi	C#
| ```
Procedure DoExample(n : Integer);
  Var
    i, j : Integer;
  Begin
    j := 6;
    For i : = 1 To n
      Do Writeln('Hello World!', i*j)
  End;
``` | ```
static void DoExample(int n) {
    int j = 6;
    for (int i = 1; i <= n; i++)
    {
        Console.WriteLine("Hello World! {0}", i*j);
    }
}
``` |
| Python | Java |
| ```
def doExample(n):
    j = 6
    for i in range(n):
        print('Hello World!', j*(i + 1))
``` | ```
public static void doExample(int n) {
    int j = 6;
    for (int i = 1; i <= n; i++) {
        System.out.println("Hello World! " + j*i);
    };
}
``` |
| VB.Net | |
| ```
Sub doExample(ByVal n As Integer)
  Dim j As Integer = 6
  For i As Integer = 1 To n
    Console.WriteLine("Hello World! {0}", i*j)
  Next
End Sub
``` | |

Figure 2.10a.15 Declaring and using local variables

Why use local variables?

Support for modularisation

Subroutines enable modularisation of a program.

A solution to a problem can be divided into separate and independent modules. These modules can be implemented as subroutines.

The aim of modularisation is to have subroutines which can be worked on independently of the rest of the program. This requires that each subroutine is **self-contained** and that its interaction with the rest of the program takes place only through the subroutine's interface, i.e. through its formal parameter(s).

Using local variables aids modularisation.

It also enables a subroutine to be reused because if a subroutine is self-contained and independent it may be lifted and used in another program.

Questions

5. What is a local variable?

6. What is the lifetime and scope of a local variable?

7. Explain why the use of local variables is considered good practice.
```

2.10a Subroutines (procedures/functions)

Questions

8 *Figure 2.10a.16* contains pseudo-code for a subroutine that returns a value. Complete the trace table for the call `D(12, 4)`.
(You may not need to use all of the rows in the table).

a	b	c

```
SUBROUTINE D(a, b)
  c ← 0
  WHILE a > 0
    a ← a - b
    c ← c + 1
  ENDWHILE
  RETURN c
ENDSUBROUTINE
```

Figure 2.10a.16

9 Explain why the subroutine call `D(12, 0)` will never return a result.

10 Modify subroutine D so that it returns -1 when called with a value for parameter b ≤ 0.

In this chapter you have covered:
- The concept of subroutines
- The advantages of using subroutines in programs
- Describing the use of parameters to pass data within programs
- Using subroutines that return values to the calling routine
- That subroutines may declare their own variables, called local variables, and that local variables usually:
    - only exist while the subroutine is executing
    - are only accessible within the subroutine.
- Using local variables and explaining why it is good practice to do so.

2 Programming

2 Programming

Learning objectives:

- *Describe the structured approach to programming*
- *Explain the advantages of the structured approach.*

2.10b Structured programming

The structured approach to program design and construction

Software artefact

The end result of program design and construction is an artefact, a piece of software that when executed solves some given problem, hopefully the one required to be solved.

Design

"Design" means to plan or mark out the form and method of solution.

Software design takes a real-world problem and produces a plan for a computer-based solution.

Structured design

Structured design is a disciplined process of deciding which components interconnected in which way will solve some well-specified problem.

Structured design relies on a principle known since the days of Julius Caesar:

DIVIDE and CONQUER

A problem is divided into smaller and smaller subproblems, so that each subproblem will eventually correspond to a **component or module of the system** which solves the problem.

The partitioning process into smaller and smaller subproblems is done until the subproblems are

- manageably small, and
- solvable separately, i.e. relatively independent of one another.

Good design

Good design is an exercise in partitioning and organising the pieces of the system so that each is

- cohesive, and
- loosely coupled (*by using subroutine interfaces to pass data in and out of the subroutine or the return statement, and relying on local variables, i.e variables declared inside subroutine - see later*).

We call the pieces of the system, **modules**.

The modules are plugged together to create the system. Modules are usually implemented as **subroutines** (procedures and functions). Subroutines are covered in *Chapter 2.10a*.

Cohesive/Cohesion

Cohesion measures the strength of the interconnection between elements within a subroutine.

Key term

Design:
To plan or mark out the form and method of solution.

Key term

Structured design:
Structured design is a disciplined process of deciding which components interconnected in which way will solve some well-specified problem.
A problem is divided into smaller and smaller sub problems, so that each sub problem will eventually correspond to a component of the system which solves the problem.
The partitioning process into smaller and smaller sub problems is done until the sub problems are
- manageably small, and
- solvable separately, i.e. relatively independent of one another.

Key principle

Good design:
Good design is an exercise in partitioning and organising the pieces of the system so that each is
- cohesive, and
- loosely coupled

2 Programming

To achieve cohesion, highly interrelated parts of the real-world **problem** should be in the same piece of the **software system**, i.e. things that belong together should go together.

Figure 2.10b.1 shows a schematic mapping from a problem in a real-world system to a highly-cohesive software architecture of a structured design for a computer-based system to solve the problem.

Figure 2.10b.2 shows a specific example of a simple calculator system. Note the one-to-one mapping between real-world system and the computer-based system.

To achieve a solution in which modules/components are highly-cohesive the software system needs to be broken down into modules

- which are highly independent and
- which accomplish a single objective.

The aim is to achieve **functional cohesion**, i.e. modules which contain only one function or perform only one logically-related task.

For example,

- CalculateSquare
- GetDate.

One good way to determine if modules are (functionally) cohesive is to write a phrase fully describing what the module does.

Analysis of this phrase can indicate whether or not the module is (functionally) cohesive. The module is not (functionally) cohesive if the result is one of the following:

- A compound sentence such as
  - Edit Student Name AND Test Scores
  - Get two operands AND Add these
- A lack of a specific object
  - Edit all Data
- Words relating to time such as
  - Initialisation
- Words such as "house-keeping" or "clean-up" because these imply more than one task.

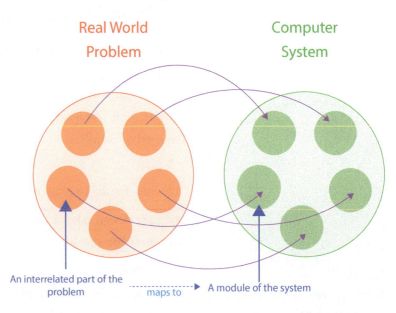

Figure 2.10b.1 Mapping of problem parts to system modules

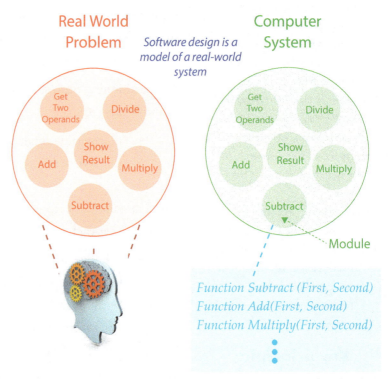

Figure 2.10b.2 Highly interrelated parts of the problem should be in the same piece of the system

The functional description should not define the code within the module but how the module appears to the coder, e.g. `Subtract`.

2.10b Structured programming

The highest level of cohesion, referred to as **functional cohesion**, is a subroutine in which
- every element is an integral part of a single function (task), and
- every element is essential to the performance of a single function (task).

Some advantages of using subroutines with high cohesion:
- The subroutine can easily be replaced by any other serving the same purpose since what it does is localised within the subroutine, i.e. it has no side-effects when it executes
- In the event of program failure,
  - it should be easier to locate the error as being in the subroutine
  - it should be easier to discount the subroutine as a source of error
- Different developers can work on individual subroutines because each is an independent unit.

> **Key terms**
>
> **Cohesion:**
> Cohesion measures the strength of the interconnection between elements within a subroutine.
>
> **Functional cohesion:**
> Functional cohesion is the highest level of cohesion. A functionally cohesive module is one in which
> - every element is an integral part of a single function (task), and
> - every element is essential to the performance of a single function (task).

Questions

1. What is the process known as design?
2. What is structured design?
3. What is meant by the term *cohesive* when applied to a module or subroutine of a system?
4. A procedure in a calculator program is described as "Adding two operands and displaying the result".
   (a) Explain why this procedure is not considered functionally cohesive.
   (b) What can be done to achieve functional cohesion in this case?
5. State **two** advantages of using modules with high cohesion.

Loosely coupled

Coupling measures the strength of relationships between subroutines (modules). The objective of structured design is to minimise the coupling between subroutines, so that they will be as independent as possible.

The lower the coupling, the less likely that other subroutines will have to be considered in order to
- create a subroutine
- understand a given subroutine
- debug a given subroutine
- change a given subroutine.

Coupling results from connections.
A connection exists when an element of code references a location defined outside the module.
Some connection must exist among subroutines in a program, or else they would not be part of the same program.
The objective is to **minimise the coupling among subroutines**.

> **Key term**
>
> **Coupling:**
> Coupling measures the strength of relationships between subroutines (modules).
> The objective of structured design is to minimise the coupling between subroutines, so that they will be as independent as possible. Coupling results from connections. A connection exists when an element of code references a location defined outside the subroutine.

> **Information**
>
> The key terms coupling, cohesion and functional cohesion are not explicitly mentioned in AQA's specification but their concept underpins structured design.

2 Programming

To minimise coupling among subroutines:
- Subroutines or modules should only be allowed to access that data which they need to perform their assigned task
- All data transfer between subroutines is visible in the subroutine parameters
- There must be no hidden flows of data via global variables or shared data areas
- There should be no control information passing between subroutines, e.g. Boolean flags
- The number of subroutine parameters should be minimal.

Loose coupling is achieved when a subroutine's data interface with other subroutines is its subroutine parameter list. Here we interpret subroutine to mean a procedure or function.

In VB.NET, a procedure `DisplayMessage` is defined with the language keywords `Sub` and `End Sub` as shown in the example in Figure 2.10b.3. In VB.NET, the term module can be interpreted as equivalent to program.

Figure 2.10b.4 shows a procedure `DisplayMessage` defined with the language keywords `Procedure` and `Begin` and `End`.

The data interface for VB.NET `DisplayMessage` is the parameter list `ByVal Message As String`.

The data interface for Pascal `DisplayMessage` is the parameter list `Message : String`.

The procedure `DisplayMessage` is called with actual parameter value "Hello World" and 'Hello World', respectively, in Figure 2.10b.3 and Figure 2.10b.4.

The Pascal program in Figure 2.10b.5 has declared a global variable `Message` which in Pascal is visible within procedure `DisplayMessage`. The procedure `DisplayMessage` has dispensed with a procedure parameter list and instead relies on accessing the global variable `Message`. The procedure `DisplayMessage` in Figure 2.10b.5 has a higher coupling with its program than `DisplayMessage` does in Figure 2.10b.4.

```
Module ProcedureInterface
    Sub Main()
        DisplayMessage("Hello World")
        Console.ReadLine()
    End Sub
    Sub DisplayMessage(ByVal Message As String)
        Console.WriteLine(Message)
    End Sub
End Module
```

Figure 2.10b.3 VB.NET program with procedure DisplayMessage

```
Program DisplayMessageExample;
Procedure DisplayMessage (Message : String);
  Begin
    Writeln(Message);
  End;
Begin
  DisplayMessage('Hello World');
  Readln;
End.
```

Figure 2.10b.4 Pascal program with procedure DisplayMessage

```
Program DisplayMessageExampleGlobal;
Var
  Message : String;
Procedure DisplayMessage;
  Begin
    Writeln(Message);
  End;
Begin
  Message := 'Hello World';
  DisplayMessage;
  Readln;
End.
```

Figure 2.10b.5 Pascal program with procedure DisplayMessage without a parameter list

Questions

6. What is *coupling* when applied to modules or components of a system?

7. Why should coupling between modules be minimised?

8. How does coupling between modules arise?

9. How can coupling between modules be minimised?

10. Give **two** reasons why the pseudo-code in *Figure 2.10b.6* could be considered a poor design by structured design standards.

11. Suggest **one** reason why the procedure `DisplayMessage` in *Figure 2.10b.7* could be considered poorly designed by structured design standards.

12. How could the design of procedure `DisplayMessage` and the program be changed to reflect good structured design?

```
Program Exercise1
Var
  No1, No2 : Integer
Procedure AddTwoNumbers
  Output No1 + No2
End Procedure
Begin
  No1 ← 4
  No2 ← 5
  AddTwoNumbers
End
```

Figure 2.10b.6 Pseudo-code to add two numbers

```
Module Module1
    Sub Main()
        DisplayMessage("hello world", False)
        DisplayMessage("hello world", True)
        Console.ReadLine()
    End Sub
    Sub DisplayMessage(ByVal Message As String, ByVal UpperCase As Boolean)
        If UpperCase Then
            Console.WriteLine(StrConv(Message, vbUpperCase))
        Else Console.WriteLine(Message)
        End If
    End Sub
End Module
```

Figure 2.10b.7 VB.NET program that uses a procedure DisplayMessage with a flag parameter

13. A procedure `Initialise` is defined with a long parameter list of reference formal parameters, i.e. each formal parameter is a pointer type which when replaced by an actual parameter will point to a variable outside the procedure:

    `Procedure Initialise(Var a, b, c, d, e, f, g, h, i, j, k, l, m, n, p : Integer)`

    Why is this considered a poor design by the standards of structured design?

2 Programming

Simple calculator example which illustrates cohesion and loose coupling

Suppose that we are required to demonstrate structured design in a simple way.

We choose to do this by designing and creating a very simple calculator that is limited to performing integer arithmetic on two given operands.

The arithmetic operations that must be supported are

1. Add
2. Subtract

The major "pieces" of the system are

1. The system must display to the user the choices which are available for arithmetic operations
2. The system must obtain the user's choice of arithmetic operation
3. The system must obtain two operands from the user
4. The system must carry out the chosen operation on the two operands
5. The system must have a "piece" to do each of the following
   5.1 Add
   5.2 Subtract
6. The system must display the result to the user.

> **Key term**
>
> **Hierarchy chart:**
> In structured design of software, the partition of a software system into its component parts can expressed as a hierarchy chart which shows the components (subroutines) and how they are interconnected.

Structured design is then used to decide which modules to use to solve this problem.

Structured design tells us that each piece identified above in 1, 2, 3, 4, 5.1, 5.2, 6 should be a module of the system - *Figure 2.10b.2*.

In this simple example, these modules can then be implemented in a programming language as **subroutines**.

Hierarchy charts

We show the **software architecture** of the simple calculator system resulting from the structured design approach in *Figure 2.10b.8*. We call this a **hierarchy chart**.

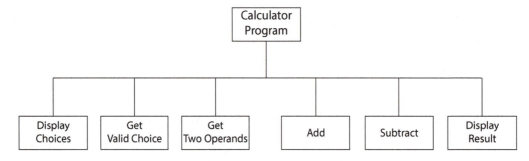

Figure 2.10b.8 Hierarchy chart showing the software architecture of the simple calculator system

This doesn't tell the whole story because the chart doesn't show the coupling between the modules/subroutines. Loose coupling is achieved when a subroutine's data interface with other subroutines is its subroutine parameter list. By adding the parameter list for each subroutine to the chart we can show that its data interface is indeed that required for low coupling - *Figure 2.10b.9*.

The meaning of the symbols used in *Figure 2.10b.9* are shown in *Figure 2.10b.10*.

2.10b Structured programming

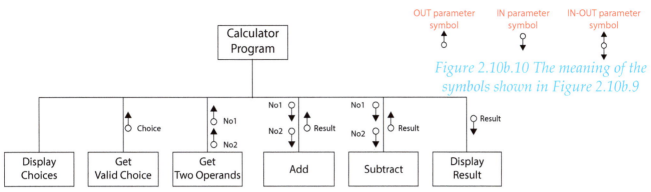

Figure 2.10b.10 The meaning of the symbols shown in Figure 2.10b.9

Figure 2.10b.9 Hierarchy chart showing the software architecture of the simple calculator system and the parameter list/data interface of each subroutine

The parameter `Choice` is the only parameter of subroutine `GetChoice`. It is an OUT parameter. The value returned by `GetChoice` is used by the Calculator Program to choose from among subroutines `Add`, `Subtract`.

Subroutine `Add` has three parameters in its data interface: `No1`, `No2` and `Result`. `No1` and `No2` are IN parameters. `Result` is an OUT parameter.

Sometimes a subroutine needs to use an IN-OUT parameter because it processes the value passed in by an IN-OUT parameter and then exports a new value from the subroutine in the same IN-OUT parameter.

The chart in *Figure 2.10b.9* just shows the architectural breakdown of the system into its software modules and the data interfaces between these modules.

Figure 2.10b.11 shows the program structure in Pascal using procedures. The program structure could also have been written using functions if required.

```
Program SimpleCalculator;
  Procedure DisplayChoices;
    Begin
    End;
  Procedure GetValidChoice(Var Choice : Char);
    Begin
    End;
  Procedure GetTwoOperands(Var No1, No2 : Integer);
    Begin
    End;
  Procedure Add(No1, No2 : Integer; Var Result : Integer);
    Begin
    End;
  Procedure Subtract(No1, No2 : Integer; Var Result : Integer);
    Begin
    End;
  Procedure DisplayResult(Result : Integer);
    Begin
    End;
Var
  UsersChoice : Char = 'A';
  FirstNo : Integer = 0;
  SecondNo : Integer = 0;
  Answer : Integer = 0;
Begin
  Repeat
    DisplayChoices;
    GetValidChoice(UsersChoice);
    GetTwoOperands(FirstNo, SecondNo);
    Case UsersChoice of
      'A', 'a' : Add(FirstNo, SecondNo, Answer);
      'S', 's' : Subtract(FirstNo, SecondNo, Answer);
      'Q', 'q' : ;
    End;
    DisplayResult(Answer);
  Until UsersChoice In ['Q', 'q'];
End.
```

Var denotes that parameter is IN-OUT but in this example it is used as an OUT parameter

Formal parameter

IN only parameters

Actual parameters

Figure 2.10b.11 Program structure in Pascal of simple calculator written as procedures

Programming task

1. Create a simple calculator program based on the program structure shown in *Figure 2.10b.9* in a programming language of your choice.

141

Structured design does not address the issue of how to write the program for the body of each procedure only the division of a system into its components and how those components fit together to produce a solution.

To write the program for the body of the procedures we use the **principles of structured programming**.

Structured programming

The principles

Structured programming advocates a *disciplined approach* to the construction of programs in order to avoid problems which can arise if the approach is not disciplined.

At the lowest level, the main principles of structured programming are concerned with the **flow of control** through a program unit such as shown in *Figure 2.10b.12*. The most fundamental idea is that the **main flow** of control through a program unit should be from **top to bottom** of the program.

This translates to **every block** (sequence, selection and iteration) should have **one entry point and one exit point**. In *Figure 2.10b.12* this means that the flow of control enters at the top of a dotted block and exits at the bottom. Within a block, the flow doesn't have to be forward, e.g. iteration.

There are three basic control constructs necessary to build any program:

- Sequence - a list of program statements which are executed one after another (i.e. in sequence),

  e.g. $x \leftarrow x + 1;\ y \leftarrow y + 2;\ z \leftarrow 6;$

- Selection - a means of choosing between two or more sequences of statements depending on the value of some condition(s),

  e.g. `If Then Else`

- Iteration - a construct to allow controlled repetition of a sequence of statements, e.g.

  `While x < 5 Do Something`.

It can be shown that these **three constructs** are sufficient to implement the control structure of any algorithm.

Structured programming is also known as gotoless programming because it avoids the use of the **Go To** control construct in all but the one case of a major error in the computation which would require, if handled in a structured programming way, convoluted and difficult-to-understand program source code to be written.

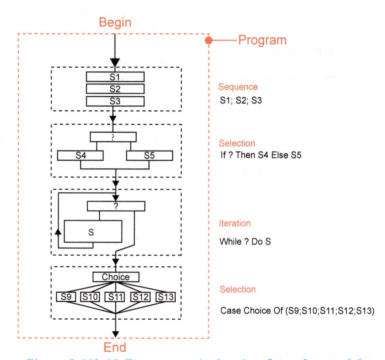

Figure 2.10b.12 Program unit showing flow of control from top to bottom through the three basic control constructs, sequence, selection and iteration

2.10b Structured programming

Structured programming requires that

1. The **main flow of control** through a program unit should be from **top to bottom** of the program.
2. **Program blocks** should have **one entry point** and **one exit point**.
3. **Meaningful identifiers** should be used for variables, subroutines (procedures and functions), etc, to aid readability and understanding.
4. **Indentation** should be used that reflects the structure of the program and which aids readability and understanding.
5. The following control constructs should be used: **sequence**, **selection** and **iteration**.
6. **Go To should be avoided** in all but the one case of a major error in the computation which would require, if handled in a structured programming way, convoluted and difficult-to-understand program source code to be written.
7. The use of **global variables** which are used in a global way **should be avoided**.
8. **Data should be passed to subroutines in subroutine parameters** and **results returned through subroutine parameters** or preferably **as a function return** datum.
9. **Local variables should be used** for handling data within subroutines.

Stepwise refinement

The focus of structured design is the identification of the components of the system and how they interact, i.e. the software architecture of the computerised system, and not on the internal design of the components.

For the **internal design of the components**, i.e. the program source code for subroutines and the program which calls these subroutines, we use structured programming.

Internal design of components is done using the control structures of structured programming, sequence, selection and iteration and a technique called **stepwise refinement**.

Stepwise refinement starts with the **major steps**.
Each major step is then refined into a **more detailed sequence of steps**.
Each one of these more detailed steps is then refined and so on until a stage is reached where the steps can be replaced by programming language statements.
Psychology research tells us that humans manage information in "chunks" and that the human brain is able to handle up to five pieces of information, maybe seven at a pinch. Stepwise refinement fits this limitation of the human brain well.

Advantages of structured programming

We use structured programming because it leads to programs which are

- **easier to understand**,
- **easier to maintain** (debug and change)
- **easier to reason about** (the program does what it is required to do).

A goal of structured programming is **to reduce the conceptual gap between the program text and the corresponding computations**. In other words, how can you be sure that your program does what it is required to do, i.e. meets its specification?

Writing programs that are **easy to understand** contributes to achieving this goal even if it is done at the expense of efficiency, e.g. execution time and memory requirements.

Subroutines produced using structured programming should be **easier to reuse** in other programs because they are loosely coupled.

2 Programming

Questions

14 Which of the following statements are requirements of structured programming:

A Use local variables

B Use Go To statements

C Data should be passed to subroutines in subroutine parameters

D Results should be returned through subroutine parameters or via a return statement

E Don't use local variables.

15 Explain **three** advantages of the structured programming approach.

In this chapter you have covered:

- Describing the structured approach to programming
- Explaining the advantages of the structured approach.

2 Programming

2 Programming

Learning objectives:
- *Be able to write simple data validation routines*
- *Be able to write simple authentication routines*
- *Understand what is meant by testing in the context of algorithms and programs*
- *Be able to correct errors within algorithms and programs*
- *Understand what test data is and describe the following types of test data: normal (typical), boundary (extreme) and erroneous data*
- *Be able to select and justify the choice of suitable test data for a given problem*
- *Understand that there are different types of error:*
  - *syntax error*
  - *logic error*
- *Be able to identify and categorise errors within algorithms and programs.*

2.11 Robust and secure programming

Be able to write simple data validation routines

In computing, the term **validation** refers to computerised data checking that is carried out with the purpose of detecting any data that is unreasonable, incomplete or not in the correct format.

Users are only human and therefore can make mistakes when entering data into executing programs.

The sensible approach, when writing programs which act on user input, is to include program code whose sole purpose is to guard against such mistakes by checking the validity of the user input, and, if necessary, rejecting and then reporting invalid input when it occurs.

Why validate?

How many times have you written programs that a user could crash by entering invalid input, often unwittingly?

Here is a typical interaction between a program and a user that goes wrong because

(a) the program does not validate user input and

(b) the user misunderstands the format required for the numeric data they are prompted to enter.

```
> Input your age as an integer between 11 and 18
sixteen
$$$ Program crashed $$$
```

Yet when this program is run again with the following interaction, it doesn't crash:

```
> Input your age as an integer between 11 and 18
16
```

In both examples, a string was entered, the first time, string `'sixteen'`, the second time, string `'16'`. Although, both strings appear valid, to the computer program only the second is valid.

The program was expecting a string containing only digits such as `'16'` that could be converted to an integer i.e. 16, and not one that could not be converted directly, i.e. `'sixteen'`.

Without any guidance on how to spot and gracefully handle this error in the string, the program crashed.

To improve a program's ability to cope with user mistakes, program code which validates a user's input is needed. This code should only allow execution to proceed if the input is valid otherwise user input should be rejected and requested again.

Validation checks that the data is reasonable not that it is accurate.

The string `'16'` is reasonable because it contains only digits but it may not be accurate.

The user may have lied about their age, they could be `'15'`.

Further checks are necessary on valid data to check its accuracy. These are called **integrity checks**.

2 Programming

Different types of validation

Length, presence, type and range checks

For the age example we would expect to check the following

- minimum length - the data entered must be a string at least two digits long
- maximum length - the data entered must be a string at most two digits long.

We call these **length checks**.

and

- string entered is not empty, i.e. nothing has been entered.

We call this a **presence check**.

and

- string consists only of character digits, i.e. characters chosen from '0'..'9'.

We call this a **type check**.

and

- integer representation of the input should be in the range 11 to 18, inclusive.

We call this a **range check**.

Failure to pass any of these checks should result in the user being

- presented with an informative message drawing attention to the specific error
- asked to try entering input again.

The validity checks should be repeated until all are passed.

The following pseudo-code shows how this might be done to achieve greater program robustness:

Validation

```
REPEAT
  valid ← True
  OUTPUT 'Input your age as an integer between 11 and 18:'
  ageStr ← USERINPUT # ageStr is a string variable
  IF LEN(ageStr) = 0 THEN
    OUTPUT 'you must enter something, please try again'
    valid ← False
  ELSE
    IF LEN(ageStr) ≠ 2 THEN
      OUTPUT 'input must be two character digits in length, please try again'
      valid ← False
    ELSE
      TRY
        age ← STR_TO_INT(ageStr) # try to convert string, ageStr, to an integer
      CATCH # catch a conversion error
        OUTPUT 'Not an integer, please try again' # deal with conversion error
        valid ← False
      ENDTRY
      IF valid THEN
        IF (age < 11) OR (age > 18) THEN
          OUTPUT 'input must be in range 11 to 18, inclusive, please try again'
          valid ← False
        ENDIF
      ENDIF
    ENDIF
  ENDIF
UNTIL valid
```

Figure 2.11.1 Validation of user input

Information

Exception handling:
Exception handling, i.e. the pseudo-code TRY CATCH ENDTRY is not in AQA GCSE Computer Science specification, but it is useful to know because using it in programs that you write is considered good programming practice.

2.11 Robust and secure programming

The code section **TRY CATCH ENDTRY** in *Figure 2.11.1* is designed to first try string-to-integer conversion on the age string. If this conversion fails then the error is 'caught', and handled by the CATCH code section thus avoiding a program crash.

We might place the validation code in *Figure 2.11.1* in a subroutine as follows

Validation routine for age
```
SUBROUTINE GetValidAge
    Code from Figure 2.11.1 goes here
    RETURN age
ENDSUBROUTINE
```

Subroutine `GetValidAge` can then be called to return a valid age

$$\text{nextAge} \leftarrow \text{GetValidAge}$$

File access errors

Any attempt by an executing program to access a file that does not exist (or does not exist in directory space accessed) will cause an execution error which could crash the program.

To avoid the program encountering such an event we need to improve the robustness of the program by checking for the existence of the file with the given filename.

We call this an **existence check**.

One way is shown in *Figure 2.11.2* which uses **TRY CATCH ENDTRY** to catch ('trap') this error. If the file `ages.txt` does not exist in the current directory then attempting to open it results in an error which is 'caught' and handled by the code in the CATCH section.

Exception handling in various programming languages

> **Key concept**
>
> **Exception handling:**
> An exception is an unexpected (or at least unusual) condition that arises during program execution, and which cannot easily be handled by the program.
> Another name for an exception is a program error.
> Such errors may be trapped using the following concept:
> TRY
>   # do some code that might
>   cause an error
> CATCH
>   # if an error is found then do
>   this code
> ENDTRY

Validation
```
fileExists ← True
TRY
    fileHandle ← OPEN('ages.txt')
    dataIN ← READLINE(fileHandle)
    CLOSE(fileHandle)
CATCH
    OUTPUT('File does not exist')
    fileExists ← False
ENDTRY
```

Figure 2.11.2 Validation of file existence

```
Program AgeConversionExceptionHandling;
{$APPTYPE CONSOLE}
{$RANGECHECKS ON}
Uses SysUtils;
Var
  age : Integer;
  ageStr : String;           Delphi/Pascal
Begin
  Try
    Write('Input your age as an integer between 11 and 18: ');
    Readln(ageStr);
    age := StrToInt(ageStr);
  Except
    Writeln('Not an integer, please try again')
  End;
  Writeln('Press return key to exit program');
  Readln;
End.
```

VB.NET

```vbnet
Module Module1
  Sub Main()
      Dim age As Integer
      Dim ageStr As String
      Try
          Console.Write("Input your age as an integer between 11 and 18: ")
          ageStr = Console.ReadLine()
          age = Integer.Parse(ageStr)
      Catch e As Exception
          Console.WriteLine("Not an integer, please try again")
      End Try
      Console.Write("Press return key to exit")
      Console.ReadLine()
  End Sub
End Module
```

C#

```csharp
using System;
namespace AgeConversionExceptionHandling
{
    class Program
    {
        static void Main(string[] args)
        {
            int age;
            try
            {
                Console.Write("Input your age as an integer between 11 and 18: ");
                String ageStr = Console.ReadLine();
                age = Int32.Parse(ageStr);
            }
            catch (Exception e)
            {
                Console.WriteLine("Not an integer, please try again");
            }
            Console.WriteLine("Press return key to exit");
            Console.ReadLine();
        }
    }
}
```

2.11 Robust and secure programming

Java

```java
import java.util.Scanner;
public class AgeConversionExceptionHandling {
  public static void main(String[] args) {
    int age;
      try
        {
            Scanner in = new Scanner(System.in);
            System.out.print("Input your age as an integer between 11 and 18: ");
            String ageStr = in.nextLine();
            age = Integer.parseInt(ageStr);

        }
        catch (Exception e)
        {
            System.out.println("Not an integer, please try again");
        }
  }
}
```

Python

```python
try:
  ageStr = input("Input your age as an integer between 11 and 18: ")
  age = int(ageStr)
except ValueError:
  print("Not an integer, please try again")
else:
  print("Conversion was successful")
```

Information

AQA pseudo-code:
The pseudo-code that AQA will use in examination material is listed in the following PDF which may be downloaded from
https://filestore.aqa.org.uk/resources/computing/AQA-8525-TG-PC.PDF

Questions

1. Write pseudo-code which prompts (asks) a user for a password, then collects a string from the user and checks that the string is at least 8 characters in length.

2. Modify your pseudo-code from Question 1 so that it repeats the action of this code until a password of valid length is entered.

3. Write pseudo-code which prompts a user to enter an integer in the range 0 to 9, then collects an integer in an integer variable, n, and checks that n is in the range 0 to 9. (Assume that only integers are entered).

4. Modify your pseudo-code from Question 3 so that it repeats the action of this code until an integer within the expected range is entered.

5. Modify your pseudo-code from Question 4 so that it traps input that is not an integer string.

2 Programming

> **Programming tasks**
>
> ① In a programming language familiar to you, write a program which implements your pseudo-code answer to Question 2.
>
> ② In a programming language familiar to you, write a program which implements your pseudo-code answer to Question 5.

User authentication is the process or action of verifying the identity of a user. It involves three distinct steps:

1. **Identification**: The identification step requires that a person identifies themselves, e.g. by means of identification string such as a username.
2. **Authentication**: Once identification has been provided, the person is required to provide evidence of their identity which could be done by password.
3. **Authorisation**: Allows an authenticated person access to the system.

Figure 2.11.3 shows pseudo-code for a very simple authentication routine, so simple that valid username and password are hard-coded into the routine. This is not how it would be done in practice but it suffices for the moment to illustrate the first two steps - identification check which if successful is followed by a password check.

In practice, usernames and passwords would be stored securely in a file that would be accessed by the program which authenticates users. Securely means stored in a form that protects usernames and passwords from unauthorised access. One way that this could be done uses encryption but this is beyond GCSE.

Figure 2.11.4 shows in principle how authentication could be done using a text file `a.txt` to store usernames and passwords each on a separate line. Validation of user input and code to deal robustly with file access have been omitted for space reasons.

> **Information**
>
> Note: file handling has been omitted from AQA's CS specification 8525.

Authentication
```
match ← False
REPEAT
  OUTPUT 'Input your user name'
  username ← USERINPUT
  IF username ≠ 'fredbloggs' THEN
    OUTPUT 'Your user name is not recognised'
  ELSE
    OUTPUT 'Input your password'
    password ← USERINPUT
    IF password ≠ 'letmein' THEN
      OUTPUT 'Your password is not recognised'
    ELSE
      match ← True
    ENDIF
  ENDIF
UNTIL match
```
Figure 2.11.3 User authentication

Authentication
```
match ← False
REPEAT
  OUTPUT 'Input your user name'
  username ← USERINPUT
  OUTPUT 'Input your password'
  password ← USERINPUT
  fileHandle ← OPEN('a.txt')
  REPEAT
    nextU ← READLINE(fileHandle) # read next username
    nextP ← READLINE(fileHandle) # read next password
    IF nextU = username THEN
      IF nextP = password THEN
        match ← True
      ENDIF
    ENDIF
  UNTIL EndOfFile OR match
  CLOSE(fileHandle)
  IF match THEN
    OUTPUT 'Welcome'
  ELSE
    OUTPUT 'Username and/or password not found'
  ENDIF
UNTIL match
```
Figure 2.11.4 User authentication with file of usernames and passwords

2.11 Robust and secure programming

Programming tasks

3. In a text editor create a file of usernames and passwords containing ten lines of text with content as shown in *Table 2.11.1*. The structure is `username` followed by its associated `password`, e.g. 'mary' followed on the next line by 'contrary5@#'. Save this text file as `a.txt`.

   In a programming language familiar to you, write a program which implements the pseudo-code in *Figure 2.11.4*.

   Check that your program works correctly with a sample of usernames from *Table 2.11.1* and their matching passwords.

   Check that your program rejects the following:
   - username correct but password incorrect
   - username entered not present in *Table 2.11.1*.

Information
Note: file handling has been omitted from AQA's CS specification 8525.

Test data
fred
letmein
mary
contrary5@#
ahmed
pass67%&
khiat
sooty58£
ashmira
opensesame

Table 2.11.1

Testing

If you have just written a program to convert raw examination marks into grades you will want to convince yourself that your program does just that accurately.

You know that a raw mark can be any integer between 0 and 100 but do you want to test that your program works for every integer in this range?

This is the dilemma facing every programmer: "How to test the reliability of their programs?"

It is all too easy to settle on checking that your program works for a couple of raw marks but this is insufficient to adequately test your program.

You need to be more systematic, but you also need to be realistic and accept that for all but the simplest of programs you will not always be able to test your program on every possible input value.

In *Figure 2.11.5*, after the raw mark has been checked to be in the range 0 to 100, inclusive, there are two possible pathways through the **IF THEN ELSE ENDIF** code section - the path for which

   `rawMark ≥ 50`

is **True** and the one for which it is **False**.

We need to select test data that tests that each pathway is followed as expected.

Being systematic about testing means that we should record what tests we plan to carry out and the results of applying these tests.

It is convenient to do this as shown in *Table 2.11.2*.

Converting raw mark to grade
```
valid ← True
REPEAT
  OUTPUT 'Input your raw mark (0-100):'
  rawMark ← USERINPUT # Integer variable rawMark
  IF (rawMark < 0) OR (rawMark > 100) THEN
    OUTPUT 'Raw mark needs to be between 0 and 100'
    valid ← False
  ENDIF
UNTIL valid
IF rawMark ≥ 50 THEN
  grade = 'PASS'
ELSE
  grade = 'FAIL'
ENDIF
OUTPUT 'Grade'
OUTPUT grade
```
Figure 2.11.5

Test number	Description	Input data	Expected outcome	Actual outcome	Test passed?
1	Test for the correct result when raw mark is greater than 50	75	PASS	PASS	✓
2	Test for the correct result when raw mark is less than 50	25	FAIL	FAIL	✓
3	Test for the correct result when raw mark is 50	50	PASS	PASS	✓

Table 2.11.2 Incomplete test plan for pseudo-code shown in Figure 2.11.4

2 Programming

The incomplete **test plan** shown in *Table 2.11.2* has three **test cases**: raw marks 75, 50 and 25.

- The test datum 75 sits in the middle of the PASS grade raw mark range.
  For this reason, it is considered representative of a set of data which we call **normal or typical test data**.
- The test datum 25 sits in the middle of the FAIL grade raw mark range.
  For this reason it is also considered representative of a set of data which we call **normal or typical test data**.
- The test datum 50 sits on the boundary between the PASS and the FAIL grade raw mark ranges.
  For this reason it is considered representative of a set of data which we call **boundary or extreme test data**.

We cannot exhaustively test a program (except the most trivial) with every possible datum so we classify test data into representative sets and use a few values from each set for testing.

If they are truly representative sets then a test result for one datum from a set should be representative of the test results for all data in the set.

The challenge is to pick a test case (instance of a test datum) which will do for all data in a particular set.

Boundary (extreme) test data

It is a well-known fact that programmers are prone to getting a boundary condition wrong, e.g. writing `rawMark > 50` when they meant to write `rawMark ≥ 50` as shown in *Figure 2.11.6*.

Table 2.11.3 shows an updated test plan with three boundary test cases whereas before there was only one. When this test plan is applied to the modified pseudo-code shown in *Figure 2.11.6* test case 3 **reveals the presence of an error**.

> **Raw mark to grade**
> ```
> IF rawMark > 50 THEN
>    grade = 'PASS'
> ELSE
>    grade = 'FAIL'
> ENDIF
> OUTPUT 'Grade'
> OUTPUT grade
> ```

Figure 2.11.6 Modified pseudo-code

Test number	Description	Input data	Expected outcome	Actual outcome	Test passed?
1	Test for the correct result when raw mark is greater than 50	75	PASS	PASS	✓
2	Test for the correct result when raw mark is less than 50	25	FAIL	FAIL	✓
3	Test for the correct result when raw mark is 50	50	PASS	FAIL	✗
4	Test for the correct result when raw mark is 51	51	PASS	PASS	✓
5	Test for the correct result when raw mark is 49	49	FAIL	FAIL	✓

Table 2.11.3 Updated but incomplete test plan for pseudo-code shown in Figure 2.11.6

It is a well-accepted fact that, in general, testing a program can never adequately prove or demonstrate the correctness of the program.

All that testing can hope to do is reveal the existence of errors as we have done and shown in *Table 2.11.3*.

The purpose of testing is to find errors.

However, it is not the purpose of testing to find solutions to errors discovered, that is the job of debugging.

> **Key fact**
> Testing a program can never adequately prove or demonstrate the correctness of the program. Generally speaking, testing can only reveal the existence of errors.

> **Key term**
> **Test case:**
> Specific sets of data are chosen to test a program to reveal errors. These sets of data are known as test data and each test is known as a test case.

2.11 Robust and secure programming

Questions

6. Draw up a test plan that relies on normal and boundary data to adequately test, using integer input, the pseudo-code shown in *Figure 2.11.7*.

```
valid ← True
REPEAT
  OUTPUT 'Input your raw mark (0-100):'
  rawMark ← USERINPUT # Integer variable rawMark
  IF (rawMark < 0) OR (rawMark > 100) THEN
    OUTPUT 'Raw mark needs to be between 0 and 100'
    valid ← False
  ENDIF
UNTIL valid
```

Figure 2.11.7

Erroneous test data

There is a third type of test data called **erroneous data**.

This is data that is invalid e.g. a letter of the alphabet is entered when an integer is expected or the value entered is outside the accepted range.

For example, in the pseudo-code in *Figure 2.11.7* because `rawMark` is a variable of data type integer, an implicit conversion from string input to integer takes place by the action of statement

`rawMark ← USERINPUT`, e.g. '75' to 75

However, if the input is, say, 'seventy five' or any string value containing non-digits, then the conversion will fail, and if the pseudo-code has been coded in an actual programming language, the program will probably crash.

In the pseudo-code in *Figure 2.11.7* the value entered for `rawMark` is required to be in the range 0 - 100 inclusive, so a value such as 200 which clearly isn't would belong in the category of erroneous data.

Questions

7. (a) Modify the pseudo-code shown in *Figure 2.11.8* so that input of erroneous data will be trapped. Use TRY CATCH ENDTRY.

```
REPEAT
  valid ← True
  OUTPUT 'Input your raw mark (0-100):'
  rawMark ← USERINPUT # Integer variable rawMark
  IF (rawMark < 0) OR (rawMark > 100) THEN
    OUTPUT 'Raw mark needs to be between 0 and 100'
    valid ← False
  ENDIF
UNTIL valid
```

Figure 2.11.8

(b) Draw up a test plan that relies on just erroneous data to test that your modified pseudo-code does now trap a conversion error.

Key term

The design of test cases can be classified as follows:

Normal test data:
Typical values.

Boundary test data:
Test cases designed to probe the boundary regions: just valid (on the boundary and just inside the boundary) and just invalid values (just outside the boundary) are tried.

Erroneous test data:
Data that is invalid e.g. a letter of the alphabet is entered when an integer is expected, or an out of range value.

2 Programming

Designing test cases

Test cases should be chosen to find errors.

The starting point is the specification of what the program is supposed to do.

Table 2.11.4 shows a specification for a program which tests three integers to see if they can be the lengths of sides of a triangle.

The analysis given for the program specification shown in Table 2.11.4 shows how challenging and time-consuming designing test cases can be.

	Program specification
Description	Program determines whether each triplet of numbers can be the length of the sides of a triangle. Each triplet of numbers must satisfy the triangle condition: **a** + **b** > **c**, **a** + **c** > **b**, **b** + **c** > **a**. For example, **a** = 3, **b** = 4, **c** = 5 is a valid triangle
Input	A triplet of positive integers excluding zero, **a**, **b**, **c**. For example, **a** = 3, **b** = 4, **c** = 5
Output	**True** if triplet of numbers can be the length of the sides of a triangle, **False** otherwise
Analysis	If **a** ≤ **b** ≤ **c** then the triplet satisfies the triangle condition if and only if **a** + **b** > **c** If **b** ≤ **a** ≤ **c** then the triplet satisfies the triangle condition if and only if **a** + **b** > **c** If **a** ≤ **c** ≤ **b** then the triplet satisfies the triangle condition if and only if **a** + **c** > **b** If **c** ≤ **a** ≤ **b** then the triplet satisfies the triangle condition if and only if **a** + **c** > **b** If **b** ≤ **c** ≤ **a** then the triplet satisfies the triangle condition if and only if **b** + **c** > **a** If **c** ≤ **b** ≤ **a** then the triplet satisfies the triangle condition if and only if **b** + **c** > **a**

Table 2.11.4 Program specification

When designing test cases you should consider trying to find if the program:

- fails to do what it is supposed to do, e.g. output False for **a** = 3, **b** = 3, **c** = 6 because this cannot be a triangle - **a** ≤ **b** ≤ **c**, but **a** + **b** > **c** is not true.

- fails to trap input which the logic of the program is not designed for or fails in its logic to cater for all logical pathways through the program.

  Figure 2.11.9 shows pseudo-code for a program that fails to prevent n being less than 0 because it has omitted to test for n < 0. This section of code is to be used in a program that needs n to be an integer between 0 and 100, inclusive.

  ```
  valid ← True
  REPEAT
    OUTPUT 'Input an integer (0-100):'
    n ← USERINPUT # Integer variable n
    IF (n > 100) THEN
      OUTPUT 'n needs to be between 0 and 100'
      valid ← False
    ENDIF
  UNTIL valid
  ```
  Figure 2.11.9

- fails to trap and report invalid input, e.g. a letter of the alphabet is entered when the program expects an integer or input not in the expected range. For example, if the string '12.5' is entered when exercising the pseudo-code in Figure 2.11.9 a string conversion error will occur because '12.5' is not a valid integer string.

- works as expected with normal, typical data, e.g. **a** = 3, **b** = 4, **c** = 5 for the program specified in Table 2.11.4.

2.11 Robust and secure programming

Questions

8 (a) The pseudo-code in *Figure 2.11.10* is written to make sure that the user enters a value within a given range.

Tick the set of test data that is the most appropriate to check that the code works as expected.

```
n ← USERINPUT # Integer variable n
WHILE (n < 0) OR (n > 10)
   OUTPUT 'Not in range 0 to 10'
   n ← USERINPUT
ENDWHILE
```
Figure 2.11.10

Test data	Tick **one** box
-1, 0, 9, 10	
0, 1, 10, 11	
-1, 0, 10, 11	
0, 1, 9, 10	

(b) Why is the set of test data that you have chosen in Question 8(a) likely to be enough to show that the code in *Figure 2.11.10* works as expected?

9 A program to calculate car insurance premiums uses information from a guidance table, *Table 2.11.5*, to decide the loading to apply to an insurance policy. Age is an integer.

Write test cases to adequately test that the program applies the guidance correctly to integer input.

Age	Message
>=21	Policy loaded by 10%
< 21	Policy loaded by 50%

Table 2.11.5

Programming task

4 In a programming language familiar to you, write a program which implements the program specification shown in *Table 2.11.4*. Use the equivalent in your programming language of TRY CATCH ENDTRY where appropriate.

Draw up a test plan and test that your program is as error-free as you are able to make it.

Why is it a good idea to draw up and use your test plan as early as possible in the development of your program?

Program errors - syntax and logic

Two types of program error are **syntax error** and **logic errror**.

Syntax error

A statement in the program violates a rule of the language; this could be a simple misspelling of a keyword, a missed punctuation mark, or a wrongly formed statement. For example,

```
Console.Writelinne("Hello World);
```
(*misspelt keyword - WriteLine - and missing quote-mark*)

Logic error

The program runs but gives the wrong answer or performs wrongly in some way (excluding 'crashing' which is another error condition called a run-time error). For example, the programmer writes

```
NetWage = GrossWage + Tax;
```
when the statement should have been written

```
NetWage = GrossWage - Tax;
```

Questions

10 (a) The pseudo-code shown in *Figure 2.11.11* contains a single syntax error and a single logic error. What are these?

```
valid ← True
REPEAT
  OUTPUT 'Input rating (1-10):'
  rating ← USERINPUT # Integer variable rating
  IF (rating < 1) OR (rating >= 10) THEN
    OUTPUT 'Rating needs to be between 1 and 10'
    valid ← Falsse
  ENDIF
UNTIL valid
```

Figure 2.11.11

11 The pseudo-code shown in *Figure 2.11.12* is supposed to output the product of a sequence of integers greater than 1 but it doesn't because it contains a logic error. What is this logic error?

```
product ← 1
REPEAT
  OUTPUT 'Input next integer greater than one (0 to exit): '
  nextInteger ← USERINPUT
  product ← product * nextInteger
UNTIL nextInteger = 0
OUTPUT 'Product = '
OUTPUT product
```

Figure 2.11.12

In this chapter you have covered:

- Writing simple data validation routines
- Writing simple authentication routines
- What is meant by testing in the context of algorithms and programs
- Correcting errors within algorithms and programs
- What test data is and the types of test data:
  - normal (typical)
  - boundary (extreme)
  - erroneous data
- Selecting suitable test data that covers normal (typical), boundary (extreme) and erroneous data
- Justifying the choice of test data
- The different types of error:
  - syntax error
  - logic error
- Identifying and categorising errors within algorithms and programs.

3 Fundamentals of data representation

3 Fundamentals of data representation

Learning objectives:

- *Understand the following number bases*
  - *decimal (base 10)*
  - *binary (base 2)*
  - *hexadecimal (base 16)*
- *Understand that computers use binary to represent all data and instructions*
- *Explain why hexadecimal is often used in computer science.*

Information
Base 10 system is an example of a positional number system. This type of system was first used by the Babylonians over 4000 years ago in Mesopotamia, modern day Iraq. Positional number systems are good for doing arithmetic with.

Key concept
Decimal:
The number base of the decimal system is ten because it has ten digits 0, 1, 2, 3, 4, 5, 6, 7, 8, 9 and the digit multiplier is a power of ten, 10^n where n is ..., −3, −2, −1, 0, 1, 2, 3, ...

Key point
To indicate the base we use a subscript attached to the numeral, e.g. 734_{10}.

Key concept
Binary:
The number base of the binary system is two because it has two digits 0, 1 and the digit multiplier is a power of two, 2^n where n is ..., −3, −2, −1, 0, 1, 2, 3, ...

3.1 Number bases

Meaning of number base

The number base system specifies how many digits are used in constructing a numeral (representation of a number) and by how much to multiply each digit.

For example, in the decimal system the numeral 734 is interpreted as meaning

$$7 \times 100 + 3 \times 10 + 4 \times 1$$

Decimal (base 10)

The number base of the decimal system is ten because it has ten digits 0, 1, 2, 3, 4, 5, 6, 7, 8, 9 and the digit multiplier is a power of ten, 10^n where n is

..., −3, −2, −1, 0, 1, 2, 3, ...

The number represented by the numeral 734 in base 10 is constructed using the place values indicated in *Table 3.1.1* as follows

$$7 \times 100 + 3 \times 10 + 4 \times 1$$

...	10^2	10^1	10^0	...
...	100	10	1	...
	7	3	4	

Table 3.1.1 Place values for the decimal system

To indicate the base we can use a subscript attached to the numeral, e.g. 734_{10}.

Binary (base 2)[1]

The number base of the binary system is two because it has two digits 0, 1 and the digit multiplier is a power of two, 2^n where n is ..., −3, −2, −1, 0, 1, 2, 3, ...

The number in decimal represented by the binary numeral 10111 is constructed using the place values in *Table 3.1.2* as follows

$$1 \times 16 + 0 \times 8 + 1 \times 4 + 1 \times 2 + 1 \times 1$$

To indicate the base we use a subscript attached to the numeral, e.g. 10111_2.

...	2^4	2^3	2^2	2^1	2^0	...
...	16	8	4	2	1	...
	1	0	1	1	1	

Table 3.1.2 Place values for the binary system

Now the quote "There are 10 types of people in the world those that understand binary and those that don't" might make more sense because

$$10_{Binary} = 2_{Decimal}$$

---

[1] There is more on binary in Chapter 3.2. For the exam you will only have to work with whole numbers up to 255 in decimal.

3 Fundamentals of data representation

Key concept

Hexadecimal:
The number base of the hexadecimal system is sixteen because it has sixteen digits 0, 1, 2, 3, 4, 5, 6, 7, 8, 9, A, B, C, D, E, F and the digit multiplier is a power of sixteen, 16^n where n is
$..., -3, -2, -1, 0, 1, 2, 3, ...$

Questions

1. What is the decimal equivalent of the binary number 11001 shown in *Table 3.1.3*?

2^4	2^3	2^2	2^1	2^0
16	8	4	2	1
1	1	0	0	1

Table 3.1.3

2. The bit pattern 11001 in *Table 3.1.3* is replaced by the bit pattern 11111 representing another number.
What is the decimal equivalent of this number?

Hexadecimal (base 16)[2]

The number base of the hexadecimal system is sixteen because it has sixteen digits 0, 1, 2, 3, 4, 5, 6, 7, 8, 9, A, B, C, D, E, F and the digit multiplier is a power of sixteen, 16^n where n is $..., -3, -2, -1, 0, 1, 2, 3, ...$

The number in decimal represented by the hexadecimal numeral D4 is constructed using the place values in *Table 3.1.4* as follows

$$13 \times 16 + 4 \times 1$$

where D has been replaced by 13.

...	16^1	16^0	...
...	16	1	...
	D	4	

Table 3.1.4 Place values for the hexadecimal system

The hexadecimal digits A, B, C, D, E and F are, in decimal, 10, 11, 12, 13, 14 and 15 respectively.

The number in decimal represented by the hexadecimal numeral 38AD4 is constructed using the place values in *Table 3.1.5* as follows

$$3 \times 65536 + 8 \times 4096 + 10 \times 256 + 13 \times 16 + 4 \times 1$$

To indicate the base we use a subscript attached to the numeral, e.g. $38AD4_{16}$.

...	16^4	16^3	16^2	16^1	16^0	...
...	65536	4096	256	16	1	...
	3	8	A	D	4	

Table 3.1.5 Some more place values for the hexadecimal system

Questions

3. What is the decimal equivalent of the hexadecimal number 51CBE shown in *Table 3.1.6*?

16^4	16^3	16^2	16^1	16^0
65536	4096	256	16	1
5	1	C	B	E

Table 3.1.6

4. The hexadecimal number 51CBE in *Table 3.1.6* is replaced by the hexadecimal number FFFFF representing another number. What is the decimal equivalent of this number?

---

[2] There is more on hexadecimal in Chapter 3.2. For the exam you will only have to work with whole numbers up to 255 in decimal.

3.1 Number bases

Binary is used to represent all data and instructions

Figure 3.1.1 shows executable binary codes called machine code instructions.

These executable binary codes or bit patterns instruct computer hardware to carry out some machine task, e.g. ADD two numbers and display the result on the screen of the visual display unit.

The language of computer hardware is binary, i.e. binary codes or bit patterns that the hardware can interpret in a meaningful way as data or instructions.

For example, the bit pattern 10010111 could represent

- a machine instruction
- an integer
- an item of text, e.g. the letter 'A'
- a pixel of a bitmap image
- a part of a sound file.

When a computer program is downloaded from the Internet it streams into your computer as a sequence of bit patterns. These bit patterns could represent any of the above.

In fact, if the bit pattern stream is downloaded as an attachment to an email it could be a computer virus. The virus arrives as data but ends up being executed as machine code which potentially does nasty things to your computer.

0000011000010000	0000000000000101	0000000001000001
0000011000010000	0000000000000110	0000000001110011
0000011000010000	0000000000000111	0000000001101101
0000011000010000	0000000000001000	0000000001010100
0000011000010000	0000000000001001	0000000001110101
0000011000010000	0000000000001010	0000000001110100
0000011000010000	0000000000001011	0000000001101111
0000011000100000	0000000000000000	0000000001110010
0000011011000000	0000000000000000	0000000000001100
0000001100000000	0000000000000000	0000000000000000
0000000000000000	0000000000000000	0000000000000000
0000000000000000	0000000000000000	0000000000000000
0000000000000000	0000000000000000	0000000000000000
0000000000000000	0000000000000000	0000000000000000
0000000000000000	0000000000000000	0000000000000000

Figure 3.1.1 Machine code displayed in binary

0610	0005	0041
0610	0006	0073
0610	0007	006D
0610	0008	0054
0610	0009	0075
0610	000A	0074
0610	000B	006F
0620	0000	0072
06C0	0000	000C
0300	0000	0000
0000	0000	0000
0000	0000	0000
0000	0000	0000

Figure 3.1.2 The same machine code expressed in hexadecimal

Question

5. The stream of bit patterns 11110010...10101101 consists of several thousand binary digits i.e. 1s and 0s of data.
State **three** possible things that this stream might represent.

Why is hexadecimal used?

Hexadecimal as shorthand for binary

Long strings of 1s and 0s are difficult for a human to work with so programmers often switch to the hexadecimal equivalent because it is much easier to work with.

Compare *Figure 3.1.1* and *Figure 3.1.2* which show respectively, a sample of machine code and its hexadecimal equivalent.

If the strings of 1s and 0s represent executable code then debugging this code is much easier if the code is displayed in hexadecimal form.

Its meaning is easier to determine than its binary form.

Similarly, writing numbers in hexadecimal form is less error prone than writing the same numbers in binary especially if the binary form consists of long strings of 1s and 0s.

Information

Debugging:

Debugging software means to identify and remove errors from the software.

Maurice Wilkes, computing pioneer:

"By June 1949, people had begun to realize that it was not so easy to get a program right as had at one time appeared. It was on one of my journeys between the EDSAC1 (World's first stored program digital computer) room and the punching equipment (programs were submitted on punched cards) that the realization came over me with full force that a good part of the remainder of my life was going to be spent in finding errors in my own programs."

3 Fundamentals of data representation

Information

In some programming languages, e.g. Java, a number represented in hexadecimal is indicated by placing **0x** before the numeral, e.g. 0x3C4.

For example, it would be cumbersome and error prone to specify the colour for text on a page of HTML in 24 binary digits, better to use the shorthand form of hexadecimal, e.g. #1F040A.

Here the # symbol is used to indicate that the numeral is in hexadecimal.

The contents of memory or registers of a computer system can be displayed for debugging purposes. It is usual for the software that is used for debugging to display these contents in hexadecimal because it is much easier for a human to read the numbers in this form as well as taking up less space on the display screen.

Software is needed because the numbers are actually stored in memory locations and registers in base 2 form.

Memory addresses are more conveniently expressed in hexadecimal than binary. For example, the memory limit of Windows 7 is 4 GiB. This requires the use of 32 binary digits to express the address of a particular memory word or location but in hexadecimal it requires only 8 hexadecimal digits. Incidently, it would require 10 decimal digits.

However, hexadecimal is more suitable when working with digital hardware than decimal because hexadecimal uses 4x fewer digits than binary ($^{32}/_4$) but decimal uses 3.2x fewer ($^{32}/_{10}$), an awkward factor to work with.

Key point

Long strings of 1s and 0s are difficult for a human to read so programmers often switch to the hexadecimal equivalent because it is
- much easier to read
- more compact,
  4x fewer digits
- less error prone
- easier to debug code expressed in hexadecimal.

Information

GiB:
The unit of storage GiB or **Gi**ga**B**yte is 2^{20} bytes

Question

6 What is wrong with this statement:
"Hexadecimal is often used instead of binary in a computer's memory because it is more compact."?

In this chapter you have covered:

- The following number bases
  - decimal (base 10)
  - binary (base 2)
  - hexadecimal (base 16)
- That computers use binary to represent all data and instructions
- Why hexadecimal is often used in computer science.

3 Fundamentals of data representation

3 Fundamentals of data representation

Learning objectives:

- *Understand how binary can be used to represent whole numbers*
- *Understand how hexadecimal can be used to represent whole numbers*
- *Be able to convert in both directions between:*
  - *binary and decimal*
  - *binary and hexadecimal*
  - *decimal and hexadecimal.*

Information

Throughout this chapter you may find Microsoft® Windows' calculator in programmer mode a handy tool with which to explore the relationship between decimal and binary, decimal and hexadecimal.

Key method

Example:
Decimal to decimal by successive division, picks out the individual digits
e.g. $n = 462_{10}$

n	n/10	r
462	46	2
46	4	6
4	0	4

Where r is the remainder. The remainder supplies the individual digits, one at a time, e.g. 2.

3.2 Converting between number bases

Converting from decimal to binary

Method 1

Using the place values in Table 3.2.1, take the decimal number to be converted and find between which two column place values it lies, e.g. 35_{10} lies between columns with place values **32** and **64**, respectively.

Place **1** in the column with the lower of the two place values and **0** in the higher of the two as shown in Table 3.2.1.

With the given example, take the place value **32** away from the decimal number, leaving 3_{10}. Place **0** in all the columns with place values greater than 3_{10}. It is then trivial to see that we need one **2** and one **1** to match 3_{10}.

...	2^6	2^5	2^4	2^3	2^2	2^1	2^0	...
...	64	32	16	8	4	2	1	...
	0	1	0	0	0	1	1	

Table 3.2.1 Some place values for the binary system and the binary representation of decimal 35

Questions

1. Convert the following numbers expressed in decimal to their binary equivalent using *Method 1*.

   (a) 33_{10} (b) 24_{10} (c) 58_{10} (d) 127_{10}

Method 2 - the method of successive division

Take the decimal number and repeatedly divide by **2** writing down the remainder each time as shown in Table 3.2.2, stopping when zero is reached.

The binary equivalent of 35_{10} is read from the remainder column beginning at the last row and working up the table.

Quotient	New number	Remainder
35/2	17	1
17/2	8	1
8/2	4	0
4/2	2	0
2/2	1	0
1/2	0	1

Table 3.2.2 Successive division by 2 method

161

3 Fundamentals of data representation

> ### Questions
> 2. Convert the following numbers expressed in decimal to their binary equivalent using *Method 2*. Show the intermediate results in a table with structure similar to *Table 3.2.2*.
>
>   (a) 33_{10} (b) 24_{10} (c) 58_{10} (d) 127_{10}

Converting from binary to decimal
See *Chapter 3.1*.

Converting from decimal to hexadecimal
We can use the method of successive division similar to the one used for decimal to binary conversions, this time dividing by 16. *Table 3.2.3* shows a worked example for n = 249_{10}. The last column is read from the last row upwards giving $F9_{16}$.

Quotient	New number	Remainder
249/16	15	9
15/16	0	15(F)

Table 3.2.3 Successive division by 16 method

> ### Questions
> 3. Convert the following numbers expressed in decimal to their hexadecimal equivalent using the method described above. Show the intermediate results in a table with structure similar to *Table 3.2.3*.
>
>   (a) 47_{10} (b) 127_{10} (c) 189_{10} (d) 255_{10}

Converting from hexadecimal to decimal
See *Chapter 3.1*.

Converting from hexadecimal to binary
This can be done in a straightforward way as follows:

```
Write down the number in hexadecimal
Replace each hexadecimal digit by its binary
equivalent using 4 binary digits
```

Figure 3.2.1 shows how this can be done with the example of $B47A_{16}$ giving the result

$B47A_{16} = 1011010001111010_2$

Figure 3.2.1 Hexadecimal to binary

The method relies on the fact that the hexadecimal digits 0 to F map to 0 to 15 in decimal and this decimal range can be coded by just four binary digits. When a number represented in four binary digits is multiplied by 16_{10}, it becomes a number represented by eight binary digits with zeroes in the least significant four bit positions, twelve binary digits when multiplied by 16_{10} again and so on.

> ### Questions
> 4. Convert the following numbers expressed in hexadecimal to their binary equivalent using the method described above.
>
>   (a) 47_{16} (b) $3A2_{16}$ (c) $6FE7_{16}$ (d) $BEEF_{16}$

3.2 Converting between number bases

Converting from binary to hexadecimal

This can be done in a straightforward way as follows:

```
Write down the number in binary
Add leading 0s to the left-hand side of the bit pattern so that the number of
bits is a multiple of 4 (if necessary)
Replace each block of four binary digits by their hexadecimal equivalent
```

Figure 3.2.2 shows how this can be done with the example of $B47A_{16}$ giving the result

$$1011010001111010_2 = B47A_{16}$$

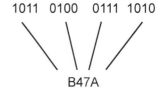

Figure 3.2.2 Binary to Hexadecimal

Questions

5. Convert the following numbers expressed in binary to their hexadecimal equivalent using the method described above.

   (a) 1111_2 (b) 10101101_2 (c) 101100_2 (d) 110011100011_2

Using binary to represent decimal whole numbers

Whole numbers are numbers without a fractional part. Whole numbers can be positive, negative or zero. In fact, whole number is another name for an integer.

You are only required to be able to represent decimal whole number values between 0 to 255 in binary.

Table 3.2.4 shows some decimal whole number values and their equivalent representation in binary.

Table 3.2.5 shows eight bits and their place values. The maximum decimal whole number that can be represented in these eights bits is 255. The binary representation of decimal 255 is 11111111 as shown in *Table 3.2.5* and calculated as follows

$$1 \times 128 + 1 \times 64 + 1 \times 32 + 1 \times 16 + 1 \times 8 + 1 \times 4 + 1 \times 2 + 1 \times 1 = 255$$

Decimal value	Binary value	Decimal value	Binary value	...	Decimal value	Binary value	Decimal value	Binary value
0	00000000	8	00001000	...	240	11110000	248	11111000
1	00000001	9	00001001	...	241	11110001	249	11111001
2	00000010	10	00001010	...	242	11110010	250	11111010
3	00000011	11	00001011	...	243	11110011	251	11111011
4	00000100	12	00001100	...	244	11110100	252	11111100
5	00000101	13	00001101	...	245	11110101	253	11111101
6	00000110	14	00001110	...	246	11110110	254	11111110
7	00000111	15	00001111	...	247	11110111	255	11111111

Table 3.2.4 Table of binary codes in eight bits and their decimal equivalent values

2^7	2^6	2^5	2^4	2^3	2^2	2^1	2^0
128	64	32	16	8	4	2	1
1	1	1	1	1	1	1	1

Table 3.2.5 Place values for binary representing whole numbers between 0 and 255

3 Fundamentals of data representation

> **Questions**
>
> 6 Express the following decimal whole numbers in binary using 8 bits.
>
> (a) 128 (b) 127 (c) 245 (d) 254

Using hexadecimal to represent decimal whole numbers

You are only required to be able to represent decimal whole number values between 0 to 255 in hexadecimal.

Table 3.2.6 shows some decimal whole number values and their equivalent representation in hexadecimal.

Table 3.2.7 shows two hexadecimal digits and their place values. The maximum decimal whole number that can be represented with two hexadecimal digits is 255. For this maximum number the hexadecimal representation is FF as shown in Table 3.2.7 and calculated as follows

$$F \times 16 + F \times 1 = 15 \times 16 + 15 \times 1 = 240 + 15 = 255$$

Decimal value	Hexa-decimal value	Decimal value	Hexa-decimal value	...	Decimal value	Hexa-decimal value	Decimal value	Hexa-decimal value
0	00	8	08	...	240	F0	248	F8
1	01	9	09	...	241	F1	249	F9
2	02	10	0A	...	242	F2	250	FA
3	03	11	0B	...	243	F3	251	FB
4	04	12	0C	...	244	F4	252	FC
5	05	13	0D	...	245	F5	253	FD
6	06	14	0E	...	246	F6	254	FE
7	07	15	0F	...	247	F7	255	FF

Table 3.2.6 Table of two digit hexadecimal codes and their decimal equivalent values

16^1	16^0
16	1
F	F

Table 3.2.7 Place values for hexadecimal representing whole numbers between 0 and 255

> **Questions**
>
> 7 Express the following decimal whole numbers in hexadecimal using two hexadecimal digits.
>
> (a) 128 (b) 127 (c) 245 (d) 254

In this chapter you have covered:

- How binary can be used to represent whole numbers
- How hexadecimal can be used to represent whole numbers
- Converting in both directions between:
  - binary and decimal
  - binary and hexadecimal
  - decimal and hexadecimal.

3 Fundamentals of data representation

3 Fundamentals of data representation

Learning objectives:

- *Know that:*
  - *a bit is the fundamental unit of information*
  - *a byte is a group of 8 bits*
- *Know that quantities of bytes can be described using prefixes:*
  - *kilo, 1 kB is 1,000 bytes*
  - *mega, 1 MB is 1,000 kilobytes*
  - *giga, 1 GB is 1,000 Megabytes*
  - *tera, 1 TB is 1,000 Gigabytes*
- *Be able to compare quantities of bytes using the prefixes above.*

3.3 Units of information

Information

We are surrounded in everyday life by information-carrying symbols or signs. For example, road signs are an expression of information for road users.

In Figure 3.3.1(a) the information conveyed is of a factual kind. Figure 3.3.1(a) has the meaning, the road ahead narrows, that is a fact.

In Figure 3.3.1(b) the information conveyed is of a instructional kind. The GIVE WAY sign has a meaning that is an instruction.

(a)   (b)

Figure 3.3.1 Some information-carrying road signs

As "pretty" as symbols/signs may be, their purpose is not decoration but instead it is communication of something. That something is **information**.

We therefore separate the symbol from the information it carries. The symbol is merely the **carrier of information**.

In digital computers, collections of binary digits or bits are used to represent information and to convey information from one place to another - Figure 3.3.2. Whilst in transit the bits are just data (uninterpreted symbols). The bits are turned into information when they are interpreted, i.e. when their meaning is extracted.

Figure 3.3.2 Two computing machines communicating in binary

The bit streams in Figure 3.3.2 being downloaded could be for example, an image or a computer program or a magazine article or a web page, etc.

The smallest unit of information being conveyed is a 0 or a 1, i.e. a **B**inary dig**IT** or **bit**, abbreviated to **b**.

Thus **the bit is the smallest unit of information**.

The meaning of a bit is not known until it is processed or interpreted, e.g. is it part of an image or a program or a web page?

For convenience, bits are grouped together into a unit called a **byte** for which the abbreviation **B** is used. **A byte is 8 bits**.

Key concept

Bit:
The bit is the fundamental unit of information.
It is abbreviated to the symbol b.

Byte:
A byte is a group of 8 bits.
It is abbreviated to the symbol B.

165

3 Fundamentals of data representation

> **Key concept**
> Information = data + meaning

> **Key concept**
> **Datum:**
> A datum (plural data) is any physical phenomenon or object that carries information, e.g. road sign object, speech. There can be no information without data. Data is how information is represented.

> **Questions**
> 1. State the information conveyed by the following symbols:
>
>   ♩ ♪ ☺ He Ar
>
>   You might need to do some research to discover some of the answers.
>
> 2. State the number of bytes in 1111000010101100.

Powers of 10

Figure 3.3.3 shows in red the decimal number corresponding to a given power of 10. The power is known as the exponent. The exponent specifies the number of zeroes in the decimal number.

To avoid writing out long strings of zeroes, the names, symbols and corresponding powers of 10 are used as shown in *Table 3.3.1*.

Name	Symbol	Power of 10
kilo	k	10^3
mega	M	10^6
giga	G	10^9
tera	T	10^{12}

Table 3.3.1 Unit name, symbol and corresponding power of 10

Power of Ten	Decimal number	Exponent
10^{12}	1000000000000	12
10^{11}	100000000000	11
10^{10}	10000000000	10
10^9	1000000000	9
10^8	100000000	8
10^7	10000000	7
10^6	1000000	6
10^5	100000	5
10^4	10000	4
10^3	1000	3
10^2	100	2
10^1	10	1

Figure 3.3.3 Powers of 10

Quantities of bytes

Storage device manufacturers measure capacity using the decimal system (base 10), so 1 gigabyte (GB) is calculated as exactly 1,000,000,000 bytes or 1 billion bytes.

Figure 3.3.4 shows the reporting of the capacity of a Western Digital hard disk.

Table 3.3.2 shows how to express a decimal numeral which is a power of 10 in units of k, M, G and T.

If the decimal numeral refers to a quantity of bytes then we can express the quantity using the units of k, M, G and T.

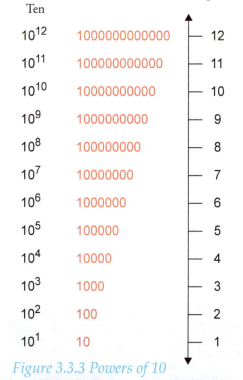

Figure 3.3.4 Exterior of a hard disk showing storage capacity of 160.0 GB

3.3 Units of information

Decimal number	Power of 10	Using units	Using symbol form of unit for quantities of bytes	Using named unit for quantities of bytes
1000	10^3	1k	1kB	1 kilobyte
10000	10^4	10k	10kB	10 kilobytes
100000	10^5	100k	100kB	100 kilobytes
1000000	10^6	1M	1MB	1 megabyte
10000000	10^7	10M	10MB	10 megabytes
100000000	10^8	100M	100MB	100 megabytes
1000000000	10^9	1G	1GB	1 gigabyte
10000000000	10^{10}	10G	10GB	10 gigabytes
100000000000	10^{11}	100G	100GB	100 gigabytes
1000000000000	10^{12}	1T	1TB	1 terabyte

Table 3.3.2 Quantities of bytes expressed in units k, M, G and T

Did you know?
Genetic information in the form of genes are instructions which together with other essential ingredients serve the purpose of controlling and guiding the development of organisms.

Background
This picture of a tree stump is an example of another type of information, environmental information. The concentric rings visible in the wood of a cut tree trunk provide information on the age of the tree and the growing conditions at the time a ring was laid down. Here the information carrier is a tree ring.

Questions

3. Express the following decimal numerals in the form 10^n
   (a) 1000   (b) 1000000   (c) 10000000

4. Convert the following quantities in bytes to kB
   (a) 1000   (b) 10000

5. Convert the following quantities in bytes to MB
   (a) 500000   (b) 2000000   (c) 30000000

Background

Historically, the terms kilobyte, megabyte, etc have often been used to represent powers of 2.
This rather confusing situation has been resolved by the gradual adoption of the International Electrotechnical Commission (IEC) standard for binary prefixes, which specify the use of **gigabyte (GB)** to strictly denote **1000000000 bytes** and **gibibyte (GiB)** to denote **1073741824 bytes**. This standard is now part of the International System of Quantities.

You are not required to know the powers of 2 alternative units. However, for the sake of completeness it is included here.

Powers of 2

Table 3.3.3 shows decimal numbers expressed as powers of 2, their equivalent binary and the corresponding unit. In 2 raised to the power of 10, 10 is known as the exponent. The exponents 10, 20, 30, 40 specify the number of zeroes in the binary numeral.

Decimal number	Power of 2	Binary number	Unit
1024	2^{10}	10000000000	kibibyte
1048576	2^{20}	100000000000000000000	mebibyte
1073741824	2^{30}	1000000000000000000000000000000	gibibyte
1099511627776	2^{40}	10000000000000000000000000000000000000000	tebibyte

Table 3.3.3 Some decimal numbers expressed as powers of 2

Background

To avoid writing out long strings of zeroes, the names, symbols and corresponding powers of 2 are used as shown in *Table 3.3.4*.

If the binary numeral refers to a quantity of bytes then we can express the quantity using the units of **Ki, Mi, Gi** and **Ti** as shown in *Table 3.3.5*.

B refers to byte.

Name	Symbol	Power of 2
kibi	Ki	2^{10}
mebi	Mi	2^{20}
gibi	Gi	2^{30}
tebi	Ti	2^{40}

Table 3.3.4 Unit name, symbol and corresponding power of 2

Key fact

kibi, Ki - 2^{10}
mebi, Mi – 2^{20}
gibi, Gi – 2^{30}
tebi, Ti – 2^{40}

kilo, k - 10^3
mega, M – 10^6
giga, G – 10^9
tera, T – 10^{12}

Decimal number	Power of 2	Using units	Using symbol form of unit for quantities of bytes	Using named unit for quantities of bytes
1024	2^{10}	1Ki	1KiB	1 kibibyte
1048576	2^{20}	1Mi	1MiB	1 mebibyte
1073741824	2^{30}	1Gi	1GiB	1 gibibyte
1099511627776	2^{40}	1Ti	1TiB	1 tebibyte

Table 3.3.5 Quantities of bytes expressed in units

In this chapter you have covered:

- That:
  - a bit is the fundamental unit of information
  - a byte is a group of 8 bits
- That quantities of bytes can be described using prefixes:
  - kilo, 1 kB is 1,000 bytes
  - mega, 1 MB is 1,000 kilobytes
  - giga, 1 GB is 1,000 Megabytes
  - tera, 1 TB is 1,000 Gigabytes
- Comparing quantities of bytes using the prefixes above.

3 Fundamentals of data representation

3 Fundamentals of data representation

Learning objectives:

- *Be able to add together up to three binary numbers*
- *Be able to apply a binary shift to a binary number*
- *Describe situations where binary shifts can be used.*

Information

You may find Microsoft® Windows' calculator in programmer mode a handy tool with which to convert between binary and decimal and vice versa.

3.4 Binary arithmetic

Adding two binary integers

The rules for adding numbers expressed in the binary numeral system are basically the same as for any other system. We add the contents of each column in turn, starting from the right with the least significant digit column and moving progressively leftward. Any carry from a column must be added to the sum of the digits in the next column as shown in *Figure 3.4.1* which shows the sum $01101100_2 + 00101010_2$ of two 8-bit binary integers.

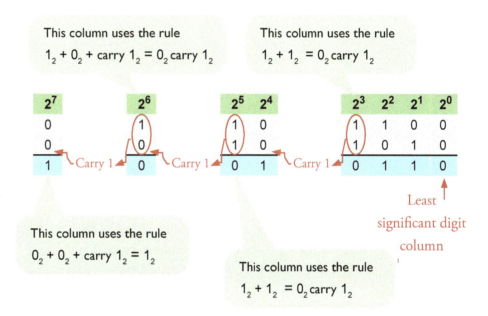

Figure 3.4.1 Addition of two 8-bit binary integers

The basic rules are as follows

$$0_2 + 0_2 = 0_2$$
$$0_2 + 1_2 = 1_2$$
$$1_2 + 0_2 = 1_2$$
$$1_2 + 1_2 = 0_2, \text{ carry } 1_2 \text{ to the next column}$$
since there is no symbol for 2.

The last rule states that $1_2 + 1_2 = 10_2$.

3 Fundamentals of data representation

If we have a carry from the previous column then the carry must be added to the sum of the two digits of the current column. So we have the additional rules

$$0_2 + 0_2 + \text{carry } 1_2 = 1_2$$
$$0_2 + 1_2 + \text{carry } 1_2 = 0_2 \text{ carry } 1_2$$
$$1_2 + 0_2 + \text{carry } 1_2 = 0_2 \text{ carry } 1_2$$
$$1_2 + 1_2 + \text{carry } 1_2 = 1_2 \text{ carry } 1_2$$

Normally addition of two binary numerals representing unsigned binary integers is set out in the manner of the example below

```
  01101011
+ 00011011
----------
  10000110
```

Questions

1. Complete the following sums

   (a) $0_2 + 0_2 =$
   (b) $0_2 + 1_2 =$
   (c) $1_2 + 0_2 =$
   (d) $1_2 + 1_2 =$
   (e) $0_2 + 0_2 + 1_2 =$
   (f) $0_2 + 1_2 + 1_2 =$
   (g) $1_2 + 1_2 + 1_2 =$

2. Complete the following additions of two 4-bit binary integers:

   (a) 0 1 1 0
      + 0 0 0 1
      ‾‾‾‾‾‾‾‾

   (b) 0 1 0 1
      + 0 1 0 1
      ‾‾‾‾‾‾‾‾

3. Complete the following additions of two 8-bit binary integers:

   (a) 0 1 1 0 1 0 1 1
      + 0 0 0 1 1 0 1 1
      ‾‾‾‾‾‾‾‾‾‾‾‾‾‾‾‾

   (b) 1 1 0 1 0 1 0 1
      + 0 0 0 1 1 1 0 1
      ‾‾‾‾‾‾‾‾‾‾‾‾‾‾‾‾

3.4 Binary arithmetic

Adding three binary integers

We add the contents of each column in turn, starting from the right with the least significant digit column and moving progressively leftward. Any carry from a column must be added to the sum of the digits in the next column.

The basic rules are as follows

$0_2 + 0_2 + 0_2 = 0_2$
$0_2 + 0_2 + 1_2 = 1_2$
$0_2 + 1_2 + 0_2 = 1_2$
$1_2 + 0_2 + 0_2 = 1_2$
$0_2 + 1_2 + 1_2 = 0_2$, carry 1_2 to the next column
$1_2 + 0_2 + 1_2 = 0_2$, carry 1_2 to the next column
$1_2 + 1_2 + 0_2 = 0_2$, carry 1_2 to the next column
$1_2 + 1_2 + 1_2 = 1_2$, carry 1_2 to the next column

If we have a carry from the previous column then the carry must be added to the sum of the three digits of the current column.

So we have the additional rules shown in *Figure 3.4.2*.

The last rule produces a carry of 10_2 not 1_2. In decimal this is a carry of 2 not 1.

Figure 3.4.3 shows the sum $01101000_2 + 00101010_2 + 01001011_2$ of three 8-bit binary integers.

$0_2 + 0_2 + 0_2 + \text{carry } 1_2 = 1_2$
$0_2 + 0_2 + 1_2 + \text{carry } 1_2 = 0_2 \text{ carry } 1_2$
$0_2 + 1_2 + 0_2 + \text{carry } 1_2 = 0_2 \text{ carry } 1_2$
$1_2 + 0_2 + 0_2 + \text{carry } 1_2 = 0_2 \text{ carry } 1_2$
$0_2 + 1_2 + 1_2 + \text{carry } 1_2 = 1_2 \text{ carry } 1_2$
$1_2 + 0_2 + 1_2 + \text{carry } 1_2 = 1_2 \text{ carry } 1_2$
$1_2 + 1_2 + 0_2 + \text{carry } 1_2 = 1_2 \text{ carry } 1_2$
$1_2 + 1_2 + 1_2 + \text{carry } 1_2 = 0_2 \text{ carry } 10_2$

Figure 3.4.2 Additional rules that apply to the addition of three binary digits

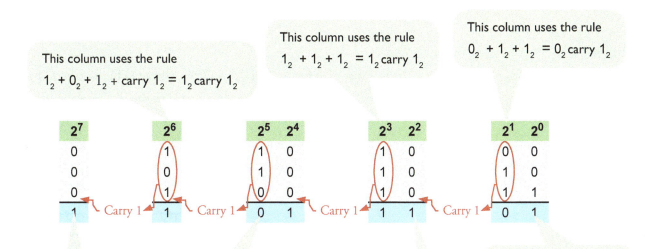

Figure 3.4.3 Addition of three 8-bit binary integers

3 Fundamentals of data representation

Normally addition of three binary numerals representing binary integers is set out in the manner of the example below

```
  01101000
  00101010
+ 01001011
----------
  11011101
```

Of course, there is nothing to stop you adding two of the three binary numbers first and then adding the third to the result!

Questions

4 Complete the following sums
(a) $0_2 + 0_2 + 1_2 =$
(b) $0_2 + 1_2 + 1_2 =$
(c) $1_2 + 1_2 + 1_2 =$
(d) $0_2 + 0_2 + 1_2 + 1_2 =$
(e) $0_2 + 1_2 + 1_2 + 1_2 =$
(f) $1_2 + 1_2 + 1_2 + 1_2 =$

5 Complete the following additions of three 4-bit binary integers:

(a) 0110
    0001
   +0110

(b) 0111
    0101
   +0001

6 Complete the following additions of three 8-bit binary integers:

(a) 01101011
    00011011
   +00011000

(b) 01010101
    00011101
   +01101001

Shifting bits in a binary number

A shift operation takes two inputs, one the number of shifts to apply, n, and the other the bit pattern to be shifted by n bits. For example, the bit pattern in *Figure 3.4.4 (a)* when shifted by one bit to the left becomes the bit pattern shown in *Figure 3.4.4(b)*.

The least significant bit position is filled with 0. The most significant bit is shifted out and discarded.

Figure 3.4.4(a) 8-bit bit pattern before it is shifted left one bit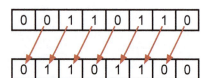

Figure 3.4.4(b) 8-bit bit pattern after it is shifted left one bit

Figure 3.4.4 is an example of a **shift left** operation.
With a **shift right** the bit pattern is moved to the right with the most significant bit position replaced by a zero. The least significant bit is shifted out and discarded.

Figure 3.4.5(a) 8-bit bit pattern before it is shifted right one bit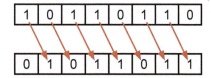

Figure 3.4.5(b) 8-bit bit pattern after it is shifted right one bit

3.4 Binary arithmetic

Situations where binary shifts are used
Multiplying by 2

The 8-bit binary number 00110110 shown in *Figure 3.4.6(a)* represents the decimal number 54.

$$00110110 = 0 \times 2^7 + 0 \times 2^6 + 1 \times 2^5 + 1 \times 2^4 + 0 \times 2^3 + 1 \times 2^2 + 1 \times 2^1 + 0 \times 2^0$$
$$= 0 \times 128 + 0 \times 64 + 1 \times 32 + 1 \times 16 + 0 \times 8 + 1 \times 4 + 1 \times 2 + 0 \times 1$$
$$= 54$$

Multiplying this decimal number by 2 we obtain 108.

$$108 = 0 \times 128 + 1 \times 64 + 1 \times 32 + 0 \times 16 + 1 \times 8 + 1 \times 4 + 0 \times 2 + 0 \times 1$$
$$= 0 \times 2^7 + 1 \times 2^6 + 1 \times 2^5 + 0 \times 2^4 + 1 \times 2^3 + 1 \times 2^2 + 0 \times 2^1 + 0 \times 2^0$$
$$= 01101100$$

One left shift operation on the binary number in *Figure 3.4.6(a)* results in the binary number 01101100 (*Figure 3.4.6(b)*), which is in decimal 108, because

$$0 \times 2^7 + 1 \times 2^6 + 1 \times 2^5 + 0 \times 2^4 + 1 \times 2^3 + 1 \times 2^2 + 0 \times 2^1 + 0 \times 2^0 = 108$$

Thus one left shift operation is equivalent to multiplying by 2.

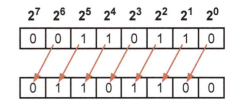

Figure 3.4.6(a) 8-bit bit pattern before it is shifted left one bit

Figure 3.4.6(b) 8-bit bit pattern after it is shifted left one bit

Two left shift operations is equivalent to multiplying by 2×2, i.e. 4 (2^2).

The resulting binary number from two left shift operations is 11011000.

In decimal, $11011000 = 1 \times 2^7 + 1 \times 2^6 + 0 \times 2^5 + 1 \times 2^4 + 1 \times 2^3 + 0 \times 2^2 + 0 \times 2^1 + 0 \times 2^0$
$$= 1 \times 128 + 1 \times 64 + 0 \times 32 + 1 \times 16 + 1 \times 8 + 0 \times 4 + 0 \times 2 + 0 \times 1$$
$$= 216$$

However, this goes wrong when a left shift is applied to a binary number with 1 in the most significant position, e.g. the binary number 11011000 which we have just calculated to be 216 in decimal.

Applying a left shift to 11011000 results in 10110000, i.e. 11011000 ↦ 10110000

But $10110000 = 1 \times 2^7 + 0 \times 2^6 + 1 \times 2^5 + 1 \times 2^4 + 0 \times 2^3 + 0 \times 2^2 + 0 \times 2^1 + 0 \times 2^0$
$$= 1 \times 128 + 0 \times 64 + 1 \times 32 + 1 \times 16 + 0 \times 8 + 0 \times 4 + 0 \times 2 + 0 \times 1$$
$$= 176$$

Doubling 216 produces 432 not 176. Decimal number 432 is too big to be represented in 8 bits which is why the left shift operation fails.

Questions

7. Show the binary number that results from 3 left shift operations on the binary number in *Figure 3.4.7*.

   Figure 3.4.7 `0 0 0 1 0 1 1 1`

8. Show the binary number that results from 3 left shift operations on the binary number in *Figure 3.4.8*. Comment on the result.

   Figure 3.4.8 `0 0 1 0 0 1 1 1`

3 Fundamentals of data representation

Dividing by 2

The 8-bit binary number 11011000 shown in *Figure 3.4.9(a)* represents the decimal number 216.

$11011000 = 1 \times 2^7 + 1 \times 2^6 + 0 \times 2^5 + 1 \times 2^4 + 1 \times 2^3 + 0 \times 2^2 + 0 \times 2^1 + 0 \times 2^0$

$\qquad = 1 \times 128 + 1 \times 64 + 0 \times 32 + 1 \times 16 + 1 \times 8 + 0 \times 4 + 0 \times 2 + 0 \times 1$

$\qquad = 216$

Dividing this decimal number by 2 we obtain 108.

$108 = 0 \times 128 + 1 \times 64 + 1 \times 32 + 0 \times 16 + 1 \times 8 + 1 \times 4 + 0 \times 2 + 0 \times 1$

$\qquad = 0 \times 2^7 + 1 \times 2^6 + 1 \times 2^5 + 0 \times 2^4 + 1 \times 2^3 + 1 \times 2^2 + 0 \times 2^1 + 0 \times 2^0$

$\qquad = 01101100$

One right shift operation on the binary number in *Figure 3.4.9(a)* results in the binary number 01101100, in decimal 108, because

$0 \times 2^7 + 1 \times 2^6 + 1 \times 2^5 + 0 \times 2^4 + 1 \times 2^3 + 1 \times 2^2 + 0 \times 2^1 + 0 \times 2^0 = 108$

Figure 3.4.9(a) 8-bit bit pattern before it is shifted left one bit

Figure 3.4.9(b) 8-bit bit pattern after it is shifted left one bit

Thus one right shift operation is equivalent to dividing by 2.

Two right shift operations is equivalent to dividing by 2×2, i.e. 4 (2^2).

The resulting binary number from two right shift operations is 00110110.

Table 3.4.1 shows successive divisions by 2 applied to the starting decimal number 216 and then the resulting decimals.

The division by 2 is a type of division called **integer division**.

In this division, the result is an integer (whole number).

For the odd decimals, 27, 13, 3 and 1, the result is a whole number and a non-zero remainder. Remainders are either 0 or 1.

Decimal no before single right shift operation	Binary no Before	Binary no After	Decimal no after single right shift operation	Remainder after division
216	11011000	01101100	108	0
108	01101100	00110110	54	0
54	00110110	00011011	27	0
27	00011011	00001101	13	1
13	00001101	00000110	6	1
6	00000110	00000011	3	0
3	00000011	00000001	1	1
1	00000001	00000000	0	1

Table 3.4.1 Successive division by 2

Questions

9 Show the binary number that results from 3 right shift operations on the binary number in *Figure 3.4.10*.

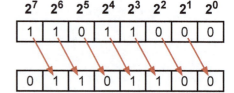

Figure 3.4.10

10 Show the binary number that results from a single right shift operation on the binary number in *Figure 3.4.11*. Comment on the result.

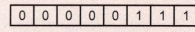

Figure 3.4.11

In this chapter you have covered:

- Adding together up to three binary numbers
- Applying a binary shift to a binary number
  - Left shift
  - Right shift
- Describing situations where binary shifts can be used
  - Multiplying by 2
  - Dividing by 2.

3 Fundamentals of data representation

3 Fundamentals of data representation

Learning objectives:
- *Understand what a character set is and be able to describe the following character encoding methods:*
  - *7-bit ASCII*
  - *Unicode*
- *Understand that character codes are commonly grouped and run in sequence within coding tables*
- *Describe the purpose of Unicode and the advantages of Unicode over ASCII*
- *Know that Unicode uses the same codes as ASCII up to 127.*

3.5 Character encoding

ASCII

Long ago, before the Internet and the World Wide Web, the only characters that mattered were unaccented uppercase and lowercase English letters based on a 26 letter alphabet, digits 0 - 9, and a variety of punctuation and special symbols.

We have learned that computers work with numbers in the form of bit patterns.

Therefore, to store letters of the alphabet and other characters we have to assign each one a number.

An encoding scheme called ASCII does just this. It was invented to encode the limited set of characters mentioned above.

In this scheme, characters are encoded using a number between 32 and 127. For example, in the ASCII character set, space is 32, and the upper case letter 'A' is 65. Device-control characters such as line feed and carriage return were added to this set of characters and allocated numbers in the range 0 to 31.

Code in decimal	Character	Code in decimal	Character	Code in decimal	Character	Code in decimal	Character
32	Space	56	8	80	P	104	h
33	!	57	9	81	Q	105	i
34	"	58	:	82	R	106	j
35	#	59	;	83	S	107	k
36	$	60	<	84	T	108	l
37	%	61	=	85	U	109	m
38	&	62	>	86	V	110	n
39	'	63	?	87	W	111	o
40	(	64	@	88	X	112	p
41	)	65	A	89	Y	113	q
42	*	66	B	90	Z	114	r
43	+	67	C	91	[	115	s
44	,	68	D	92	\	116	t
45	-	69	E	93	]	117	u
46	.	70	F	94	^	118	v
47	/	71	G	95	_	119	w
48	0	72	H	96	`	120	x
49	1	73	I	97	a	121	y
50	2	74	J	98	b	122	z
51	3	75	K	99	c	123	{
52	4	76	L	100	d	124	|
53	5	77	M	101	e	125	}
54	6	78	N	102	f	126	~
55	7	79	O	103	g	127	DEL

Table 3.5.1 ASCII code lookup table

In all, the entire character set is encoded using numbers in the range 0 to 127.

To represent this number range in the language of the machine, binary, requires 7 bits.

Table 3.5.1, shows 96 of the possible 128 (2^7) codes.

For example, from *Table 3.5.1* the ASCII code for the letter A is 1000001 in binary and 65 in decimal whilst the ASCII code for the minus sign symbol - is 0101101 in binary which is 45 in decimal.

ASCII was invented in the 1960s so that information could be exchanged over telephone wires between data processing equipment.

ASCII stands for American Standard Code for Information Interchange.

3 Fundamentals of data representation

All 128 codes are called **character codes** because they encode what is collectively known as **characters**.

However, only 95 codes are actually used for symbols, the other 33 are **control codes**, codes 0 to 31 and the code 127 which is reserved for an instruction *delete a character code*.

Table 3.5.2 shows a lookup table for ASCII control codes, 0 to 31.

The codes in *Table 3.5.2* with a blank character field are codes used for controlling communication over a telephone line.

Line feed and carriage return are used to break a long string of characters into separate lines.

When characters are organised on a line-by-line basis we call this text, e.g. the text that you are reading on this page.

Text files therefore consist of one long string of ASCII character codes with the line breaks marked by a combination of ASCII code 10 (line feed) and ASCII code 13 (carriage return).

These control codes reposition a VDU's cursor at the beginning of the next line when displaying a text file on a VDU.

Code in decimal	Character	Code in decimal	Character
0	Null	16	
1		17	
2		18	
3		19	
4		20	
5		21	
6		22	
7	Bell	23	
8	Backspace	24	
9	Horizontal tabulation	25	
10	Line feed	26	
11	Vertical tabulation	27	Escape
12	Form feed	28	
13	Carriage return	29	
14		30	
15		31	

Table 3.5.2 ASCII code lookup table for some control codes

Questions

1. State the ASCII character code for
   (a) the letter H   (b) the decimal digit 3   (c) the symbol ?

2. What is the symbol or character corresponding to the following ASCII character codes
   (a) 97   (b) 37   (c) 48?

3. Encode the message "Hello" in ASCII.

4. Encode the text

   "Hello

   World!"

   in ASCII.

5. Convert the following string of ASCII character codes to its equivalent text form

   72 101 108 108 111 10 13 87 111 114 108 100 33

Key concept

ASCII or American Standard Code for Information Interchange:
In ASCII, the symbols corresponding to the letters of the alphabet (upper case and lower case), punctuation marks, special symbols and the decimal digits 0 to 9 are assigned different 7-bit binary codes according to a look up table.

3.5 Character encoding

Unicode

Logogram-based languages such as Chinese have characters that number in the tens of thousands. These characters will never fit a 7-bit encoding scheme.

It is impossible, therefore, to represent a string such as 你好 世界 in any of the ASCII 7-bit encoding schemes.

The answer to this problem is an encoding scheme called **Unicode** (www.unicode.org).

Unicode covers all of the characters in all of the world's writing systems, plus accents and other special marks and symbols, and control codes such as tab and carriage return, and assigns each one a standard number called a **Unicode code point**.

Unicode version 8 defines code points for over 120,000 characters in well over 100 languages and scripts but not Klingon, which was rejected in 2001 by the Unicode Technical Committee.

The Unicode Glossary defines a **character** as:

- The smallest component of written language that has semantic value, i.e. meaning
- The basic unit of encoding for Unicode character encoding
- The English name for the ideographic written elements of Chinese origin.

UTF-32 is the simplest Unicode encoding form.

Each Unicode code point is represented directly by a single 32-bit code unit. Because of this, UTF-32 has a one-to-one relationship between encoded character and code unit; it is a fixed-width character encoding form.

Whilst UTF-32 provides the simplest mapping, it **uses much more space than is necessary** - 4 bytes for every Unicode code point or character.

Most computer-readable text is in **ASCII**, which requires only 7 bits which can be accommodated in 1 byte (8 bits).

In fact, all the characters in widespread use still number fewer than 65,536, which can be coded in 16 bits or 2 bytes. This gave rise to two other Unicode encoding forms - **UTF-16** and **UTF-8** of 16 bits and 8 bits respectively.

Figure 3.5.1 shows the three Unicode encoding forms - UTF-32, UTF-16, UTF-8. In UTF-8 as many bytes as needed are allocated, e.g. the uppercase letter A is allocated one byte (8 bits) which is the hexadecimal code 41. This is exactly the same code that ASCII uses (or its 8-bit ANSI standard).

In fact, **Unicode uses the same codes as ASCII up to 127**, albeit in 8 bits rather than 7 bits.

Key term

Unicode: Unicode is a computing industry standard for the consistent encoding, representation, and handling of text expressed in most of the world's writing systems. Unicode provides a unique number for every character: no matter what the platform; no matter what the program; no matter what the language.

Information

Unicode code charts: http://www.unicode.org/charts/ **Knowledge of the detail of UTF-32, UTF-16 and UTF-8 is not required for GCSE.**

Information

Characters: Characters are represented by code points that reside only in a memory representation as strings in memory, on disk, or in data transmission. For example U+0041 is Latin capital letter A.

The Unicode Standard Version 8.0 - Core Specification: http://www.unicode.org/versions/Unicode8.0.0/ch02.pdf

The Unicode Standard deals with character codes.

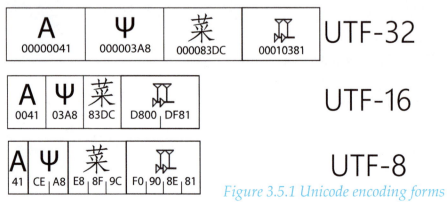

Figure 3.5.1 Unicode encoding forms

3 Fundamentals of data representation

> ## Questions
>
> **6** 你 is one example of the set of 50000 Chinese characters. What character coding scheme could you use to represent these 50000 Chinese characters and why?
>
> **7** State **one** advantage of Unicode over ASCII.
>
> **8** Why is it possible to use Unicode to represent 7-bit ASCII?

Code in decimal	Symbol
48	0
49	1
50	2
51	3
52	4
53	5
54	6
55	7
56	8
57	9

Table 3.5.3 ASCII codes for the decimal digit symbols 0 to 9

Character form of a decimal digit

Table 3.5.3 has been constructed by copying the ASCII code points for the decimal digits 0 to 9 from *Table 3.5.1*.

Humans work with numerals consisting of decimal digits, e.g. 261, when they do a calculation or record a number. If a decimal numeral sent from one computer or computer component to another is used by a human at the receiving end for a calculation, the decimal digits of the numeral must first be mapped to their ASCII code equivalents before sending, and mapped back on receipt from ASCII code to decimal digit form.

For example, if 261 is typed at the keyboard, the sequence of ASCII codes 50, 54, 49 is generated and sent. A visual display unit (VDU) receiving these ASCII codes knows that it should display 261 on its screen - see *Figure 3.5.2*.

Figure 3.5.2 From decimal numeral to ASCII codes and back to decimal numeral

The ASCII codes 50, 54, 49 are called the **character code form of the decimal digits** 261 e.g. 50 is the character code form of the decimal digit 2. To convert this character code form 50 into the number 2 we should subtract 48. The character code form of the decimal number 2 in 7-bits is 0110010 whereas its **pure binary representation** is 000 0010 in 7-bits.

Symbolically, the character code form 50, 54, 49 can be written as '2' '6' '1'. The single apostrophes around each digit are used to differentiate the character form from the decimal digit form.

Grouping of character codes

Table 3.5.3 reflects how character codes are grouped within the ASCII coding table. For example, the decimal character digits '0' to '9' are assigned codes that run in a sequence that matches the sequence of decimal character digits, 48 ↦ '0', 49 ↦ '1', 50 ↦ '2', etc.

This means that the codes for character digits '1' to '9' can be calculated once the code for character digit '0' is known.

Code	Letter
65	A
66	B
67	C
68	D
69	E
70	F
71	G
72	H
73	I
74	J
75	K
76	L
77	M
78	N
79	O
80	P
81	Q
82	R
83	S
84	T
85	U
86	V
87	W
88	X
89	Y
90	Z

Table 3.5.4 ASCII codes for the uppercase letters

Similarly, *Table 3.5.4* reflects how character codes for the uppercase letters are grouped within the ASCII coding table. For example, the character 'A' has the code 65, the character 'B' the code 66. The codes for uppercase letter characters run in a sequence that matches the sequence of uppercase character letters, 65 ↦ 'A', 66 ↦ 'B', 67 ↦ 'C', etc.

This means that the codes for characters digits 'B' to 'Z' can be calculated once the code for character 'A' is known.

Questions

9. The ASCII character code for the decimal character digit '0' is 48.
   Without using an ASCII code table, calculate what the ASCII character code is for the decimal character digit '3'.

10. The ASCII character code for the character 'A' is 65.
    Without using an ASCII code table, show how you would calculate the ASCII character code for the character 'D'.

11. Show by calculation how to convert the following ASCII codes to their equivalent decimal digit value (not their equivalent decimal character digit), given that decimal character digit '0' has ASCII code 48 and decimal digit value 0.
    (a) 51   (b) 53   (c) 57

12. What is the ASCII character code form of the following decimal digits and combination of decimal digits (note that 6 is not the same as '6', 34 is not the same as '34', etc)
    (a) 6   (b) 34   (c) 908   (d) 444?

13. Why is it difficult to do arithmetic with the character form of a decimal number?
    What would need to be done with the character form of a decimal numeral in order to do arithmetic in the conventional way?

14. What is the ASCII character code form of the following characters and character strings
    (a) '6'   (b) '54'?

In this chapter you have covered:

- What a character set is and the following character encoding methods:
  - 7-bit ASCII
  - Unicode
- That character codes are commonly grouped and run in sequence within coding tables
- The purpose of Unicode and the advantages of Unicode over ASCII
- That Unicode uses the same codes as ASCII up to 127.

3 Fundamentals of data representation

3 Fundamentals of data representation

Learning objectives:

- *Understand what a pixel is and be able to describe how pixels relate to an image and the way images are displayed*

- *Describe the following for bitmaps:*
  - *size in pixels*
  - *colour depth*

- *Know that the size of a bitmap image is measured in pixels (width x height)*

- *Describe how a bitmap represents an image using pixels and colour depth*

- *Describe using examples how the number of pixels and colour depth can effect the file size of a bitmap image*

- *Calculate bitmap image file sizes based on the number of pixels and colour depth*

- *Convert binary data into a bitmap image*

- *Convert a bitmap image into binary data.*

Key concept

Pixel:
A pixel is the smallest addressable region or element of a digital image or dot of colour. Each pixel is a sample of the original image.

3.6 Representing images

What is a pixel?

Light reflected by an object may be captured by a digital camera as shown in *Figure 3.6.1*. The digitised image is made up of pixels.

A pixel is the smallest addressable region ("point") or element of a digital image. The term pixel is short for **picture element**.

Each pixel is a sample of the original image. **A pixel is a single dot of colour**.

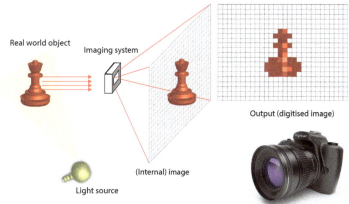

Figure 3.6.1 Digital camera imaging system

Each "square" in the pixel grid of rows and columns shown in *Figure 3.6.2* is known as a **pixel** or **picture element**.

The pixel at the row position 12 and column position 17 in *Figure 3.6.2* is a mix of red, green and blue.

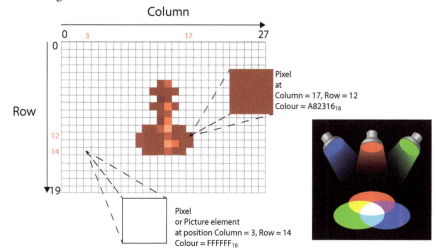

Figure 3.6.2 Pixel grid made up of 28 x 20 = 560 pixels

- the red component has an 8-bit value representing its intensity of $A8_{16}$ or 168_{10} (measured on a scale that ranges from 0 to 255)
- the green component (8-bits) has an intensity of 23_{16} or 35_{10}
- the blue component (8-bits) has an intensity of 16_{16} or 22_{10}

At position Row = 14 and Column = 3, the corresponding red, green and blue intensities are each represented by FF_{16} or 255_{10}, the maximum value.

3 Fundamentals of data representation

Questions

1. *Figure 3.6.3* shows an image captured and saved with three different settings of a digital camera. Give **one** reason why the quality of the three images appears to improve from image (a) to image (c).

(a)   (b)   (c)

Figure 3.6.3

Displaying an image

Visual Display Units (VDUs) display pictures (images) by dividing the display screen into thousands (or millions) of pixels, arranged into rows and columns as shown in *Figure 3.6.4*.

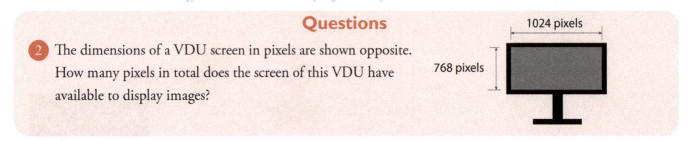

Figure 3.6.4 Visual Display Unit of 1080 x 1920 pixels

Questions

2. The dimensions of a VDU screen in pixels are shown opposite. How many pixels in total does the screen of this VDU have available to display images?

Image size of a bitmap

The pixel grid shown in *Figure 3.6.2* is made up of 28 x 20 = 560 pixels.

The colour of each pixel is recorded in 24 bits, 8 bits per primary colour (the primary colours are red, green and blue).

The total collection of bits for the entire 560 pixels making up the digitised image is called a **bitmap** and the digitised image, a **bitmap image**. To store a digitised image we store its bitmap.

Key concept

Bitmap size in pixels:
Bitmap size = W x H
where
W = width of image in pixels
H = width of image in pixels

The size of a bitmap image is expressed directly as width of image in pixels by height of image in pixels using the notation **width x height**, e.g. 28 x 20. A bitmap image's **resolution** can be expressed in terms of its **image size** in pixels, i.e. **image resolution = width in pixels x height in pixels**.

Colour depth of a bitmap

Colour depth, also known as **bit depth**, is expressed as **the number of bits used to indicate the colour of a single pixel in a digitised image**, e.g. 24 bits.

The bitmap of an image records for each pixel a whole number (integer) encoded in the given bit depth.

Visual Display Units use each integer in the bitmap when displaying the image to select the corresponding colour to display for each pixel.

> **Key concept**
>
> **Colour depth or bit depth:** Colour depth, also known as bit depth, is expressed as the number of bits used to indicate the colour of a single pixel in a digitised image, e.g. 24 bits.

Suppose the colour depth of each pixel is recorded using **8** bits per pixel, then the possible whole numbers (integers) that can be represented lie in the range **0** to **255** in decimal.

If instead **16** bits are used per pixel then the range is greater and from **0** to **65535**.
More bits means more colours can be represented, a different colour can be chosen for each integer in this range.

If the colour depth of each pixel is recorded using **2** bits per pixel, then the possible whole numbers (integers) that can be represented lie in the range **0** to **3** in decimal.

Fewer bits means fewer colours can be represented.

Given a colour depth of **24** bits allocated as follows:

- 8 bits to represent **red** intensity
- 8 bits to **green** and
- 8 bits to **blue**,

The integer values for **each primary colour** can range from 0 to 255 in decimal.

Figure 3.6.5

Ignoring the 8 bits for green and the 8 bits for blue and focussing just on the 8 bits allocated to red, *Figure 3.6.5* shows some selected values from the possible range 0 to 255 for red intensity and their corresponding "redness". Note that when the value is 0 the redness manifests itself as black, an absence of colour.

Each possible combination of the coded red, green and blue intensities represents a different resultant colour.
The number of different bit patterns of 24 bits is 2^{24} = 16777216.
Thus a colour depth of 24 bits allows for 16777216 different colours.

Questions

3. State the maximum number of different colours that can be encoded when using two bits for each pixel.

4. What is meant by colour depth?

5. State the minimum number of bits need to encode 256 different colours.

3 Fundamentals of data representation

How does a bitmap represent an image?

If we wish to store a digitised image, such as the one shown in *Figure 3.6.2*, then information about the colour of each element of the image, i.e. each pixel, must be stored.

This is done by recording for each pixel, the number (from the range allowed by the chosen colour depth) representing its digitised intensity. *Figure 3.6.6* shows a section of memory from locations 308 to 335 and the corresponding row of pixels that it maps to in *Figure 3.6.2*.

Note that the white pixels in this row are stored as FFFFFF and the non-white pixels as either A82316, CA1719, or F29476.

We say that the image is mapped to bits in memory.

The stored bits in memory are a digital representation of this image, a **bitmap**.

Any **bitmap image** is a pixel-based digital image.

Figure 3.6.6 shows a section of memory from locations 308 to 335 and the corresponding row of pixels that they map to.

Bitmap image file sizes

The digitised image shown in *Figure 3.6.2* consists of 28 x 20 = 560 pixels.

The colour information for each pixel requires 24 bits of storage space because the colour depth is 24 bits.

Therefore, the size in bits of this digitised image is as follows

Size in bits = Width x Height x Colour depth

Size in bits = 28 x 20 x 24

= 13440

The size in bytes of this digitised image is as follows

Size in bytes = (Width x Height x Colour depth)/8

= 13440/8

= 1680

For this image, a minimum file size of 1680 bytes will be required to store the image's bitmap.

If colour depth was changed to 8 bits then the minimum file size will be (28 x 20 x 8)/8 = 560 bytes.

Example

Width = 1920 pixels
Height = 1080 pixels
Colour depth = 24 bits

Size in bits = Width x Height x Colour depth
Size in bits = 1920 x 1080 x 24
= 49766400

The size in bytes of this digitised image is as follows

Size in bytes = (Width x Height x Colour depth)/8
= 49766400/8
= 6220800

Size in megabytes = 6220800/1000000
= 6.2208 MB

For this image, a minimum file size of 6.2208 MB will be required to store the image's bitmap.

> **Key concept**
>
> **Bitmap image or bitmap:**
> A bitmap image is a pixel-based digital image.
> The digitised image is mapped to bits in memory representing the intensity and colour of each pixel.

> **Key point**
>
> **Bitmap image file sizes:**
> Size (in bits) = W x H x D
> Size (in bytes) = (W x H x D)/8
> where
> W = width of image in pixels
> H = height of image in pixels
> D = colour depth in bits

3.6 Representing images

Questions

6. The 640 x 480 digitised image shown in *Figure 3.6.7* uses a colour depth of 24 bits.
   How would the size of its bitmap be affected if colour depth was changed to 8 bits?

7. Calculate the size in bytes of the bitmap for the 640 x 480 digitised image of colour depth 24 bits shown in *Figure 3.6.7*.

Figure 3.6.7

Converting a digitised black and white image[1] into binary data

The image shown in *Figure 3.6.8* is made up of a 5 by 5 pattern of black and white squares.

Digitising this image onto a 5 x 5 grid of pixels results in the grid shown in *Figure 3.6.9*.

If we use a colour depth of 1 bit and encode black with the bit value 0 and white with the bit value 1 then the binary encoding of each row of the digitised image shown in *Figure 3.6.9* is as shown in *Figure 3.6.10*.

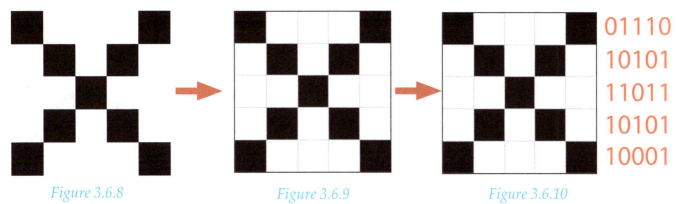

Figure 3.6.8   *Figure 3.6.9*   *Figure 3.6.10*

It would be wasteful but perfectly possible to use a colour depth of 2 bits and encode black with the bit value 00 and white with the bit value 11.

The binary encoding of each row would then be as shown in *Figure 3.6.11*.

With a colour depth of 1 bit the bitmap for the digitised image shown in *Figure 3.6.10* is   01110
10101
11011
10101
10001

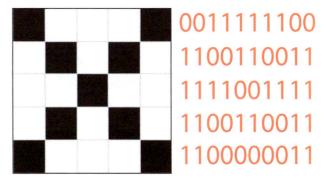

Figure 3.6.11

With a colour depth of 2 bits the bitmap for the digitised image shown in *Figure 3.6.11* is   0011111100
1100110011
1111001111
1100110011
1100000011

The displayed image appears the same (*Figure 3.6.9*) but its bitmap requires more storage space. However, the unused bit patterns 01 and 10 could be used for two different shades of grey.

---
[1] AQA's 8525 specification refers to this task as converting a bitmap image into binary data

3 Fundamentals of data representation

Questions

8 The grid shown in *Figure 3.6.12* represents a bitmap image of colour depth 1 bit.
   The corresponding bitmap uses bit value 0 to encode a black pixel and bit value 1 to encode a white pixel. Copy *Figure 3.6.13* and write the bit patterns corresponding to each row of pixels shown in *Figure 3.6.12*.

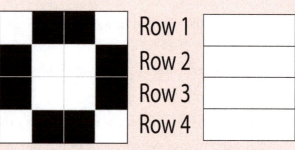

Figure 3.6.12   *Figure 3.6.13*

Converting binary data into a bitmap image

Using a colour depth of 1 bit to encode black with the bit value 0 and white with the bit value 1, the following binary encoding of each row of a digitised image was produced as shown in *Figure 3.6.14*.

From the bitmap of 0s and 1s shown in *Figure 3.6.14* it is possible to deduce that the digitised image has 4 columns and 5 rows of pixels.

Figure 3.6.15 shows a reconstruction of the 5 x 4 grid.

To recreate the digitised image we read the bitmap data row by row, from left to right, starting with the first row.

When a 0 is encountered the corresponding pixel is made black and when a 1 is encountered the corresponding pixel is made white as shown in *Figure 3.6.16*.

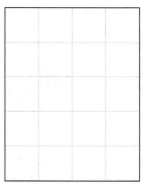

Figure 3.6.15

Reading direction →

0101
1010
0101
1010
0101

Figure 3.6.14

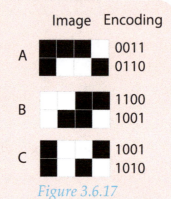

Figure 3.6.16

Questions

9 *Figure 3.6.17* shows three digitised black and white images. The corresponding bitmaps use bit value 0 to encode a black pixel and bit value 1 to encode a white pixel.
   Only **one** bitmap is correctly encoded.
   State which bitmap is correctly encoded.

Image   Encoding

A   0011
     0110

B   1100
     1001

C   1001
     1010

Figure 3.6.17

In this chapter you have covered:
- What a pixel is and describing how pixels relate to an image and the way images are displayed
- The following for bitmaps:
  - size in pixels
  - colour depth
- Know that the size of a bitmap image is measured in pixels (width x height)
- How a bitmap represents an image using pixels and colour depth
- Describing using examples how the number of pixels and colour depth can affect the file size of a bitmap image
- Calculating bitmap image file sizes based on the number of pixels and colour depth
- Converting binary data into a bitmap image
- Converting a bitmap image into binary data.

3 Fundamentals of data representation

3 Fundamentals of data representation

Learning objectives:

- *Understand that sound is analogue and that it must be converted to a digital form for storage and processing in a computer*

- *Understand that analogue signals are sampled to create the digital version of sound*

- *Describe the digital representation of sound in terms of:*
  - *sampling rate*
  - *sample resolution*

- *Calculate sound file sizes based on the sampling rate and the sample resolution.*

3.7 Representing sound

Sound is analogue

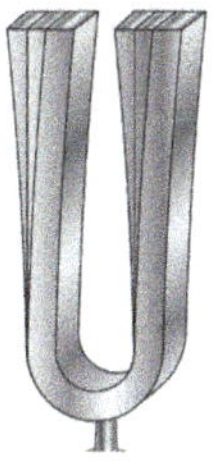

When the forks of a tuning fork vibrate naturally, the oscillations caused in the surrounding air are perceived as a pure sound tone by the brain "hearing them".

The ear of the listener converts the tuning-fork-induced air pressure fluctuations into an equivalent oscillating electrical signal that then travels to the brain for processing.

We can see the shape of these oscillations by converting the smooth and continuous fluctuations in air pressure into an equivalent oscillating electrical voltage by using a microphone and displaying this voltage as a function of time on the screen of an oscilloscope, a sophisticated kind of voltmeter, as shown in *Figure 3.7.1*.

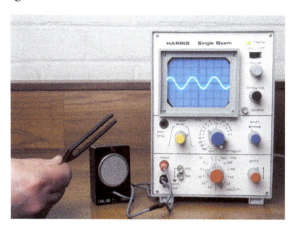

Figure 3.7.1 Oscilloscope displaying the oscillations of a tuning fork via a microphone

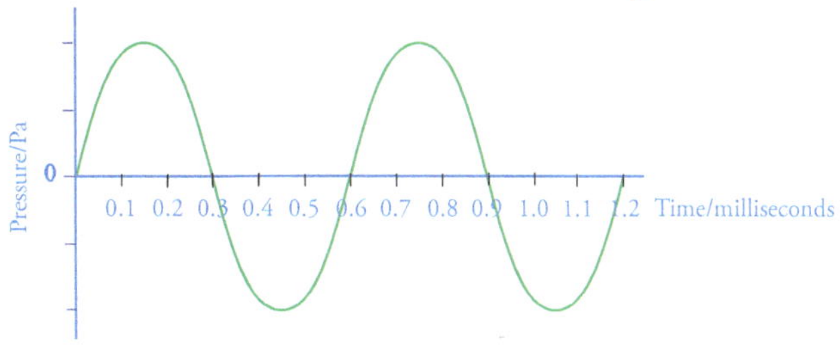

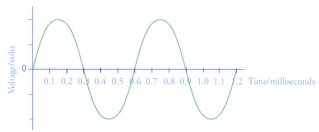

Figure 3.7.2 Fluctuations in air pressure caused by a vibrating tuning fork as a function of time

The fluctuations in air pressure that we experience as sound vary in a continuous manner.

For the vibrating tuning fork, we get a smooth and continuous variation in air pressure as shown in *Figure 3.7.2*, which travels as a sound wave to the microphone. The voltage (and current) the microphone generates in response also varies in a smooth and continuous manner and is similar in shape to the sound vibrations picked up by the microphone.

By shape is meant waveform - see *Figure 3.7.3*.

Sound is analogue in form because it (the air pressure fluctuations) varies in a continuous manner.

The voltage (or current) generated by the microphone is an electrical signal.

This electrical signal (voltage or current) is also analogue because it too varies in a continuous manner and its variation is similar in shape to that of the sound.

Figure 3.7.3 Fluctuations in voltage induced in a microphone by a vibrating tuning fork as a function of time

3 Fundamentals of data representation

Recording sound in digital form

The language of digital computers is binary. Therefore, if we want to record sound in a digital computer we must represent the sound as a sequence of bit patterns, i.e. a sequence of numbers.

To get these numbers, we must first sample the analogue waveform of the sound, or more correctly its electrical equivalent - an analogue signal.

We must do this at regular points in time and when we sample, we must also measure the height (amplitude) of the analogue waveform as shown in Figure 3.7.4.

> **Key term**
> **Sample:**
> A sample is a measure of amplitude at a point in time.

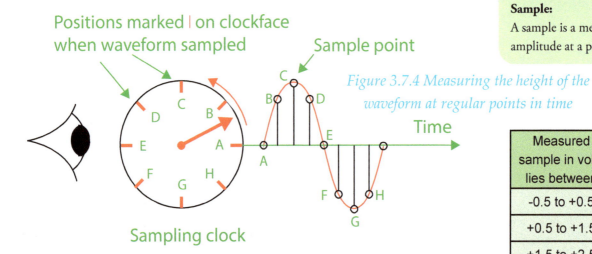

Figure 3.7.4 Measuring the height of the waveform at regular points in time

Measured sample in volts lies between	Binary Number
-0.5 to +0.5	0000
+0.5 to +1.5	0001
+1.5 to +2.5	0010
+2.5 to +3.5	0011
+3.5 to +4.5	0100

Table 3.7.1 Part of conversion table used when measuring a sample and assigning a binary number

A conversion table such as shown in Table 3.7.1 is then used to decide which binary number (bit pattern) to use for the measured height.

Table 3.7.1 assumes that the binary numbers are restricted to using 4 bits. If greater measurement precision is required then more bits must be used, e.g. if voltage measurement ranges for samples of, say, -0.25 to + 0.25 volts, +0.25 to + 0.5 volts, etc, are required then more than 4 bits must be used.

If less precision is acceptable then fewer bits can be used as shown in Figure 3.7.6.

Figure 3.7.5 shows an enlargement of a measurement ruler that corresponds to Table 3.7.1. The voltage interval between consecutive binary numbers is 1 volt.

Figure 3.7.6 shows an enlargement of a measurement ruler that uses three bits for sample height measurement and therefore less precision - difference between consecutive binary numbers is now 2.25 volts.

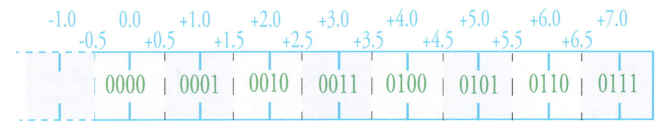

Figure 3.7.5 Enlargement of a measurement ruler that encodes sampled waveform height using 4 bits

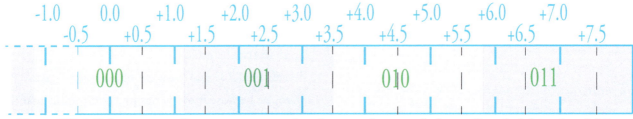

Figure 3.7.6 Enlargement of a measurement ruler that encodes sampled waveform height using 3 bits

3.7 Representing sound

Questions

1. What is meant by saying that sound is analogue in form?

2. *Table 3.7.2* shows five stages in converting sound into a digital form.
State the correct order for the five stages using the given labels A - E.

Label	Stage
A	Amplitude of waveform measured at a specific point in time
B	Converted to an electrical analogue signal
C	Binary representation stored
D	Microphone picks up sound waves
E	Amplitude measurement assigned a binary number

Table 3.7.2

Sampling rate

The **sampling rate is the number of samples taken in a second** and is usually **measured in Hertz** (1 Hertz = 1 sample per second).

For example, the sampling rate used in audio recordings on a Compact Disc (CD) is 44.1 kHz, i.e. 44100 samples per second (1 kHz = 1000 Hz).

This is approximately twice the maximum analogue frequency of 20 kHz of any audio signal.

A raw, uncompressed, sampling of sound lasting 60 seconds will consist of
$$60 \times 44100 \text{ samples or } 2646000 \text{ samples.}$$

Digital telephone lines are sampled at a rate of 8 kHz or 8000 samples per second, and assume that the maximum analogue frequency present in speech carried by a digital telephone line is 4 kHz.

Therefore, one minute of sampled speech sent along a digital telephone line will consist of
$$60 \times 8000 \text{ samples or } 480000 \text{ samples.}$$

Information

Sound:
In physics, sound is a vibration that travels as a mechanical wave of pressure (and displacement), through a medium such as air or water. In physiology and psychology, sound is the reception of such waves and their perception by the brain.
Humans can hear sound waves with frequencies between about 20 Hz and 20 kHz. Sound above 20 kHz is ultrasound.

Questions

3. Digital Audio Tapes (DAT) used a sample rate of 48 kHz to record sampled audio on magnetic tape.
How many samples are taken per second?

4. *Figure 3.7.7* shows sampling of an analogue electrical signal from a microphone. Samples are taken at time = 0 and every millisecond from thereon.

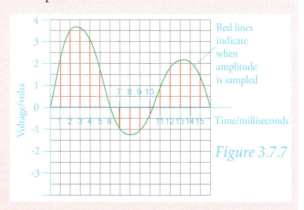

Figure 3.7.7

(a) What is the sampling frequency in Hertz?
(b) What is the measured voltage at time = 1 millisecond?
(c) Convert this voltage to binary using *Table 3.7.1*.

Information

Audio:
Audio is sound within the range of frequencies that humans can hear. The limits of human hearing fall within the range, 20 to 20000 Hz.

Audio signal:
An audio signal is a representation of sound, typically as an electrical voltage.

3 Fundamentals of data representation

Sample resolution

Sample resolution is the number of bits allocated to each sample (number of bits per sample).

Each sample sent along a digital telephone line is encoded in 8 bits.

Therefore, a minute of sampled speech will consist of the following number of bits

$$60 \times 8000 \times 8 = 3840000 \text{ bits}$$
$$= 480000 \text{ bytes}$$
$$= 480 \text{ kB}$$

The audio recorded on CD is of higher quality than speech audio sent along a telephone line. This higher quality is achieved by allocating more bits per sample, 16 bits, in fact. We say that the sample resolution of audio CDs is **16 bits**.

Therefore, a minute of uncompressed sampled sound will consist of the following number of bits

$$60 \times 44100 \times 16 = 42336000 \text{ bits}$$
$$= 5292000 \text{ bytes}$$
$$= 5292 \text{ kB}$$
$$= 5.292 \text{ MB}$$

> **Key term**
>
> **Sample resolution:** Sample resolution is the number of bits allocated to each sample (number of bits per sample).
>
> **Sampling rate:** Sampling rate is the number of samples taken in a second and is usually measured in Hertz (1 Hertz = 1 sample per second).

Questions

5. The sample resolution of a DVD-Audio is 24 bits. What does this mean?

Calculating sound file sizes

Uncompressed sampled sound may be stored in a file with a format such as Wave or AIFF.

Wave files have the extension WAV (.wav). The Wave file format was created by Microsoft.

Audio Interchange File Format (AIFF) is an audio file format standard developed by Apple Inc and used for storing sound. The file extension for the standard AIFF format is .aiff or .aif.

To calculate the file size of a Wave or AIFF file (ignoring any metadata) we may use

file size (bits) = sampling rate x sample resolution x number of seconds of recorded sound

For a WAV audio file,

$$\text{Sampling rate} = 44.1 \text{ kHz}$$
$$\text{Sample resolution} = 16 \text{ bits}$$

Therefore, the file size of a WAV file that stores 5 minutes of sampled sound is calculated as follows

$$\text{File size (bits)} = 44100 \times 16 \times 5 \times 60$$
$$= 211680000$$
$$\text{File size (bytes)} = (44100 \times 16 \times 5 \times 60)/8$$
$$= 26460000$$
$$\text{File size (megabytes)} = (44100 \times 16 \times 5 \times 60)/(8 \times 1000000)$$
$$= 26.46$$

Questions

6 Calculate the file size in bits for a three minute sound recording that has used a sample rate of **1000** Hertz (Hz) and a sample resolution of **6** bits.

7 The sample resolution of a DVD-Audio is **24** bits. The sampling rate is **48** kHz.
10 minutes of sound recorded in uncompressed sampled form is stored in a file on a DVD-Audio disc.
(a) What is the size in bits of this file?
(b) What is the size in bytes of this file?
(c) What is the size in kilobytes of this file?

In this chapter you have covered:

- That sound is analogue and that it must be converted to a digital form for storage and processing in a computer
- That analogue signals are sampled to create the digital version of sound
- Describing the digital representation of sound in terms of:
  - sampling rate
  - sample resolution
- Calculating sound file sizes based on the sampling rate and the sample resolution.

3 Fundamentals of data representation

3 Fundamentals of data representation

Learning objectives:

- *Explain what data compression is*
- *Understand why data may be compressed and that there are different ways to compress data*
- *Explain how data can be compressed using Huffman coding*
- *Be able to interpret/create Huffman trees*
- *Be able to calculate the number of bits required to store a piece of data compressed using Huffman coding*
- *Be able to calculate the number of bits required to store a piece of uncompressed data in ASCII*
- *Explain how data can be compressed using run length encoding (RLE)*
- *Represent data in RLE frequency/data pairs.*

Key principle

Compression:

Data can be compressed because its original representation is not the shortest possible. The original data has redundancies (redundancy = not needed) and compressing the data reduces or eliminates these redundancies, e.g. "AT" is replicated three times in the text "THE BLACK CAT SAT ON A MAT.". Non-random data is non-random because it has structure in the form of regular patterns. It is this structure that is the cause of redundancy in the data. Random data has no structure and therefore has no redundancy. Therefore, random data cannot be compressed.

3.8 Data compression

What is data compression and why compress?

Essentially, data compression squeezes data into a smaller number of bytes than the data would occupy if not compressed.

There are two main reasons why data are compressed:

- To reduce the amount of storage space required to store the data
- To reduce the time taken to transmit the data because fewer bytes need to be transmitted.

For example, text may be compressed by replacing each common character/letter combination with a single byte-coded integer number as in *Table 3.8.1*.

Integer Code	Character Combination
1	'TH'
2	'BL'
3	'CK'
4	'AT'
5	'ON'

Table 3.8.1 Codes for common character combinations

Uncompressed text = "THE BLACK CAT SAT ON A MAT."

Compressed text = "1E 2A3 C4 S4 5 A M4."

If each character in the uncompressed text is coded in one byte (including spaces and full stop) then this text requires 27 bytes of storage.

For the compressed text the storage requirement is just 20 bytes, a saving of seven bytes. This represents a 26% saving, approximately.

This example is just one way that data may be compressed.

There are other ways depending on the type of data (text, images, audio, etc). Each method of data compression works best with a particular data type.

Although we used the term "squeeze", compressing data is not actually done by squeezing data, but by removing any **redundancy** (unnecessary data duplication).

Data with redundancy can be compressed by removing some or all of the redundancy.

Data without any redundancy cannot be compressed without loss of information.

3 Fundamentals of data representation

> **Questions**
> 1. What does it mean to compress data?
> 2. Give **two** reasons why data are compressed.
> 3. Why is it possible to compress data that has structure without losing information?
> 4. Give **two** reasons why it is desirable to compress data.

Huffman coding
Fixed-size coding versus variable-size coding

Before a computer can store and process data, the data must be expressed in the language of the computer, i.e. binary (0s and 1s).

Figure 3.8.1 shows an upside down tree which can be used to encode data in numeral form chosen from the range 0 to 7.

For example, the numeral 3, is encoded as 011 as shown in *Figure 3.8.3* by following the instructions

- Start at root
- Take route along branches to numeral
- Note each red numeral in the order encountered, 011.

Table 3.8.2 shows the codes for the numerals 0 to 7.

This is a **fixed-size coding scheme** with each numeral encoded using a binary digit string of length 3.

Using a fixed-size code is a natural choice because it makes it easy for software applications to handle.

Figure 3.8.2 Upside down tree with root at top, and leaves at the bottom

Numeral	Code
0	000
1	001
2	010
3	011
4	100
5	101
6	110
7	111

Table 3.8.2 Codes for the numerals 0 to 7

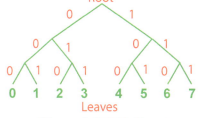

Figure 3.8.1 Coding tree

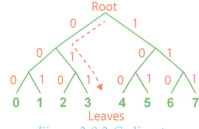

Figure 3.8.3 Coding tree

For example, we could use this encoding scheme to encode strings such as

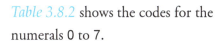

However, this is not normally the best option for encoding strings in which some numerals occur more often than others.

In such cases, it is normally better to use a **variable-size coding scheme**.

Suppose the numerals 0, 1, 2 occur with the same frequency but more frequently than the numerals 3, 4, 5, 6, 7 and numerals 5, 6 and 7 occur with the same frequency but more frequently than 3 and 4 which occur with the same frequency as each other.

Numeral	Code
0	00
1	01
2	10
3	11000
4	11001
5	1101
6	1110
7	1111

Table 3.8.3 Codes for the numerals 0 to 7

To take into account the difference and similarity in frequency of occurrence, a shorter code can be allocated to 0, 1 and 2 as shown in *Table 3.8.3* and longer codes for 3, 4, 5, 6 and 7 according to their comparative frequency.

Figure 3.8.4 shows the coding tree for this variable-size coding scheme.

Table 3.8.4 shows that fewer bits are required to encode the given numeral strings when the coding tree for variable-size codes is used instead of the coding tree for fixed-size codes.

Numeral string	Coding scheme	Binary-coded strings
2222000001111663 4557711112222000	Variable-size coding	10101010000000000101010111 10111011000110011101111111 11010101011010101000000000
2222000001111663 4557711112222000	Fixed-size coding	01001001001000000000000000 01001001001110110011100101101 11111100100100100101001001001 0000000000

Table 3.8.4 Comparison of fixed-size and variable-size coding

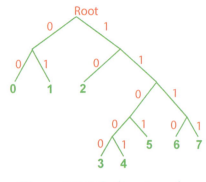

Figure 3.8.4 Coding tree for scheme that uses variable-size codes

Compressing text

A common form of data is text.

In meaningful English text, some letters such as "e", "a", and "t" occur often, whilst some letters such as "q" and "z" occur less often. This suggests that text could be compressed by using variable-size coding.

One binary coding scheme commonly used by computers is ASCII, a fixed-size code of 7 bits. Unicode is another.

Text encoded in ASCII is likely to contain redundancy because it assigns to each character, common or rare, the same number of bits.

The solution is to remove this redundancy by assigning variable-size binary codes to the characters.

Common characters are assigned short binary codes and less common characters, long binary codes.

This is precisely how **Huffman coding** works.

We have seen Huffman coding in action already in the coding scheme shown in *Figure 3.8.4*.

To understand how short codes and long codes can be assigned to text consider the following simple example.

The words referee, freeze, reefer suggest a possible Huffman coding tree as shown in *Figure 3.8.5*. *Figure 3.8.6* shows a tree built for fixed-size coding.

Table 3.8.5 shows that Huffman coding produces fewer bits than fixed-size coding when coding these words. Later you will see that this saving in bits can be considerable when the fixed-size coding uses ASCII coding.

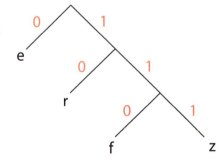

Figure 3.8.5 Huffman coding tree

Word	Coding scheme	Binary-code
referee	Huffman coding	10 0 110 0 10 0 0
referee	Fixed-size coding	01 00 10 00 01 00 00
freeze	Huffman coding	110 10 0 0 111 0
freeze	Fixed-size coding	10 01 00 00 11 00
reefer	Huffman coding	10 0 0 110 0 10
reefer	Fixed-size coding	01 00 00 10 00 01

Table 3.8.5 Comparison of fixed-size and Huffman coding

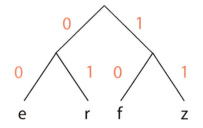

Figure 3.8.6 Fixed-size coding tree

3 Fundamentals of data representation

> **Questions**
>
> 5. By definition, random data is data in which each datum occurs just as often as any other datum. Can random data be compressed?
>
> 6. Using the Huffman coding tree shown in *Figure 3.8.5*, encode the following words
>   (a) reef (b) freer (c) refreeze
>
> 7. Using the Huffman coding tree shown in *Figure 3.8.5*, decode the binary code 110100010.

Table 3.8.6 shows a Huffman code based on statistical analysis of English language texts for the 26 letters of the alphabet.

The length of the code depends upon how often the letter appears in English text. The shortest code (3 bits) is assigned to the letter "e", the most common letter, and the longest code (7 bits) is assigned to the least common, letters "q" and "z".

Letter	Huffman Code	Letter	Huffman Code	Letter	Huffman code
a	0011	j	111100	s	10001
b	11010	k	111101	t	0010
c	10100	l	10011	u	10101
d	10010	m	10110	v	11101
e	000	n	0101	w	11011
f	10111	o	0100	x	111110
g	11100	p	11000	y	11001
h	10000	q	1111110	z	1111111
i	0111	r	0110		

Table 3.8.6 A Huffman code for the 26 letters of the alphabet

> **Questions**
>
> 8. (a) Using 7-bit ASCII, calculate the number of bits required to encode the vowel string "aeiou".
>   (b) Using the Huffman code in *Table 3.8.6*, calculate the number of bits required to encode the vowel string "aeiou".
>   (c) Calculate the difference in number of bits between the two coding methods.

Worked example of a Huffman tree constructed from specific text
Context

Figure 3.8.7 shows a Huffman tree for the text TESS SAW A RAT UP A TREE.

Each character of this text has been placed at a position in the tree determined by how often the character is used in the text.

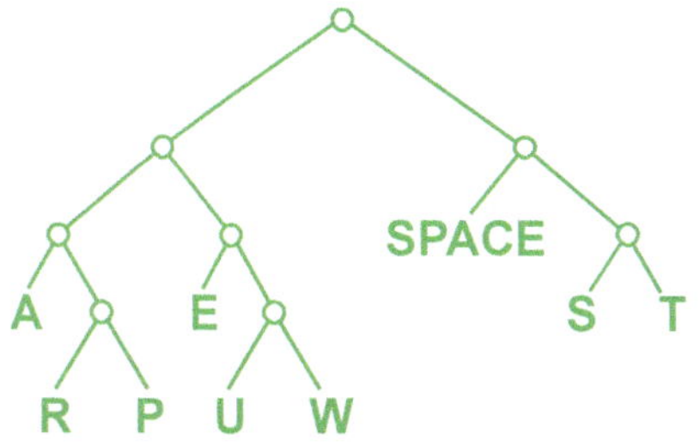

Using this Huffman tree, the Huffman coding for the character E would be the bit pattern 010 because from the top of the tree E is to the left, then right and then left.

The character S is represented by the bit pattern 110 because from the top of the tree S is to the right, then right again and then left.

Figure 3.8.7 Huffman tree

3.8 Data compression

Question

Using Huffman code defined by the tree in *Figure 3.8.7*, complete *Table 3.8.7* to show the Huffman coding for the characters A, SPACE and U.

Word	Huffman coding
A	
SPACE	
U	

Table 3.8.7 Huffman coding

Solution

Starting from the top of the tree, the character A is reached by going left, then left again and left again. A is therefore represented by 000.

Starting from the top of the tree, the SPACE character is reached by going right, then left.

SPACE is therefore represented by 10.

Starting from the top of the tree, the character U is reached by going left, then right, then right again and finally left. U is therefore represented by 0110.

Word	Huffman coding
A	000
SPACE	10
U	0110

Table 3.8.8 Huffman coding solution

Question

Using Huffman coding, the text TESS SAW A RAT UP A TREE can be stored in 71 bits.

Calculate how many additional bits are needed to store the same text using ASCII. Show your working.

Solution

Each character is coded in 7 bits using 7-bit ASCII.

There are 24 characters in the text including the SPACE character.

Therefore, using ASCII, the total number of bits = 24 x 7 = 168 bits

An additional 97 bits are therefore required.

Questions

9. *Figure 3.8.8* shows a Huffman tree for the text MY PET BEE HAS NAME MANNY. Each character of this text has been placed at a position in the tree determined by how often the character is used in the text. Using this Huffman tree, the Huffman coding for the character E would be the bit pattern 010 because from the top of the tree E is to the left, then right and then left.

The character M is represented by the bit pattern 110 because from the top of the tree M is to the right, then right again and then left.

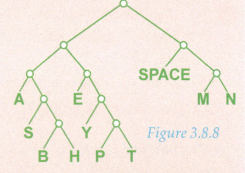

Figure 3.8.8

(a) Using Huffman code defined by the tree in *Figure 3.8.8*, complete the table to show the Huffman coding for the characters N, SPACE and P.

Word	Huffman coding
N	
SPACE	
P	

(b) Using Huffman coding, the text MY PET BEE HAS NAME MANNY can be stored in 81 bits.

Calculate how many additional bits are needed to store the same text using ASCII. Show your working.

3 Fundamentals of data representation

Constructing a Huffman tree (this section is not in 8525 specification but has been included for interest)

For the word *refreeze* the letters occur with the frequencies shown in Table 3.8.9. Table 3.8.10 shows these frequencies expressed as a fraction of the total number (4 + 2 + 1 + 1 = 8). We call this the probability of a particular letter appearing in the set of words, e.g. the letter 'e' has probability 0.5.

To create a Huffman coding tree for the letters with the probabilities shown in Table 3.8.10, we arrange the letters in descending order of probability as shown in Figure 3.8.9.

We then start from the left with the two letters with the lowest probabilities. We link these as shown into a new node 'fz' and from now on, we ignore nodes 'f' and 'z'.

We also note that the probability of finding 'f' or 'z' is 0.125 + 0.125 = 0.25.

We now combine the nodes with the two lowest probabilities, i.e. 'r' and 'fz' into a new node 'rfz'.

We note that the probability of finding 'r' or 'f' or 'z' is 0.25 + 0.25 = 0.5.

From now on, we ignore nodes 'r' and 'fz'.

We now combine the nodes with the two lowest probabilities, i.e. 'rfz' and 'e' into a new node 'erfz'.

We note that the probability of finding 'e' or 'r' or 'f' or 'z' is 0.5 + 0.5 = 1.

Now, we assign 0 to each upper branch and 1 to each lower branch as shown in Figure 3.8.9. We could equally have chosen to do the opposite and assigned 1 to the upper branch and 0 to the lower. It is quite arbitrary which labelling is used. Figure 3.8.9 now translates into the Huffman coding tree shown in Figure 3.8.10.

We could have set up Figure 3.8.9 with 'f' and 'z' swapped around since both have letter probability 0.125. This would mean that 'f' and 'z' would have to swap positions in the Huffman tree in Figure 3.8.10. However, this would make no difference to the average size of the code which is given by the following calculation:

Letter	Frequency
e	4
r	2
f	1
z	1

Table 3.8.9 Letter frequencies

Letter	Frequency
e	4/8 = 0.5
r	2/8 = 0.25
f	1/8 = 0.125
z	1/8 = 0.125

Table 3.8.10 Letter frequencies

Probability of finding letter in text shown in black

Figure 3.8.9 Construction of Huffman tree from letter probablities

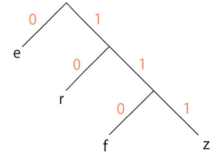

Figure 3.8.10 Huffman coding tree

> Letter 'e' occurs with probability 0.5 and requires 1 bit to encode, so contributes 0.5 x 1.
> Letter 'r' occurs with probability 0.25 and requires 2 bits to encode, so contributes 0.25 x 2.
> Letter 'f' occurs with probability 0.125 and requires 3 bits to encode, so contributes 0.125 x 3.
> Letter 'z' occurs with probability 0.125 and requires 3 bits to encode, so contributes 0.125 x 3.
> Therefore, average size of code = 0.5 x 1 + 0.25 x 2 + 0.125 x 3 + 0.125 x 3 = 1.75 bits/letter.
> With four letters, the minimum uncompressed code would require 2 bits/letter.

Questions

10 (a) Create a Huffman coding tree for the letters shown in Table 3.8.11.

(b) What is the average size of code? Show your working.

11 (a) Create a Huffman coding tree for the letters shown in Table 3.8.12. (Note that there is more than one possible tree).

(b) What is the average size of code? Show your working.

Candidates are not required to know how to create a Huffman tree.

Letter	Frequency
A	1/30
B	1/30
C	1/30
D	2/30
E	3/30
F	5/30
G	5/30
H	12/30

Table 3.8.12 Letter frequencies

Letter	Frequency
e	1/3
a	1/4
d	1/6
n	1/6
b	1/12

Table 3.8.11 Letter frequencies

Run length encoding (RLE)

In **run length encoding** a **run** of contiguous bytes all with the same value can be condensed into two bytes, one byte that stores the count (or run length) and a second byte that stores the value in the run. These two bytes are sometimes called a **frequency/data pair**.

Figure 3.8.11 shows run length encoding applied to a run of six contiguous bytes each of value 128. The amount of data stored is reduced from 6 bytes to 2 bytes by this data compression method.

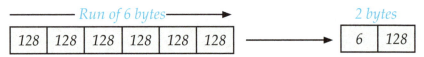

Figure 3.8.11 Run length encoding compression of 6 bytes into 2 bytes

RLE can be used to **compress bitmap images**.

Each run of pixels of the same colour is encoded as a frequency/data pair (run length/pixel colour value).

Information

Contiguous: Means next to each other or together in sequence.

The following example shows how RLE could be applied to a bitmap that encodes the intensity of each pixel in 8 bits and that starts with the sequence

15, 15, 15, 15, 15, 15, 15, 15, 46, 81, 123, 58, 98, 98, 98, 98, 7, 7, 7, 8, ···

The compressed sequence of bytes is

8, 15, 1, 46, 1, 81, 1, 123, 1, 58, 4, 98, 3, 7, 1, 8, ···

where the red values indicate counts.

The original 20 bytes in the example have been reduced to 16 bytes.

Example

Black and white images such as shown in outline in Figure 3.8.12 can be encoded using 1 to represent a white pixel and 0 to represent a black pixel.

The two-dimensional grid of pixels making up a black and white image may then be represented in a bitmap by rows of 0s and 1s, one row per pixel row.

The ellipsis symbol ··· indicates more black or white pixels.

Suppose a row of this bitmap consists of the following run of 0s and 1s

0000000111111111110000000111111

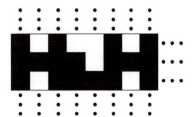

Figure 3.8.12 Part of a black and white image made up of rows of pixels

3.8 Data compression

3 Fundamentals of data representation

Using run length encoding this row becomes

7 0 12 1 6 0 7 1

This is a simplification because the amount of storage space allocated to each frequency/data pair has been ignored.

> ### Questions
>
> **12** Bit patterns are often compressed.
> Compress the following bit pattern using run length encoding.
> 1111 0000 0111 0000 0001 1111

In this chapter you have covered:

- What data compression is
- Why data may be compressed and that there are different ways to compress data
- How data can be compressed using Huffman coding
- Interpreting and creating Huffman trees
- Calculating the number of bits required to store a piece of data compressed using Huffman coding
- Calculating the number of bits required to store a piece of uncompressed data in ASCII
- How data can be compressed using run length encoding (RLE)
- Representing data in RLE frequency/data pairs.

4 Computer systems

4 Computer systems

Learning objectives:

- *Define the terms hardware and software and understand the relationship between them.*

4.1 Hardware and software

What is hardware?

The hardware of a computer is the **physical components, electronic and electrical**, that it is assembled from. It is the **platform on which software executes**.

What is software?

Software consists of **sequences of instructions** called programs which can be **understood and executed by the hardware** in its digital electronic circuits or a virtual machine equivalent.

> **Key concept**
>
> **Hardware:**
> The hardware of a computer is the physical components, electronic and electrical, that it is assembled from. It is the platform on which software executes.

> **Key concept**
>
> **Software:**
> Consists of sequences of instructions called programs which can be understood and executed by the hardware in its digital electronic circuits or a virtual machine equivalent.

> **Questions**
>
> 1. What is meant by hardware?
> 2. What is meant by software?

In this chapter you have covered:

- The terms hardware and software and the relationship between them.

4 Computer systems

4 Computer systems

Learning objectives:

- *Construct truth tables for the following logic gates:*
  - *NOT*
  - *AND*
  - *OR*
  - *XOR*

- *Construct truth tables for simple logic circuits using combinations of NOT, AND, OR and XOR gates*

- *Interpret the results of simple truth tables*

- *Create, modify and interpret simple logic diagrams*

- *Create and interpret simple Boolean expressions made up of NOT, AND, OR and XOR operations*

- *Create the Boolean expression for a simple logic circuit*

- *Create a logic circuit from a simple Boolean expression.*

4.2 Boolean logic

Background to logic gates

An electrical circuit such as shown in Figure 4.2.1 is made with wires, a switch, batteries and lamps.

When the switch labelled X is closed the lamp Q is lit (ON) and when X is open, the lamp Q is not lit (OFF).

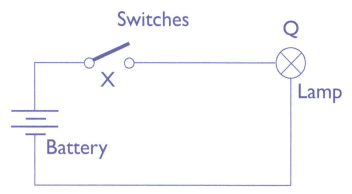

Figure 4.2.1 Simple electrical circuit

Questions

1. Switch X has two possible positions, open or closed. What position must the switch be in for the lamp Q to be lit?

Table 4.2.1 shows the possible states of lamp Q for the two possible states of switch X.

State of switch X	State of lamp Q
OPEN	OFF
CLOSED	ON

Table 4.2.1 Possible states of switch X and lamp Q

It is more convenient to express the possible states of switch X by answering the question: "Is switch X closed?". Table 4.2.2 shows the possible answers expressed using values NO and YES.

Is switch X closed?	Meaning
NO	Switch X is not closed
YES	Switch X is closed

Table 4.2.2 Possible answers to the question

201

4 Computer systems

The corresponding question for lamp Q is "Is lamp Q on?".

Table 4.2.3 shows the possible answers expressed using values NO and YES.

Is lamp Q on?	Meaning
NO	Lamp Q is not on
YES	Lamp Q is on

Table 4.2.3 Possible answers to the question

Questions

2. Figure 4.2.2 shows an electrical circuit with two switches X and Y, and one lamp Q.

   Copy and complete Table 4.2.4 by writing YES or NO in the blank rows.

Is switch X closed?	Is switch Y closed?	Is lamp Q on?
NO	NO	NO

   Table 4.2.4

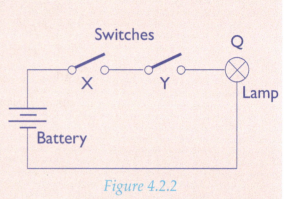

Figure 4.2.2

Truth tables

Now we move from questions to statements which are either true or false.

If the statement "Switch X Closed" is true for the circuit shown in Figure 4.2.1 then the statement "Lamp Q On" is true.

If the statement "Switch X Closed" is false for the circuit shown in Figure 4.2.1 then the statement "Lamp Q On" is false.

This is summarised for the circuit if Figure 4.2.1 in a truth table as shown in Table 4.2.5.

Switch X Closed	Lamp Q On
FALSE	FALSE
TRUE	TRUE

Table 4.2.5

Truth tables deal with statements considered either true or false.

Questions

3. Figure 4.2.3 shows an electrical circuit with two switches X and Y, and one lamp Q.

   Copy and complete Table 4.2.6 by writing TRUE or FALSE in the blank rows.

Switch X Closed	Switch Y Closed	Lamp Q On
FALSE	FALSE	FALSE

   Table 4.2.6

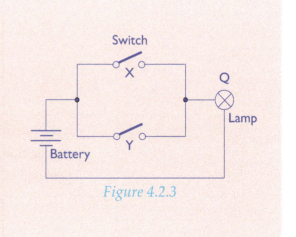

Figure 4.2.3

4.2 Boolean logic

Logic gates

You must be able to construct truth tables for NOT, AND, OR and XOR logic gates and simple logic gate circuits as well as be able to create, modify and interpret simple logic gate circuit diagrams. However, you are not required to know or understand the various technologies from which logic gates are constructed.

NOT logic gate

Consideration of one technology from the past may, however, make the use of logic gates easier to accept. For this reason, we will consider how a particular logic gate called a **NOT gate** can be made using relay technology.

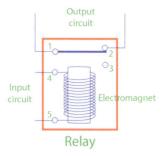

Figure 4.2.4

A relay uses an electromagnet to close or open a switch in an "output" circuit depending on how the output circuit is wired to the relay. *Figure 4.2.4* shows a relay in which the output circuit is wired between poles 1 and 2 of the relay. The output circuit could equally well have been wired between poles 1 and 3.

If the electromagnet is energised, its iron core becomes magnetic, which in turn pulls on the flexible metal contact moving it away from pole 2 and into contact with pole 3. Whereupon, the output circuit becomes disconnected if connected between poles 1 and 2 and vice versa if connected between poles 1 and 3.

Figure 4.2.5 shows an output circuit which is connected between poles 1 and 2. On the input circuit side, poles 4 and 5 connect the electromagnet of the relay to a battery and a single switch X.

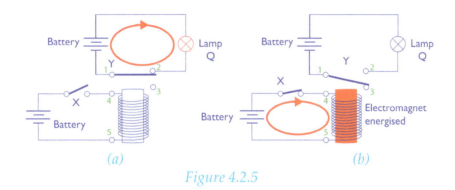

Figure 4.2.5

In *Figure 4.2.5(a)*, switch X is open in the input circuit and switch Y in the output circuit is in the position which connects the battery to lamp Q. The lamp is lit.

In *Figure 4.2.5(b)*, switch X is closed in the input circuit and switch Y in the output circuit is in the position which disconnects the battery from lamp Q. The lamp is not lit.

Table 4.2.7 shows the truth table for the operation of the circuit shown in *Figure 4.2.5*.

Switch X Closed	Lamp Q On
FALSE	TRUE
TRUE	FALSE

Table 4.2.7 Truth table for circuit shown in Figure 4.2.5

We simplify this truth table as shown in *Table 4.2.8*. What is of interest is whether there is current flowing in the input circuit (TRUE or FALSE) and similarly, whether there is current flowing in the output circuit (TRUE or FALSE.

Input	Output
FALSE	TRUE
TRUE	FALSE

Table 4.2.8 Simplified truth table for circuit shown in Figure 4.2.5

4 Computer systems

Figure 4.2.6 shows the relay circuit used in *Figure 4.2.5* rejigged with the relay and battery used in the output circuit partially obscured in a red/blue box. Switch X has been replaced by a switch that can connect to the 5 volts terminal of a battery used to energise the electromagnet or its 0 volts terminal to remove its energy supply.

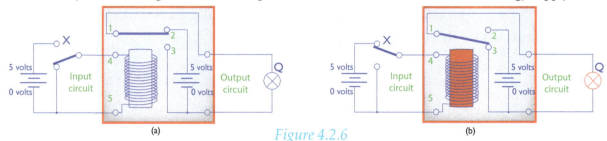

Figure 4.2.6

Table 4.2.9 shows an alternative representation within the truth table, one which uses voltages with 5 volts corresponding to TRUE and 0 volts corresponding to FALSE (the two voltages just have to be sufficiently different to be distinguishable).

Input	Output
0 volts	5 volts
5 volts	0 volts

Table 4.2.9 Truth table for circuit shown in Figure 4.2.6

If we let binary 1 stand for 5 volts or any energising voltage and binary 0 for 0 volts then *Table 4.2.9* can be simplified to the representation shown in *Table 4.2.10*.

The circuit at the heart of *Figure 4.2.6* is called a **NOT logic gate**. It is also shown in *Figure 4.2.7(a)*.

Input	Output
0	1
1	0

Table 4.2.10 Truth table for circuit shown in Figure 4.2.6

Table 4.2.10 is the truth table for this **NOT gate**.

Figure 4.2.7(b) shows the equivalent ANSI/IEEE standard 91-1984 standard symbol for a **NOT gate**.

Figure 4.2.8 shows this NOT gate symbol being used in a circuit. *Figure 4.2.9* shows all that is needed to understand the effect of the NOT gate on its input. *Figure 4.2.10* shows the input generalised to **X** and the output to **Q**. *Table 4.2.11* shows the **truth table for a NOT gate in terms of input X and output Q.**

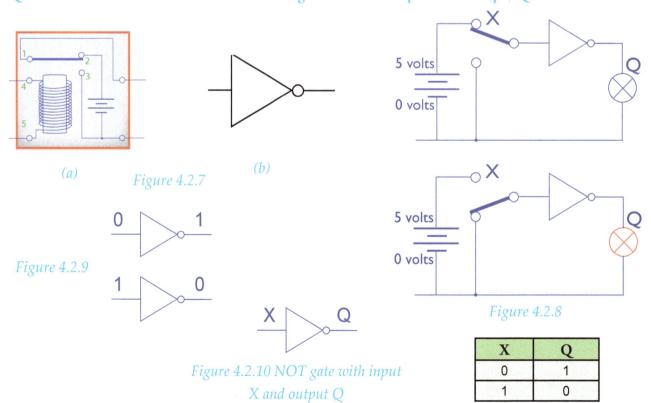

Figure 4.2.7

Figure 4.2.9

Figure 4.2.10 NOT gate with input X and output Q

Figure 4.2.8

X	Q
0	1
1	0

Table 4.2.11 Truth table for NOT gate

AND logic gate

Another logic gate is the **AND gate**. This has two inputs and one output as shown in *Figure 4.2.11*. The lamp is lit because both inputs are connected to **5** volts otherwise the lamp would not be lit.

Its truth table is shown in *Table 4.2.12* with one particular ordering of rows. *Figure 4.2.12* shows its IEEE logic gate symbol.

X	Y	X AND Y
0	0	0
0	1	0
1	0	0
1	1	1

Table 4.2.12 Truth table for AND logic gate with inputs X and Y and output X AND Y

Figure 4.2.12 AND logic gate IEEE symbol

Figure 4.2.11 AND logic gate with inputs X and Y, and output Q

OR logic gate

Another logic gate is the **OR gate**. This has two inputs and one output as shown in *Figure 4.2.13*. The lamp is lit because at least one input is connected to **5** volts otherwise the lamp would not be lit.

Its truth table is shown in *Table 4.2.13* with one particular ordering of rows. *Figure 4.2.14* shows its IEEE logic gate symbol.

X	Y	X OR Y
0	0	0
0	1	1
1	0	1
1	1	1

Table 4.2.13 Truth table for OR logic gate with inputs X and Y, and output X OR Y

Figure 4.2.14 OR logic gate IEEE symbol

Figure 4.2.13 OR logic gate with inputs X and Y, and output Q

Information
You may experiment with virtual logic gates using an online simulator at
https://academo.org/demos/logic-gate-simulator/

XOR logic gate

Another logic gate is the **eXclusive-OR** or **XOR gate**. This has two inputs and one output as shown in *Figure 4.2.15*. The lamp is lit if X is connected to **5** volts and Y is connected to **0** volts or if X is connected to **0** volts and Y is connected to **5** volts. However, if both X and Y are **0** volts or **5** volts, the lamp is not lit.

Its truth table is shown in *Table 4.2.14* with one particular ordering of rows. *Figure 4.2.16* shows the logic gate symbol used by AQA.

X	Y	X XOR Y
0	0	0
0	1	1
1	0	1
1	1	0

Table 4.2.14 Truth table for XOR logic gate with inputs X and Y, and output X XOR Y

Figure 4.2.16 XOR logic gate AQA symbol

Figure 4.2.15 XOR logic gate with inputs X and Y, and output Q

Information
ANSI/IEEE XOR symbol

4 Computer systems

Questions

4. Identify the logic gate with inputs X and Y, and output Q whose truth table is shown in Table 4.2.15.

5. Identify the logic gate with inputs X and Y, and output Q whose truth table is shown in Table 4.2.16.

6. Identify the logic gate with inputs X and Y, and output Q whose truth table is shown in Table 4.2.17.

X	Y	Q
1	1	1
0	0	0
1	0	0
0	1	0

Table 4.2.15

X	Y	Q
1	1	1
0	0	0
1	0	1
0	1	1

Table 4.2.16

X	Y	Q
1	1	0
0	0	1
1	0	1
0	1	0

Table 4.2.17

Constructing truth tables for simple logic circuits

Figure 4.2.17 shows a simple logic gate circuit consisting of an AND gate and a NOT gate.

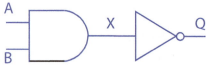

Figure 4.2.17 Logic gate circuit

You are required to be able to construct truth tables which contain up to three inputs. In Figure 4.2.17, A and B are inputs, X is an intermediate value which forms the input to the NOT gate.

Its truth table is shown in Table 4.2.18. The inputs to the AND gate are A and B. The output X from the AND gate forms the input X to the NOT gate. The output from the NOT gate is labelled Q.

A	B	X	Q
0	0	0	1
0	1	0	1
1	0	0	1
1	1	1	0

Table 4.2.18

Figure 4.2.18 shows another logic gate circuit consisting of an OR gate, an AND gate and a NOT gate.

Its truth table is shown in Table 4.2.19. The inputs to the OR gate are A and B. The output X from the OR gate forms the first input to the AND gate. The second input to this AND gate comes from B.

The output from the AND gate is labelled Y.

This forms the input Y to the NOT gate.

The output from the NOT gate is labelled Q.

Figure 4.2.18 Logic gate circuit

A	B	X	Y	Q
0	0	0	0	1
0	1	1	1	0
1	0	1	0	1
1	1	1	1	0

Table 4.2.19

Figure 4.2.19 shows a logic gate circuit with three inputs A, B and C.

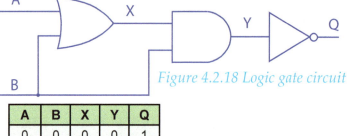

Figure 4.2.19 Logic gate circuit

Its truth table is shown in Table 4.2.20. It has eight rows since there are eight possible different combinations of three inputs, each input consisting of 0 or 1.

A	B	C	X	Q
0	0	0	0	0
0	0	1	0	0
0	1	0	0	0
0	1	1	0	0
1	0	0	0	0
1	0	1	0	0
1	1	0	1	0
1	1	1	1	1

Table 4.2.20

The inputs to the first AND gate are A and B. The output X from this AND gate forms the first input to the second AND gate. The second input to this AND gate is C. Its output is Q.

4 Computer systems

Questions

7 Complete the truth table shown in *Table 4.2.21* for the logic gate circuit shown in *Figure 4.2.20*.

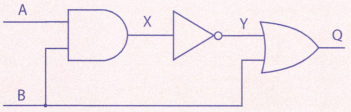

A	B	X	Y	Q
0	0			
0	1			
1	0			
1	1			

Figure 4.2.20 Logic gate circuit

Table 4.2.21

Creating logic gate circuits

You are expected to be able to construct simple logic circuit diagrams which contain up to three inputs.

Consider the following example for which the specification is as follows:

> A logic circuit is being developed for an automatic alarm system protecting a store room:
> - The alarm system has two sensors, sensor A and sensor B. Sensor A is activated if the front door to the store room is open. Sensor B is activated if the back door to the store room is open.
> - The alarm system can be turned on/off using a manual switch, S. The alarm system is not enabled unless S is on.
> - The alarm is to sound if either door or both are open and the manual switch is on otherwise the alarm is to be silent.
> - The output from this logic circuit is Q.

Complete the logic circuit diagram shown in *Figure 4.2.21* for this system:

```
A ──

B ──                    ── Q

S ──
```

Figure 4.2.21 Logic gate circuit

The way to tackle a logic circuit design problem is to
- identify the inputs
- identify the output
- look for the following keywords/key phrases
  - Either … or
  - Or both
  - But not both
  - And
  - And both
  - Not

4.2 Boolean logic

In the given alarm system specification we can identify:

> "The alarm is to sound if **either** door **or both** are open",
> "Sensor A is activated if the front door to the store room is opened",
> "Sensor B is activated if the back door to the store room is opened".
> This suggests an OR logic gate with inputs A and B as shown in *Figure 4.2.22*.
> When sensor A is activated its output is 1 otherwise its output is 0.
> When sensor B is activated its output is 1 otherwise its output is 0.
> "The alarm is to sound if either door or both are open **and** the manual switch is on otherwise the alarm is to be silent".
> When the switch S is on its output is 1 otherwise its output is 0.
> This suggests an AND logic gate with inputs X and S as shown in *Figure 4.2.23*.

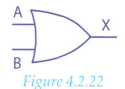

Figure 4.2.22

Figure 4.2.23

The solution is therefore obtained by combining these two logic circuits as shown in *Figure 4.2.24*.

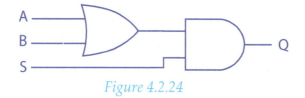

Figure 4.2.24

Questions

8 A logic circuit is being developed for an automatic plant watering system:

- The plant watering system has two sensors, sensor A and sensor B. Sensor A is activated when the soil in the plant pot is dry. Sensor B is activated when the light level is above a threshold value.
- The plant watering system can be turned on/off using a manual switch, S. Plant watering will not occur unless S is on.
- Plant watering is to occur when the soil is dry and the light level is above the threshold value and the manual switch is on.
- The output from this logic circuit, for whether plant watering occurs or not, is Q.

Complete a copy of the logic circuit diagram for this system:

A ——

B ——   —— Q

S ——

9 In a cockpit warning system for an aircraft's landing gear, a warning lamp is lit if the left landing wheel is up and the right landing wheel is down, or vice versa, otherwise the warning lamp is not lit. Each landing wheel has its own sensor which senses the wheel's state and outputs a 0 if the landing wheel is up and a 1 if it is down. The left landing wheel's sensor is labelled A and the right wheel's sensor B. The output from the logic circuit which performs the warning function is Q.

Complete a copy of the logic circuit diagram for this system:

A ——

                                       —— Q

B ——

Questions

10 A logic circuit is being developed to control a motor system:

- The motor can be in one of three possible states at any one moment in time:
  - Rotating forwards
  - Rotating backwards
  - Stopped
- The electric motor system has two sensors, sensor A and sensor B. Sensor A is activated when a control paddle is in the down position. Sensor B is activated when the control paddle is in the up position. When the control paddle is in the neutral position, sensor A and sensor B are deactivated.
- The electric motor system can also be turned on/off using a manual switch, S. The electric motor cannot be on if S is off.
- The motor is to rotate forwards when the control paddle is in the down position and S is on.
- The motor is to rotate backwards when the control paddle is in the up position and S is on.
- The motor is to be stopped if the control paddle is in the neutral position.
- There are two outputs from this logic circuit, U and D. Output U is connected to one side of the motor and output D is connected to the other side. If U = 1 and D = 0 then the motor rotates forwards. If U = 0 and D = 1 then the motor rotates backwards. If U and D are both the same, the motor is stopped.

Complete a copy of the logic circuit diagram for this system:

A ──

S ──

B ──

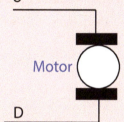

11 The following logic circuit consists of inputs X and Y and output Z.

Modify this circuit so that its new output Q is as shown in *Table 4.2.22*.

X	Y	Q
0	0	1
0	1	1
1	0	1
1	1	0

Table 4.2.22

12 A logic circuit is being developed for a room protected by an interlocked door system:

- The room is entered by passing through two doors in succession, door A and door B.
- The system must prevent door A and door B from being open at the same time.
- The system has two sensors, sensor X and sensor Y. Sensor X is activated when door A is open. Sensor Y is activated when door B is open.
- The output from this logic circuit, Q, when activated is used to prevent both doors from being open at the same time. This is done by making Q active if door A is open and door B is closed or if door B is open and door A is closed.
- Activated corresponds to logic value 1 and not activated to logic value 0.

Complete a copy of the logic circuit diagram for this system:

Sensor X ──

── Q

Sensor Y ──

4.2 Boolean logic

Boolean variables

In 1847 George Boole, an English mathematician, introduced a shorthand notation for a system of logic originally set forth by Aristotle. Aristotle's system dealt with statements considered either true or false. Here are two examples:

It is sunny today.

Today is Tuesday.

Quite clearly these two statements are either True or False. If today is Wednesday then the statement "Today is Tuesday" is False. Table 4.2.23 shows the possible outcomes of examining the truth of each statement.

Statement	Outcome	
It is sunny today	False	True
Today is Tuesday	False	True

Table 4.2.23 Possible outcomes for truth of statements

Just as we might use an integer variable G to record the number of goats in a farmer's field so we can use variable X as shorthand for "It is sunny today", and Y for "Today is Tuesday". The values that G can be assigned are the natural or counting numbers. For X and Y, we have only two possible values, True or False, to assign. We call X and Y Boolean variables, after George Boole who introduced this form of algebra called Boolean algebra. Table 4.2.24 shows the Boolean variable equivalent of Table 4.2.23 for "It is sunny today" expressed as Boolean variable X. Boolean algebra deals with Boolean values that are typically labelled True/False (or 1/0, Yes/No, On/Off).

X (It is sunny today)	Meaning
False	It is not sunny today
True	It is sunny today

Table 4.2.24 Boolean variable representation of truth statements

As digital computers rely for their operation on using the binary number system, Boolean algebra can be applied usefully in the design of the electronic circuits of a digital computer. Using Boolean values 1 and 0 instead of True and False, True in Table 4.2.24 becomes 1 and False becomes 0 as shown in Table 4.2.25. X = 1 now means that "It is true that it is sunny today" and X = 0 means "It is not true that it is sunny today".

X	Meaning
0	It is not sunny today
1	It is sunny today

Table 4.2.25 Boolean variable representation of truth statements using 0 in place of False and 1 in place of True

It is then a small step to use Boolean variables to represent the state of components such as switches and indicator lamps as follows:

- a switch can be either closed (1) or open (0) and
- an indicator lamp can be either on (1) or off (0).

4 Computer systems

Boolean expressions

In *Figure 4.2.25*, the output Q is determined by the operation of the OR gate on the two Boolean inputs X and Y which may be 0 volts (binary 0) or 5 volts (binary 1).

We can write this as OR(X, Y) or (X OR Y) where OR denotes the operation performed by the OR gate on inputs X and Y. The outcome is Q.

However, we can write this another way as a Boolean expression using the Boolean variables X and Y and the OR operator symbol + as follows

$$X + Y$$

The evaluation of this expression by the OR logic gate produces output Q. Writing Q as a Boolean variable we obtain

$$Q = X + Y$$

The truth table for this expression is shown in *Table 4.2.26*.

For AND(X, Y) or (X AND Y) where AND denotes the operation performed by the AND gate on inputs X and Y (*Figure 4.2.26*), we can write the equivalent expression using the Boolean variables X and Y and the AND operator symbol • as follows

$$X \cdot Y$$

The evaluation of this expression by the AND logic gate produces output Q. Writing Q as a Boolean variable we obtain

$$Q = X \cdot Y$$

The truth table for this expression is shown in *Table 4.2.27*.

In *Figure 4.2.27*, the output Q is determined by the operation of the NOT gate on the Boolean input X.

For NOT(X) or (NOT X) where NOT denotes the operation performed by the NOT gate on input X, we can write the equivalent expression using the Boolean variable X and the NOT operator symbol ‾ as $\overline{X}$.

The evaluation of this expression by the NOT logic gate produces output Q. Writing Q as a Boolean variable we obtain

$$Q = \overline{X}$$

The truth table for this expression is shown in *Table 4.2.28*.

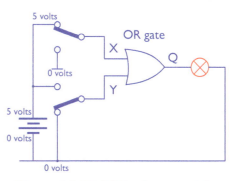

Figure 4.2.25 OR logic gate with inputs X and Y, and output Q

X	Y	X + Y
0	0	0
0	1	1
1	0	1
1	1	1

Table 4.2.26 Truth table for the Boolean expression X + Y

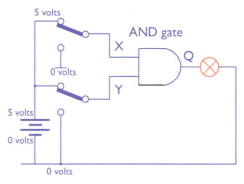

Figure 4.2.26 AND logic gate with inputs X and Y, and output Q

X	Y	X • Y
0	0	0
0	1	0
1	0	0
1	1	1

Table 4.2.27 Truth table for the Boolean expression X • Y

X	$\overline{X}$
0	1
1	0

Table 4.2.28 Truth table for the Boolean expression $\overline{X}$

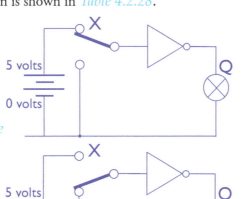

Figure 4.2.27 NOT logic gate with input X and output Q

For XOR(X, Y) or (X XOR Y) where XOR denotes the operation performed by the XOR gate on inputs X and Y (*Figure 4.2.28*), we can write the equivalent expression using the Boolean variables X and Y and the XOR operator symbol ⊕ as follows

$$X \oplus Y$$

The evaluation of this expression by the XOR logic gate produces output Q. Writing Q as a Boolean variable we obtain

$$Q = X \oplus Y$$

The truth table for this expression is shown in *Table 4.2.29*.

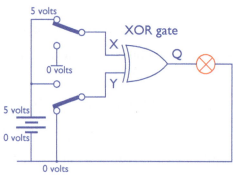

Figure 4.2.28 XOR logic gate with inputs X and Y, and output Q

X	Y	X ⊕ Y
0	0	0
0	1	1
1	0	1
1	1	0

Table 4.2.29 Truth table for Boolean expression X ⊕ Y

Examples

Ex1: We may write the expression (NOT A) AND (NOT B) using operator notation as follows

$$\overline{A} . \overline{B}$$

(For convenience, the • operator is just written as .)

Figure 4.2.29 shows the equivalent logic gate circuit for the Boolean expression $\overline{A} . \overline{B}$

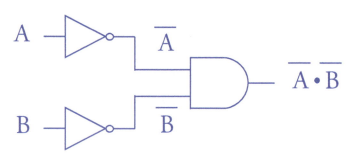

> **Information**
>
> **Writing A • B as A.B or AB**
> We can write A • B as A.B
> We can even omit the • operator and write the Boolean variables one after another, e.g. A • B as AB.

Figure 4.2.29 The equivalent logic circuit for the Boolean expression $\overline{A} . \overline{B}$

Ex 2: We may write the expression (A AND B) OR (NOT C) using operator notation as follows

$$(A . B) + \overline{C}$$

Figure 4.2.30 shows the equivalent logic gate circuit for this Boolean expression

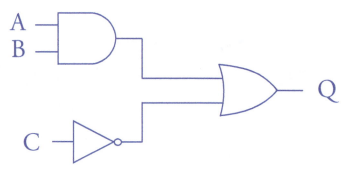

Figure 4.2.30 The equivalent logic circuit for the Boolean expression $(A . B) + \overline{C}$

4 Computer systems

Ex 3: We may write the expression (A AND B) OR (A AND C) using operator notation as follows

A.B + A.C

Figure 4.2.31 shows the equivalent logic gate circuit for this Boolean expression

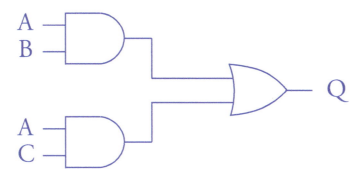

Figure 4.2.31 The equivalent logic circuit for the Boolean expression A.B + A.C

Ex 4: We may write the expression (A AND (NOT B)) OR ((NOT A) AND B) using operator notation as follows

$(A \cdot \overline{B}) + (\overline{A} \cdot B)$

Figure 4.2.32 shows the equivalent logic gate circuit for this Boolean expression

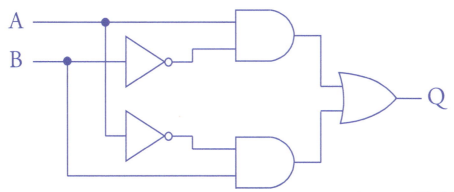

Figure 4.2.32 The equivalent logic circuit for the Boolean expression $A \cdot \overline{B} + \overline{A} \cdot B$

Questions

13 Write the Boolean expression for the following
(a) ((NOT A) OR B) AND (A OR (NOT B))
(b) ((NOT A) AND (NOT B)) OR (A AND B)
(c) (A XOR B) AND C
(d) NOT(A AND B)
(e) NOT((A AND B) OR (A AND C))

14 Write the Boolean expression for the logic circuit shown in Figure 4.2.33.

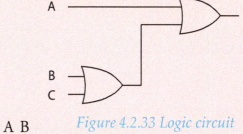

Figure 4.2.33 Logic circuit

15 Write the Boolean expression for the logic circuit shown in Figure 4.2.34.

16 Draw the logic circuit for the Boolean expression
(a) A ⊕ B
(b) A + (B + C)
(c) (A . B) + (A . C)
(d) (A + B) . (A + C)

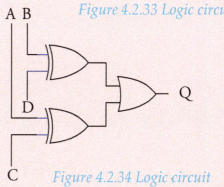

Figure 4.2.34 Logic circuit

4.2 Boolean logic

In this chapter you have covered:

- Truth tables for the following logic gates:
  - NOT
  - AND
  - OR
  - XOR
- Constructing truth tables for simple logic circuits using combinations of NOT, AND, OR and XOR gates
- Interpreting the results of simple truth tables
- Creating, modifying and interpreting simple logic diagrams.
- Creating and interpreting simple Boolean expressions made up of NOT, AND, OR and XOR operations. Using the following symbols
  - • or . to represent AND gate
  - + to represent OR gate
  - ⊕ to represent XOR gate
  - Overbar or ‾ to represent the NOT gate
- Creating the Boolean expression for a simple logic circuit
- Creating a logic circuit from a simple Boolean expression.

Logic gate	Symbol	Truth table
NOT		X | NOT X 0 | 1 1 | 0
AND		X | Y | X AND Y 0 | 0 | 0 0 | 1 | 0 1 | 0 | 0 1 | 1 | 1
OR		X | Y | X OR Y 0 | 0 | 0 0 | 1 | 1 1 | 0 | 1 1 | 1 | 1
XOR		X | Y | X XOR Y 0 | 0 | 0 0 | 1 | 1 1 | 0 | 1 1 | 1 | 0

4 Computer systems

4 Computer systems

Learning objectives:

- *Explain what is meant by:*
  - *system software*
  - *application software*
- *Give examples of both types of software*
- *Understand the need for, and functions of, operating systems (OS) and utility programs*
- *Understand that the OS handles management of the:*
  - *processor(s)*
  - *memory*
  - *I/O devices*
  - *applications*
  - *security.*

> **Key concept**
>
> **System software:**
> A layer or layers of software which enables users to operate the computer without having to be familiar with its internal workings.

> **Key concept**
>
> **Application software:**
> Application software is an application program or programs designed to support user-oriented tasks which would need to be carried out even if computers did not exist.

> **Key concept**
>
> **Software:**
> Consists of sequences of instructions called programs which can be understood and executed by the hardware in its digital electronic circuits or a virtual machine equivalent.

4.3 Software classification

Computer software may be classified as follows:

1. The **system programs** (or system software), which control the operation of the computer itself, e.g. the operating system.
2. The **application programs** (or application software), which solve problems for their users, e.g. constructing a letter using word processing software for printing and sending to someone.

What is system software?

A computer system uses a layer or layers of software to enable users to operate the computer without having to be familiar with its internal workings. This layer or layers is called systems software and includes the operating system and other forms of systems software such as anti-virus software, disk defragmenters, backup software.

What is application software?

Applications software is an application program or programs designed to support user-oriented tasks which would need to be carried out even if computers did not exist. For example, communicating in written form, placing orders for goods, looking up information.

Application software cannot execute unless it has been first translated into the language of the computer, machine code, or a form that is executable by a computer.

It needs to be loaded into main memory and it needs to obtain input from input devices such as keyboards and to write output to output devices such as printers and it may need to communicate with other computers.

Application software may need to store information permanently and to subsequently access stored information. The stored information should be backed up so, if necessary, it may be restored from a back-up copy. These services are provided by the operating system and utility software without which it would not be possible to run application software.

Application software may be classified as

- **General purpose application software:** software that is appropriate for many application areas is described as general-purpose application software. For example, word processing can be applied in writing-up project work, in personal correspondence, writing memos, writing a book, creating standard business letters. The software is relatively cheap

215

because its development costs are spread among all the purchasers of the software, which in the case of popular application software will be a large number. It is likely to be very reliable because it has been produced by an experienced team of programmers and tested on a large customer base.

- **Special purpose applications software:** special purpose application software is used for a particular application. For example, a dentist might use application software written specifically to record and process dental treatments, a task that every dentist needs to do. A business might use an accounting package for its accounts of sales. It is likely to be very reliable because it has been produced by an experienced team of programmers and tested on a large but specialised customer base.

- **Bespoke software:** when no general purpose or special purpose software exists that could do the job, software must be written from scratch to solve the specific problem or to support the required task. This software is called bespoke (tailor-made) software. For example, a teacher interested in finding out how frequently his students logged on to the college's computer network and for how long, wrote a program using the programming language C to handle this task because no application program existed which could do this job.

> **Key concept**
>
> **Different types of application software:**
> 1. General purpose
> 2. Special purpose
> 3. Bespoke.

Questions

1. Explain what is meant by:
   (a) system software   (b) application software.
2. Give one example of system software and one example of application software.

Understand the need for, and functions of, operating systems (OS) and utility programs

Systems software can be classified as follows:

- **Operating system software:** an operating system is a program or suite of programs which controls the entire operation of a computer

- **Utility programs:** a utility program is a systems program designed to perform a common place task, for example, formatting and partitioning a disk or checking a disk for viruses. Some utility programs are supplied with the operating system, others can be installed at a later time.

> **Key concept**
>
> **System software classification:**
> 1. Operating systems
> 2. Utility programs.

4.3 Software classification

The most fundamental of all the system programs is the operating system.

An operating system performs several major functions:

- **Hiding the complexities of the hardware** from the user so that the user is presented with a machine which is much easier to use.

- **Managing the hardware resources** to give an orderly and controlled allocation of the processors and processor time, memories and input/output (I/O) devices among the various programs competing for them, and manage data storage.

  - The operating system (OS) will need to schedule processor time for each executing program loaded into RAM. In a single processor system, this may be done on a round robin basis or some other way of allocating processor time fairly and appropriately. The task becomes a little more challenging if there is more than one processor.

  - The OS will need to manage the allocation of space in RAM to programs and unload programs that have finished their execution - memory management.

  - The OS will need to manage the allocation and release of areas of storage, e.g. disk blocks - disk management.

  - It will also need to manage the file/directory system which structures storage into files and directories - file management.

  - The OS will need to respond to I/O devices that need attention, e.g. when a key on the keyboard has been pressed or when a disk block of file data has finished being transferred into RAM. It will need to know how to "drive" I/O devices because the OS will be responsible for handling the transfer of data between the processor/RAM and I/O devices, e.g. writing a disk block of data to a disk file. The OS will rely on pieces of software to do this called device drivers. Their software will have been written for a specific device or type of device, e.g. a disk device driver.

- **Managing the loading, unloading of application software**.

- **Managing user accounts, passwords** and **access to the system** in order to secure the system against unauthorised access, alteration and deletion of data.

> **Key concept**
>
> **Functions of an operating system:**
> 1. Hiding the complexities of the hardware from the user so that the user is presented with a machine which is much easier to use.
> 2. Managing the hardware resources to give an orderly and controlled allocation of the processors and processor time, memories and input/output (I/O) devices among the various programs competing for them, and manage data storage.
> 3. Managing the loading and unloading of application software.
> 4. Managing user accounts, passwords and access to the system in order to secure the system against unauthorised access, alteration and deletion of data.

Questions

3. Explain the purpose of an operating system.

4. Give **one** example of a utility program.

4 Computer systems

In this chapter you have covered:

- What is meant by:
  - system software
  - application software
- Examples of both types of software
- The need for, and functions of, operating systems (OS) and utility programs
- That the OS handles management of the:
  - processor(s)
  - memory
  - I/O devices
  - applications
  - security.

4 Computer systems

4 Computer systems

Learning objectives:

- *Know that there are different levels of programming language:*
  - *low level language*
  - *high-level language*
- *Explain the main differences between low-level and high-level languages*
- *Know that machine code and assembly language are considered to be low-level languages and explain the differences between them*
- *Understand that ultimately all programming code written in high-level or assembly languages must be translated into machine code*
- *Understand that machine code is expressed in binary and is specific to a processor or family of processors*
- *Understand the advantages and disadvantages of low-level language programming compared with high-level language programming*
- *Understand that there are three common types of program translator:*
  - *interpreter*
  - *compiler*
  - *assembler*
- *Explain the main differences between these three types of translator*
- *Understand when it would be appropriate to use each type of translator.*

Information
EDSAC film:
https://www.youtube.com/watch?v=6v4Juzn10gM
Maurice Wilkes' 1976 commentary on the 1951 film about how EDSAC was used in practice.

4.4 Classification of programming languages and translators

Levels of programming language

There are two levels of programming language:

- low-level language
- high-level language.

Low-level programming languages

There are two levels of low-level programming languages:

- machine code
- assembly language.

EDSAC and machine code

On May 6th, 1949, EDSAC ran its first program which printed a table of squares for integers in the range 0 to 99. The program took two minutes to run. The program of order codes had been punched on paper tape as 5-bit binary codes (see *Figure 4.5.1.3* in *Chapter 4.5.1*).

The order codes represented arithmetic and logical orders, shifts, jumps, data transfer orders, input and output orders and stop orders.

The word "order" was literally an order for EDSAC to do something.

These order codes were the first programming language, a low-level language known as **machine code** that was interpreted directly by the hardware of EDSAC.

Two examples of these order codes are shown in *Table 4.4.1* where each 5-bit order code is expressed as a single letter.

The single letter order codes were typed on a machine that punched the corresponding 5-bit code directly onto paper tape (see Information panel opposite for the 1951 film on how EDSAC was used in practice).

Addresses were also expressed in decimal and then translated into binary.

Letter form of order code	5-bit binary equivalent of order code	Address	Description
A	11100	n	Add the content of location n to the accumulator.
S	01100	n	Subtract the content of location n from the accumulator.

Table 4.4.1 Examples of EDSAC order codes

4 Computer systems

> **Key concept**
>
> **Machine code:**
> Machine code is a language consisting of bit patterns/binary codes that a machine can interpret, i.e. execute. For this reason, machine code is referred to as executable binary code.

Figure 4.4.1 shows a snippet of an EDSAC order code program. Each character represents a 5-bit code.

> T123SE84SPSPSP10000SP1000SP100SP10SP1S
>
> QS#SA40S!S&S@SO43SO33SPSA46S
>
> T65ST129SA35ST34SE61ST48SA47ST65SA33SA40S

Figure 4.4.1 EDSAC order code

Machine code is a language consisting of **bit patterns/binary codes** that a machine can interpret, i.e. execute. For this reason, machine code is referred to as **executable binary code**. For example, the EDSAC executable binary code instruction

$$0010100000010101$$

means "transfer the content of the accumulator to storage location 21."

> **Key concept**
>
> **Machine code instruction:**
> A machine code instruction is an operation which a machine is capable of carrying out.

A **machine code instruction** is an operation which a machine is capable of carrying out, i.e. the processor in the central processing unit. This direct relationship with the hardware gives machine code instructions their **low-level classification**. Therefore, higher-level operations for which there is no direct machine counterpart have to be broken down into a sequence of machine code instructions.

Each type of processor or family of processors, e.g. ARM Cortex, has its own specific machine code instruction set. Today, the set of order codes of the EDSAC would be called its instruction set.

> **Key concept**
>
> **Low-level programming language:**
> The direct relationship with the hardware gives machine code instructions their low-level classification.

What is a machine code program?

A **machine code language program** is a program consisting of executable binary codes.

> ### Questions
>
> 1. What is machine code?
> 2. What is a machine code instruction?
> 3. Why is machine code classified as a low-level programming language?

Assembly language

Writing programs directly in machine code is challenging.

The EDSAC programmers wrote their programs using letters for the operation to be performed and addresses in decimal using the digit characters '0'..'9'.

The hardware on which they typed these letters and digit characters was wired to punch paper tape with the 5-bit equivalent of each.

We would call the form of the program shown in *Figure 4.4.1* which uses letters, **an assembly language program**.

In assembly language, a (**symbolic**) **name** is assigned to each operation/instruction code.

The operation/instruction code name is called a **mnemonic** or memory jogger.

4.4 Classification of programming languages and translators

The operation code mnemonic should describe in some way what the instruction does, e.g. LDR means LoaD a Register, ADD means add - see *Table 4.4.2.* The address field &1234 is expressed in hexadecimal (& is used to indicate this).

Assembly language	Description
LDR R_d, &1234	LDR means LoaD a Register with content of a memory location or word, R_d is the symbolic name for the register, &1234 is the memory location's address expressed in hexadecimal.
ADD R_d, R_n, R_m	ADD means add content of registers R_n and R_m, store result in register R_d.
STR R_d, &4321	STR means STore the content of the specified Register in a memory location or word.

Table 4.4.2 Some assembly language instructions

There is a **ONE-to-ONE mapping** between an assembly language instruction and its equivalent machine code language instruction.

For example,

LDR R_d, &1234 might be assembled to 000000 0001 01001000110100

The one-to-one mapping makes translating instruction mnemonics into the binary of machine code a simple task that can be assigned to a computer. The translator is called an **assembler**.

Assembly language is often used to develop software for embedded systems and for controlling specific hardware components.

An embedded computer system is loosely defined as any device that includes a programmable computer but which is not intended to be a general purpose computer like a desktop PC. Cars are full of embedded computer systems such as an antilock brake system (ABS) and an engine management system. Embedded systems interface with sensors and actuators (a device for controlling a mechanism) at a very low level. Hence, the need to program at a low level.

The Internet of Things (IoT) is connecting to more and more remote devices consisting of sensors and actuators in embedded systems. This has resulted in a rising demand for assembly language programmers to program these systems.

The input/output hardware controllers of devices such as hard disks operate at a low level. It is therefore appropriate to use assembly language for programming these components of a computer system. These programs are called device drivers.

Key concept

Assembly language:
Assembly language is the symbolic form of machine code. Each operation/instruction code of machine code is assigned a symbolic name or mnemonic describing what the instruction does, e.g. ADD.
There is a ONE-to-ONE mapping between an assembly language instruction and its equivalent machine code language instruction.

Questions

4. What is assembly language code?

5. What is the mapping between assembly language instructions and machine code?

6. What language translator is required to translate assembly language into machine code?

4 Computer systems

> **Key concept**
>
> **High-level programming language (HLL):**
> High-level programming languages are problem-oriented and therefore closer to English than they are to the machine. This means that the mapping from a high-level language statement to machine code will be a one-to-many mapping because each high-level language statement will need to be broken down into several machine code operations.

> **Information**
>
> **GNU Fortran:**
> GNU Fortran is the primary open source version of the Fortran compiler widely used both in and out of academia. It is one of the Fortran compilers available for the Raspberry Pi.

> **Key fact**
>
> **Advantages of programming in machine code and assembly language:**
> Hand-coded assembly language when assembled can
> - achieve a smaller memory footprint in machine code than compiled high-level language code
> - achieve better code optimisation than compiled high-level language code and therefore code that will run faster
> - directly access registers and low-level operating system routines which is not possible with most high-level programming languages.

High-level languages (HLL)

As the 1951 EDSAC film showed, a problem had to be recast by hand into a form that could use the machine code language of EDSAC. Wouldn't it be much better if the problem could be expressed in a programming language much closer to the problem space (i.e. in a language easier for programmers to understand), leaving the task of translating to machine code to the computer? This thought led to the development in the 1950s of high-level languages, some of which are still used. For example, Fortran (1957) was designed for numerical applications and is still used by mathematicians, scientists and engineers, today.

High-level languages (HLL) are closer to English than they are to the machine. This means that the mapping from a high-level language statement to machine code will be a *one-to-many mapping* because each high-level language statement will need to be broken down into several machine code operations. For example, the assignment statement

$$x = y + z$$

when translated could become in the assembly language form of machine code

$$LDR\ R_0, \&1234$$
$$LDR\ R_1, \&1235$$
$$ADD\ R_2, R_0, R_1$$
$$STR\ R_2, \&1236$$

> **Questions**
>
> 7 What is meant by the term *high-level programming language*?
>
> 8 What is the mapping between high-level language statements and machine code?

Advantages of programming in machine code and assembly language compared with HLL programming

High-level language programs are converted into machine code by a translator called a *compiler*. Most compilers attempt to optimise the machine code which is produced. The compiler scans the machine code to see if it contains any unnecessary code which it then attempts to remove or adapt. Fewer machine code instructions means the code will take up less memory (smaller footprint) as well as running more quickly when executed. However, the process is not perfect, for example, where floating-point operations are concerned. In embedded computer systems, where speed of execution is paramount or memory is at a premium, the compiled code can be examined by hand and sections that are not already optimised replaced by hand-coded assembly language code, which is then assembled into machine code.

For short sections of code which need to run quickly or take up little space, it may be better to code directly in assembly language. Some high-level programming languages allow assembly language code to be embedded (inline) in the HLL program to take advantage of the time and space efficiency of assembly language coding.

Assembly language and machine code programming allow **direct access to registers** and low-level operating system routines which is not generally possible with most high-level language programming languages.

> ## Questions
>
> 9. State **three** advantages of programming in assembly language compared with programming in a high-level language.

Disadvantages of programming in machine code and assembly language compared with HLL programming

Code written in assembly language or machine code is **less readable** than code written in a high-level language and therefore **more difficult to understand and maintain**, **debug** and **write without making errors**. Code written in assembly language or machine code uses the instruction set of a particular processor (processor family). It is therefore **machine dependent** and will only execute on processors that use this instruction set. High-level languages are **machine independent**. An HLL program is expressed in an **English-like language** which is turned into machine code by a compiler. As long as a compiler exists for a particular instruction set, the HLL program may be **ported to** and its compiled version run on a computer with a different instruction set processor from the one it was written on. HLL programs are **easier to understand** and therefore **maintain** than assembly language programs because they are written using statements that are close to English. They are **less error-prone** when writing for the same reason.

> ## Key fact
>
> **Disadv. of programming in machine code and assembly language:**
> Code written in assembly language or machine code is less readable than code written in a high-level language and so more difficult to
> - understand and maintain
> - debug
> - write without making errors
>
> Code written in assembly language or machine code is machine dependent making it difficult to port to a different instruction set processor compared with code written using high-level languages which do port readily because they are not machine-oriented.

> ## Questions
>
> 10. State **three** disadvantages of programming in assembly language compared with programming in a high-level language.

Types of program translator

There are three types of program translator:

- Assembler
- Compiler
- Interpreter.

Role of an assembler

Programs written in assembly language have to be translated into machine code before they can be executed. This is done with an **assembler**.

Machine code is a language that the machine can execute, i.e. it is executable binary code (binary patterns for which machine operations are defined).

Assembly language is the mnemonic form of these executable binary codes. Thus there is a one-to-one correspondence between an assembly language statement and its machine code equivalent: one assembly language statement maps to one machine code statement. This is in contrast to a high-level language statement which typically maps to several machine code statements.

Role of a compiler

A **compiler** is a program that reads a program (**the source code**) written in a high-level programming language (the source language) and translates it into an equivalent program (**the object code**) in another language - the target language. As an important part of this translation process, the compiler reports the presence of errors in the source code program.

A compiler translates (compiles) a high-level programming language source code program into a **separate and independently executable object code target language program**. The target language program or object code produced by the process could be

- Machine code of an actual machine (in which case the compiler is called a native language compiler)
- Intermediate code which can, if necessary, be interpreted by an interpreter, e.g. Java bytecode is an intermediate language produced by a Java compiler
- Executable code for execution by a virtual machine.

A compiler translates one high-level language statement into several machine code or target language statements.

A compiler only translates a high-level language program (the whole of the program), it does not execute it.

The process that the compiler engages in is called **compiling**.

Key principle

Assembler:
An assembler translates assembly language into machine code.
One assembly language statement maps to one machine code statement.

Key principle

Compiler:
A compiler translates a high-level programming language source code program into a separate and independently executable object code target language program. Object code is typically machine code.

A compiler translates one high-level language statement into several machine code or target language statements.

4.4 Classification of programming languages and translators

> **Did you know?**
>
> **A compiler consists of several stages:**
> - Lexical analysis – splits the source into user-defined "words", e.g. variable identifiers and language-defined "words", e.g. While
> - Syntax analysis – checks that statements are grammatically correct
> - Semantic analysis – e.g. type checking, "A" + 3.142 is incorrect as you can't add a real to a string
> - Intermediate code generation
> - Code optimising
> - Code generation

Role of an interpreter

An interpreter is a program that executes a high-level programming language program, statement by statement, by recognising the statement type of a statement, e.g. X = X + 1, and then calling a pre-written procedure/function for the statement type, to execute the statement. Therefore, an interpreter does not, unlike a compiler, produce an independently executable target language equivalent of the source language program. The application of interpreter to a source code program is called interpreting.

The differences between compilation and interpretation

The major differences between the compilation and interpretation are:

- An interpreter both "translates" and executes whereas a compiler only translates.
- A compiler produces a separate independently executable form of the source code program whereas an interpreter does not.
- A compiler is not needed when target form of source program is executed whereas in the case of the interpreter, execution requires the source code form of the program together with the interpreter, i.e. the interpreter needs to be available on the machine where the program is being run.
- If an interpreter is used then only the source code form of program is needed to execute the program whereas, if a compiler is used then the object code form of program is needed in order to execute the program.
- Interpreters are usually easier to write than compilers.
- With the compiler approach, if an error is discovered while the program is executing, the source form of program must be located. An editor and the source form of the program must be loaded. The error must be pin-pointed which is not always easy and then corrected. The compiler must be loaded and a compilation carried out. The new target form of program must then be loaded and executed. With an interpreter, the execution is halted at the point where the error occurs. The interpreter gives precise details of location of error. The error is corrected with an editor which may be co-located with interpreter. If it isn't, an editor will have to be loaded. However, no time-consuming compilation is involved and execution can resume immediately.

> **Key principle**
>
> **Interpreter:**
> An interpreter is a program that executes a high level programming language program, statement by statement, by recognising the statement type of a statement and then calling a pre-written procedure/function for the statement type, to execute the statement.

> **Key principle**
>
> **Interpreter vs compiler:**
> An interpreter both "translates" and executes whereas a compiler only translates.

> **Key principle**
>
> **Interpreter vs compiler:**
> A compiler produces a separate independently executable form of the source code program whereas an interpreter does not.

> **Key point**
>
> **Ultimately all programming code written in high-level or assembly languages must be translated into machine code:**
> An electronic digital computer can only execute machine code instructions. Therefore assembly and High Level Languages (HLL) cannot be executed directly without the use of a translator.
> A HLL may be executed indirectly by using an interpreter but the interpreter in order to execute must be presented to the computer in machine code form.
> Remember that the language of an electronic digital computer is binary.

Key principle

When to use assembly language:
Where speed of execution and/or direct access to hardware is required, use assembly language and an assembler.

Key principle

Interpreter vs compiler:
Compiled code which has been compiled into machine code of the computer will execute a lot faster than its interpreted source code equivalent (i.e. interpreter + the source code equivalent of the compiled code).

Key principle

Interpreter vs compiler:
Where rapid debugging and immediate feedback on errors is required including pinpointing the location of both syntax and runtime errors, use an interpreter.

Key principle

Interpreter vs compiler:
Where a separate executable that can execute independently of its source code equivalent is required, use a compiler.

Questions

13. Give **two** reasons why programs are still written in assembly language.

14. Given a choice, under what circumstances would it be preferable to use:
    (a) a compiler;
    (b) an interpreter?

Questions

11. Explain the role of each of the following:
    (a) assembler (b) compiler (c) interpreter

12. State **three** differences between compilation and interpretation.

Situations in which assemblers, compilers and interpreters would be appropriate

Assemblers

For time-critical sections of code where execution speed is important, e.g. interrupt service routines, assembly language still has a role to play because in the hands of a skilled programmer, assembly language code can be written that is highly optimised for speed. As an assembler simply translates one assembly language statement into one machine code statement, that optimisation is preserved. Compilers can optimise code but the result cannot be guaranteed to be fully optimised for the given hardware. In the pecking order of execution speed, interpreters come after compilers.

Assembly language is still used where direct access to hardware is required e.g. processor registers or I/O controller registers. This is the case when writing device drivers, e.g. a screen driver. In this instance an assembler would be required to translate the assembly language program into machine code.

Compilers and interpreters

It is considerably more productive to write programs in high-level languages than in assembly language. There are relatively few programmers who are skilled in writing assembly language programs compared with the number of programmers skilled in writing in one or more high-level programming languages.

Compiled code which has been compiled into machine code of the computer will execute a lot faster than its interpreted source code equivalent (i.e. interpreter + the source code equivalent of the compiled code).

The immediate feedback and ease of locating errors in source code give interpreters an advantage over compilers when developing programs. This advantage is particularly beneficial for novice programmers or when programs are being prototyped and the write, compile, debug, edit cycle can be too time consuming.

Compiling has an advantage over interpreting because it produces a separate executable which means that the source code program does not have to be distributed. There are plenty of situations where this is desirable such as when producing commercial software or where there is a requirement is to protect the algorithm or coding technique used.

4.4 Classification of programming languages and translators

Questions

15 Two computer programs that add two integers are shown in *Table 4.4.3*.

One is written in a high-level language and one is written in a low-level language.

Table 4.4.4 gives three correct reasons why computer programs are most commonly written in high-level languages (HLL) instead of low-level languages are true. Tick these **three** correct reasons.

High-level program	Low-level program
r = 5	0100 0101
s = 3	0100 0011
t = r + t	1000 0000
	0001 0010
	1100 0011
	1110 1100

Table 4.4.3

Reason	Tick three boxes
A HLL programs are easier to debug.	
B HLL programs always run faster.	
C Less time-consuming for a programmer to write a HLL program.	
D HLL program code can be easier for humans to understand.	
E Computers understand only HLL programs.	

Table 4.4.4

16 The low-level program shown in *Table 4.4.3* is written in machine code.

Give **two** reasons why it would have been better for the programmer to have used assembly language instead of machine code.

In this chapter you have covered:

- That there are different levels of programming language:
  - low level language
  - high-level language
- The main differences between low-level and high-level languages
- That machine code and assembly language are considered to be low-level languages
- The differences between machine code and assembly language
- That ultimately all programming code written in high-level or assembly languages must be translated into machine code
- That machine code is expressed in binary and is specific to a processor or family of processors
- The advantages and disadvantages of low-level language programming compared with high-level language programming
- That there are three common types of program translator:
  - interpreter
  - compiler
  - assembler
- The main differences between these three types of translator
- When it would be appropriate to use each type of translator.

4 Computer systems

4 Computer systems

Learning objectives:

- *Explain the von Neumann architecture.*

4.5.1 Systems architecture

Von Neumann architecture

Between 1945 and 1951 John von Neumann (*Figure 4.5.1.1*) created a design for a digital electronic computer as a system consisting of

- a memory called **Main Memory**, containing instructions and data
- a calculating unit called the **Arithmetic and Logic Unit** (ALU), for performing arithmetic and logical operations
- a **Control Unit**, to fetch and interpret (decode and execute) instructions stored in main memory
- an input device and an output device
- a method of connecting these together called a **bus** consisting of a collection of wires (this bus is called the **System Bus**).

Figure 4.5.1.1 John von Neumann

Figure 4.5.1.2 shows the basic architecture of John von Neumann's computer.

The combination of **Control Unit + Arithmetic and Logic Unit (ALU)** is called the **Central Processing Unit (CPU)** in modern computer systems.

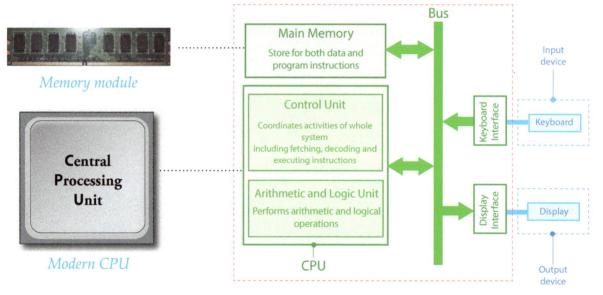

Figure 4.5.1.2 Von Neumann architecture

Lesson activity

1. Download Activity 1 from www.educational-computing.co.uk/GCSE/Ch4.5.1/Activity1.pdf.
   This activity consists of the six people engaging in executing a list of numbered instructions.
   The six people are required to perform the following roles

   1. Memory   2. Control Unit   3. Arithmetic and Logic Unit
   4. Keyboard   5. Display   6. Bus

4 Computer systems

The von Neumann architecture was an improvement over the program-controlled computers of the 1940s, such as Colossus and ENIAC, which had no memory so had to be programmed by inserting patch leads (cables) to route data and control signals between various functional units - Figure 4.5.1.4.

In the ENIAC, patch leads needed to be unplugged and then re-plugged in a new position to reprogram the computer to complete a different task.

Von Neumann's design is much more flexible because it can be reprogrammed by simple loading a different program, as well as the program's data, into read-write main memory (random access memory (RAM)).

Programs and their data are kept ready to be loaded into main memory from another storage medium called **backing store** (or **secondary storage** to differentiate this type of storage from main memory (primary memory)). Punched paper tape was used for secondary storage in the early days (Figure 4.5.1.3).

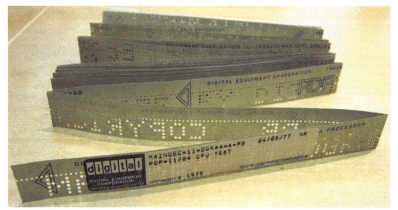

Figure 4.5.1.3 Paper tape used to store data and computer programs in the 1950's

A paper-tape reader attached to the keyboard was used to input a program and its data from the paper tape on which the program and its data were represented by a series of punched holes.

Computers based on von Neumann's architecture are sometimes called **stored-program computers** because their programs and data, if necessary, can be loaded into main memory from a secondary storage medium, e.g. magnetic disk.

Once finished with they are unloaded (removed from main memory) and replaced in main memory by another program until needed again.

Loading and unloading are operations carried out by the stored-program computer.

Information

The University of Manchester's Small-Scale Experimental Machine is generally recognised as the world's first electronic computer that ran a stored program - an event that occurred on 21st June 1948. However, the EDSAC (designed and built at Cambridge University) is considered the first complete and fully operational electronic digital stored program computer. It ran its first program on 6th May 1949. The design was inspired by John von Neumann's First Draft of a Report on the EDVAC.
EDVAC, America's first electronic digital stored program computer wasn't available to run until August 1949.

Figure 4.5.1.4 ENIAC computer being reprogrammed by changing the wiring (U.S. Army photo, http://ftp.arl.army.mil/~mike/comphist/)

4.5.1 Systems architecture

Questions

1. Von Neumann's design for a digital electronic computer consisted of an input device, an output device and four other components. Name these **four** other components.

Lesson activity

2. Download Activity 2 from www.educational-computing.co.uk/GCSE/Ch4.5.1/Activity2.pdf.
This activity is similar to Activity 1 in using six people to perform the roles of the parts of a computer system but differs in the way that the two integers are obtained. This time the two integers are fetched from memory.

Characteristics of the von Neumann architecture

A computer system with a von Neumann architecture is characterised by

- Memory (common name Main Memory) which is used to store both program instructions and data
- Data from Main Memory and from devices are accessed in the same way via the bus system
- Data and instructions in Main Memory are indistinguishable from each other.

In a digital computer, instructions and data are represented internally by numbers. If these numbers are stored together in Main Memory then it becomes difficult without guidance to distinguish numbers which represent instructions from numbers which represent data.

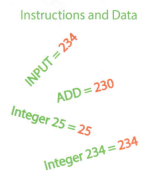

For example,

- The instruction INPUT might be represented internally by the number 234 and
- A datum (value) which is to be interpreted as the integer 234 might also be represented internally by the number 234
- The contents of Main Memory from beginning to end just consists of numbers - *Figure 4.5.1.5*
- Some numbers represent instructions
- Some numbers represent data (values to be manipulated by instructions or values which are the results of such manipulation or values from input devices)
- Some numbers represent memory addresses, and
- Some numbers are simply rubbish left over from previous computer activities.

It is the logic in computer programs that instructs a computer to treat one number as an instruction and another as a value.

Sometimes the logic of a computer program is faulty and the computer tries erroneously to execute data. This situation is exploited by computer viruses which are first downloaded as data but then, by a bit of trickery, can be treated as programs and executed.

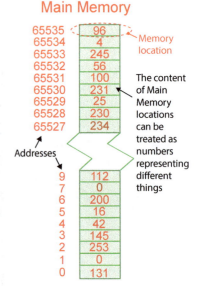

Figure 4.5.1.5 Main Memory consisting of consecutively numbered storage locations

Questions

2. Select the letter from the list below which labels the answer which you think best describes what Main Memory stores temporarily in a digital electronic computer based on von Neumann's architecture
   - **A** Instructions
   - **B** Data
   - **C** Data or instructions, but not both
   - **D** Data and instructions

3. Explain what is meant by "Data and instructions in Main Memory are indistinguishable from each other".

4. Select the letter from the list below which labels the answer which you think best describes how data from Main Memory and from devices are accessed in von Neumann's architecture
   - **A** Via the keyboard
   - **B** Via the bus system
   - **C** Via the control unit
   - **D** Via the Arithmetic and Logic Unit

Lesson activity

3. Download Activity 3 from www.educational-computing.co.uk/GCSE/Ch4.5.1/Activity3.pdf.
   In both Activity 1 and Activity 2, the operations performed by six people were coordinated by arrangement but not by time. If the operations are to be coordinated by time then a clock is required.

Von Neumann computer system as a collection of subsystems

Figure 4.5.1.6 shows the major subsystems (components) of a computer system based on the von Neumann architecture.

The subsystems are classified as either **internal** or **external**.

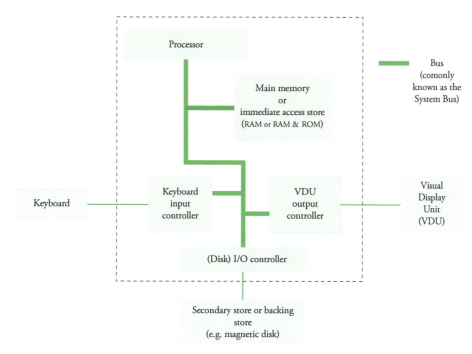

Figure 4.5.1.6 Block diagram of the von Neumann architecture

4.5.1 Systems architecture

Internal subsystems

The internal components are

- **Processor or Central Processing Unit (CPU)** - contains the control unit, the arithmetic and logic unit, registers (a register is a store with its own identity used for storing a single number temporarily which could represent an address, a value, an instruction or the status of something), and a clock for sequencing operations within the computer system

- **Main memory** (normally a mix of RAM and ROM)

- **I/O controllers** - input only, output only, both input and output - which connect the CPU to input and output devices, and secondary storage

- **Bus** - a collection of wires connecting the internal components, data/signals are transmitted along the bus from one component to another.

External components

The external components do not interact directly with the CPU but are largely on the periphery of the computer system and are known, therefore, as peripherals or peripheral devices - for example, the keyboard, visual display unit (e.g. flat screen monitor), printer, magnetic disk drive.

Interaction between CPU and peripherals

The main processor, or CPU, exchanges data with a peripheral device through an **I/O controller**.

Peripheral devices are not connected directly to the CPU because the former often operate with signal levels, protocols and power requirements which are different from those used by a CPU.

Therefore, peripherals are not under the direct control of the CPU instead they are controlled indirectly through an I/O controller.

> **Key concept**
>
> **Peripheral:**
> A peripheral is a device that is connected to the computer system but which is not under the direct control of the processor. Instead the processor interacts with the peripheral indirectly via the peripheral's I/O controller which sits electrically between the peripheral and the system bus. Examples of peripherals are keyboard, VDU, mouse, printer.

In this chapter you have covered:

- The von Neumann architecture
    - internal components
        - processor or Central Processing Unit (CPU)
        - main memory (RAM or a mix of RAM and ROM)
        - I/O controllers - input only, output only, both input and output
        - bus - collections of wires connecting components
    - external subsystems
        - components not connected directly to the processor (CPU)
        - they are called peripherals, e.g. keyboard, printer, flat screen monitor, magnetic disk drive.

4 Computer systems

4 Computer systems

Learning objectives:

- *Explain the role and operation of main memory and the following major components of a central processing unit (CPU) within the von Neumann architecture:*
  - *arithmetic logic unit*
  - *control unit*
  - *clock*
  - *register*
  - *bus.*

4.5.2 Systems architecture

Main memory

The basic requirement of memory is to be able to write some information into it, leave it there, and return later to read it.

- Main memory serves this purpose in von Neumann's architecture.

Figure 4.5.2.1 Single memory cell

- It consists of a collection of individual storage cells, each capable of storing a single bit - *Figure 4.5.2.1*.

These are grouped together into rows of a fixed size, e.g. 8 cells, and called **memory locations**. *Figure 4.5.2.2* shows a single row or memory location with contents 01011100.

| 0 | 1 | 0 | 1 | 1 | 1 | 0 | 0 |

Figure 4.5.2.2 Single memory location consisting of eight memory cells

- Each memory location is assigned a unique physical address and the memory locations are organised together as shown in *Figure 4.5.2.3* with addresses from 0 upwards.

In *Figure 4.5.2.3*, addresses are expressed in 8-bit binary.

The lowest memory location is assigned the unique memory address 00000000, the next 00000001, and so on, with the memory address increasing by one each time.

The highest memory location is assigned the last possible address in 8-bit binary, 11111111.

In this example, there are **256** memory locations.

The size in bits of a memory location is normally a power of 2, e.g. $2^3 = 8$ bits as shown in *Figure 4.5.2.3*.

Information

Magnetic core memory was the predominant form of random access main memory (RAM) for 20 years between about 1955 and 1975. Such memory was often just called core memory, or, informally, core.
Magnetic-core memory uses the magnetisation of tiny magnetic rings, the cores, to write and read information.

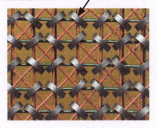

Each core represents one bit of information. When not being read or written, the cores maintain the last value they had, even when power is turned off. This made them non-volatile.

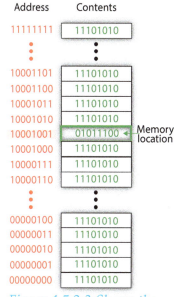

Figure 4.5.2.3 Shows the current contents of a block of 256 memory locations, with each location designed to store 8 bits

4 Computer systems

> **Key concept**
> **Memory location:**
> A memory location is the smallest addressable unit of memory.

A memory location is the smallest addressable unit of memory:

- Nothing smaller than a memory location can be accessed directly
- The contents of a memory location are read by selecting it by address and copying the contents,
  e.g. the memory location in *Figure 4.5.2.3* with address **10001001** has contents **01011100** expressed in binary
- The contents of a memory location are changed by selecting it by address and replacing its current contents by another value.

Figure 4.5.2.4 shows a single location selected by address when the CPU sends the location's address, encoded as on and off signals, along the bus connecting the CPU to the main memory. This bus is called the **system bus**.

If the requested action is reading from memory then the contents of the memory location shown in *Figure 4.5.2.4* appear on the bus wires connecting main memory to CPU.

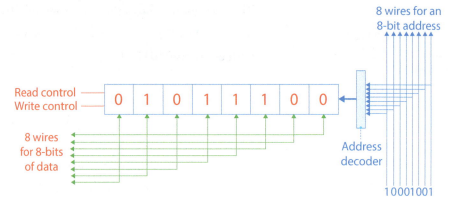

Figure 4.5.2.4 Single memory location consisting of eight memory cells

In von Neumann's architecture, reading from and writing to main memory is made possible by dividing the system bus[1] into address bus, data bus and control bus as shown in *Figure 4.5.2.5*.

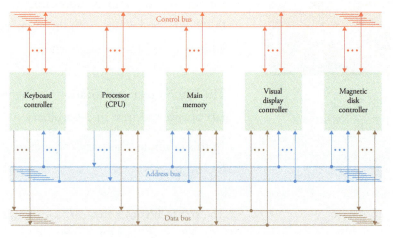

Figure 4.5.2.5 Von Neumann architecture showing the subdivision of the system bus into data bus, address bus and control bus

---

1 You do not need to know that the system bus is divided into address, data and control bus.

4.5.2 Systems architecture

Reading from main memory

The 256 main memory locations shown in *Figure 4.5.2.3* are shown in *Figure 4.5.2.6* packaged into a single memory chip (integrated circuit) of 256 locations each capable of storing one byte of data which can be any of the following

- an instruction
- a number
- an address
- a letter.

For a program to be executed it must first be loaded into the main memory of the computer. The computer can then start the execution as follows[2]:

- The CPU sends an address to main memory to start retrieving the program
- This address just consists of a series of 1s and 0s encoded as on and off signals on the address bus wires connecting the CPU to the main memory
- The main memory doesn't do anything with this address until the CPU turns on the Read wire
- When the Read wire is turned on by the CPU, the main memory automatically sends whatever is in the addressed main memory location back to the CPU via the data bus wires connecting the main memory to the CPU. The Read wire connects the CPU to the Read pin on the memory chip.

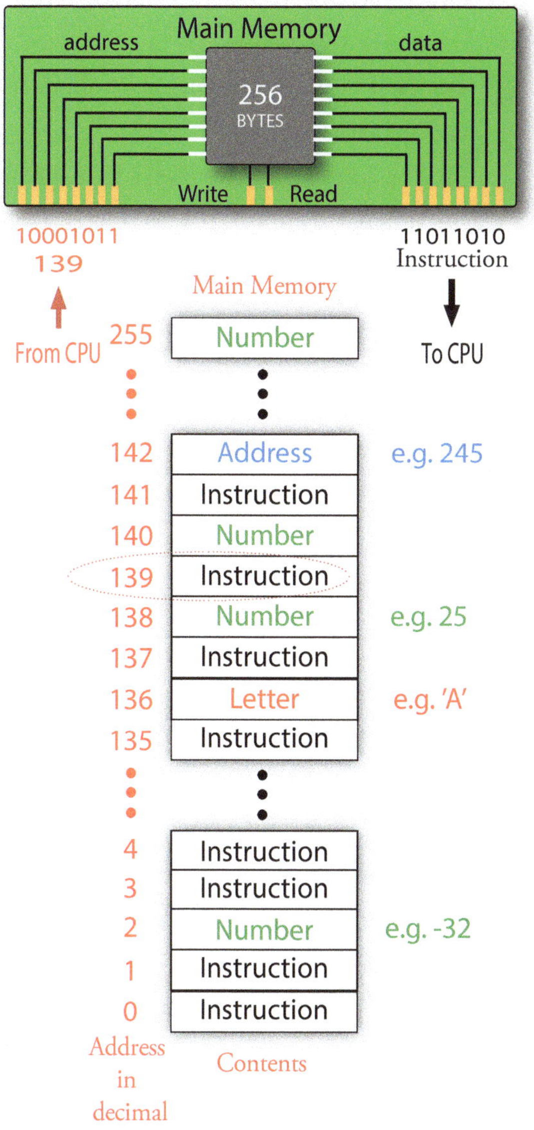

For example, to fetch the instruction at memory address decimal 139 (binary 10001011), the CPU sends 10001011 to the address input of the memory chip (*yellow pins connected to address wires in Figure 4.5.2.6*).

On turning on the Read wire connected to the read pin of this memory chip, the addressed memory location's contents, 11011010, appear on the data pins (*yellow pins connected to the data wires in Figure 4.5.2.6*). This instruction is retrieved by the CPU from the data bus connected to the data pins and processed. Once the CPU has dealt with this instruction it sends another address to main memory, turns on the Read wire and gets the next addressed location's contents. This process is repeated until the program has finished executing.

Writing to main memory

Writing to a memory location in main memory is done as follows

- The CPU sends the address of the memory location from CPU to main memory along the address bus wires of the system bus
- The CPU sends what it wants to write to main memory along the data bus wires of the system bus
- The Write wire is turned on and contents of the memory location are then changed.

---

2   The remainder of this "Reading from main memory" section whilst useful to know, covers more detail than required for AQA's GCSE specification 8525.

Figure 4.5.2.6 A 256 byte memory chip mounted on a circuit board for main memory

4 Computer systems

> **Questions**
>
> ① For each of the statements below indicate whether the statement is true or false by choosing the appropriate letter.
>
> (a) The contents of a memory location are read by selecting it by address and copying the contents.
>
> **A** True
>
> **B** False
>
> (b) A memory location is made up of a collection of memory cells each of which can store one bit.
>
> **A** True
>
> **B** False
>
> (c) The contents of a memory location are changed by selecting it by address and replacing its current contents by another value.
>
> **A** True
>
> **B** False

> **Key term**
>
> **Random Access Memory (RAM)**
>
> Memory that permits access to any of its address locations (cells) in any desired sequence with similar access time to each location.
>
> The term, as commonly used, denotes a read/write memory with unlimited data rewrite capability and similar read and write times.

RAM

Memory is labelled **random access** if

- Cells can be accessed in any order
- The time to access any cell is the same wherever it is in memory.

Today's computers use a type of semiconductor memory for main memory called **dynamic RAM** or **DRAM**.

Information/data stored in modern RAM is lost when the power is removed. Therefore, modern RAM is said to be **volatile**.

ROM

- There is another type of random-access memory called **Read Only Memory** or **ROM** that can also be present in main memory, i.e. its memory locations can be addressed by the processor (CPU) in any order.

> **Key term**
>
> **Volatile memory:**
> A memory in which the data content is lost when electrical power is removed.

- This is memory that can be read from but not written to (during normal operation).

  It is also **non-volatile** which means that information/data stored in ROM is retained when the power is removed.

ROM was used in early desktop computers (PCs) for the BIOS.
Software stored in the BIOS

> **Key term**
>
> **Non-volatile memory:**
> A memory in which the data content is retained when electrical power is removed.

- initialises and tests the system hardware components
- loads a boot loader or an operating system from a storage device.

> **Information**
>
> **Flash ROM:**
> Modern PCs, use a different technology called Flash ROM for the BIOS. This is non-volatile random-access memory which can be read from and, if necessary, written to.

> **Information**
>
> **ROM:**
> Technically, the ROMs in use today are actually non-volatile RAM because they can be written to or erased by the processor. However, the convention is to use the term ROM because erasing and rewriting is expected to be rare.

4.5.2 Systems architecture

PC activity

1. Download CPU-Z from http://www.cpuid.com/softwares/cpu-z.html. Using CPU-Z record the following:
   (a) The CPU that your computer is using
   (b) The type of RAM your system is using.

Questions

2. For each of the two statements below indicate whether the statement is true or false by choosing the appropriate letter.
   (a) ROM is volatile memory.
      A True
      B False
   (b) RAM used in main memory can be read from and written to.
      A True
      B False

Key concept

Bus:
A bus is a collection of wires through which data/signals are transmitted from one component to another. The external or system bus in a computer consists of a collections of wires providing pathways between the CPU, memory modules (RAM), chipsets, secondary storage and peripherals.

Key term

Bus width:
The number of bits that can be placed on the bus in any one go.

Information

The chipset is the link between the individual components of a computer, ensuring that all components can communicate successfully with each other. Different voltage levels, clock frequencies and protocols are taken into account and converted among each other so that the different components of the computer system work together as intended.

System bus

A bus is a collection of wires through which data/signals are transmitted from one component to another.

The width of a bus is the number of bits that can be placed on the bus in one go.

The external or system bus in a computer consists of a collections of wires providing pathways between the CPU, memory modules (RAM), chipsets, secondary storage and peripherals.

The classic "system bus" is a shared bus.

It has largely disappeared from today's computer architectures and been replaced, instead, by different serial and parallel bus systems designed and developed to meet specific requirements - *Figure 4.5.2.7*.

Although no system-wide system bus exists in today's computer systems, *logically*, the manner of driving memory and peripherals has remained the same.

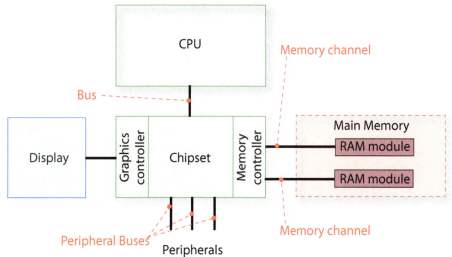

Figure 4.5.2.7 Shows main memory linked to the CPU via a memory controller located in a chipset module

Key term

(Beyond 8525 specification)
Static RAM (SRAM):
SRAM is semiconductor memory in which memory content is stored by means of flip-flops, a type of logic gate circuit with two stable states - flip and flop. Static RAM holds its contents as long as power is available and doesn't need refreshing. However, the consequence is higher power consumption than DRAM and therefore the generation of more heat.
SRAM is expensive compared with DRAM because fewer bits can be stored per SRAM chip than per DRAM chip. Therefore SRAM is restricted to storage of low capacity size, i.e. L1, L2 and L3 cache or buffer memory and registers where its superior speed of operation can be exploited. DRAM is much slower than SRAM.

Information

DRAM (beyond 8525 specification) consist of lots of tiny capacitors each of which store an amount of electrical charge to represent a single bit, more charge for 1 and less charge for 0.
Even when connected to electrical power, any stored charge drains away from the cell quite quickly so the cell needs to be refreshed every few milliseconds to reliably store data. This refreshing with electrical charge gives the memory its dynamic name.
Information/data stored in DRAM is lost when the power is removed. Therefore, DRAM is said to be volatile (RAM is not necessarily volatile - see information panel on magnetic core memory on the first page of this chapter).
Nowadays, the term RAM has come to mean random-access memory that is both read and write.

Arithmetic and Logic Unit (ALU)

The Arithmetic and Logic Unit (ALU) performs arithmetic and logical operations on data supplied in registers, storing any result in a register as shown in *Figure 4.5.2.8*.

It can perform, for example, addition and subtraction, fixed and floating point arithmetic, Boolean logic operations such as AND, OR, XOR and a range of shift operations.

The ALU[3] operation shown in *Figure 4.5.2.8* adds integer 3 to integer -5 to produce the result -2.

Information

Knowledge of specific registers is not required.

The Status Register indicates a negative result by setting its N bit to 1. In addition to the Status Register three other registers are used, $Register_A$, $Register_B$ and $Register_C$.

- A register is a store with its own identity used for storing a single number temporarily.
- It is usually constructed from the same semiconductor memory type as Static RAM or SRAM. This is semiconductor memory which is much faster to read from and write to than DRAM.

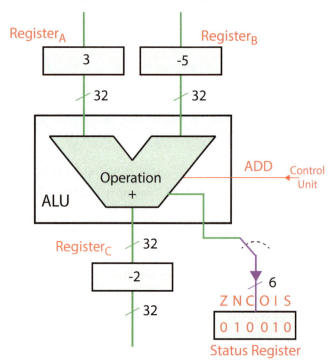

Figure 4.5.2.8 ALU performing an ADD operation

Key term

Register:
A register is a store with its own identity used for storing a single number temporarily. A central processing unit contains several registers performing different roles. Registers are usually constructed from the same semiconductor memory type as Static RAM or SRAM. This is semiconductor memory which is much faster to read from and write to than DRAM.

---

3   The remainder of this "Arithmetic and Logic Unit" section whilst useful to know, covers more detail than required for AQA's GCSE specification 8525 with the exception of the general role of registers.

4.5.2 Systems architecture

Control Unit

The control unit of the processor shown in *Figure 4.5.2.9* controls fetching, loading and storing operations.[4]

It **fetches an instruction** into the **Current Instruction Register** via the **Memory Buffer Register** and the data bus.

The control unit also

- **Decodes** the instruction to determine if it is a load, store, arithmetic operation, or logic operation
- **Executes** the instruction by
  - using the instruction's operand fields as addresses to use in load or store operations, if required, or
  - loading a memory word into a register, or
  - changing a word of memory in a store operation, or
  - controlling an arithmetic operation, e.g., ADD, or a logical operation, e.g., AND, in the Arithmetic and Logic Unit (ALU) using as operands the instruction's operand fields.

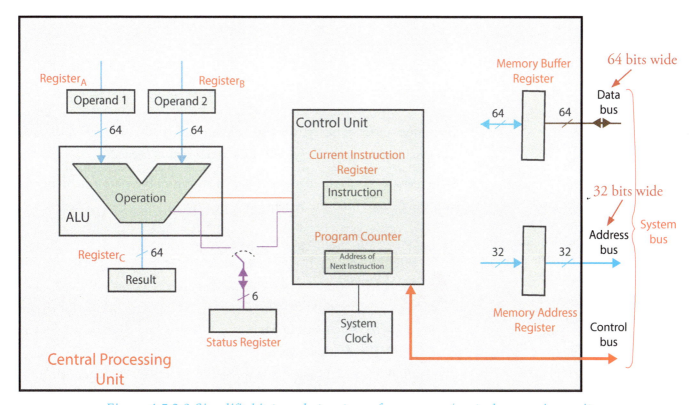

Figure 4.5.2.9 Simplified internal structure of a processor/central processing unit

---

4   The remainder of this "Control Unit" section following this sentence whilst useful to know, covers more detail than required for AQA's GCSE specification 8525.

4 Computer systems

Information

Timing:

For the computer system to work properly things must happen at the right time. This is achieved by timing signals. For example, the correct sequence for writing data to memory is first to send out the address on the address bus, and then send out the data on the data bus a few clock ticks later. Finally a pulse has to be sent out on the Write wire to actually write the data into memory. This is an example of timing.

Information

Intel CPUs are sold to operate at a specific, fixed CPU clock frequency if locked. This clock frequency is set well below the maximum frequency at which the CPU can operate. Therefore, Intel offer a variant for sale which is unlocked, i.e. the CPU clock frequency may be varied considerably. This unlocked variant is indicated by adding a "k" to the CPU's identifier, e.g. Intel's 7th generation i7 processors have a fixed CPU clock frequency version, Intel® Core™ i7-7700 and an unlocked version, Intel® Core™ i7-7700k. The locked CPU has a clock frequency of 3.6 GHz whilst the unlocked CPU's clock frequency may be overclocked up to 4.9 GHz.

Information

Timing:

The CPU needs to perform more operations per second than the motherboard, its clock (the CPU clock), is generated by taking the system clock and multiplying it by a number which is either fixed or if the CPU is unlocked, a number which can be set by the user. If unlocked then the CPU's clock can be overclocked by changing a BIOS setting, to give a higher operating clock frequency.

Clock

The operations of all components on the motherboard are synchronised by the **system clock**.

This is an oscillator which is controlled by a quartz crystal so that it produces very stable and unvarying timing signals similar to those produced by the quartz crystal controlled oscillator inside a wristwatch.

Chaos would reign if say, the CPU got out of step with main memory when fetching, decoding and executing instructions. The situation would be akin to missing the bus to school because your alarm clock went off late because it was running slow.

Each component on the motherboard takes the system clock's timing signals (a continuous train of on-off pulses as shown in *Figure 4.5.2.10*) and derives their own timing signals.

Figure 4.5.2.10 Continuous train of on-off pulses produced by clock

The various buses in the system also need timing signals, their bus clocks are also synchronised with the system clock and scaled as needed.

Main memory needs timing signals as well and again these are synchronised with and derived from the system clock.

PC activity

2. Using CPU-Z obtained from http://www.cpuid.com/softwares/cpu-z.html record the following:
   (a) The core speed in MHz
   (b) The multiplier value
   (Both displayed values, core speed and multiplier, may fluctuate in CPU-Z, so take the steadiest)
   Calculate core speed/multiplier value. This should be the system clock frequency for the motherboard. This is also the frequency of the bus connecting CPU to RAM, which is called bus speed.

Key term

Clock:

The operations of all components on the motherboard are synchronised by the system clock.

This is an oscillator which is controlled by a quartz crystal so that it produces very stable and unvarying timing signals similar to those produced by the quartz crystal controlled oscillator inside a wristwatch.

4.5.2 Systems architecture

Questions

3. Four components of a CPU are given below. For each row in *Table 4.5.2.1*, choose the letter A, B, C, or D that best matches the description.

   A. Clock
   B. Control Unit
   C. Register
   D. Arithmetic Logic Unit

Description	Letter
Decodes the current instruction	
A store with its own identity used to store a small number of bits temporarily	
A source of a continuous train of electronic pulses	
Performs a calculation	

Table 4.5.2.1

In this chapter you have covered:

- The role and operation of main memory and the following major components of a central processing unit (CPU) within the Von Neumann architecture:
  - arithmetic logic unit
  - control unit
  - clock
  - register
  - bus.

4 Computer systems

4 Computer systems

Learning objectives:
- *Explain the effect of the following on the performance of the CPU:*
  - *clock speed*
  - *number of processor cores*
  - *cache size*
  - *cache type.*

4.5.3 Systems architecture

Effect of clock speed on CPU performance

To understand the effect of clock frequency on the performance of the CPU we need to study a little background first. The following background detail is for information only.

Figure 4.5.3.1 shows a motherboard example in which

- 133 MHz SDRAM main memory is connected by a 133 MHz data bus to a 1 GHz CPU
- The motherboard's system clock operates at a speed or frequency of 133 MHz
- The motherboard's BIOS contains configuration datum 7.5 for the CPU clock multiplier
- The system clock actually oscillates at a frequency of 133.33 MHz, even though its quoted frequency is 133 MHz.
- The data bus is clocked at a frequency/speed of 133 MHz (133.33 MHz), the same as the system clock.
- The CPU obtains a value of 7.5 to use as its clock multiplier from the BIOS. The CPU clock frequency is then generated by multiplying the system clock frequency by 7.5 giving 1 GHz, **a higher frequency than its external data bus, but still synchronous with it**.

The CPU clock frequency is calculated as follows

CPU clock frequency = 133.33 MHz x 7.5 = 1000 MHz = 1 GHz.

> **Information**
>
> **Synchronous:**
> Synchronous means to be in step in time or occur at the same time.

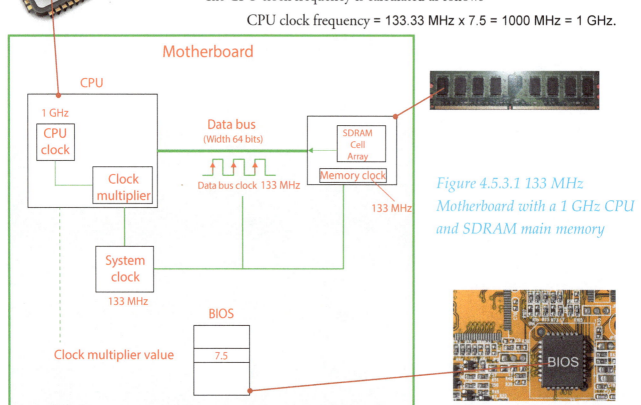

Figure 4.5.3.1 133 MHz Motherboard with a 1 GHz CPU and SDRAM main memory

4 Computer systems

Clearly, if the system clock is up-rated to operate at a higher frequency then the components that use the system clock will operate more quickly provided that these components are also up-rated.

Figure 4.5.3.2 shows some of these up-rated components on a motherboard that operates with a system clock frequency of 200 MHz.

- The processor now operates at 2.4 GHz, a frequency derived from the system clock frequency of 200 MHz multiplied by a clock multiplier of 12.
- The bus connecting this processor to the chipset of logic gates driving the memory controller and graphics controllers uses a clock frequency of 800 MHz. This is derived from the system clock.
- The memory bus uses a clock frequency of 400 MHz as the memory is now double-rate, double frequency DRAM, DDR2 - see *Figure 4.5.3.3*.

Information

AQA's specification does not require you to know the detail in Figure 4.5.3.2. This figure is included here to provide a modern context for the theory.

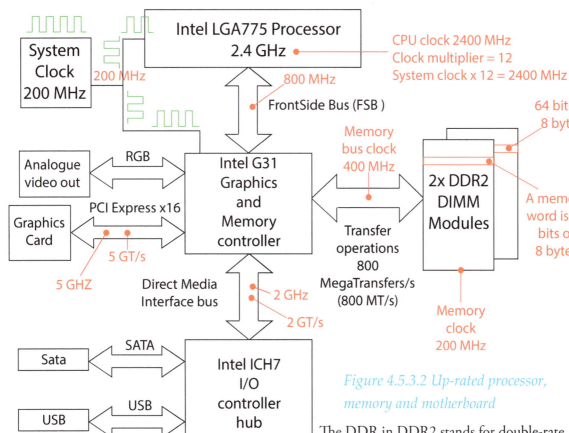

Figure 4.5.3.2 Up-rated processor, memory and motherboard

The DDR in DDR2 stands for double-rate. DDR means that two memory words can be placed on the memory bus in one memory bus clock cycle - one word on the rising edge ↑ and one word on the falling edge ↓. The 2 in DDR2 means that memory words are clocked onto the memory bus at twice the rate of the memory clock.

The latest DDR memory is DDR4. The meaning of DDR is as stated above. The 4 means that memory words are clocked onto the memory bus at four times the rate of the memory clock.

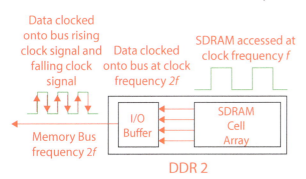

Figure 4.5.3.3 DDR2 main memory module 4 transfers per memory clock, 2 per memory bus clock

4.5.3 Systems architecture

- Let's say that the CPU executes an instruction in 2 clock cycles of the CPU clock, on average.
- If the CPU clock frequency is 1 GHz then one clock cycle lasts one nanosecond (1.0×10^{-9} seconds - light travels 30 cm in this time).
- A clock cycle is one on-off pulse of the clock signal as shown in Figure 4.5.3.4.
- Therefore on average, an instruction in this 1 GHz CPU takes 2 nanoseconds to execute.
- If the CPU clock frequency is changed to 2.4 GHz, not one but 2.4 instructions are executed in 2 nanoseconds, all other things being equal.

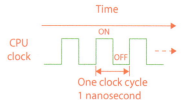

Figure 4.5.3.4 CPU clock cycles for a CPU clock frequency of 1 GHz

Information

GigaHertz (GHz):
1 GHz = 1 000 000 000 cycles per second = 1.0×10^9 cycles per second.

However, raw clock speed is not a good way to compare CPUs, unless they are from the same manufacturer, model, and family.

The reason is that the average number of cycles per instruction varies between manufacturer, model and family because CPU architecture can be different.

For example, the first Pentium CPU executed about twice as many instructions in a given number of cycles as its predecessor, the 80486 CPU.

Therefore, given the same clock speed, a Pentium I is twice as fast as a 80486 CPU. Consequently, a 133 MHz 486 CPU (such as the Intel 80486-133) is not even as fast as a 75 MHz Pentium.

Cache Memory

As CPU processor speeds were increased (i.e. CPU clock frequency increased), memory speeds (memory bus clock frequencies) were unable to keep up.

Trying to run a CPU faster than the memory from which it gets instructions and data has an adverse effect on CPU performance.

Main memory and the memory bus became a bottleneck (Figure 4.5.3.5) that slowed the flow of data and instructions between main memory and the processor in the CPU.

Figure 4.5.3.5 A bottleneck slows the flow

The solution is cache memory.

In its simplest terms, cache memory is a high-speed memory that temporarily stores data/instructions, so that the processor does not have to go to the slower main memory to get every program instruction or datum individually.

Instead the processor can access a whole block of instructions or data pre-loaded from main memory into the cache.

Information

Using the scenario from Figure 4.5.3.1, main memory is Synchronous Dynamic RAM (SDRAM) which operates synchronously with the data bus clock signal which itself is derived from the system clock, say 133 MHz.
The DRAM's internal clock, the memory clock, operates at the bus speed 133 MHz.
The clock cycle time for the memory is therefore 7.5 nanoseconds.
It takes several memory clock cycles to set up a single read access to memory. This set up time could be as many as 8 memory clock cycles or 8 x 7.5 nanoseconds = 60 nanoseconds.
So the total time to read a single word from memory is 60 + 7.5 nanoseconds = 67.5 nanoseconds.
In this time, the CPU can execute approximately 34 instructions on average. However, it will be held up waiting 67.5 nanoseconds until the next word of memory arrives.

4 Computer systems

Information

Kibibyte(KiB):
A kibibyte (a contraction of kilo binary byte) is a unit of information or computer storage, symbol KiB.
1 KiB = 2^{10} bytes = 1024 bytes.

Mebibyte(MiB):
A mebibyte (a contraction of mega binary byte) is a unit of information or computer storage, symbol MiB.
1 MiB = 2^{20} bytes
= 1048576 bytes
= 1024 kibibytes.

Key term

Cache:
A cache is a smaller, faster memory, closer than main memory to a processor core, which stores copies of data/instructions the processor is most likely to need in advance of these actually being needed.

Cache memory sits between the processor in the CPU and main memory as shown in *Figure 4.5.3.6*.

Figure 4.5.3.6 Cache memory situated between processor and main memory

However, a cache is more than a simple high-speed memory.

It is designed to hold the data/instructions the processor is most likely to need in advance of these actually being needed.

This enables the processor to continue working at either full speed or close to it without having to wait for the data/instructions to be retrieved from slower main memory. For this to be achieved, a **cache controller** (the "brain") is needed which selects and fills the cache memory with just those data/instructions which it anticipates the processor is most likely to need.

Cache memory is usually made up of static RAM (SRAM).
SRAM is faster to access than the DRAM used for main memory.
Nowadays cache memory is integrated into the CPU whereas a long time ago, it was provided in chipsets on the motherboard.

Effect of cache type and cache memory size on CPU performance (Cache type not in AQA specification 8525)

Typically, processors work with multi-level caches that are different in size and speed - *Figure 4.5.3.7*. The closer the cache is to the processor in the CPU, the smaller and faster it works.

If there is more cache, there is a higher probability that data and instructions being fetched will be in the cache which is quicker to access than main memory.

If instructions and data processed by instructions can be fetched directly from cache rather than the slower main memory then the time taken to execute a program can be reduced.

L1 cache / first-level cache

As a rule, L1 cache is not particularly large - 16 to 64 kibibytes[1] - thus making it faster to access than L2 and L3 caches which are larger. This cache is often subdivided into two caches, one for program instructions and one for data. It runs at the same speed as its CPU. The cache controller in modern CPUs usually has a hit-rate of around 90%, i.e. 90% of the time the processor gets its data/instructions from L1 cache.

L2 cache / second-level cache

L2 cache, is primarily used for data - typically 3 x 2048 kibibytes in size. If in the CPU, it runs at the same speed as the CPU clock. There is more of it than L1 cache but for this reason it is slightly slower to access than L1 cache.

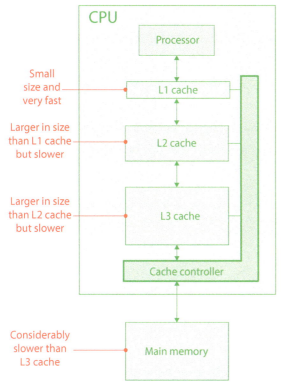

Figure 4.5.3.7 Cache memory hierarchy

---

[1] You are not required to know the units kibibyte and mebibyte. Both are similar but slightly different in magnitude from the units kilobyte and megabyte which you are required to know.

4.5.3 Systems architecture

L3 cache / third-level cache

L3 cache is the slowest to access of the three types of cache because there is more of it than L1 and L2 cache. It is used in multi-core CPUs, i.e. CPUs with more than one processor (core) - typically, 8 mebibytes in size. In multi-core CPUs the L3 cache is often shared amongst the cores. If in the CPU it runs at the clock speed of the CPU.

Questions

1. You try out a newly opened noodles bar and order a bowl of Tom Yum soup which takes 10 minutes to arrive. You get through this dish in two minutes by eating at the rate of one mouthful every 10 seconds. You then order Singapore noodles which takes 10 minutes to arrive. You eat this dish at the same rate as before. To summarise, your eating experience at the noodles bar consists of periods of waiting, followed by short bursts of actual eating at full speed.

   You return to the noodles bar at the same time, twice a week for the next nine weeks, to eat the same two dishes at the same table. On the third week, your regular waiter anticipates your arrival and orders your two dishes so that the first is on your table ready for you to eat immediately and the second is on your table when you finish the first.

   If this scenario is considered to model a processor requesting and operating on data from memory then main memory is the kitchen where the food is prepared and you are the processor consuming data (the food). To model *L1 cache* and the *cache controller* we need to involve the waiter and the table where you are seated. What role would you allocate to

   (a) the waiter?

   (b) the table?

   (c) Explain your choice for cache controller and L1 cache.

2. On the tenth week you arrive exactly on time and start with the usual Tom Yum soup which the waiter has anticipated you will, so there is no waiting.

   However, just as you finish the soup, and exactly as the waiter is placing the Singapore noodles on your table, you ask for Penang Laksa. Oh calamity, the waiter has guessed wrong. For you the consequence is a full ten minute wait as the kitchen prepares your Laksa. In the cache analogy of question 1 this is known as a cache miss. Suggest how the noodles bar could reduce your waiting time for other dishes, e.g. Penang Laksa, to significantly less than ten minutes.

3. Explain why having cache memory can improve the performance of the Central Processing Unit (CPU).

PC activity

1. Download CPU-Z from http://www.cpuid.com/softwares/cpu-z.html.
   Using CPU-Z record the following for the CPU in your computer:

   (a) The size and type of each cache memory.

   (b) The CAS latency of DRAM main memory in clock cycles (CAS = delay time between the READ command and the moment the data is available).

   (c) The DRAM clock speed (DRAM frequency).

   (d) Calculate the access time to a word of main memory in your computer using your answer to (b) / your answer to (c).

4 Computer systems

Effect of Number of processor cores on CPU performance

CPU clock speeds cannot be increased indefinitely because of various problems, one of which is heat generation in the CPU.

CPU manufacturers have settled on a limit of about **4 GHz** for CPU clock speed.

In single-core CPUs the processing unit is a single core or processor (registers, control unit, ALU, internal buses).

The restriction imposed by an upper limit on clock speed has led to CPU manufacturers making CPUs with multiple-cores or processing units. *Figure 4.5.3.8* shows a dual-core CPU in which each core has its own L1 and L2 cache whilst sharing the L3 cache.

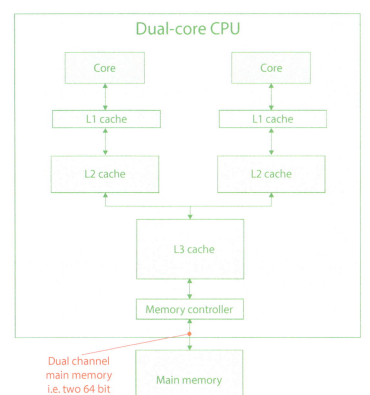

With multiple cores, a running application can spread its processing load (program instructions) across several processing units or cores.

Of course, this requires the executing application to be capable of being distributed across multiple cores, plus the hardware in the CPU to support this distribution.

Essentially, a single program instruction could be distributed across multiple cores with each core applying this instruction to a different part of the data to be processed, e.g. different pixels of a bitmap. Alternatively, different instructions could be executed in parallel on different parts of the data, e.g. add, subtract, multiply.

The outcome in both cases is an application that runs more quickly on multiple-cores than it would on a single core CPU.

Figure 4.5.3.8 Multi-core CPU consisting of two cores

Not all applications lend themselves to distribution across multiple-cores. Applications which can benefit from multiple-cores are those in which a single instruction can be applied to a different part of the data to be processed e.g. image processing including 3-D rendering (*Figure 4.5.3.9*), video processing, and audio processing, or where the some of application's instructions can be executed in parallel, e.g. machine learning applications.

Many applications do not require considerable computing power, e.g. word processing, or cannot be divided up in a way that can exploit multiple-cores. In these types of application a single-core is sufficient. However, an operating system designed to use multiple-cores can still bring about an increase in performance by running more than one application at the same time, with each application executing on its own CPU core.

Figure 4.5.3.9 3-D scene rendering

4.5.3 Systems architecture

In the history of multi-core processors, the adoption of dual-core CPUs over single-core CPUs immediately resulted in less power being consumed because the cores ran at a lower clock rate then single-core CPUs. Performance also increased especially for those applications able to exploit dual-cores. Having dual-cores is like having two diesel locomotives pulling a train on a railway track with an upper speed limit of 100 mph:

- overkill if the load being pulled doesn't need two diesel locomotives to achieve the maximum speed
- necessary when the load being pulled is heavy and the maximum track speed needs to be achieved.

A multiple-core CPU still has to work with a single main memory but their added complexity has led to the memory controller being integrated into the CPU in the latest CPUs. The memory controller works with motherboards that use dual-channel DIMM sockets for memory modules (the modules are paired). Each channel transfers a **64** bit memory word at the same time. This fits well with a dual-core CPU with the first channel's memory word going to one core and the second channel's memory word to the other.

Questions

4. Give **one** reason why a CPU with two cores might perform faster than an equivalent CPU with only one core.

PC activity

2. Download PerfMonitor2 from http://www.cpuid.com/softwares/perfmonitor-2.html.
   Using PerfMonitor2 record the following for the CPU in your computer:
   (a) The number of cores.
   (b) The L2 cache hit ratio which measures as a percentage the number of times the data required is present in the cache.
   (c) How many cores are more than 5% active at the same time.

3. Run CPU-Z and PerfMonitor2 so that the windows of both are visible.
   Switch to the Bench tab in CPU-Z. Leave the reference field unselected.
   Click on the Stress CPU button in CPU-Z and note what you observe in the PerfMonitor2 window.
   Click on the Stop button in CPU-Z and note what you observe in the PerfMonitor2 window.

4.5.3 Systems architecture

In this chapter you have covered:

- The effect of the following on the performance of the CPU:
  - clock speed
  - number of processor cores
  - cache size
  - cache type.

4 Computer systems

4 Computer systems

Learning objectives:

- *Understand and explain the Fetch-Execute cycle.*

4.5.4 Systems architecture

Fetch-Execute cycle

A machine code program is made up of machine code instructions which are fetched from main memory, one at a time, and executed in the processor/CPU.

A processor executes each machine code instruction by breaking its execution into a three-step sequence with the execution synchronised by the system clock and controlled by the control unit.

This sequence of three steps is called the **Fetch-Execute cycle** or **instruction cycle**. This cycle is repeated continuously until the CPU is instructed to halt or the last machine code instruction is reached and executed.

The first step is a fetch operation, the second a decode operation and the third step is execution.

These steps are as follows:

(Fetch phase)

> The next instruction to be executed is fetched to the CPU from main memory

(Decode phase)

> The instruction is decoded in order that the CPU knows what operation to carry out.

(Execute phase)

> The instruction is executed, i.e. carried out. This may include reading/writing from/to main memory.

> **Key term**
>
> **Fetch-Execute cycle:**
> A processor executes each machine code instruction by breaking its execution into a three-step sequence with the execution synchronised by the system clock and controlled by the control unit.
> The three steps are:
> 1. Fetch
> 2. Decode
> 3. Execute.

Task

1. Run and observe the Fetch-Execute cycle at
   http://www.hartismere.com/20398/CPU-Fetch-Decode-Execute-Animation
   Describe how the machine code program is executed.

Question

1. Processor (CPU) and main memory are two essential components of a computer system. Explain, with reference to both processor and main memory, how a computer executes a machine code program.

In this chapter you have covered:

- The Fetch-Execute cycle.

4 Computer systems

4 Computer systems

Learning objectives:

- *Understand the different types of memory within a computer:*
  - *RAM*
  - *ROM*
  - *Cache*
  - *Register*
- *Know what the different types of memory are used for and why they are required.*
- *Understand the differences between main memory and secondary storage*
- *Understand the differences between RAM and ROM*
- *Understand why secondary storage is required*
- *Be aware of different types of secondary storage (solid state, optical and magnetic)*
- *Explain the operation of solid state, optical and magnetic storage*
- *Discuss the advantages and disadvantages of solid state, optical and magnetic storage*
- *Explain the term 'cloud storage'*
- *Explain the advantages and disadvantages of cloud storage when compared to local storage*
- *Understand the term 'embedded system' and explain how an embedded system differs from a non-embedded system.*

4.5.5 Systems architecture

Different types of memory, what they are used for and why they are required

RAM and ROM - see page 236.
Cache memory - see Page 244.
Register - see page 238.

Differences between main memory and secondary storage

Main memory is directly accessible by the processor (CPU) which is why it once went by the name immediate access store.

Secondary storage is persistent storage (non-volatile) that is not directly accessible by the processor. Instead the processor must place a request to read or write data to secondary storage with an interface controller.

RAM main memory is not persistent storage (volatile). Remove the power and the contents of RAM are lost. Although some parts of main memory may use ROM which is persistent, non-volatile storage.

Main memory and secondary storage also differ in capacity and speed of access.

The cost per bit is generally lower for secondary storage than main memory so affordable secondary storage units can be built with storage capacities far exceeding what is affordable for main memory.

However, the technology of main memory and its direct accessibility mean it is much faster to access than secondary storage.

The capacity of main memory is also limited by the fact that it is directly addressable by the processor and processors are designed with a limited address range.

The technology of RAM main memory is different from secondary storage technology.

Differences between RAM and ROM

See page 236.

Why is secondary storage used?

The technology that primary storage (RAM) is built from and which supports read and write random access to individual words/locations requires a continuous supply of electrical energy at the correct voltage level in order to work. Unfortunately, when the supply of electrical energy is removed or disrupted, the information stored in memory is lost. We say that read/write main memory is **volatile** (analogous to liquids which disappear by the process of evaporation). To retain information and programs after electrical power is removed requires a different form of storage, one which is **non-volatile**. There are three technologies with which such storage is built currently:

1. Magnetic
2. Optical
3. Solid-state.

4 Computer systems

If we want to retain a program we have created in RAM, or some information we have written to RAM, then we must transfer both to a non-volatile secondary storage device. The commonest form of read/write secondary storage is a **magnetic hard disk** encased in a **magnetic hard disk drive (HDD)** - *Figure 4.5.5.1*.

A newer form of read/write secondary store that is now shipping in desktop PCs, laptops and tablets is a **solid-state disk (SSD)**.

Compact Disc (CD) and **Digital Versatile Disc (DVD)** storage are optical media that can be used for secondary storage. There are read only (CD-ROM, DVD-ROM), write once read many times (CD-R, DVD-R) and read/write versions (CD-RW, DVD-RW) of these.

> ### Questions
> Why is secondary storage needed?

Magnetic storage

Magnetic storage comes in two forms:

1. Magnetic tape
2. Magnetic disk.

Magnetic disks

IBM developed magnetic disk drives in the late 1950s. The disk drive allows rapid random (direct) access to large amounts of data.
All disk drives use a thin circular platter made of non-ferrous metal or plastic which is rotated at up to 10,000 revolutions per minute beneath a read-write head that moves radially across the surface of the platter.
Figure 4.5.5.1 shows a hard disk drive with the cover removed. The platter and read-write head can be clearly seen as well as the photographer's reflection in the platter.
The platter is coated with an emulsion of iron or cobalt oxide (or a cobalt-based alloy) particles that act as tiny magnets. Binary data is recorded by aligning these tiny magnets in one direction to represent a binary 0 and in the opposite direction to represent a binary 1. Binary data is recorded in concentric rings, or tracks, subdivided into sectors that hold a fixed number of bytes, such as 512. A hard disk can store and retrieve a large volume of data.

To read data stored on the hard disk, the read-write head moves to the desired track and waits for the relevant sector to pass beneath it. When data is transferred from the hard disk to the computer and vice versa, a whole sector of a track is read or written each time. A whole sector of a track is often called a **disk block** or a block. For this reason, a magnetic

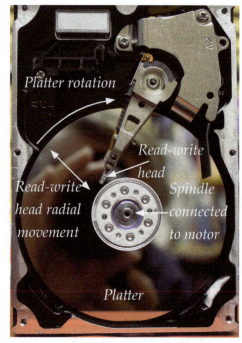

Figure 4.5.5.1 Hard disk drive with cover removed

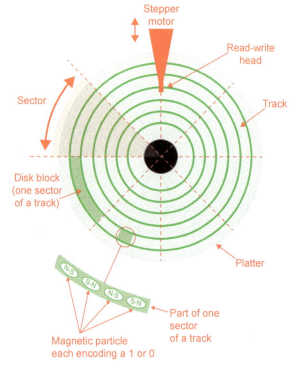

Figure 4.5.5.2 Hard disk platter showing concentric tracks and sectors

hard disk drive is known as a block-oriented storage device. The smallest unit of transfer is a block which is typically 512 bytes.

The top and bottom surfaces of a platter may be used to store data. A block address for a single-platter system is composed of a **surface address**, a **track address** and a **sector address**. Typically, the surfaces are numbered 0 and 1, the tracks 0 to 7,000 and the sectors 0 to 63. *Figure 4.5.5.2* shows a schematic for one surface of a magnetic hard disk.

Modern hard disks for a PC system are sealed units, called Winchester disks, containing several platters mounted on a common spindle. The platters are sealed inside an assembly which allows the disk to operate with minimal risk of damage from contaminants. The read-write heads are built into the assembly with one head per surface. The greater the number of platters, the greater the storage capacity.

Questions

2. Explain the principle of operation of a magnetic disk drive.

Magnetic tape

Figure 4.5.5.3 shows a magnetic tape cartridge used to store backup data or archived data. In late 2017 IBM, using a new magnetic tape prototype, achieved a storage capacity of 330 TB of uncompressed data on a palm-sized cartridge, breaking the world record and far exceeding any single magnetic hard drive solution.

Figure 4.5.5.3 Magnetic tape data cartridge

The information that needs to be stored doubles every two years, tape storage offers the most cost-effective solution.

Tape storage is used extensively in today's modern data centres for backup and archiving. Numerous studies confirm that the Total Cost of Ownership (TCO) for tape is much lower than disk when it comes to backup and data archiving applications.

Did you know?

Backing up data means taking a copy of data and storing it somewhere safe, e.g. in a fireproof safe or off-site. Archiving data means removing it from the online storage medium, usually to free up space. Data qualifies for archiving if it has not been accessed recently and will not be accessed regularly in the future. Programs and data may be backed up and archived.

IBM obtained the technology for making magnetic disks from Manchester University where a one kilobyte magnetic disk had been made on a one metre-wide platter.

4.5.5 Systems architecture

Key concept

Track:
One of the concentric rings on a platter of a hard disk.

Sector:
A subdivision of a track.

Disk block:
The smallest unit of transfer between a computer and a disk. A disk block is one sector of a track.

Did you know?

In 2015, the fastest rotation speeds of consumer disk drives was 10,000 revolutions per minute.

Background

Disk buffer:
Executing programs do not write directly to magnetic hard disks. Instead, they write to an area of main memory (RAM) called a disk buffer. Before a program can write to a file, it has first to open the file, if it exists, or create the file if it doesn't. This open/create action creates a disk buffer in main memory (RAM) which is then associated with the file. The program writes to this buffer. When the buffer becomes full or the program closes the corresponding file, the operating system writes the buffer to disk. The size of the buffer matches the size of a disk block or a multiple of this.

To read a file it must first be opened. This creates a disk buffer which receives a block at a time belonging to the file. The program that opened the file then reads from this buffer. When the buffer becomes empty, the operating system transfers the next disk block belonging to the file into this buffer.

4 Computer systems

> **Key fact**
>
> **Optical disc:**
> An optical disc is a flat, usually circular disc which encodes binary data (bits) in a special reflective layer. In one form of optical disc, binary data is encoded in the form of pits and lands on a reflective material, usually metallic, on one of its flat surfaces. The pits reflect less light than the lands and this is used to encode 0s and 1s.

> **Did you know?**
>
> **CD-R:**
> Write Once, Read Many (WORM) times optical disc.
> CD-R can record about 650 - 900 MiB of data.
>
> **CD-RW:**
> CD-ReWritable disc that can be read and written to over and over again.
>
> **DVD-ROM:**
> Digital versatile disc or digital video disc (DVD) is an optical standard offering much greater storage capacity than CDs. Storage capacity of a single-layer DVD-ROM is 4.3 GiB (4.7 GB).
>
> **DVD-R:**
> DVD-R is a WORM format similar to CD-R.
>
> **DVD-RW:**
> The DVD-RW format provides a rewritable optical disc with a typical capacity of 4.3 GiB (4.7 GB).
>
> **DVD+RW:**
> A competing rewritable format to DVR-RW.
>
> **DVD-RAM:**
> DVD-RAM is a rewritable format that has built-in error control and a defect management system, so it is considered to be better than the other DVD technologies for tasks such as data storage, backup and archiving. The on-disc structure of DVD-RAM is closely related to hard disk technology, as it stores data in concentric tracks.
>
> **Blu-ray disc:**
> A Blu-ray disc (BD) is a high-density optical disc capable of storing 23.3 GiB (25 GB) in a single-layer which is considerably more than a DVD can store.

Optical storage

An optical disc is a flat, usually circular disc which encodes binary data (bits) in a special reflective layer. In one form of optical disc, binary data is encoded in the form of pits (binary value of 0 due to lack of reflection when read) and lands (binary value of 1 due to a reflection when read) on a reflective material, usually metallic, on one of its flat surfaces as shown in *Figure 4.5.5.4*.

CD-ROM

The success of compact discs (CDs) for storing audio led to a new format, CD Read-Only Memory (CD-ROM). Introduced early in 1985, this format was initially used to publish encyclopedias, reference works, professional directories and other large databases. CD-ROMs were ideal for this because they had (for the time) a high storage capacity of 600–700 million bytes, offered fast data access and were portable, rugged and read-only. Today, CD-ROMs are also used for software distribution.

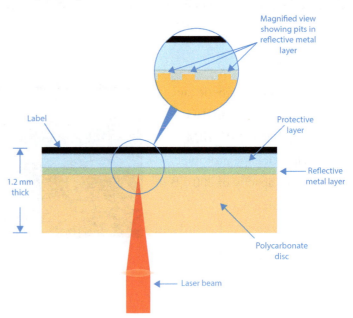

Figure 4.5.5.4 CD-ROM cross-section through its layers

The data is written on the discs using disc-mastering machinery that impresses pits (physical depressions) into a continuous spiral track. The silvery data surface contains pits in a single track 3.5 miles (5.6 km) long. The disc spins at 200-500 revolutions per minute depending on which part of the track is being read.

A data bit is read by focusing a laser beam onto a point in the reflective metal layer where the pits are impressed (*Figure 4.5.5.4*).

More laser light is reflected from the unpitted surface than from the pitted surface. This is detected by a photodiode that outputs an equivalent electrical signal. After some conditioning, the result is a digital signal representing a single data bit. Without going into the fine detail, the amount of reflection is used to encode a data bit as 0 or 1.

4.5.5 Systems architecture

Solid state storage

Solid state storage relies on a technology called **flash memory** derived from EEPROM technology (electrically eraseable ROM).

Flash memory falls into four categories:

1. SD (used in cameras), MMC (used in video cameras), compact flash (used in video cameras) and Sony® memory stick (used in Sony cameras and other products) (Figure 4.5.5.5)
2. USB flash/stick/pen/thumb drive (Figures 4.5.5.6 and 4.5.5.7)
3. Embedded flash (eMMC, UFS)
4. Flash-based solid state drives (SSDs) designed to replace conventional hard drives (Figure 4.5.5.8).

Flash is a type of non-volatile semiconductor memory designed to provide individual memory cells in an addressable matrix similar to DRAM memory (see Chapter 4.5.2). The fundamental flash memory cell is based on the floating-gate MOSFET transistor.

A cell stores a bit as a level of electrical charge.

Unlike a DRAM cell, this charge may be stored in a flash storage cell for up to 100 years, it is claimed, and without the need to be connected to any form of electrical power - hence the label, non-volatile - to retain data.

Unfortunately flash memory cells have a limitation that is not present in SRAM or DRAM memory cells (see Chapter 4.5.2): flash memory cells may be written to and/or erased only a certain number of times. This may be as little as 1000 write/erase cycles but it can be up to 100,000.

Writing data to flash memory is done in two stages. The first stage erases the memory cells involved which consists of setting them all to 1. The second stage consist of changing those cells that need to be 0.

In general, the individual cells in flash devices all work the same way. The difference between flash devices depends to some extent on how these cells are arranged and interconnected on the silicon semiconductor chip from which the flash storage is created.

SD memory card

Compact flash

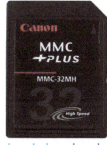

(© Ralf Roletschek roletschek.at)
Figure 4.5.5.5
Flash memory cards

Figure 4.5.5.6 USB thumb drive

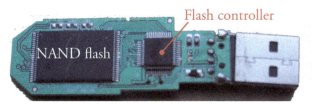
Figure 4.5.5.7 USB thumb drive interior

© D-Kuru/ Wikimedia Commons

Figure 4.5.5.8 Solid-state disk drive

> **Did you know?**
>
> There are currently two very different architectures:
>
> - **NOR flash:** May be written and read down to a single memory word, which can be anywhere from 8 bits to 64 bits.
>   It is faster to read but slower to write and erase than NAND flash.
>   It can support in-place execution of code and is commonly used for storing firmware (software that is retained when the power is removed) in embedded devices.
>
> - **NAND flash:** has to be accessed in larger units called pages of 512 or 4096 bytes.
>   Pages are combined into blocks of typically 16 KB or more.
>   NAND flash is read and written in pages, but erased only in blocks. Fresh pages for writing to can only be obtained from an erased block.
>   The smallest unit that may be read or written to in a single operation is a page.
>   However, to change a page a copy is altered, and then written to a page that has not been written to since erasure (all bits will be set to 1 after erasure).
>   This means that NAND flash does not allow data to be rewritten "in place" which would be necessary for operation as RAM.
>   Therefore, in-place execution of code is generally not possible due to lack of support for rapid random access to the flash array of cells.
>   Instead, NAND flash was designed to act as mass storage (secondary storage) rather than non-volatile RAM. Cameras use NAND flash memory in the form of SD cards. Cameras use the fact that NAND flash is faster to write but is slower to read which is perfectly acceptable when storing photographic images for processing later in image processing software such as Adobe® Photoshop.

eMMC

This type of flash storage is soldered to a circuit board for a smartphone or a tablet and therefore is not removable storage. It goes under the name embedded MMC or eMMC where MMC is short for Multi-Media Controller which refers to a package consisting of flash memory and a flash memory controller. Almost all mobile phones and tablets use this form of flash for main storage. The latest version of the eMMC standard (released February 2015) has speeds rivalling discrete SATA-based Solid State Drives (400 MB/s). *Figure 4.5.5.9* shows eMMC soldered to the Tiva microcontroller board.

Figure 4.5.5.9 eMMC 512KB

Flash-based Solid-state disk (SSD)

The solid-state disk (SSD) in a solid-state disk drive (*Figure 4.5.5.8*) is a form of flash memory which operates by trapping electrons in a wafer of semiconducting material. These electrons and their electric charge remain trapped even when electric power is removed, i.e. SSD is non-volatile storage. Binary 0 is represented by trapped electrons and binary 1 by absence of trapped electrons.

The sites (floating gate transistors) where these electrons are trapped are organized in a grid. The entire grid layout is referred to as a **block**, while the individual **rows** that make up the grid are called a **page**.

Common page sizes are 2KiB, 4KiB, 8KiB, or 16KiB, with 128 to 256 pages per block. Block sizes are typically between 256KiB and 4MiB. For example, the Samsung™ SSD 840 EVO has blocks of size 2MiB, and each block contains 256 pages of 8 KiB each. The Samsung SSD 840 EVO comprises 8 NAND flash chips, each of capacity 64 GiB. Each Samsung flash chip contains 32 blocks.

4.5.5 Systems architecture

Unlike magnetic disk drives, solid-state drives contain no moving parts or spinning disks. The absence of moving parts means that solid state disk drives can operate at speeds far above those of a typical hard disk drive.

Access time for a typical hard drive is on average 10-15 milliseconds whereas access time for an SSD drive is 25-100 microseconds (access time for RAM is typically 40 -100 nanoseconds).

The technology used is NAND flash memory.

A solid-state disk is a block-oriented storage device which has to erase a block first in order to rewrite it because unlike magnetic hard disk drives, NAND flash memory can't overwrite existing data. Erasing a block in the SDD means "untrapping" electrons.

The solid-state disk drive requires an onboard controller which consists of an embedded microprocessor with RAM buffer to perform reading and writing to the solid state disk (Figure 4.5.5.10). The controller is a very important factor in determining the speed of the SSD drive.

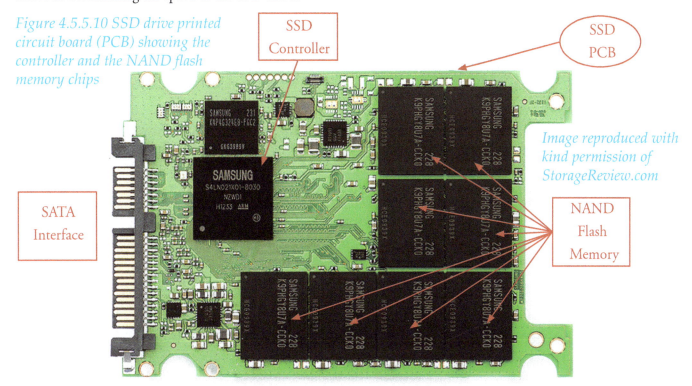

Figure 4.5.5.10 SSD drive printed circuit board (PCB) showing the controller and the NAND flash memory chips

Image reproduced with kind permission of StorageReview.com

To alter the contents of a particular memory location of SSD storage, an entire page must be constructed containing the new information and written to a page which is in the "free" state, i.e. has not been used since erasure.

When data is changed, the content of the page is copied into an internal register, the data is updated, and the new version is stored in a "free" page, an operation called "read-modify-write".

SSD secondary storage is increasingly being used in laptops, tablets and is an option now for desktop PCs. The attraction is lower power consumption and faster booting of the operating system.

Pages cannot be overwritten, and once they become stale, i.e. used but data stored is no longer needed, the only way to make them free again is to erase them. However, it is not possible to erase individual pages. It is only possible to erase whole blocks at once. Erasure is triggered automatically by a garbage collection process in the SSD controller when it needs to reclaim stale pages to make free space.

Questions

3. Explain how data is written to flash memory.

4. In what devices or systems are the following flash memories used:
   (a) eMMC? (b) Compact flash? (c) SSD?

4 Computer systems

Advantages and disadvantages of solid state, optical and magnetic storage

A flash memory device is solid-state, i.e. has no moving parts, it is therefore less affected by shock than a spinning magnetic disk.

Flash memory is ideal as non-volatile RAM (NVRAM) in tablets and mobile phones and can also store the devices' operating system including the file system. Wear-level management in flash NVRAM is now very good and operating systems used in most tablets and mobile phones are not a Windows-based design which would soon wear out the flash memory by frequent writing of registry settings to NVRAM (every second).

SSDs consume less power than magnetic disk drives but the latter offers a more cost effective storage solution. In 2017 SSDs are more expensive than hard drives in terms of pound sterling per gigabyte.

A PC or Mac with an SSD boots faster, launches and runs applications faster, and transfers files faster than magnetic hard disk.

There is a limit to how small magnetic hard drives can be manufactured because they rely on spinning platters. SSDs have no such limitation, so they can be made to fit a form factor much smaller than the smallest magnetic hard disk form factor which is currently at 1.8 inches.

Even the quietest hard drive emits noise when it is in use from the drive spinning or the read arm moving back and forth. Faster hard drives will make more noise than those that are slower. SSDs make virtually no noise at all, since they are non-mechanical.

Both flash and optical storage are more portable than magnetic disk drives. The former are removable media whereas the latter are not meant to be removed from a computer system.

Both magnetic disk and SSD storage have been optimised for high speed access, DVDs and CDs are fast enough to play movies and music but are slower than magnetic disks and SSDs.

Optical media and their drives are considerably cheaper than magnetic disk drives and SSDs (but not when compared per byte).

Magnetic disks and SSDs have storage capacities much greater than current optical media. Blu-ray optical disks can store up to 50 billion bytes (25-50 GB) whereas magnetic disk drives and SSDs currently can store trillions of bytes (TB). In 2017 Seagate® announced a 60 TB SSD.

Optical media can suffer damage from surface scratches which can render them useless. Magnetic disks and flash devices have greater protection because they are located inside protective sealed units. However, unlike optical and solid state media, magnetic disks can be damaged by strong magnetic fields.

> **Information**
>
> **SSD vs other flash-based devices:**
> SSDs are much faster than any of the other flash-based portable drives, e.g. USB thumb drive.

Questions

5. An SSD device is a type of solid state storage.
   State **two** advantages of solid state storage compared to magnetic storage.

6. Why are optical media not suitable as general purpose secondary storage but instead are used for backing up data and distributing software?

7. Some desktop computers have both magnetic hard drives and solid state drives.
   What would each be used for and why?

8. Describe how data is stored on, and read from
   (a) a magnetic hard disk (b) a CD-ROM.

4.5.5 Systems architecture

Cloud storage

Figure 4.5.5.11 shows the interior of one of Google's data centres which provides remote storage for multiple users in racks of commodity servers with hard disks or solid state disks attached.

Users access this remote storage over the Internet through a web-based interface.

An example of a web-based interface is shown in *Figure 4.5.5.12* for CertainSafe®'s cloud storage service.

Users pay only for the storage capacity used (beyond a certain capacity in the case of some providers, e.g. after 2GB).

Cloud storage is a **storage service** in which data is stored on remote servers accessed from the Internet, or "cloud", and maintained, operated and managed by a cloud storage service provider on storage servers that are built on virtualisation techniques (*Figure 4.5.5.11* shows some of Google's server racks in a data centre). Cloud storage is scalable on demand according to users' needs and made possible by virtualisation.

In virtualisation a single physical computer is "broken" into smaller pieces, with each one able to act like a computer of its own, a virtual computer. Cloud computing enabled the building of large clusters of physical computers, which could then be leased out as smaller virtual ones by the hour.

Virtualisation enables storage hardware to appear as a single unit of local storage belonging to one user or organisation when in fact the storage hardware may be located across several servers in different server racks as shown in *Figure 4.5.5.13*. These servers and their storage units store data belonging to many users and organisations without the latter being aware that this is happening.

Figure 4.5.5.11 Racks of commodity servers with storage at one of Google's data centres (image Google/Connie Zhou)

Figure 4.4.5.12 CertainSafe®'s Digital Safety Deposit Box web interface

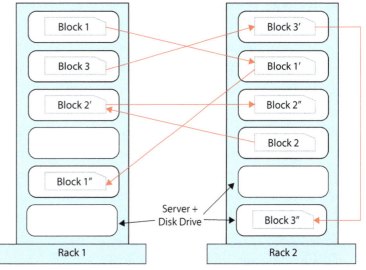

Figure 4.5.5.13 The data blocks of a user's file may be spread and replicated three times over several hard disks or SSDs in several servers in different racks

Each user gets a container to store their data. The container has a globally unique name and a few other options which the user can set such as the type of disk required (SSD or magnetic) and where this disk should live (ie, Europe or the US). The big difference is that this "disk" is extraordinarily large in that there's no limit to how many bytes can end up in a container. The only limit is that each file in the container can be up to **5 Terabytes**. The container itself is replicated and spread across many physical disks in order to maintain high levels of durability and availability - see *Figure 4.5.5.13*.

Some examples of cloud storage services available to the general public are Microsoft® OneDrive, Google® Drive, Apple® iCloud, Dropbox, and CertainSafe Digital Safety Deposit Box.

Advantages and disadvantages of cloud storage compared with local storage

Advantages of cloud storage compared with local storage

1. Files stored in the cloud and accessible from the Internet:
   (a) *May be accessed from anywhere*, e.g. from smartphone on the train, from tablet in your hotel room. With local storage only, a file on a system at work or school cannot be accessed away from work/school without taking a copy home. With no local storage a file may still be accessed, e.g. from smartphone with Internet access.
   (b) *May be accessed from any computer with an Internet connection*, e.g. smartphone, tablet, laptop, desktop.
   (c) *Can be shared and worked on by more than one user making collaboration possible*. The cloud service manages the collaboration by queuing edits so that none are lost or overwritten.
   (d) *Avoids working with separate local copies* instead users can jointly work on the cloud copy of the file, e.g. a document, performing edits, adding comments etc, which all can see.
   (e) *Avoids having multiple out-of-sync copies* scattered across local storage on different systems which on merging can result in the *loss of vital edits/changes* if overwritten.
   (f) *Don't have to rely on carrying files around on USB thumb drives/memory sticks which could get lost or stolen easily or have to rely on email to send files to yourself*. Instead, users undergo an authentication process to secure access to the files in the cloud.

2. Files stored in the cloud:
   (a) As a part of their support for collaboration s*ome cloud providers* also *offer office productivity tools* such as word processing *as part of the deal* which otherwise would have to be paid for separately if processing is done with files in local storage.
   (b) If files are downloaded from the cloud to be worked on locally and offline (i.e. not connected to the Internet), *cloud storage services usually provide a mechanism by which the cloud copy can be synchronised with the updated local copy when it comes back online*. This relieves users from managing the syncing of multiple local copies of the same file in a way that preserves all the edits/changes.
   (c) *Relieves the user of backup management*. The cloud service provider usually offers this as part of the service.
   (d) Users of cloud storage services also *do not have to worry about local hard disk crashes/damage* due to natural disasters such as fire or flooding because their *files are now stored in redundant storage arrays* in the cloud, the maintenance of these being the responsibility of the cloud service provider.
   (e) Users of cloud storage services *do not have to worry about loss of data and loss of privacy* from someone breaking into their home, *stealing their computer and then examining the contents of the local storage unit*.
   (f) Cloud storage can be an *exceptionally good fit for situations where you don't know (or can't know) what your storage will look like, either many years in the future, or tomorrow*. Anytime a situation arises where more storage is needed the elastic nature of cloud storage will meet this need quickly and more cheaply than purchasing more local storage capacity with attendant configuration issues.

Disadvantages of cloud storage compared with local storage

1. When you use cloud storage you are relying on storage in a data centre which doesn't belong to you unlike local storage. This **means giving up some control over your assets** (such as data or program source code) in exchange for other benefits (such as flexibility or lower costs).
   You can expect your data to be stored in encrypted form in the Cloud. In one cloud storage scheme, the cloud storage provider keeps a copy of the encryption key so when you ask for your data, it can be returned to you decrypted. However, this also means if the cloud storage provider were to receive a court order, they do have the technical ability to comply with it and decrypt your data without your consent.

2. Cloud service providers are **high profile and subject to concerted and sophisticated attacks from hackers**. Several of the well-known providers have suffered security breaches. Dropbox had to fix a security hole recently, and got breached a few years ago. Google Drive, OneDrive, and Dropbox accounts are vulnerable to man-in-the-middle attacks.

3. Most cloud storage providers **charge a subscription for storing users' data** with only a small amount of storage being subscription-free. This is an ongoing cost which must be compared with the one-off cost of local storage. Other factors need to be considered such as the cost of Internet access and the speed of access.

4. Without Internet access **you will not be able to access your files in cloud storage**.

Questions

9. What is cloud storage?
10. Discuss the advantages and disadvantages of cloud storage.

Embedded system

We can think of a laptop as a computer which can be used to do all sorts of things users want to do from surfing the Web to word processing essays. For this reason a laptop is considered a general purpose computer system. But this is not the only type of computer system.

Another type is an embedded computer system.
Loosely defined, **an embedded computer system is any device that includes a programmable computer but is not itself intended to be a general purpose computer**. For example, a clock built from a microprocessor is an embedded computing system as is a washing machine with a microprocessor-controlled washing cycle.

Many of today's cars operate an embedded computer system with over 100 million lines of code running on 40 to 100 microprocessors monitoring whether seat belts are in use to managing and controlling the running of the car's engine.

Another example of an embedded system is a portable music player. The cheapest portable music players are essentially USB thumb drives with a two-line LCD display, a headphone jack and a couple of buttons. To reduce cost, the audio codecs and UI manager on such devices often run in the flash controller microprocessor alongside the flash controller software. Music is saved to flash memory so that it is retained when the portable music player is switched off. USB thumb drives need only about 512 bytes of volatile RAM for buffering a page to be written to flash memory. Therefore, a portable music player will have much more non-volatile memory than volatile memory. The programs to decode and play the stored music, and music data are stored in and accessed by the processor from flash memory - *Figure 4.5.5.14*.

4 Computer systems

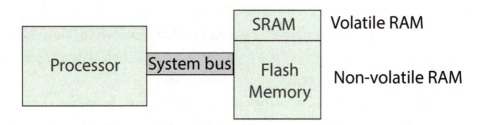

Figure 4.5.5.14 Portable music player

Characteristics of embedded systems

An embedded system has a **dedicated purpose**, has a **limited or non-existent user interface**, and is designed to **operate completely or largely autonomously within other machinery**, e.g. an engine management system. They also have **limited memory capacity**.

Operating systems for embedded systems are designed to **work with the constraints of limited memory size** and **limited processor performance**. In portable embedded systems, the operating system must also take account of limited battery life.

Characteristics of non-embedded systems

Non-embedded systems do not suffer the constraints of embedded systems. They form the bedrock of general purpose computers and as such have **operating systems which are much more complex** and **powerful** than embedded operating systems. They will have **more volatile RAM** secondary storage, **more powerful processors** (CPUs), probably multicore. They are also likely to have **separate graphics processors** (GPUs) and support to plug expansion boards such as graphics cards into the motherboard. They will have a **user interface**, usually both graphical and command line (text-based). They will **support a wide range of peripherals** from mice and keyboards to printers, scanners and DVD players.

Questions

11 What is meant by an embedded system?

12 Explain how an embedded system differs from a non-embedded system.

13 Give **one** example of an embedded system and **one** example of a non-embedded system.

14 Embedded systems normally have less volatile RAM in main memory and more non-volatile RAM or ROM than non-embedded systems. Explain why?

In this chapter you have covered:

- The different types of memory within a computer: RAM; ROM; Cache; Register
- What the different types of memory are used for and why they are required
- The differences between main memory and secondary storage
- The differences between RAM and ROM
- Why secondary storage is required
- That there are different types of secondary storage (solid state, optical and magnetic)
- The operation of solid state, optical and magnetic storage
- The advantages and disadvantages of solid state, optical and magnetic storage
- The term 'cloud storage'
- The advantages and disadvantages of cloud storage when compared to local storage
- The term 'embedded system' and how an embedded system differs from a non-embedded system.

5 Fundamentals of computer networks

5 Fundamentals of computer networks

Learning objectives:

- *Define what a computer network is*
- *Discuss the advantages and disadvantages of computer networks*
- *Describe the main types of computer network including:*
  - *Personal Area Network (PAN)*
  - *Local Area Network (LAN)*
  - *Wide Area Network (WAN)*
- *Understand that networks can be wired or wireless*
- *Discuss the advantages and disadvantages of wireless networks as opposed to wired networks*
- *Describe the following common LAN topologies:*
  - *star*
  - *bus*
- *Define the term network protocol.*

Figure 5.3 Ethernet switch with exposed CAT 5 cable showing four wires, two per circuit (one outgoing, one incoming)

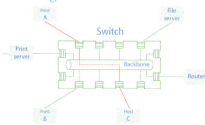

Figure 5.4 Internal operation of switch connects two nodes together temporarily so that they can communicate with each other.

5a Computer networks

What is a computer network?

A computer network is a collection of connected computers.

Figure 5.1 shows three computers, labelled Host A, Host B and Host C, connected together via a switch and cabling. The switch could be an Ethernet switch such as the one shown in *Figure 5.3* operating as shown in *Figure 5.4*.

Key term

Computer network: A computer network is a collection of connected computers.

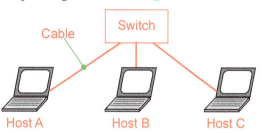

Figure 5.1 Wired computer network

The connection between computers can be done with cabling, in which case the connection is said to be **wired**, or with radio waves, in which case the connection is said to be **wireless**.

Computers on a network are called **hosts** or **nodes**.

Questions

1. What is a computer network?

Advantages of networking

Computers are connected together in a network so that resources such as a printer or a file server or a connection to the Internet may be shared amongst computers in the network. Communication between computers is also improved which means that updates and new software may be installed from a centrally managed server. The activities of computer users may be also be monitored centrally by observing network traffic. Users benefit because their work may be backed-up and managed centrally, and users will be able to store and access their files centrally from any computer.

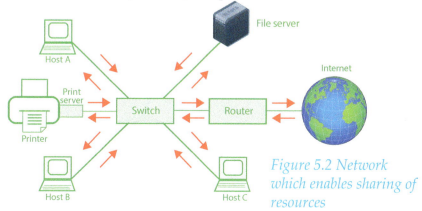

Figure 5.2 Network which enables sharing of resources

5 Fundamentals of computer networks

Questions

2. Give **three** examples of the advantages of connecting computers in a network.

Disadvantages of networking

Local area networks (LANs) share data, processing and communication. Therefore they are at risk of the following:

1. As the geographical area spanned by a LAN increases, say from a single office to a building and then a site, so does the chance of interception and leakage of information especially if the network is wireless.
2. An unauthorised user gaining access to one computer may then have access to the whole network including sensitive and confidential information stored on a file server.
3. A virus downloaded on one computer may then go on to infect other LAN-connected computers.
4. A single point of failure, e.g.
   a. central switch failure may bring down the operation of the whole network denying all users access to their data stored on a network file server.
   b. failure of a domain server used to authenticate users will prevent users from logging in and being able to use network resources.
   c. file server failure will mean that users' files will become inaccessible.

Questions

3. Give **three** examples of the disadvantages of networking.

The main types of computer network

> **Information**
> **PAN** - Only Bluetooth needs to be considered.

Personal Area Network (PAN)

A personal area network (PAN) is a computer network organized around an individual person, and that's set up for personal use only. A PAN typically involves a computer, mobile phone, tablet and/or some other personal device like bluetooth headphones. *Figure 5.5* shows an example of PANs in use at an airport.

Personal area networks can be wireless (Bluetooth, ZigBee, Wireless USB, IrDA, an infrared connection) or constructed with cables (wired PAN using USB or FireWire). Wireless PANs are called WPANs.

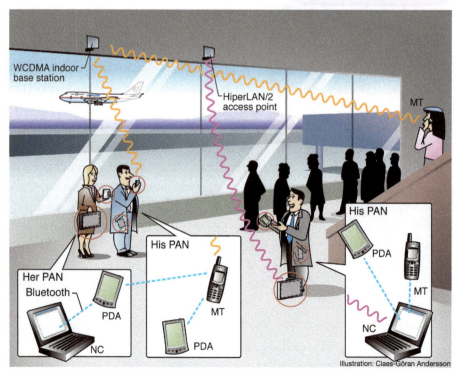

Figure 5.5 Use of PANs at an airport - for PDA read tablet computer

The reason PANs are classified apart from other network types like LANs, WLANs, and WANs (see later in chapter for a description of these network types) is because they transmit information between devices that are nearby.

For example, a Bluetooth enabled keyboard connects to a nearby tablet which itself may control a nearby smart light bulb.

A PAN might also consist of small, wearable or embedded devices that can communicate upon nearby contact with other wireless devices.

The reach of a PAN varies from a few centimetres to several metres depending on the technology used.

Although PANs are personal, by definition, they can still access the Internet by connecting to a LAN which has access to the Internet.

> **Key term**
>
> **Pan Area Network (PAN):**
> A personal area network (PAN) is a computer network organized around an individual person, and that's set up for personal use only. A PAN typically involves a computer, mobile phone, tablet and/or some other personal device like bluetooth headphones.
> A PAN transmits information between devices that are nearby, e.g. a few centimetres or metres away.

Questions

4. What is a Personal Area Network (PAN)?

5. Give **two** examples of the use of a PAN.

Local Area Network (LAN)

Local area networks (LANs) emerged in the early 1970s when companies realised that desktop computers could share peripherals, such as printers, and could share data, if all were interconnected.
The interconnections became the local area network.
A computer that is not interconnected is known as a stand-alone computer. A stand-alone computer needs its own printer, hard disk storage, and local installation of application software whereas LAN-connected computers can share printers, hard disk storage and download application software from an application server.
Figure 5.2 shows an example of computers sharing the following resources via a LAN: a printer and print server, a file server and a connection (router) to the Internet.
LANs cover a relatively small geographic area such as a single building or a school site. The close proximity of computers to each other in a LAN enables communication links to be used that have higher speeds and lower error rates than in wide area networks (WANs).

LAN ownership

LANs are usually owned and controlled/managed by a single person if it is a home network, or an organisation if it is, for example, a school network.

> **Key term**
>
> **Local Area Network (LAN):**
> A Local Area network consists of linked computers in close proximity, e.g. a single building or site occupying a relatively small geographic area.

> **Information**
>
> **Difference between a wireless PAN and a wireless LAN:**
> Conceptually, the difference between a PAN and a wireless LAN is that a PAN tends to be centred around one person while a wireless LAN is a local area network (LAN) that is connected without wires and which serves multiple users.
> Some other examples of wireless PAN, or WPAN, devices include mobile phone headsets, wireless mice, printers, bar code scanners and game consoles.

Questions

6. What is a Local Area Network (LAN)?

5 Fundamentals of computer networks

Wide Area Network (WAN)

Wide Area Networks (WANs) were invented to solve the problem of connecting a LAN to a distant computer or to a remote LAN - *Figure 5.6*.

LANs are perfect for sharing resources within a building or over a single site, but they cannot be used to connect distant sites.

Wide Area Networks serve this need.

Expressed simply, a wide area network is a set of connections between geographically remote local area networks.

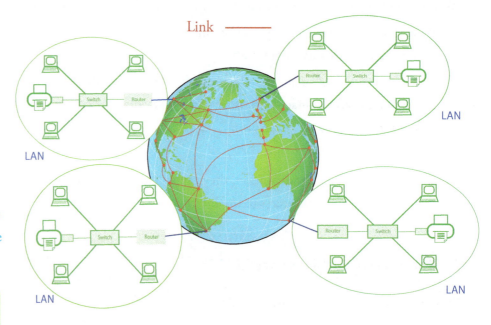

Figure 5.6 A WAN linking computers in geographically remote locations

Key term

Wide Area Network (WAN): A set of links that connect geographically remote computers and local area networks.

Key fact

Internet: The Internet is the largest example of a WAN.

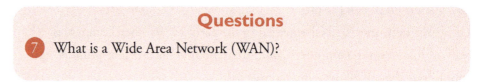

Questions

7 What is a Wide Area Network (WAN)?

The Internet WAN

When two LANs are interconnected by a WAN so that computers or nodes on one network are able to communicate with computers or nodes on the other network, and vice versa, the two LANs are said to be internetworked or to form an internet (note the use of lowercase "i"). The publicly accessible internet known as the Internet is the largest example of a WAN.

WAN ownership

A WAN has to operate at high-speed, with high bandwidth connections and high-performance routers connecting together LANs.

This connection infrastructure is sometimes referred to as the backbone of the WAN.

WAN backbones are expensive to install, operate and maintain.

For this reason WANs are often under collective or distributed ownership.

For example in the UK, Janet (**J**oint **A**cademic **NET**work) is the name of a high-speed network for the UK's research and education community. It is owned by JISC, a not-for-profit company that was originally set up and funded directly by the British government. This WAN connects universities, Further Education (FE) colleges and research establishments in the UK from Lands End to John O'Groats and everywhere in between.

It serves some 18 million users and has over 5,000 km of optical fibre capable of running at either 100 Gbit/s or 2 Tbit/s.

Each university, FE or research establishment owns and operates its own LANs but all rely on the JISC-owned backbone to interconnect these LANs. They pay money to JISC for the privilege of being connected to Janet.

Questions

8. Give **three** reasons why WANs are often under collective or distributed ownership.

Who owns the largest WAN in the world, the Internet?

The physical network that carries Internet traffic between different computer systems is the Internet backbone system.

It is split into continental and national backbones - *Figure 5.7*.

These backbones are owned by a number of different commercial companies or state-owned companies (e.g. People's Republic of China) but these companies have restricted control and ownership over the Internet because it was designed to:

1. Not rely on any form of **central control**
2. Use **global network policies** determined by independent public bodies not by companies
3. Rely on the **end-to-end principle**, i.e. the hosts/nodes at each end of the communication are given control of their communication.

For the above reasons, we say that ownership of the Internet is distributed.

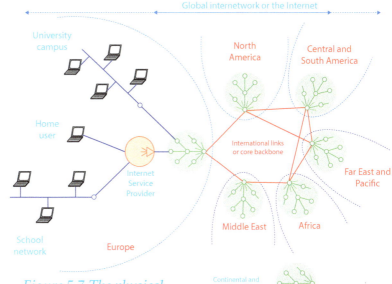

Figure 5.7 The physical structure of the Internet

Information

There are many organizations, corporations, governments, schools, private citizens and service providers that all own pieces of the infrastructure, but there is no one body that owns it all.

No one actually owns the Internet, and no single person or organisation controls the Internet in its entirety.

Wired and wireless networks

Wired networks use different kinds of cabling to carry data depending on speed and bandwidth requirements. The two main choices of material for the physical wiring of a wired network are

1. Copper
2. Fibre optic.

Fibre optics refers to technology that transmits data through thin strands of a highly transparent material that usually is either glass or plastic.

Fibre optic transmission is faster then copper wire and when travelling over a long distance, fibre optic cables experience less signal loss than copper cabling.

Wireless networks use radio waves to carry data.

Advantages and disadvantages of wireless networks as opposed to wired networks

Questions

9. Give **two** reasons why wired networks might be preferred to wireless networks and **two** reasons why wireless networks might be preferred to wired networks.

Wireless networks eliminate much of the cost of cabling that occurs with wired networks but may not provide as much bandwidth as wired networks, i.e. wireless networks could be slower. However, it is usually much easier and cheaper to add extra devices via Wi-Fi to a wireless network than to cable these devices to a wired network. Also, the wired option is not always possible because some wireless devices don't support a wired connection. Wireless devices are more flexibly relocated because no re-cabling is involved, e.g. can be used outdoors, but depending on location may suffer from an unreliable signal and therefore disruption to transmissions.

But care has to be taken because now that communication takes place via radio waves, transmissions are much easier to intercept than is the case with wired networks.

In a wireless network without encryption, it is possible to eavesdrop on traffic intended for other computers.

5 Fundamentals of computer networks

> **Key term**
> **Topology:**
> In the context of networking, the shape, layout, configuration or structure of the connections that connect devices to the network.

Star network topology

In the star network topology, cabling is configured as shown in Figure 5.8 as a star.

The centre of the star is either a network switch or a central computer.

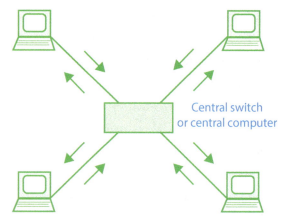

Figure 5.8 Star network topology

In a traditional star network, each link from node to central computer is an **independent link**. Each link is therefore **secure** from eavesdropping by other nodes.

If a link to a node goes down, the other links and nodes are unaffected. However, if the central computer / central switch goes down, the whole network will fail.

In a true star-based network, the speed of each link to the central computer should remain high, because the links are not shared.

Bus network topology

Figure 5.9 shows the layout of a bus network.

Each computer "taps in" to the transmission medium, i.e. the bus. Bus networks used to be cabled with coaxial cable, a form of copper cable. Each computer was then physical attached to coaxial cable via taps called T-piece connectors - Figure 5.10 and Figure 5.11.

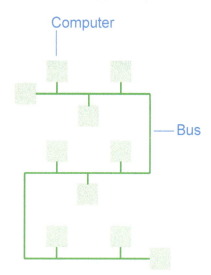

Figure 5.9 Bus network topology

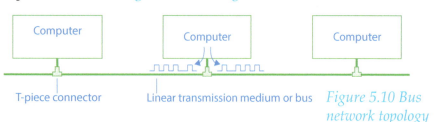

Figure 5.10 Bus network topology

A bus is a linear transmission medium.

The same linear behaviour is now achieved with a switch and CAT 5 cabling as shown in Figure 5.3 and Figure 5.4, at the beginning of this chapter, even though the wiring to the switch resembles a star network.

The bus transmission medium is a shared medium, only one computer can send at a time. In the coaxial-cabled bus network this means that every connected computer is able to "see" each transmission. A computer then selects the transmissions it should receive based on the address information contained in the transmission. In a switch-cabled network only two computers are ever connected as a bus, at a time, so only these see their transmission.

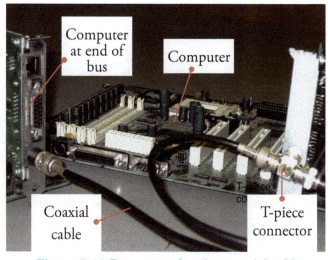

Figure 5.11 Bus network using coaxial cable

Questions

 Describe the network topologies star and bus.

When would each topology be used?

The wired bus system in which each computer on a network is connected directly to the next computer in a linear fashion is now obsolete.

This network topology was originally used because running a single cable past all the computers in the network was easier and used less wiring than other topologies.

The network connection would start at the server and end at the last computer in the network - see *Figure 5.9*.

The original wired-as-a-bus network used a networking protocol called Ethernet. Ethernet lives on in the wired-as-a-star network that uses a switch at the centre of the star configuration.

The switch creates a temporary and short duration linear Ethernet bus connection/pathway between two network computers (*Figure 5.4*) that wish to communicate. At the end of the communication, the connection is broken so that another two computers may connect temporarily. The temporary linear connection behaves as a bus.

With the **wired-as-a-star switch network**, each sending client computer (host) is able to **use the full bandwidth** of the network when transmitting because **no data/packet collisions** will occur with other sending computers (a temporary link is made between sending and receiving computer).

It is also **easy to connect new devices** and the **failure of one client computer will not affect others**. Also, **eavesdropping (packet sniffing) is made difficult** as the packets are only sent to the intended device.

In the now obsolete coaxial cable wired-as-a-bus networks, packets could be sniffed because the bus cabling was a shared medium. Also, as the bandwidth was shared by all the computers, performance could be slower then wired-as-star switched bus networks because data/packet collisions occur. There is a **noticeable and significant gain in performance of wired-as-star switched bus networks** over wired-as-a-bus networks.

Coaxial cable bus networks were first replaced by hubs which effectively allowed the network to be wired as a star but behaviour was equivalent to the shared bandwidth bus medium it replaced. It was only the transition from Ethernet hubs to Ethernet switches that brought about the improved performance.

> **Information**
>
> **Ethernet bus and wired-as-a-star network:**
>
> Ethernet lives on in the wired-as-a-star network that uses a switch at the centre of the star configuration. The switch creates a temporary and short duration linear Ethernet bus connection/pathway between two network computers that wish to communicate.

Questions

 An Ethernet bus network is wired as a star using a switch.
Explain how this wired as a star network topology behaves as a bus network.

12 State **two** advantages of the wired-as-a-star Ethernet bus network over the wired-as-a-bus Ethernet bus network.

Network protocol

A protocol provides agreed signals, codes and rules for data exchange between systems.

A network protocol makes possible communication between processes executing on different hosts whilst hiding the complexities of the underlying network from these processes. (A process is an instance of a program in execution).

5 Fundamentals of computer networks

In this chapter you have covered:

- Defining what a computer network is
- The advantages and disadvantages of computer networks
- The main types of computer network including:
  - Personal Area Network (PAN)
  - Local Area Network (LAN)
  - Wide Area Network (WAN)
- That networks can be wired or wireless
- The advantages and disadvantages of wireless networks as opposed to wired networks
- The following common LAN topologies:
  - star
  - bus
- The definition of the term network protocol.

> **Key term**
>
> **Network protocol:**
> A network protocol makes possible communication between processes executing on different hosts whilst hiding the complexities of the underlying network from these processes. A process is an instance of a program in execution.

5 Fundamentals of computer networks

5 Fundamentals of computer networks

Learning objectives:

- *Define the term 'network protocol'*
- *Explain the purpose and use of common network protocols including:*
  - *Ethernet*
  - *Wi-Fi*
  - *TCP (Transmission Control Protocol)*
  - *UDP (User Datagram Protocol)*
  - *IP (Internet Protocol)*
  - *HTTP (Hypertext Transfer Protocol)*
  - *HTTPS (Hypertext Transfer Protocol Secure)*
  - *FTP (File Transfer Protocol)*
  - *Email protocols:*
    - *SMTP (Simple Mail Transfer Protocol)*
    - *IMAP (Internet Message Access Protocol).*

5b Network protocols

What is a network protocol?

All communication needs protocols so it goes smoothly and without errors. A protocol is a set of agreed signals, codes and rules for data exchange between systems. A network protocol makes possible communication between processes executing on different hosts whilst hiding the complexities of the underlying network from these processes. (A process is an instance of a program in execution).

> **Questions**
> 1. What is a network protocol?

Common network protocols
Ethernet

A computer communicates on the network through a network interface card or network adapter. A network adapter plugs into the motherboard of a computer and into a network cable or it may already be integrated into the motherboard. Network adapters perform all the functions required to communicate on a network. They convert data between the form stored in the computer and the form transmitted or received on the cable (*Figure 5.12*).

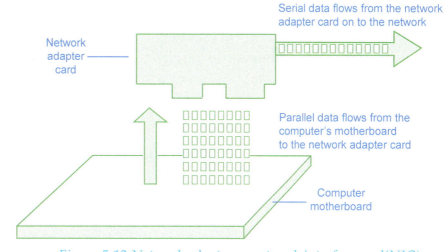

Figure 5.12 Network adapter or network interface card(NIC)

The data is transmitted in packets called frames. The format and size of a frame is defined by the Ethernet bus protocol, a Local Area Network (LAN) protocol.

Figure 5.13 shows this frame structure. Note that the data part of the frame can be any number of bytes between **46** and **1500**, inclusive.

Figure 5.13 Ethernet frame

5 Fundamentals of computer networks

Ethernet is a family of related protocols. The family supports three different transmission speeds:
- 10 Mbps (standard Ethernet)
- 100 Mbps (fast Ethernet)
- 1000 Mbps (gigabit Ethernet).

It uses 48-bit addresses for both destination (where the frame is going) and source (where it comes from).

Questions

2. "A computer communicates on a network through a network interface card or network adapter." Explain this statement with reference to the bus protocol, Ethernet.

3. Why is Ethernet referred to as a family of protocols?

Wi-Fi

Wi-Fi was invented to provide a wireless connection between computing devices and to enable these devices to connect to the Internet via a bridge between a wireless LAN (WLAN) and a wired LAN known as an **access point** - *Figure 5.14*.

WiFi or Wi-Fi® is officially called IEEE 802.11, because of the naming scheme that the IEEE (Institute of Electrical and Electronic Engineers) uses to name their standards. The 802 part means a Local Area Network (LAN), and the .11 part is for wireless. Thus Wi-Fi® which is a trademark of the Wi-Fi Alliance is a WLAN. It is a LAN because wireless is short-range.

The Wi-Fi channel through which the Wi-Fi signals travel is a shared medium, shared between devices on this channel, e.g. channel 36. For this reason, we say it is multi-access or a **multiple access medium**. Access must be coordinated and controlled. Hence the need for a Wi-Fi protocol.

Wi-Fi® is a family of protocols, e.g. 802.11a, 802.11b, 802.11g, etc.

Figure 5.15 shows a configuration screen for setting up a WLAN. The configuration allows the system to negotiate the most appropriate Wi-Fi® protocol for the WLAN.

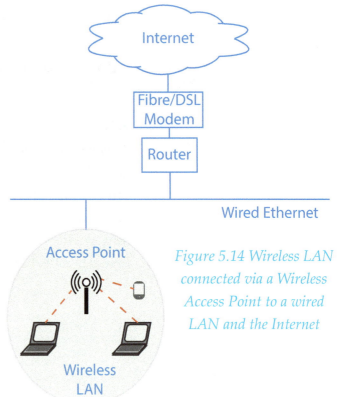

Figure 5.14 Wireless LAN connected via a Wireless Access Point to a wired LAN and the Internet

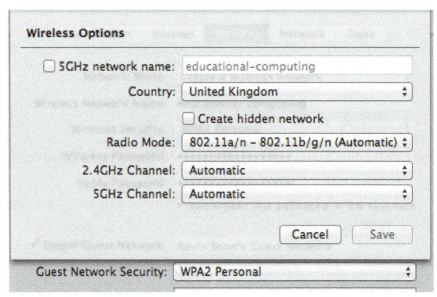

Figure 5.15 Wireless radio frequency options for wireless networks with identifier educational-computing

Questions

4. What is the purpose of a Wireless LAN (WLAN) and what is its relationship with the term Wi-Fi?

TCP (Transmission Control Protocol)

When two people make a land line telephone call, switches are closed in telephone exchanges to create a continuous end-to-end connection between the telephone handsets used by the two people. This connection is not shared with anyone else and is held for the duration of the telephone call. When the call is finished the connection is broken. What happens when a person interacts via a web browser with a web server to download a web page is completely different. The web page must travel through a packet-switched network. This requires that the web page is first split into a number of smaller units called packets. Each packet is labelled with a sequence number before being dispatched into the packet-switched network as shown in *Figure 5.16*. Packets travelling through the packet-switched network do not necessarily follow the same path which can result in some packets arriving at their destination out of sequence.

To illustrate what happens, let's consider a simple example of sending the text shown in *Table 5.1*. It is first split into numbered packets as shown in *Table 5.2*.

These are then sent independently of each other through a packet-switched network arriving at their destination out of order, possibly, as shown in *Table 5.3*.

It is software implementing the **Transmission Control Protocol (TCP)** which breaks text/long messages into shorter segments which are numbered before being sent as separate packets known as **TCP segments**. Similar software implementing TCP at the destination then uses the sequence number assigned to each packet to reassemble them into the correct order.

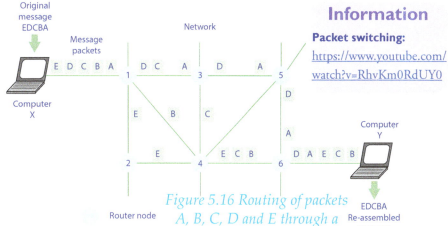

Figure 5.16 Routing of packets A, B, C, D and E through a packet-switched network

Information

Packet switching:
https://www.youtube.com/watch?v=RhvKm0RdUY0

Let me not to the marriage of true minds
Admit impediments. Love is not love
Which alters when it alteration finds,
Or bends with the remover to remove:
O, no! it is an ever-fixed mark,
That looks on tempests and is never shaken;
It is the star to every wandering bark,
Whose worth's unknown, although his height be taken.
Love's not Time's fool, though rosy lips and cheeks
Within his bending sickle's compass come;
Love alters not with his brief hours and weeks,
But bears it out even to the edge of doom.
If this be error and upon me prov'd,
I never writ, nor no man ever lov'd.

Table 5.1 Shakespeare's Sonnet 116

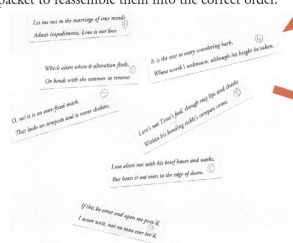

Table 5.2 Shakespeare's Sonnet 116 split into numbered packets

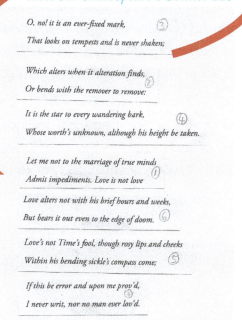

Table 5.3 Shakespeare's Sonnet 116 received out of sequence

5 Fundamentals of computer networks

The TCP software also provides **reliable transport of packets by detecting and handling errors in packet transmission**.

If the destination's TCP software receives a packet containing error(s) it requests the packet to be sent again. The sender's TCP software expects the destination's TCP software to acknowledge successful receipt of each packet sent. If an acknowledgement is not received within a certain time period, the sender sends the packet again.

To the web browser that requested the web page and to the web server with that web page, TCP appears

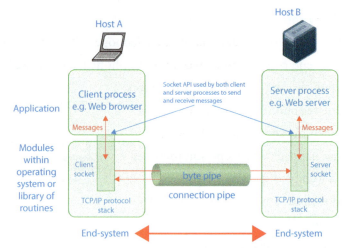

Figure 5.17 Sending and receiving messages using TCP

to **establish a reliable two-way connection for data flows in either direction between the two end-systems** as shown in *Figure 5.17*.

This connection appears to both web browser and web server to support a reliable byte-stream communication channel (pipe).

This connection has to be set up and then at the end of the message transmission, broken down (this process is called teardown).

In addition, TCP:

- Performs flow control by speed matching sender and receiver
- Provides congestion control when parts of the network are congested (packet acknowledgements don't arrive within the allotted time period). TCP will resend packets along a less congested route.

> **Questions**
>
> 5 Explain the purpose of TCP (Transmission Control Protocol).
>
> 6 Give **one** example of network communication which involves the use of TCP.

UDP (User Datagram Protocol)

When you post a letter into a Post Office pillar box, you expect the letter to get to the address on the envelope, eventually, but you have no control over the delivery part of the process only control over the writing and posting part. The letter may get lost in the post or arrive so damaged (the dog chewed it up) that it goes straight into a bin. You will just assume that your letter got through. UDP is a bit like this.

UDP, like TCP, breaks a message down into smaller-sized packets which end up being sent through a packet-switched network to their destination. These packets are called **datagrams**.

However, unlike TCP, **UDP does not establish end-to-end connections** between communicating end systems. Therefore, **no check is made by the sender's UDP software that the packets reach their destination**. **Nor does the destination's UDP software request a resend if an error is detected in a received packet**. The packet is simply discarded.

Also, **UDP does not insert sequence numbers**.

The packets are expected to arrive as a continuous stream or they are dropped. However, the receiver can signal the sender to slow down.

UDP is used because it can offer a very efficient communication transport to some applications, but it has no inherent reliability.

For example, UDP is an ideal protocol for network applications in which delay in receiving packets is critical such as gaming, voice and video communications.

These can cope with some data loss from lost or corrupted received packets without adversely affecting perceived quality.

Figure 5.18 Approximate location of some UK telephone exchanges

Questions

7 Explain the purpose of UDP (User Datagram Protocol).

8 Give **one** example of network communication which involves the use of UDP.

IP (Internet Protocol)

In order to understand the Internet Protocol and IP addressing which is what this protocol is about, we will first consider another system, the land line telephone system in the UK, which like IP uses a uniform addressing scheme of unique addresses to identify devices.

The map of the UK in Figure 5.18 shows the approximate location of some telephone exchanges in the network of exchanges. Figure 5.19 shows the telephone numbers of some land line telephones connected to local telephone exchanges in Aylesbury and High Wycombe, Buckinghamshire.

To phone High Wycombe land line number 433014 from Aylesbury requires that 01494 433014 is dialled where 01494 is the area code number for High Wycombe telephone exchange.

To phone Aylesbury land line telephone 433014 from High Wycombe requires that 01296 433014 is dialled where 01296 is the area code number for Aylesbury telephone exchange.

Figure 5.20 shows a label stuck to the base of a telephone handset. This label lists the serial number 1633082361 for this phone.

Why are phone numbers used instead of phone serial numbers when dialling? The answer is that it would be very inconvenient to use phone serial numbers because every time a household changes its phone for another, the phone number would have to change if it was based on phone serial number.

It is much easier to manage call routing and telephone directories if the phone network assigns logical telephone numbers, such as 433014, instead of physical device serial numbers.

For example, the telephone number 433014 assigned to a phone linked to Aylesbury's telephone exchange remains this household's telephone number no matter how many times the household changes its phone.

Figure 5.19 Example of UK telephone numbering system

Figure 5.20 Base of telephone handset showing serial number (S/N)

Key principle

End-to-end principle:
The end-to-end principle of the Internet requires that the two endpoints, the hosts, are responsible for establishing, supervising and maintaining a connection between two communicating processes, one on each host. This is done by a piece of software in each host known by the name Transmission Control Protocol (TCP).

5 Fundamentals of computer networks

The UK's telephone numbering system uses a uniform numbering scheme in which each telephone number (area code number + local number) is unique, e.g.

- 01494 433014 uniquely identifies a telephone (ignoring extension lines) located in High Wycombe
- 01296 433014 uniquely identifies a telephone (ignoring extension lines) located in Aylesbury.

The end-to-end principle requires that each computer using the Internet should be uniquely identified. Vint Cerf and Robert Kahn proposed that each computer be labelled with a globally unique address known as an **IP address**. Their numbering system, called **IPv4**, is used today and allows 2^{32} different addresses. All these unique addresses make up a single logical address space.

At the binary level, an **IPv4** address consists of 32 bits (4 bytes).

Cerf and Kahn split an IP address into two parts (*Figure 5.21*):

- bits that identify the network connected to the Internet (NetID)
- bits that identify a host (strictly speaking a network interface) connected to the network (HostID).

```
31                          0
| NetID      |    HostID    |
```

Figure 5.21 IPv4 address structure

The thinking behind this was that since the Internet is made up of networks, being able to identify each network would help routers (equivalent of telephone exchanges) enormously in the task of routing packets to the correct destination network.

Key concept

Host:
The end-systems, e.g. computers, are referred to as hosts because they host (i.e. run) application programs such as a Web browser program, a Web server program, an email client program.

For example, the network shown in *Figure 5.22* has NetID 10.120.61. This network is shown as having eight hosts with HostIDs:

5, 9, 10, 15, 16, 21, 25, 26.

An IP address is usually expressed in **dotted decimal notation**, where each byte of the 32-bit IP address is written in decimal, separated by a dot.

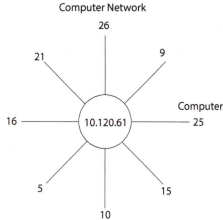

Figure 5.22 Network with network ID (NetID) 10.120.61 and eight hosts with HostIDs 5, 10, 15, etc

For example, the IP address of host with HostID 21 in *Figure 5.22* is 10.120.61.21 (NetID + HostID)

```
                 BYTE 4    BYTE 3    BYTE 2    BYTE 1
In binary this is  00001010 01111000 00111101 00010101
```

Every organisation that wishes to send and receive e-mail, or gain access to the Internet, needs at least one globally unique IP address.

An organisation is typically assigned more than one unique IP address as a block of contiguous addresses.

Key term

IPv4:
Internet numbering system of unique IP addresses that make up a single logical address space. IPv6 will eventually replace IPv4. IPv6 is also an Internet numbering system like IPv4 but it consists of 128 bits whereas IPv4 has only 32 bits.

The NetID part of the block of 32-bit IP addresses in IPv4 is indicated by expressing it in dotted decimal notation form as follows a.b.c.d/x, where x indicates the number of bits for the NetID.

For example, 129.12.0.0/16 means that the NetID is the first 16 bits, i.e. 129.12. This happens to be the NetID for the University of Kent. 192.195.42.0/23 means that the NetID is the first 23 bits, i.e.

11000000 11000011 00101010 00000000 = 11000000 11000011 0010101

This leaves 9 bits for hostIDs.

5b Network protocols

Just like the telephone network, IP protocol software defines an addressing scheme that is independent of the underlying physical addresses of the hosts. In computer networks, the physical address is the "serial number" of the host/device's network adapter, a **48-bit** number called its MAC address embedded within the adapter. It is a network adapter which enables a device to connect to a network. The network adapter shown in *Figure 5.23* has MAC address 74:D4:35:94:AD:53 expressed in hexadecimal.

Figure 5.24 shows three LANs connected by routers. Routers are used because it is not practical to connect every host directly to every other host. Instead a few hosts connect to a router, which connects to other routers, and so on, to form a network.

A **router receives packets** from one host or router and **uses the destination IP address** that they contain **to pass on the packets**, correctly formatted, to another host or router.

In the Internet, data packets flow essentially unaltered with their source and destination addresses (IP addresses) that of the endpoint systems (now referred to as **end-systems**) sending and receiving the packets, respectively. The Internet is a distributed network of switch nodes (routers) resembling a 'fishnet' as shown in *Figure 5.25*.

> **Key concept**
>
> **Uniform addressing scheme:** A uniform addressing scheme is a logical addressing scheme, independent of the underlying physical network. Each address conforms to a common format defined by a standard, e.g. IPv4.

Figure 5.23 Network adapter

> **Key term**
>
> **Internet:** A network of computer networks, computers and devices with computing capability using globally unique IP addresses and TCP/IP.

> **Key term**
>
> **Packet switching:** Messages to be sent are split into a number of segments called packets. The packets of a message are allowed to travel along independent paths through a network of routers. Routers use a packet's destination IP address to route the packet, taking account of how congested particular routes are.
>
> This network resembles a fishnet of switching nodes called routers connected by links in a way that allows multiple pathways through the network between endpoints.

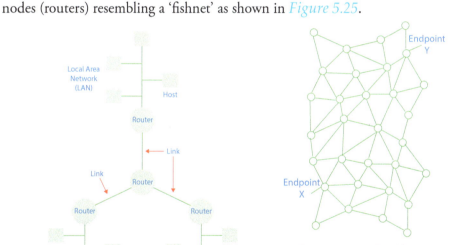

Figure 5.24 Connecting three LANs by routers

Figure 5.25 Distributed network of switching nodes (routers) resembling a 'fishnet'

Tasks

1. Visit https://ipinfo.io/countries/gb to view the range of IP address allocated to various organisations.
   Why do you think that Virgin Media Ltd, Sky UK Ltd have been allocated 9000000⁺ and 7000000⁺ IP addresses, respectively?

2. Click on the hyperlink https://ipinfo.io/AS5607 for Sky Ltd to view how Sky's IP addresses are organised into networks.

3. What is the IP address of a network computer that you have access to? To find out go to Start>Run>Cmd>IPConfig<Return key>. on a Windows machine.

On an Apple Mac or Linux machine use ifconfig from a Terminal window and look for inet.

5 Fundamentals of computer networks

> **Questions**
>
> 9 Explain the purpose of IP addressing in the Internet Protocol.
>
> 10 What device or devices in network communication other than the sending and receiving hosts use IP addresses?

HTTP (Hypertext Transfer Protocol)

Hypertext Transfer Protocol (HTTP) is a very simple application-level protocol. In this protocol, a client computer sends a request message to the server and the server responds with a response message (*Figure 5.26*).

Figure 5.26 HTTP request-response messages

In the example in *Figure 5.26* the file `index.html` has been requested. The response message may contain many forms of data. The most popular form of data is text formatted using Hypertext Markup Language (HTML).

TCP establishes a connection between the client computer and the server computer so that HTTP has a pathway for its request and response messages.

The simplest request message is

```
GET / <Return key pressed>
<Return key pressed>
```

This gets the default web page, `index.html`, for the given site.

HTTP finishes with the connection after the response message is sent; the TCP connection is broken unless specifically requested to stay connected.

A web page returned by an HTTP GET request is a text file containing content to be displayed together with instructions on how to style and structure this content when displayed.

HTTPS (Hypertext Transfer Protocol Secure)

Hypertext Transfer Protocol over Secure Sockets (HTTPS) is a web protocol that encrypts and decrypts user page requests as well as the pages that are returned by the web server. HTTPS uses the Secure Sockets Layer (SSL) beneath the HTTP application layer. HTTPS uses port 443 instead of port 80 in its interactions with TCP/IP. *Figure 5.27* shows the SSL sublayer which encrypts the HTTP GET / request before sending it through the TCP connection to the Web server www.site.co.uk. Both the request and the response are encrypted.

HTTPS has been used for a long time for securing payment transactions on the Web but it is now being more widely used for general Web access.

> **Key term**
>
> **Port number:**
> Two applications sending to and receiving from each other, are identified by numbers called port numbers (see *Figure 5.28*).

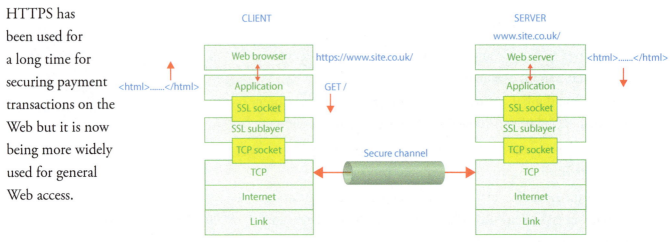

Figure 5.27 Fetching a Web page using HTTPS

FTP (File Transfer Protocol)

File Transfer Protocol (FTP) is an application layer protocol that enables files on one host, computer B, to be copied to another host, computer A. One host runs an FTP client and the other an FTP server.

FTP servers use two ports: port 21 for commands and port 20 for data.

Figure 5.28 shows an FTP client connected to an FTP server via TCP so that it can send a command request for a file `Test.txt` located on the FTP server. The FTP response is to send file `Test.txt` through the TCP connection to the FTP client.

Port 57359 is bound to the TCP socket on the client side, whilst on the server side, port 21 is bound to the command socket and port 20 to the data socket.

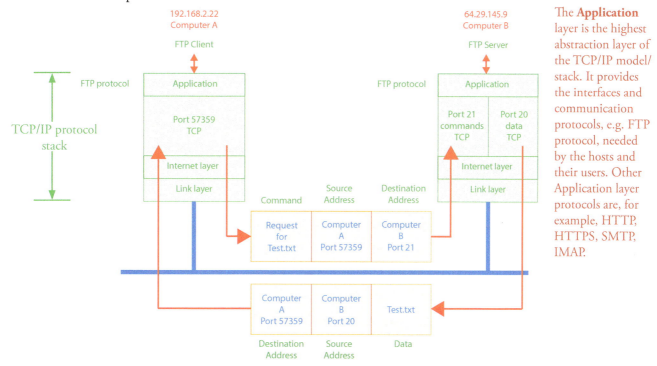

The **Application** layer is the highest abstraction layer of the TCP/IP model/stack. It provides the interfaces and communication protocols, e.g. FTP protocol, needed by the hosts and their users. Other Application layer protocols are, for example, HTTP, HTTPS, SMTP, IMAP.

Figure 5.28 FTP transfer of file Test.txt from Computer B to Computer A

The client may need to navigate the directory structure of the server, create new directories, rename files and directories, delete files and directories. These are sent to the server as command requests.

Figure 5.29 shows FTP client software (FileZilla) running on a computer with IP address 192.168.2.22 connected to an FTP server running on a computer with IP address 64.29.145.9. This server is located in the USA whilst the client computer is in the UK.

The FTP client and FTP server software rely on the FTP protocol embedded in the Application layer of the TCP/IP protocol stack to communicate.

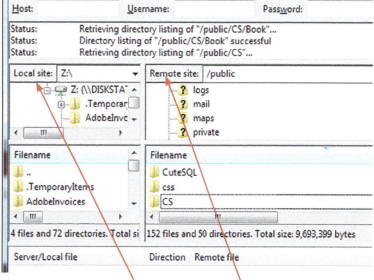

Figure 5.29 FTP client using FileZilla FTP client software connected to an FTP server

Questions

11. Explain the purpose of FTP (FileTransfer Protocol).

5 Fundamentals of computer networks

Email protocols

Simple Mail Transfer Protocol (SMTP)

Simple Mail Transfer Protocol (SMTP) is used by e-mail clients to send e-mail. It is a relatively simple text-based protocol.

One or more recipients of a message are specified then SMTP is used by the email client to transfer the message text to a mail server listening on port 25. The mail server takes care of delivering the mail to the ultimate destination using SMTP.

For creating and sending email the SMTP protocol supports commands such as

- `MAIL FROM:` - defines the e-mail address of the sender of the message.
- `RCPT TO:` - defines the e-mail address of a recipient of the message. Repeating this command once for each recipient means you can send one piece of mail to many users without having to repeat the entire process over and over again.
- `DATA` marks the start of the data portion of the message, essentially everything that you would consider "content", this includes the "To:", "From:", "CC:" etc. as these are not commands but simple informational components making up a header which the e-mail client picks out of the content and displays in a far nicer format. Just as a reminder - anything which is in the content can be faked as it is content and so consequently cannot be validated.

Internet Message Access Protocol (IMAP)

IMAP is a protocol that was designed to allow access to emails stored on a remote server. Users essentially connect to an IMAP server to read and organise their emails. Remote access from any user device is supported, e.g. smart phone, tablet, PC. New emails are cached locally so that they are available to read again without needing to contact the server. The user may configured the emails stored on the server into folders, mark emails as read, etc. One can think of the service provided by IMAP as a kind of cloud storage.

Questions

12. Which of the networking protocols labelled A .. E would be used to
    (a) make a payment securely when purchasing goods from a website?
    (b) send an email?
    (c) view email stored on a server?
    (d) transfer a file between hosts?
    (e) retrieve a web page insecurely?

    A   FTP
    B   SMTP
    C   IMAP
    D   HTTPS
    E   HTTP

Layer	Order (1-4)
Server responds by sending web page	
Server receives request for web page	
Web browser requests web page	
Web browser receives web page	

Table 5.4

13. A user accesses a web page stored on a remote web server through a web browser. *Table 5.4* shows the actions that need to take place to make this possible. Put these actions in the correct order (1-4, where 1 is the first action that needs to take place and 4 is the last). What application protocol could have been used to obtain this web page?

In this chapter you have covered:

- Defining the term 'network protocol'
- The purpose and use of common network protocols including:
    - Ethernet
    - Wi-Fi
    - TCP (Transmission Control Protocol)
    - UDP (User Datagram Protocol)
    - IP (Internet Protocol)
    - HTTP (Hypertext Transfer Protocol)
    - HTTPS (Hypertext Transfer Protocol Secure)
    - FTP (File Transfer Protocol)
    - Email protocols:
        - SMTP (Simple Mail Transfer Protocol)
        - IMAP (Internet Message Access Protocol).

5 Fundamentals of computer networks

5 Fundamentals of computer networks

Learning objectives:

- *Understand the need for, and importance of, network security*

- *Explain the following methods of network security:*
  - *authentication*
  - *encryption*
  - *firewall*
  - *MAC address filtering.*

Key term

Network security:
Network security consists of the measures and policies put in place by a network administrator to prevent and monitor unauthorised access, denial of service, misuse, modification, and destruction of network-accessible resources, e.g data including network password lists.

Key term

Data security:
Data security means protecting against unauthorised access, alteration or destruction. A greater level of data security can be achieved by the use of data security methods, authentication, encryption, firewall and MAC address filtering, in combination.

5c Network security

The need for and importance of network security

In the physical world, locks are placed on doors and alarm systems are fitted to property to protect against theft of assets and personal harm.

In the digital world, every computer system needs similar protection especially against the serious consequences of the loss of business or personal data whether from theft or otherwise. Businesses can fail as a result. For example, according to SC Magazine, the company Code Spaces was closed down after its Amazon Elastic Compute Cloud control panel was hacked and data, backups, and off-site backups were erased.

Security breaches do not just affect businesses. The computer systems of individuals are also vulnerable. Individuals can lose money if their online bank details are stolen by hackers or if their identities are stolen.

Connecting a computer or computing device to a network increases the risk that the computer could be attacked and data stolen or damaged. In fact, poor security on a network computer could allow unauthorised access to the whole network with potentially serious consequences. That is why network security is important especially if connection to the Internet is supported because many of the protocols used in the Internet do not provide any security.

Tools to "sniff" passwords on the network are in common use by malicious hackers. Thus, applications which send an unencrypted password over the network are extremely vulnerable.

Network security methods
Network security

Network security consists of the measures and policies put in place by a network administrator to prevent and monitor unauthorised access, denial of service, misuse, modification, and destruction of network-accessible resources, e.g data including network password lists.

Where data is concerned security refers to the protection of data against unauthorised access/disclosure, alteration, or destruction.

Questions

1. Why is network security important?

2. What is meant by network security?

5 Fundamentals of computer networks

Authentication

Network security systems are designed to let authorised people into the network, and to keep unauthorised people out. This involves three distinct steps:

1. **Identification**:

    The identification step requires that a person identifies themselves, e.g. by means of identification string such as an email address or userID.

2. **Authentication**:

    Once identification has been provided, the person is required to provide evidence of their identity which could be one or more of the following
    - Something they know, e.g. a password or a PIN
    - Something they have, e.g. a smart card or a token/security device
    - Some aspect of a person's physiology such as their fingerprint or iris pattern of their eye. This is called biometrics.

3. **Authorisation**:
    - Allows an authenticated person access to the system with the authority to carry out certain permitted operations such as read/write and delete specific data in an area of storage allocated to them.

Figure 5.30 Banking security device token

Key term

Authentication: The process or action of verifying the identity of a user or process.

Authentication by password is considered vulnerable because humans find it difficult to remember a password that an attacker would find difficult to guess. An improvement is to use a one-time-password (OTP) generated by a token or security device such as the one shown in *Figure 5.30*.

Tokens are designed to generate seemingly random passwords that are synchronized with a token server. When an OTP is combined with a Personal Identification Number (PIN), two-factor authentication is achieved because the client needs to have something (the token) and know something (the PIN). The user enters their PIN into the token (using keypad such as the one shown in *Figure 5.30*) they hold to get the next one-time password. The token shown in *Figure 5.30* has an internal clock which was synchronised with the bank's token server clock when the token was issued. The software in the token that generates the next password relies on this clock time to set the time period for which the password is valid. This enables the token server to generate the corresponding password so that submission of the next one-time password can be matched at the token server to authenticate the user.

Biometric authentication uses the person's body as their "password". Instead of the "password" being something that the person knows, it is something **physical** and **unique** that they possess.

A user might use biometrics to authenticate themselves to a system or might use biometrics to authenticate themselves to a local system (a smart card or token) The card/token then authenticates itself to a remote system.

Questions

3. What is authentication in the context of computer security?
4. Methods used separately or in combination to verify the identity of a user attempting to log in to a computer network are classified as follows:

    Something they know,
    Something they have,
    Something of the person

    Give **one** example of each of these methods.

5c Network security

Encryption

If authentication uses cryptography, then an attacker listening to the network gains no information that would enable them to falsely claim another's identity. Passwords sent across the network in plain text form can be intercepted and subsequently used by eavesdroppers to impersonate a user.

Encrypting data, including passwords, sent across a network can therefore improve network security.

Encryption mathematically converts data into a form that is not directly readable. Therefore, an attacker who is eavesdropping on the network will not be able to decode passwords and data sent over the network in encrypted form.

Figure 5.31 shows part of a bank login screen that uses the secure web protocol HTTPS (Hypertext Transfer Protocol over Secure Sockets).

HTTPS is a web protocol that encrypts and decrypts user page requests as well as the pages that are returned by the web server. A user's username and password will therefore be sent encrypted to HSBC®'s authentication server.

Figure 5.31 Bank login screen showing use of the secure web protocol HTTPS

> **Key point**
>
> **Encryption and authentication:** If authentication uses cryptography, then an attacker listening to the network gains no information that would enable it to falsely claim another's identity.

> **Did you know?**
>
> **Securing wireless networks:** User's data sent between two devices, e.g. a wireless station and an access point needs to be private to those two devices, i.e. kept confidential by securing against unauthorised access. Unfortunately, radio transmissions over a wireless network are easily intercepted and read by third parties unless encrypted.
> Wi-Fi Protected Access (WPA) and Wi-Fi Protected Access II (WPA2) are two security protocols developed by the Wi-Fi Alliance to secure wireless computer networks.

> **Did you know?**
>
> Authentication can also be strengthened through the use of public key cryptography. For example, a user has a smart card that contains a public key and a matching private key.
> The user's public key is placed on file at the remote server.
> To authenticate the user, the remote server sends the user a random challenge (a random number).
> The user signs the challenge with their private key to create a digital signature and sends this signature to the remote server, which verifies the signature with the public key that it has on file.
> In this way, the remote system can verify that the user has possession of the private key without ever needing sight of it and the user has no need to use a password.

> **Information**
>
> **HTTPS:**
> HTTPS will encrypt payment details such as credit card number and credit card security code when purchasing goods from a website, thus enabling the payment to be made securely.
> In addition, HTTPS will assure the payee that the website is genuine because HTTPS will use the website's digital certificate issued by a trusted authority.

Questions

5 Why is it considered a good idea to encrypt network communication?

5 Fundamentals of computer networks

Firewall

A **firewall** is a combination of hardware and software that isolates an organisation's internal network from the Internet at large, allowing some packets to pass and blocking others. *Figure 5.32* shows a firewall located between an organisation's local area network and the router that connects, via an ISP, the organisation's network to the Internet.

With all network traffic entering and leaving the organisation's network passing through the firewall, the firewall is able to allow authorised traffic through whilst blocking unauthorised traffic. The firewall is positioned as shown in *Figure 5.32* so that it watches over all traffic crossing the gateway point, acting like a sentry or doorman. A doorman/sentry positioned at the entrance or exit of a building watches for unauthorised attempts to enter the secure area. Some people are allowed to enter, others are prevented.

Figure 5.32 Local Area Network behind a firewall

Questions

6. What purpose is served by a network firewall, and typically where would a firewall be located in a network?

> **Key term**
>
> **Firewall:**
> A firewall is a combination of hardware and software that isolates an organisation's internal network from the Internet at large. It monitors incoming and outgoing network traffic and decides whether to allow or block specific traffic based on a defined set of security rules.

MAC address filtering

MAC addresses are **48**-bit addresses uniquely assigned to each network interface card (NIC). Alternative name for a NIC is network adapter.

In **MAC address filtering**, an internal table (in Wi-Fi router in wireless networks or in a managed switch in wired networks) of MAC addresses is consulted to decide whether to permit access to the network or not. If the MAC address is on this list then the device with this MAC address may join the network. If its MAC address is not on the list then any attempt made to join the network will be rejected.

However, MAC filtering can be defeated by a spoofer who learns the MAC address of a valid network interface card, i.e. one on the list, by scanning network traffic. A MAC address is "glued" into a network card, but it is possible to command the operating system to change information about the MAC address in every data packet it sends out to the network. If a spoofer were to do this to the network interface card in their machine then the spoofer could gain access to the MAC address list protected network.

Questions

7. Describe MAC address filtering.

8. Describe how the methods of authentication, encryption, firewalls and MAC address filtering could be used in combination to secure a network against unauthorised access, alteration or destruction.

> **Key term**
>
> **MAC address filtering:**
> In MAC address filtering, an internal table (in Wi-Fi router in wireless networks or in a managed switch in wired networks) of MAC addresses is consulted to decide whether to permit a device access to the network or not on the basis of its MAC address. The MAC address is a physical address embedded within the device's network adapter.

In this chapter you have covered:
- The need for, and importance of, network security
- The following methods of network security:
  - authentication
  - encryption
  - firewall
  - MAC address filtering.

5 Fundamentals of computer networks

5 Fundamentals of computer networks

Learning objectives:

- *Describe the four layer TCP/IP model:*
  - *application layer*
  - *transport layer*
  - *internet layer*
  - *link layer*

- *Understand that the HTTP, HTTPS, SMTP, IMAP and FTP protocols operate at the application layer*

- *Understand that the TCP and UDP protocols operate at the transport layer*

- *Understand that the IP protocol operates at the network layer.*

5d Four layer TCP/IP model

The four layer TCP/IP model

Networking protocols were designed to make possible communication between application programs executing on different hosts whilst hiding the complexities of the underlying network from these application programs.
A **host**, or host computer, is any computer system that connects to an internet and runs applications.
The term **process** is used for an instance of a program in execution, so it is actually processed in different hosts connected by a network that are communicating.

Layered organisation

Networking protocols are usually developed in layers.
Each layer is responsible for a different part of the communication process.
The software that implements a protocol is called **protocol software** and the software that implements a suite of protocols such as TCP/IP, is called a **protocol stack**.
The **TCP/IP protocol suite** consists of four conceptual layers as shown in *Figure 5.33*:

- Application layer
- Transport layer
- Internet or IP layer
- Link layer.

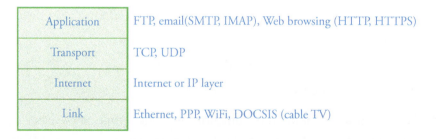

Figure 5.33 The four layers of the TCP/IP protocol suite and stack

It is implemented in software as the **TCP/IP protocol stack** in separate software modules corresponding to the individual layers of the protocol suite.

Each layer and therefore each software module has a different responsibility. The protocol stack is installed on each computer either as a part of the operating system or as a software library.

Key terms

Host:
A host is any computer system that connects to an internet and runs applications.

Process:
An instance of a program in execution.

Key terms

Protocol:
A protocol provides agreed signals, codes and rules for data exchange between systems.

Networking protocols:
Networking protocols make possible communication between processes executing on different hosts whilst hiding the complexities of the underlying network from these processes.

TCP/IP protocol suite:
The TCP/IP protocol suite consists of four conceptual layers: application, transport, internet or IP, and link.

TCP/IP protocol stack:
Implements the TCP/IP protocol suite in software.

Key term

Application layer:
Application layer protocols are used to exchange data between programs running on the source and destination hosts. It is the application layer that provides the interface between these programs and the underlying network over which the programs' messages are transmitted, e.g. HTTP message GET / which fetches the default Web page from a Web server.

Key term

Transmission Control Protocol (TCP):
TCP enables applications executing on two hosts to establish a connection and exchange application-layer messages through a reliable byte-stream channel (pipe) for data flows between the two end systems.

Application programs interact with the software stack via an **Application Programming Interface (API)**. The de facto standard is the **socket API**.

The following Python code snippet shows a client application using the socket API to set up a socket to send a message to a server:

```
clientSocket = socket(socket.AF_INET, socket.SOCK_STREAM)
message = "Hello Server"
clientSocket.sendTo(message, (serverName, serverPort))
```

Figure 5.34 shows a client process and a server process that use the socket API

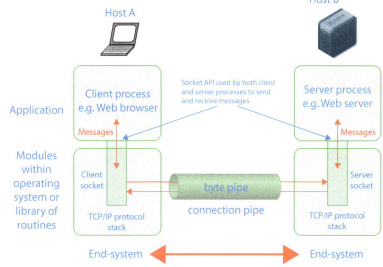

Figure 5.34 Sending and receiving messages using the socket API

from the TCP/IP protocol stack to send and receive messages via a TCP/IP connection pipe established between client and server.

Application layer

A process in one end-system (host) uses the application layer of TCP/IP to exchange packets of information with a process in another end-system. The packets of information at the application layer are called **messages**.

The **application layer** uses different application-layer protocols for different applications. For example, if the application is designed to enable Web pages to be fetched from a Web server then the application will use either the HTTP application-layer protocol or the HTTPS application-layer protocol. An application-layer protocol defines the kind of messages to send. In the case of HTTP or HTTPS, one such message could be a GET message.

Transport layer

The **transport layer** of the protocol stack is a piece of software in each host. This software implements the two transport protocols **Transmission Control Protocol (TCP)** and **User Data Protocol (UDP)**. TCP enables applications executing on two hosts to establish a two-way connection and exchange application-layer messages through a reliable byte-stream channel (pipe) for data flows in either direction between the two end-systems as shown in *Figure 5.34*. It also allows the connection to be terminated.

TCP breaks long messages into shorter segments which it sends as separate transport-layer packets known as **TCP segments**.

The application at the sending side (e.g. a Web browser using the application-layer protocol HTTP) pushes messages (e.g. GET) through a **TCP/IP socket**. The transport-layer protocol TCP has the responsibility of getting the messages to the socket of the receiving application process, e.g. a Web server listening on port 80. Port numbers such as port 80 are 16-bit numbers used for application (specific instance of a Web browser request) and service identification on the Internet (a Web server).

TCP does everything in its control to guarantee delivery of the application-layer message and also guarantee that the received TCP segments will be reassembled in the correct order to form the message to be passed to the application-layer and then the corresponding application process.

During set up TCP establishes the maximum size of the packets (Maximum Segment Size or Maximum Transmission Unit) it can use through the network - see http://www.tp-link.com/us/FAQ-190.html for an exercise that you can do to establish the maximum packet size.

Once the TCP has established a connection it:

- Monitors the connection for transmission errors and responds when an error is detected by retransmitting the segment that suffered the error
- Detects when a connection is broken
- Performs flow control by speed matching sender and receiver
- Provides congestion control when the network is congested.

Internet or IP (Internet Protocol) layer

The transport layer uses the IP layer to carry its segments. Each TCP segment is encapsulated in an IP packet before it is sent across the internet.

The IP layer adds source and destination IP addresses to packets on their way from the transport layer to the link layer, and removes source and destination IP addresses from packets on their way from the link layer to the transport layer.

The **internet or IP layer** in hosts and routers move these packets known as **IP or Internet Protocol packets** from one host to another without regard to whether these hosts belong to the same network or different networks.

The Internet Protocol is a connectionless protocol which just provides a best effort but not guaranteed way of delivering packets called **datagrams**. The reliability of the transmission is left to the layer above, the transport layer.

Getting to the destination host may require many hops via intermediate routers along the way.

Both hosts and routers need to use the internet or IP layer of the TCP/IP protocol stack but since the job of a router is dedicated to routing packets, **a router only requires use of the internet and link layers of the TCP/IP stack**. The IP layer in a router must have sufficient knowledge of other routers and links in its internet to be able to make routing decisions for packets that pass through it.

Together TCP and IP hide the differences between the underlying networks through which packets pass when going from source to destination host.

> **Key term**
>
> **Function of Transport layer:**
> The basic function of the transport layer is to
> - accept messages/data from the layer above it
> - split these into smaller units called segments if necessary (segment size determined at TCP connection set up time)
> - pass these segments to the internet or IP layer
> - ensure that all the segments arrive correctly at the other end
> - reassemble the received segments, which it gets from the internet layer, in the correct order to form the message/data to pass to the layer above.
>
> The transport layer is a true end-to-end layer which carries messages/data all the way from the source to the destination.

> **Key term**
>
> **Internet or IP layer:**
> The internet or IP layer of the TCP/IP protocol stack in hosts and routers is responsible for moving IP-layer packets from one host to another without regard to whether these hosts are on the same network or not. It adds source and destination IP addresses to packets on their way from the transport layer to the link layer, and removes source and destination IP addresses from packets on their way from the link layer to the transport layer.

5 Fundamentals of computer networks

Link layer

The link layer handles all the physical details of interfacing with the network cable or wireless connection. It includes the network interface card (network adapter) and a device driver (installed in operating system). TCP/IP protocol supports many different types of link layer, depending on the type of networking hardware being used. One example is Ethernet.

The link layer adds source and destination hardware addresses (e.g. MAC addresses) to packets that it receives from the IP layer then dispatches the packets onto the local cable or wireless connection.

If the packet is destined for a host on another network, the link layer destination address is the hardware address of the gateway (router) to the internet which the other network is connected to.

In an Ethernet local area network (LAN) these hardware addresses are Ethernet card (Network Interface Card) addresses, or MAC addresses. *Figure 5.35* shows a packet despatched by the link layer of a host with IP address 174.89.0.54 to a remote host with IP address 210.5.0.67. *Figure 5.35* shows the first, second and last hop of many hops.

Note that the link layer hardware address changes from hop to hop whilst the source and destination IP addresses remain constant.

This is because the link layer's role is to stream bytes between directly connected machines, hosts and routers.

It is the link layer that puts bits onto the network cable or wireless connection. Sending to a remote machine is done in hops where each hop is a direct connection (link) between a host and a router, a router and a host, a router and another router, or two directly connected hosts.

> **Key term**
>
> **Link layer:**
> The link layer handles all the physical details of interfacing with the network cable or wireless connection.
> The link layer adds source and destination hardware addresses (e.g. MAC addresses) to packets that it receives from the IP layer then despatches the packets onto the local cable or wireless connection.

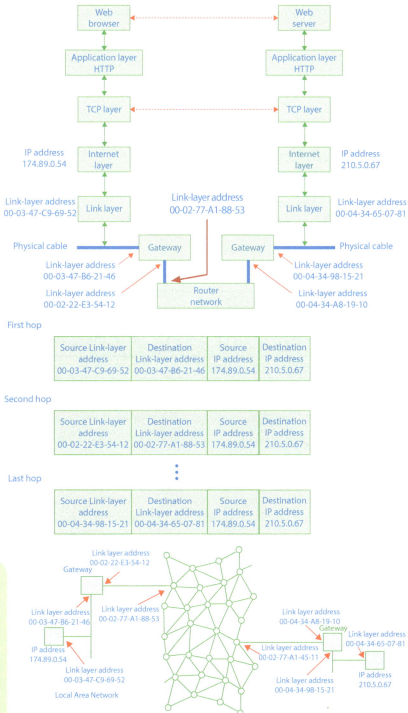

Figure 5.35 TCP/IP protocol stack and the role of the link layer (or link layer) in the communicating hosts and intermediate routers

5d Four layer TCP/IP model

Questions

1. TCP/IP is a four-layer protocol stack used in networking.

   Complete the table, using each number from 1-4 once, to indicate the correct order for these layers (where 1 is the top layer and 4 is the bottom layer).

Layer	Order (1-4)
Internet	
Application	
Link	
Transport	

2. *Figure 5.36* shows the address part of a packet sent between two computers A and B on the same local area network.

Source link-layer address	Destination link-layer address	Source IP address	Destination IP address

   Figure 5.36

   The MAC addresses of their network interface cards are as follows

   Computer A: 00-03-47-C9-69-52

   Computer B: 00-03-47-C9-44-35

   Their IP addresses are as follows

   Computer A: 212.168.0.54

   Computer B: 212.168.0.32

   Complete the table for the address part of a message packet sent from A to B.

Layer	Address
Source link-layer address	
Destination link-layer address	
Source IP address	
Destination IP address	

3. Computer B is now relocated to a different local area network on the other side of the world from computer A but it is still reachable from A across the Internet. Computer A addresses a message packet and despatches it to computer B. The message packet successfully reaches B. Which address in the packet must have been changed by computer A for the packet to be successfully routed to B?

4. Describe the roles of the application layer and the data link layer in the four-layer TCP/IP model.

- The four layer TCP/IP model:
  - application layer
  - transport layer
  - internet layer
  - link layer
- That the HTTP, HTTPS, SMTP, IMAP and FTP protocols operate at the application layer
- That the TCP and UDP protocols operate at the transport layer
- That the IP protocol operates at the internet layer.

6 Cyber security

6 Cyber security

Learning objectives:

- *Be able to define the term cyber security and be able to describe the main purposes of cyber security*
- *Understand and be able to explain the following cyber security threats:*
  - *social engineering techniques*
  - *malicious code (malware)*
  - *pharming*
  - *weak and default passwords*
  - *misconfigured access rights*
  - *removable media*
  - *unpatched and/or outdated software*
- *Explain what penetration testing is and what it is used for.*

> **Key term**
>
> **Cyber security:**
> Cyber security consists of the processes, practices and technologies designed to protect networks, computers, programs and data from attack, damage, or unauthorised access.

> **Key term**
>
> **Social engineering:**
> Social engineering is the art of manipulating a person, or group of people, into providing information or a service they would otherwise never have given.

6.1 Cyber security threats

What is cyber security?

Cyber security consists of the processes, practices and technologies designed to protect networks, computers, programs and data from attack, damage, or unauthorised access.

When computers or networks and their programs and data are attacked, the attacker attempts to bypass the security of these systems in order to "hack" into them. Hence the use of the term hacker for an attacker.

The main purpose of cyber security is to minimise the chances of an attacker hacking into a system, and exploiting this access for personal gain or malicious intent, e.g. to steal confidential information such as passwords.

6.2 Social engineering threats

Every major study on technical vulnerabilities and hacking says the following:

- Users are the weakest link, whether on purpose or by mistake
- Users and their actions represent a giant security hole that simply can't ever be completely plugged.

Social engineering provides a low tech approach to attacking a system. Social engineering is the art of manipulating a person, or group of people, into providing information or a service they would otherwise never have given.

Social engineers prey on people's natural desire to help one another, their tendency to defer to authority, their ignorance, greed and response to fear of consequences, e.g. your email account will be suspended unless you login and confirm your identity.

> **Questions**
>
> 1. You are asked by your network's administrator to provide your password. How would you respond?
>
> 2. You are surfing the Web and a pop-up box appears in your browser window to tell you that a virus has been detected on your system. To remove this virus you are told to click on a link. Would you click on the link? Explain your answer.
>
> 3. An advert appears in the side window of your browser when you are visiting a games website. The advert is offering a free game which may be downloaded immediately by clicking on a download button. Would you click on the download button? Explain your answer.

6 Cyber security

> **Information**
>
> **Spam:**
> Unsolicited email or messages that are sent to groups of people.
>
> **Distributed denial-of-service:**
> A distributed denial-of-service (DDoS) attack occurs when multiple systems flood the bandwidth or resources of a targeted system, usually one or more web servers. The targeted system is unable to cope and the service it provides becomes unavailable.

> **Key term**
>
> **Pharming:**
> Pharming is a cyberattack intended to redirect a website's traffic to a fake or bogus website.

> **Key term**
>
> **Domain Name Service (DNS):**
> The domain naming system relies upon DNS servers to handle the conversion of the letter-based (symbolic) website names, which are easily recalled by people into the machine-understandable digits (numeric addresses).

> **Key point**
>
> Pharming (pronounced 'farming') is a form of online fraud very similar to phishing as pharmers rely upon the same bogus websites and theft of confidential information. However, where phishing must entice a user to the website through 'bait' in the form of a phony email or link, pharming re-directs victims to the bogus site even if the victim has typed the correct web address. This is often applied to the websites of banks or e-commerce sites.

Malicious code(malware)

Malicious code (malware) is software that sets out to:
- Intentionally harm a computer system and other systems that it connects to
- Steal confidential information such as passwords
- Take control of a computer system for purposes such as sending spam or taking part in a Distributed Denial of Service (DDoS) attack
- Hold you to ransom (ransomware) by demanding payment to unencrypt your files
- Cause physical damage to machinery or systems controlled by a computer system, e.g. STUXNET malware causing damage to the operation of centrifuges used by Iran in its nuclear bomb programme.

The attacker might send an email containing a link that the recipient is asked to click. The link won't be so blatant as to use the label "Click me to download malicious code" but if the email comes from an unknown source the likelihood is that this will be the effect of clicking the link.

Pharming

Pharming is an "under the counter, sleight of hand" technique used by cybercriminals to redirect you from a legitimate site that you have specified to a bogus copy website elsewhere thus allowing criminals to steal the information that you enter.

Pharming exploits the fact that when the numerical addresses of the Internet (IP addresses, e.g. 123.123.123.123), which are used for routing packets of data on the Internet, became too inconvenient to remember, they were given corresponding, easier to remember, symbolic names called domain names, like umobank.co.uk.

Every time a form of a symbolic address is entered, e.g. www.umobank.co.uk, it has to be turned back into its corresponding IP address.

A Domain Name Service (DNS) server on the Internet handles this conversion process, unless either a "local host file" on your computer or a local cache on your computer already provides this.

When you enter, for example, a website address into your browser, e.g. www.umobank.co.uk, your computer contacts a DNS server and requests the corresponding and genuine IP address, 123.123.123.123.

Hackers can subvert this process in two ways:

- They can send out a Trojan horse that rewrites the local host file on your computer, so that it associates the domain name with a bogus website, e.g. www.umobank.co.uk ↔ 97.86.14.35. You are then directed to the bogus website with IP address 97.86.14.35, even though you entered the correct symbolic website address, e.g. www.umobank.co.uk.
- Alternatively, they can alter the DNS itself, i.e. alter its records so that anyone who tries to visit that symbolic address is directed to the bogus website. Compromised DNS servers are sometimes referred to as "poisoned".

By only attempting to connect to a website with SSL/TLS protection, i.e. prefix https:// in the web address and 🔒 Secure in the browser, your browser will be able to check with a Certificate Authority that the certificate associated with the site corresponds to the one for the legitimate website. If a hacker tries to mimic a secure site, a message will warn that the site's certificate does not match the address being visited.

If you see a warning that a site's certificate is not valid or not issued by a trusted authority, you should not enter the site.

The URL is also a great place to check. Always ensure that, once the page has loaded, that the URL is spelt correctly and hasn't redirected to a slightly different spelling, perhaps with additional letters or with the letters swapped around. If you examine the web address in *Figure 6.2.1* you will observe that umo is spelt u r n o.

Figure 6.2.1 Bogus site with a slightly different spelling of umo

Weak passwords

The length of a password, and the size of the character set from which its characters are chosen, can dictate the vulnerability of a system to penetration by an attacker, i.e. how easy is it to guess the password and using this knowledge gain access to a system.

For example, if passwords are restricted in length to a maximum of 3 letters, chosen from the 26 lowercase letters of the English alphabet then the maximum number of permutations of these letters is

$$26 \times 26 \times 26 = 17576$$

A computer might take only a few seconds in a brute-force attack to try each permutation in turn until the password is found that enables access to a system. Three letter passwords would be considered very weak. Even extending the choice to the 95 characters (letters and symbols) on a computer keyboard (26 uppercase, 26 lowercase, 10 digits and 33 punctuation and special symbols) would not significantly improve matters.

Weak passwords are also ones that use predictable patterns, e.g. the most common passwords of 2016 include "123456", "password", "qwerty" and "111111", according to a recently released compilation[1].

Using common words, i.e. words that would be found in a dictionary, or a list of people's names or place names also produces weak passwords. Use of such passwords can be discovered by a dictionary attack. A dictionary attack is one that attempts to discover a password by trying words found in dictionaries. The dictionary is organised by length of word so it tries single letter words then double letter words next and so on.

[1] https://blog.keepersecurity.com/2017/01/13/most-common-passwords-of-2016-research-study/

6.2 Social engineering threats

Key fact

Weak passwords:
Attackers know that many people use passwords comprised of easy-to-remember lowercase letters. Attackers typically work on those combinations first.

Key points

Strong passwords:
Length and complexity of password also adds security. Adding numbers, symbols, and using both lowercase and uppercase characters significantly increases the time needed to decipher a password.

Task

1. Read the following article on creating a secure password you will actually remember:
http://lifehacker.com/four-methods-to-create-a-secure-password-youll-actually-1601854240

Key point

Graphic cards:
Graphic cards are cheap, and can be programmed to do basic computations very quickly such as trying to guess password combinations.

Key fact

Weak passwords:
Many people use weak passwords because it can be difficult to remember strong passwords.

> **Did you know?**
>
> There are still systems that do not allow passwords longer than eight characters and no additional security measures such as two-stage authentication.
>
> In June 2014, an ATM belonging to the Bank of Montreal was successfully hacked by two fourteen year-olds using an old online ATM operator's manual that showed how to log into the cash machine's administrator's account.
>
> During a school lunch break, one day, they decided to conduct an experiment with one of the bank's ATM cash machines.
>
> Expecting little success they tried a six-digit password which to their surprise got them into the system. Rumour has it that the password they tried was '123456'.
>
> They immediately went into the bank and told staff that the security on their ATM was woefully inadequate. The bank staff did not believe the two students initially until they received a demonstration. The students were then interviewed by the branch manager and sent back to school with a note explaining that they were late because they had been assisting the bank with their security. Don't try this yourself!

Recent tests[2] cracked eight-character passwords in less than two hours by using clusters of graphic cards programmed to try permutations of the 95 characters found on a computer keyboard (*Figure 6.2.2*). **An eight-character password is thus now considered weak.** The testers concluded that the same processing power applied to twelve-character passwords was likely to take a minimum of 17134 years. A twelve-character password is thus considered very strong.

Figure 6.2.2 Computer keyboard

Passwords can be difficult to remember, which is one reason why people choose short simple passwords containing predictable sequences of letters forming a memorable name or word contained in a dictionary.

The **best kind of password** is one that is **long and random**, or at least appears to be random. A trick to creating a strong password is to **use a sentence or phrase** that is meaningful and easy to remember. For example, the password Mio68whiJ£76# was created by taking the initial letters of the words in the following sentence, substituting '£' for ',' and # for '.' and including the digits directly:

"My innings of 68 was hit in July, 76."

- Recent research has shown that changing passwords frequently is no better than not changing passwords, although people still argue that it is.
- Don't re-use passwords and use a different password for each system that you log into.
- The use of a single password such as your Facebook or Google password is not recommended because if this is stolen then all the systems that you use this password for will be compromised.
- It is alright to write passwords down in a notebook as long as the notebook can be kept somewhere safe away from the computer(s) that you use and from being accessed by anyone but you.

> **Task**
>
> ② Read the following article on the potential consequences of the use of weak passwords.
>
> Virgin Media router security flap follows weak password exposé:
>
> https://www.theregister.co.uk/2017/06/23/virgin_media_router_security_flap/

---

2   http://www.rh.gatech.edu/news/341201/teraflop-troubles-power-graphics-processing-units-may-threaten-worlds-password-security

6.2 Social engineering threats

Questions

4. Which of the following statements would you judge to be true (you may want to use *Figure 6.2.2* to help you answer this question):

    A   123456 is a very weak password.

    B   google is a very weak password.

    C   \zxcvbn,./ is a strong password.

    D   Ms?niW£si36# is a very strong password.

    E   1q2w3e4r5t6y7u8i9o is a very strong password.

5. There are many free online password strength checkers.

    (a) Explain why for security reasons you should avoid using a password checking service.

    (b) Explain how you would choose a strong password so that you would not need to rely on an online password checking service.

Key term

Default password:
A default password is a password assigned to equipment and software systems for the administrator's account, along with the account's username, e.g. admin.
Such default passwords used by manufacturers and software systems are not particularly secret and so systems that they are meant to protect are vulnerable to being hacked and worse they grant the highest possible access rights.

Default passwords

New computers with an operating system already installed, hardware such as routers, wireless security cameras, baby monitors, and database engines such as MySQL, for example, come set up with a **default password for the administrator's account**, and the account's username, e.g. admin.

An administrator's account has the highest possible access rights and therefore full control to do anything to the system.

It is not difficult for a hacker to obtain the default password used by a particular manufacturer or installer for the systems sold. Armed with a knowledge of the default password for the administrator's account an attacker could take control of a system in order to profit in some way from the gift of unfettered access.

It is very important to change the default password for the administrator's account when setting up a new system and before going live.

Internet of Things (IoT) devices connect to wireless networks and are therefore vulnerable to being "hacked". Tens of billions of these devices have been deployed. If they are password protected then they could have been sold with a default password and username. The Mirai malware let attackers hijack thousands of Internet of Things devices and carry out distributed denial-of-service attacks.

Users should reset the default password when they get an IoT device.

Did you know?

Linksys®, a manufacturer of routers, is now using WPA2 passwords which are unique on each device.

Task

3. Read the following article on the failure to change the default password:
Webcam spying disaster: http://www.telegraph.co.uk/technology/picture-galleries/11279102/The-six-worst-tech-disasters-of-2014.html?image=1

Questions

6. Explain why generating a one-time password that a user is forced to reset as part of setting up a device could help to solve the default password issue.

6 Cyber security

> **Key term**
>
> **Misconfigured access rights:**
> Misconfigured access rights occur when user accounts have incorrect permissions.
> A user whose status dictates that they should have restricted access rights could have been granted less restricted access rights by mistake.
> This could cause problems. For example, less restrictive access rights could grant access to private information which the user does not have authority to view.

Misconfigured access rights

A basic underlying principle for securing computer systems and data is the principle of least privilege. This means that users are only granted those access rights and permissions they need to perform their official duties, role or work. Access rights determine, for example, what files may be accessed and in what modes - read only, read/write, delete, execute; what programs may be run and whether the user may install programs; what operating system commands may be run, e.g. none, a restricted subset, all including the most powerful.

Access rights are misconfigured when user accounts have incorrect permissions granting them the authority to do things that they shouldn't be allowed to do. For example, less restrictive access rights and permissions might be granted in error to a user of insufficient status or trust allowing the user to do any of the following and more:

- to run executables
- to read data belonging to a certain account
- to run powerful operating system commands which could compromise a computer or computer network, etc.

The consequences could be, for example, that private information such as employee records, customer data, medical records, student records, passwords, etc, could be accessed and passed on. This is not only a security breach but also potentially breaks legislation, e.g. the Data Protection Act 1998 (and its replacement in 2018 the GDPR) - "Data should be kept secure: Appropriate technical and organisational measures shall be taken against unauthorised or unlawful processing of personal data and against accidental loss or destruction of, or damage to, personal data".

Also, if the user was a disgruntled employee, more damage might be done to the business with an incorrect elevated level of access such as granting the power to delete, or read and possibly leak important files.

A hacker could exploit a user's elevated access rights and do harm to the system or take over the system in both cases by gaining access to the user's account which might not be so well protected, e.g. by a strong password or two-factor authentication, as user accounts belonging to users with higher status within the organisation, and therefore elevated access rights.

> **Key principle**
>
> **Least privilege principle:**
> To reduce the likelihood of a data security breach or harm being done to a computer system requires policies and procedures to be implemented and maintained based on the least-privilege principle.
> The least-privilege principle means that users should be given only the minimum access to sensitive data or computer system necessary to perform a job function and that access should only be granted for the minimum time necessary.

Questions

7. Which of the following statements are always true?

   A   The principle of least privilege states that users are only granted those access rights and permissions they need to perform their official duties.

   B   Access rights determine, among other things, what files may be accessed.

   C   Misconfigured access rights occur when user accounts have correct permissions.

   D   A network manager of a school's computer network would be granted full access rights.

   E   Misconfigured access rights occur when user accounts have incorrect permissions.

Removable media

An infection of Manchester City Council's IT system caused an estimated £1.5m worth of disruption in February 2009. The use of USB flash drives was banned, as this was believed to be the cause of the initial infection.

Care in dealing with external devices is necessary because of the threat of malware infection by means of AutoRun and external drives/media. Malware infection of computer systems by Autorun and USB flash drive was documented in a 2011 Microsoft study[3]. The study found that **26** percent of all malware infections of Windows systems were due to USB flash drives exploiting the AutoRun feature in Microsoft Windows.

AutoRun, and the companion feature AutoPlay, are components of the Microsoft Windows operating system that dictate what actions the system takes when a drive is mounted, e.g. a CD-ROM or a USB flash drive.

An entry in the Windows Registry controls whether AutoRun is enabled or disabled for a particular drive.

If AutoRun is enabled then a text file autorun.inf, if present, is opened and any **commands present are executed**. Such commands include very powerful operating system commands. *Figure 6.2.3* shows the contents of a sample autorun.inf file which tells Windows to run Setup.exe program located in the CD root folder. Also it specifies that Windows should use the first icon from Setup.exe to display this CD in Explorer.

Variants of the deadly Conflicker worm are spread through removable media (e.g. flash drives) exploiting the AutoRun feature of the Windows operating system.

```
[autorun]
open=Setup.exe
icon=Setup.exe,1
```

Figure 6.2.3 autorun.inf example contents

The United States Computer Emergency Readiness Team (US-CERT[4]) recommends disabling AutoRun to prevent malware from spreading through removable media. *Figure 6.2.4* shows the result of running Kaspersky Lab software on a computer with autorun enabled.

Figure 6.2.4 Warning message from Kaspersky Lab software

If copying to removable media is permitted then the system is potentially open to confidential information being stolen. The National Security Agency (NSA) had classified information copied and leaked by Edward Snowden in 2013 without authorization.

Questions

10. Why should AutoRun be disabled in computers running a Windows operating system?

---

3 http://download.microsoft.com/download/0/3/3/0331766E-3FC4-44E5-B1CA-2BDEB58211B8/Microsoft_Security_Intelligence_Report_volume_11_English.pdf
4 https://www.us-cert.gov/

6.2 Social engineering threats

Questions

8. Explain what is meant by access rights.

9. Why it is important to assign access rights to user accounts?

Key fact

AutoRun and removable media:
AutoRun and the companion feature AutoPlay are components of the Microsoft Windows operating system that dictate what actions the system takes when a drive is mounted, e.g a CD-ROM or a USB flash drive.

Key fact

Removable media and malware:
Removable media can be a source of malware which can infect a computer system.

Did you know?

Use of autorun.inf commands to protect music CDs:
An audio CD, that a user would not expect to contain software at all, can contain a data section with an autorun.inf file of shell commands. Some companies, such as Sony BMG, have used this to install their software that attempts to protect against copying of the audio tracks.

Information

Worm:
A computer worm is a standalone malware computer program that replicates itself in order to spread to other computers.

6 Cyber security

Unpatched and/or outdated code

Malicious persons can take advantage of unpatched computer vulnerabilities. Such persons search non-stop for software vulnerabilities to exploit. For example, software vulnerabilities have been found in outdated or unpatched versions of Adobe Flash, Oracle's Java, Microsoft's SQL Server, Apache web server, and operating systems such as Android, Windows and Linux.

The cycle proceeds as follows:

Software containing vulnerabilities:
> A software vendor releases software that contains security-related bugs.

Malicious persons (or a Government agency, e.g. NSA):
> Identify the security-related bugs in the software.

Exploit code:
> Malicious persons develop code that can exploit the bugs in the software.

Vendor response:
> The software vendor becomes aware of the situation and issues a patch to correct the bugs.

User response:
> Users apply the patch to their system to make them secure for the time being.

> **Key term**
>
> **Software patch:**
> A software patch is a piece of software designed to update a computer program or its supporting data, to fix or improve it. This includes fixing security vulnerabilities and other bugs.

> **Did you know**
>
> Java and Flash versions on browsers are most likely outdated. As a safety measure many companies uninstall Java and Flash from browsers. "Outdated, Unpatched Software Rampant in Businesses" article in Threat Post.
> https://threatpost.com/outdated-unpatched-software-rampant-in-businesses/117976/

The Slammer worm which exploited vulnerable versions of Microsoft's SQL Server was the fastest computer worm in history. It is estimated that as many as 90% of the vulnerable servers online were infected within ten minutes. The Slammer worm spread at a time when a patch for the vulnerability it exploited had been available for six months. Named MS02-039, the patch should have ideally been installed on the vulnerable servers long before the worm started its chaotic journey across the Internet.

Proper patch management is very important. Software updates should be automatically managed, if possible, so that identified vulnerabilities are removed before they can be exploited. Don't keep or use out of date software on your computer, especially if patches for newly identified bugs are no longer supported, e.g. Windows XP operating system.

Figure 6.2.5 shows Kaspersky Lab software reporting multiple vulnerabilities in CPython software installed on a computer system. The offending sofware was removed from this computer.

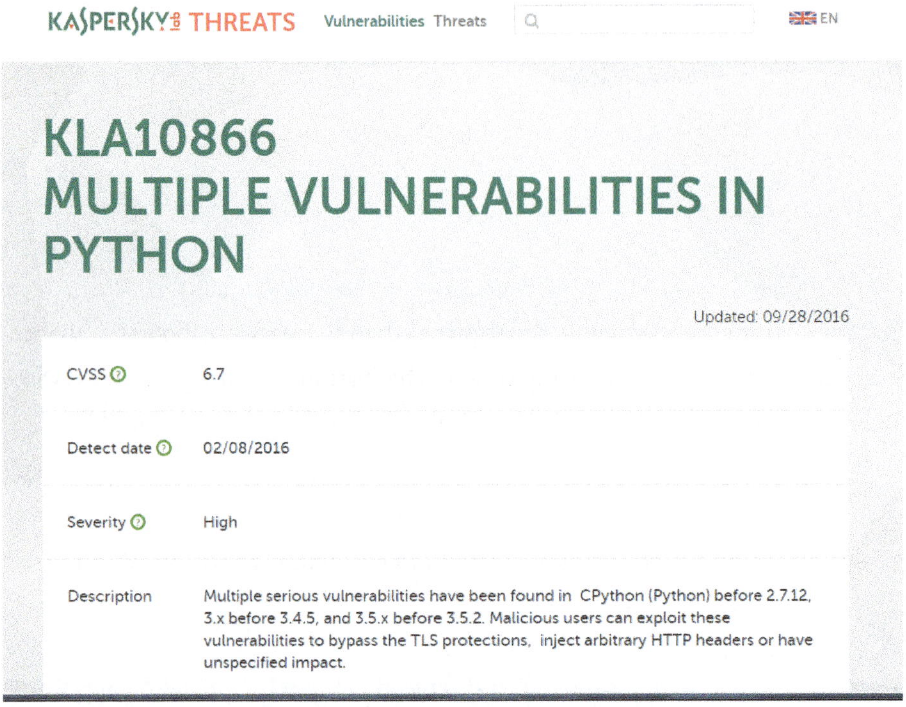

Figure 6.2.5 Warning message from Kaspersky Lab software

6.2 Social engineering threats

Figure 6.2.6 shows Microsoft Windows 7 update configuration settings screen.

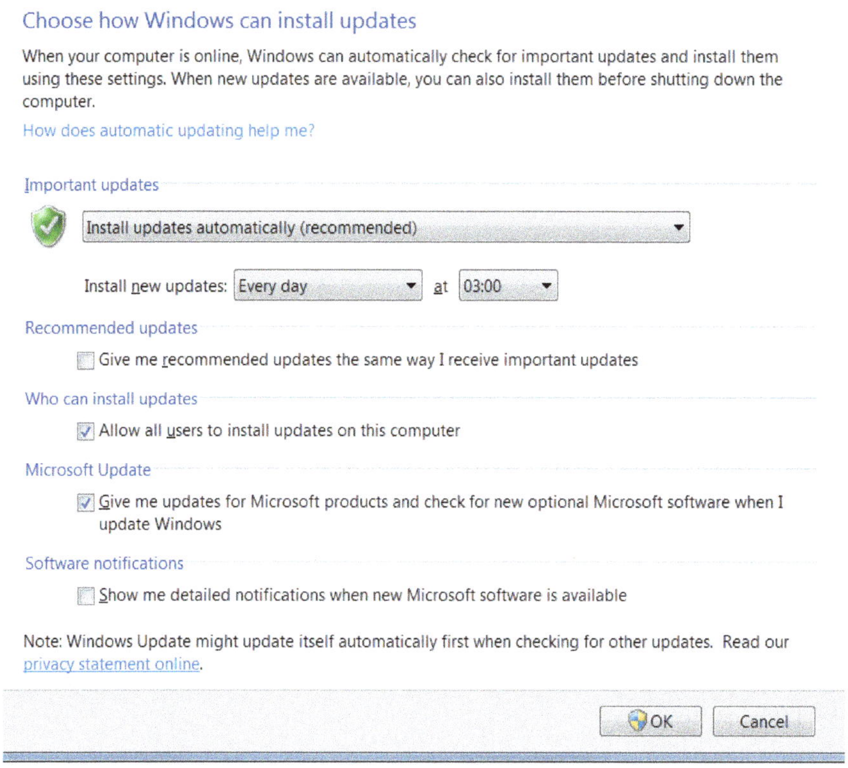

Figure 6.2.6 Microsoft Windows 7 update configuration settings screen

> **Key points**
>
> **Strategy for dealing with vulnerabilities from unpatched and/or outdated software:**
> 1. Apply patches to fix software with identified vulnerabilities.
> 2. Apply patch as soon as it becomes available.
> 3. Stop using software identified as vulnerable until patch becomes available.
> 4. Check for software updates regularly and automatically.
> 5. Remove outdated software.
> 6. Consider removing software altogether if it is not possible to update automatically
> 7. Remove software that is no longer supported because vulnerabilities yet to be discovered will not be patched.

Questions

11. Why are software patches required?
12. (a) Why may software on a computer be vulnerable to attack from attackers with malicious intent?
    (b) What needs to be done to improve security against such attacks on vulnerable software?

Penetration testing

A penetration test, is a survey, assessment, and test of the security of a given organization's computer systems carried out by a penetration tester (pentester) using the same techniques, tactics, and tools that a malicious hacker would use.

In simpler terms, it is the process of attempting to gain access to resources without knowledge of usernames, passwords and other normal means of access.

The main differences between a malicious hacker and a pentester are

- A pentester attempts to find security weaknesses in a system but does not attempt, unlike a malicious hacker, to exploit them only report them to the owner of the system.
- A pentester has permission, both legal and otherwise, from the owner of the system that will be evaluated whereas a malicious hacker does not.

A penetration tester, or pentester, is either an employee of the owner of the system or an external contractor hired on a per-job or per-project basis.

Pentesters are required to never reveal the results of a test to anyone except those designated by their client.

> **Key term**
>
> **Penetration testing:**
> A penetration test, is a survey, assessment, and test of the security of a given organization's computer systems carried out by a penetration tester (pentester) using the same techniques, tactics, and tools that a malicious hacker would use. In simpler terms, it is the process of attempting to gain access to resources without knowledge of usernames, passwords and other normal means of access.

6 Cyber security

> **Key term**
>
> **White-box penetration testing:**
> The aim of white-box penetration testing is to quickly detect problems and fix them before an external party locates and exploits them.
> It is commonly performed by internal teams who simulate a malicious insider with full knowledge of the structure and makeup of the target system.
>
> **Black-box penetration testing:**
> Black-box testing is a type of test that most closely resembles the type of situation that an outside attack presents and is sometimes known as an external test. Essentially, the aim of black-box penetration testing is to simulate an external hacking or cyber warfare attack where the attacker has no knowledge of any credentials for the target system.

White-box penetration testing

The aim of white-box penetration testing is to quickly detect problems and fix them before an external party locates and exploits them.

It is commonly performed by *internal teams* who simulate a malicious insider with full knowledge of the structure and makeup of the target system.

The time and cost required to find and resolve the security vulnerabilities is significantly less than with the black-box approach.

Black-box penetration testing

Black-box testing is a type of test that most closely resembles the type of situation that an outside attack presents and is sometimes known as an *external test*.

Essentially, the aim of black-box penetration testing is to simulate an external hacking attack or a cyber warfare attack where the attacker has no knowledge of any credentials for the target system.

To perform this test a pentester will execute the test from a remote location much like a real attacker.

The pentester will have nothing other than the name of the company to go on. The pentester will log and keep track of the vulnerabilities of the system under test and report on these.

> **Questions**
>
> **13** What is penetration testing?
>
> **14** Which of the following statements are true?
>
> A   Black-box penetration testing finds vulnerabilities of a system more quickly than white-box penetration testing.
>
> B   White-box penetration testing is conducted remotely.
>
> C   White-box penetration testing uses the full knowledge of the structure and makeup of the target system.
>
> D   Black-box penetration testing simulates external hacking.
>
> E   A black-box penetration tester has little knowledge of the target system to go on.
>
> **15** What is meant by white-box penetration testing?
>
> **16** What is meant by black-box penetration testing?

> **Task**
>
> **4** Visit the following site and explore some of the world's biggest hacks:
> http://www.informationisbeautiful.net/visualizations/worlds-biggest-data-breaches-hacks/

In this chapter you have covered:

- The meaning of the term cyber security and the main purposes of cyber security
- The following cyber security threats:
  - social engineering techniques
  - malicious code (malware)
  - pharming
  - weak and default passwords
  - misconfigured access rights
  - removable media
  - unpatched and/or outdated software
- What penetration testing is and what it is used for.

6 Fundamentals of cyber security

6 Fundamentals of cyber security

Learning objectives:

- *Define the term social engineering*
- *Describe what social engineering is and how it can be protected against*
- *Explain the following forms of social engineering:*
  - *blagging (pretetxting)*
  - *phishing*
  - *shouldering (or shoulder surfing).*

6.2.1 Social engineering

What is social engineering?

Social engineering is the art of manipulating people so that they give up confidential information. It is a mind game in which social engineers play with human psychology to gain confidence and win confidential information. Social engineering is used to realise a number of outcomes:

1. Financial fraud
2. Identity theft
3. Unauthorized access to protected systems.

Social engineering involves tricking a person into divulging confidential information that may then be used, for example, to gain access to the person's computer system, bank account, etc, or to steal their identity and exploit this theft for financial gain by obtaining, say, a bank loan in the person's name. The social engineer sets up and defines a situation where it will seem natural, normal, or helpful for the person being socially engineered to provide the requested information or to click the link that's displayed.

To extract information from the unsuspecting, social engineers rely on creating a sense of urgency in their victims, so that they will respond immediately and without thinking. It is human nature to be helpful, to avoid trouble or conflict, and to try to fix things when they break.

> **Key term**
>
> **Social engineering:** Social engineering is the art of manipulating people so that they give up confidential information.

> **Information**
>
> Accounts used to share files and images such as Google Drive, Adobe Creative Cloud, and Dropbox are the most effective lures used by social engineers according to a report, The Human Factor 2017, by Proofpoint®, Inc. (www.proofpoint.com).

> *Example 1 - The "colonel effect"*
>
> The "colonel effect" experiment was conducted by Aaron J. Ferguson at West Point Military Academy in America. He sent a bogus email message with the subject heading "Grade Report Problem" to 500 cadets, asking them to click a link to confirm that the grades on their last grade report were correct or otherwise to report any problems. The email was signed Colonel Robert Melville but there was no such colonel at West Point.
>
> Over 80% of recipients clicked the link in the message. In response, they received a notification that they'd been duped and a warning that their behaviour could have resulted in downloads of spyware, Trojan horses and/or other malware.
>
> The "colonel effect" refers to a form of social engineering which exploits a culture in which an action such as clicking on a link is executed regardless of its nature because the message purports to come from an authority figure. It is also known as the "CEO fraud" or "Chief Executive Officer fraud".

> **Example 2 - Playing on the urgency of addressing a security issue**
>
> You are contacted by phone by a person claiming to be from the security department of Microsoft. The person says that your Microsoft Cloud account's security has been compromised and they need to ask you a few questions before the security issue can be fixed. The questions are as follows
>
> 1. What is your full name and address?
> 2. What is your username?
> 3. Have you ever written down your password where someone else can find it?
>
> Your answers to these questions are
>
> 1. Fred Bloggs, 55 Acacia Avenue, Dingley Dell
> 2. FredB
> 3. No I don't need to.
>
> "That is excellent especially the fact that you haven't written down your password", replies the person. "How do you manage to remember your password, I never can says the person?" To which you reply, "because it is my sister's first name". "Ah that is good because we will also need to talk to your sister because, according to our records, her Cloud account has been compromised as well. To save time and because the problem needs to be fixed urgently, can you answer the first two questions for her now." You are concerned that your sister's Cloud account is potentially vulnerable so you oblige and supply your sister's full name, address and username, after all where is the harm you think to yourself, her surname and address is the same as mine.
>
> (a) How do you know that the person is genuinely from Microsoft?
> (b) How did the person obtain your password?
> (c) Why might the person want your username and password for your Microsoft account?

> **Example 3 - Presenting a situation and then explaining the consequences of delay or inaction.**
>
> A person receives the following email message purportedly from Yahoo mail:
>
> "Due to the congestion in the Yahoo mail system, Yahoo mail will shut down all unused accounts. You must confirm your email by filling out your login information below and then clicking the Reply button. Failure to do so will result in account suspension."
>
> This message contains several social engineering tricks:
>
> 1. Relying on the tendency of humans to be helpful by reducing account congestion
> 2. Informing the reader that failure to comply with the request will result in account suspension and loss of access to their email
> 3. Giving the reader no choice but to click on the Reply button (a hyperlink to a website), threatening account suspension for failure to comply
> 4. A reason why this email has been sent: Account congestion and removal of unused accounts

6.2.1 Social engineering

> ### Questions
>
> 1. You have just entered your keypad code into an electronic lock to let yourself into the office building where you are working during your summer holidays. A senior looking person follows you in and says he is glad that you were around as he had forgotten his keypad code. It would have been very embarrassing for him to be locked out, he says, as he is late for a meeting with the CEO. He asks you to remind him what the keypad code is, to save him the hassle of contacting security.
>
>   (a) Would you let him in? Justify your answer.
>
>   (b) Would you divulge the keypad code to him? Justify your answer.
>
>   (c) Would your decision have depended on whether the person carried an air of authority?
>
> 2. You receive an email with subject "Confirm your availability for the first eleven for next Saturday's football fixture against Bash Street Academy".
>
>   You are asked in the body of the email to click on a link to confirm your availability or unavailability. The email is signed Head of Games and nothing else.
>
>   The email rings true because according to the fixture list, next Saturday's game is against Bash Street Academy and you do play in the first eleven football team.
>
>   (a) What about this email might be considered suspicious?
>
>   (b) What about this email might be considered authentic?
>
>   (c) How might genuine information included in this email have been obtained?

How to protect against social engineering

Protecting yourself from social engineering requires being aware of the potential security risks, and taking steps to minimise them.

1. Never reveal personal, financial, or other sensitive information over the phone or the Internet.
2. Never reveal any of the usernames and passwords that you use.
3. Never reveal answers to typical security questions. These are often relied on when you reset passwords. For example, any of the following
    a. What is the name of your favourite pet?
    b. What is the name of the town/city where you were born?
    c. What is your favourite colour?
    d. Etc.
4. Be mindful of information that you post on the Internet, and understand that it could be visible to strangers.
5. If a caller claiming to be from some company, financial institution or organisation asks for confidential information then always ask for their contact information which you should then verify is real using some independent and reliable means such as a phone book or the company's website.
6. Ignore spam and steer clear of clicking links in Tweets, Facebook pages, etc.
7. Remove access to PowerShell code from your user account - PowerShell is a tool that delivers power and control over the Windows operating system and the underlying hardware.
8. Remove admin rights from your user account so that you cannot have control over the Windows operating system and the underlying hardware.
9. Disable macros or only use macros that can be trusted, i.e. macros which are digitally signed by a trusted source.
10. Be wary of rigged Word documents sent to you and which encourage you to "enable content". This action could install malware in your computer's RAM with unfortunate consequences.

6 Fundamentals of cyber security

> **Key term**
>
> **Blagging (pretexting):** Blagging is the act of creating and using an invented scenario to engage a targeted victim in a manner that increases the chance the victim will divulge information a blagger wants, e.g. sensitive or personal nature such as passwords, or perform actions that would be unlikely in ordinary circumstances, making a payment by credit card to the blagger to fix a non-existent problem with your computer.

Blagging (pretexting)

Blagging, a form of social engineering, is the act of creating and using an invented scenario to engage a targeted victim in a manner that increases the chance the victim will divulge information or perform actions that would be unlikely in ordinary circumstances. For example, you might be contacted by telephone by someone claiming to be from Microsoft, say, who claims that there is a problem with your computer. After some discussion they ask for your username and password. This is a fairly blatant and unsubtle attempt to get you to reveal information of a sensitive or personal nature. However, the telephone call could be much more subtle as illustrated in Example 2 on page 302. The reason why this example might work is that people are easily manipulated into giving away information if they believe it is in their best interest to do so, or because they believe they are helping in some way. Especially if the person claims to be in some position of authority, because the target of the blag believes that the "attacker" has the right to know - see the "colonel effect" example on page 301. We have been brought up to answer and work with authority figures, and not question them!

Shouldering (or shoulder surfing)

Shouldering is observing a person's private information over their shoulder, e.g. cashpoint machine PIN numbers.

> **Key term**
>
> **Shouldering (shoulder surfing):** Shouldering is observing a person's private information over their shoulder, e.g. cashpoint machine PIN numbers.

Questions

 A person is contacted by telephone by someone claiming to be from their bank. They say recent activity on the account leads them to believe that this bank account has been hacked. Before they proceed any further they would like to ask some security questions. They conversation proceeds as follows

"Bank": What is your date of birth?

Person: 23/06/1998.

"Bank": Name one direct debit set up on your account.

Person: Vodaphone.

"Bank": What are the first and fourth digits of your PIN?

Person: 8 and 9.

Person: Sorry, I didn't catch that, what did you say are the second and third digits of your PIN?

Person: 3 and 2.

"Bank": What is your mother's maiden name?

Person: Smith.

"Bank": Thank you very much. I can now confirm that your account is secure and it has not been hacked.

(a) What should the person have done to decide whether or not it was safe to proceed with this telephone conversation?

(b) What confidential information has the person given away that could enable his or her bank account to be illegally accessed and money to be stolen?

6.2.1 Social engineering

Phishing

Phishing is a technique of fraudulently obtaining private information, often by using a legitimate-looking email or SMS in which a lure is dangled in front of an unsuspecting user of the Internet.

A phishing email or SMS message purports to come from a legitimate and/or trusted source, e.g. a bank, and attempts to fool you into revealing login credentials, financial details, and/or sensitive information that can later be used to commit fraud or access accounts.

Phishing casts a big net to catch a few fish. It uses unsolicited email (spam), text messages, or other forms of communication sent out in bulk, i.e. to many people. While many people will dismiss the message, a few will respond to it.

> **Key term**
>
> **Phishing:** Phishing is a technique of fraudulently obtaining private information, often by using email or SMS.

> **Key term**
>
> **Spam:** Unsolicited email or messages that are sent to groups of people.

Scenario 1 - stealing credentials

One phishing technique sends an email containing a link which you are invited to click, say, to reset the password that you use to login into a service, e.g. gmail.

Clicking this link will take you to a bogus website, that looks like the real thing, in which you are invited to enter your username and password.

Of course, this fake web site is designed to collect the unsuspecting user's username and password so that the attacker can gain access to the person's gmail account and emails associated with this account.

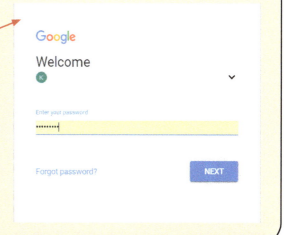

Scenario 2 - exploiting security vulnerabilities in web browsers

Another phishing technique sends an email containing a link which you are invited to click on but this time the recipient of the email is taken to a website page with an exploit kit. The exploit kit relies on an out of date browser being used with security vulnerabilities and which the kit can exploit to download malware.

Once installed, the malware can steal passwords, install a backdoor into the compromised computer or even encrypt all files on the computer (ransomware).

Many people think phishing is only a credential problem (i.e. usernames and passwords). They believe that they are safe as long as they don't enter their credentials after clicking on the phishing link.

This isn't true as can be demonstrated with the above exploit kit scenario.

In this case, just clicking the link results in your browser and computer being completely compromised.

Information

Download from KnowBe4 the 22 social engineering red flags to watch out for in any email document:

https://cdn2.hubspot.net/hubfs/241394/Knowbe4-May2015-PDF/SocialEngineeringRedFlags.pdf

Scenario 3 - malicious attachments

Another phishing technique sends an email containing a malicious attachment. Malicious attachments come in many forms, e.g. Word documents, HTML files, zip files or even executable programs (.exe, .jar, etc). The recipient of the email is tricked into downloading and opening/executing the attachment.

The most common malicious attachments are Word (or any Microsoft Office tools) document files. In this case, the attachments which are macros contain malicious code. Malicious macros are typically bits of code designed to damage the user's device (computer) when the code is run. The macro could execute a command to wipe the entire contents of a disk or it could execute code that downloads and executes other malware. Microsoft knows that letting macros run automatically is dangerous, so they prompt you to see if you want to execute the macro. If you do not trust the source you should decline or even safer decline full stop! However, attackers have got "smarter" and try to trick you by making the document say something like, "this document is encrypted for your protection, enable macros to decrypt the contents."

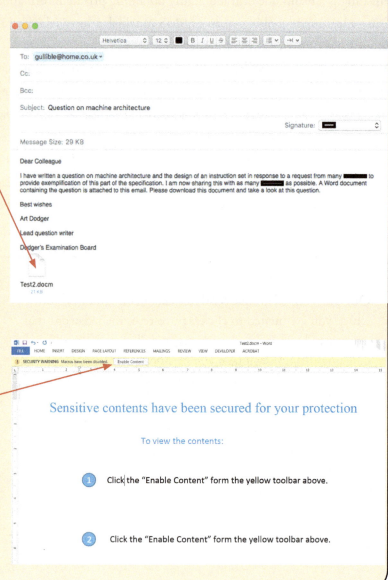

Scenario 4 - pop-up ads

When you browse the web, you might see a pop-up ad or a page warning you about a problem with your device. These alerts are pop-up ads, designed to trick you into calling a phoney support number or buying an app that claims to fix the issue. Don't call the number. Simply close the pop-up ad, or navigate away from that page and continue browsing.

A trio of terms captures just about every phishing attack: imitate, motivate, and act (click a link, reply to an e-mail, or whatever).

Imitate: A phishing message strives to look like it comes from some particular organization.

Motivate: Motivation is the social engineering part of a phishing attack.

Act: The visible hook in a phishing attack is the form that users are requested to fill out. To access this form, users must take action (click a link, send a reply, etc). An invisible hook may also lurk in a phishing attack, i.e. the phishing page visited may cause a drive-by download of malware. If this happens, even users who don't bite the visible hook and fill out the form may still fall prey to the invisible hook if the malware download succeeds. The victim is then stuck with a keylogger and a backdoor Trojan that he or she may not know about for some time.

6.2.1 Social engineering

Antivirus software cannot protect against all malware attacks.

Therefore, computers are not entirely safe from malware, so avoidance, i.e. don't reply to the email or click the link, remains the best strategy.

These signs can help you identify phishing scams:

- The sender's email address or phone number doesn't match the name of the company that it claims to be from.
- Your email address or phone number is different from the one that you gave that company.
- The message starts with a generic greeting, like "Dear customer." Most legitimate companies will include your name in their messages to you.
- A link appears to be legitimate but takes you to a website whose URL doesn't match the address of the company's website.
- The message looks significantly different from other messages that you've received from the company.
- The message requests personal information, like a credit card number or account password.
- The message is unsolicited and contains an attachment.

Questions

4. The email shown in *Figure 6.2.1.1* purports to come from PayPal, an American company operating a worldwide online payments system that supports online money transfers.
   (a) Give **two** reasons for thinking that this is a phishing email.
   (b) Give **two** security risks that the recipient of this email could face by clicking on the link "click here …".
   (c) What aspect(s) of human nature do you think that this phishing email is exploiting?

5. Give **three** signs that can help to identify phishing scams.

---

service@intl.paypal.co.uk   8 July 2017 at 13.06

To: customer

Resolution of Buyer Complaint Case # PP-001-811-430-813

Hello,

After careful consideration of the evidence provided in the case detailed below, we have completed our investigation and decided in favor of the buyer. Under terms of our User Agreement, we have debited the following amount from your PayPal account as a refund to the buyer: 450.00 EUR

……

……

Case number: PP-001-811-430-813

Click here to resolve the problem right now

……..

Please do not reply to this email. This mailbox is not monitored and you will not receive a response. For assistance login to your PayPal account and click the Help link in the top right corner of any PayPal page

……..

Figure 6.2.1.1

6 Fundamentals of cyber security

In this chapter you have covered:

- Defining the term social engineering
- Describing what social engineering is and how it can be protected against
- Explaining the following forms of social engineering:
  - blagging (pretetxting)
  - phishing
  - shouldering (or shoulder surfing).

6 Fundamentals of cyber security

6 Fundamentals of cyber security

6.2.2 Malicious code

Learning objectives:
- *Define the term 'malware'*
- *Describe what malware is and how it can be protected against*
- *Describe the following forms of malware:*
  - *computer virus*
  - *trojan*
  - *spyware.*

Malware

Malware is any software that's installed on a computer with the intention of executing malicious code and/or causing damage such as corrupting data.

In the UK, under the Computer Misuse Act, it is criminal offence, punishable by imprisonment for up to 10 years, to develop malware and/or disseminate malware.

Figure 6.2.2.1 shows a list of all processes loaded into the RAM of a Windows XP computer. A process is an instance of a program in execution.

This list shows that three instances of an executable program lsass.exe have been loaded into RAM.

Each process has its own identifier called its PID (**P**rocess **ID**entifier).

For example, the first copy of lsass.exe has PID 680.

A process started by another process will have a **P**arent **P**rocess **ID**entifier or PPID. For example, the first copy of lsass.exe has a parent whose PID is 624, the second and third 668.

This is suspicious because lsass.exe should always be started by winlogon.exe and winlogon.exe has PID 624. The second and third copies of lsass.exe have PID 668 which is an instance of the program services.exe!

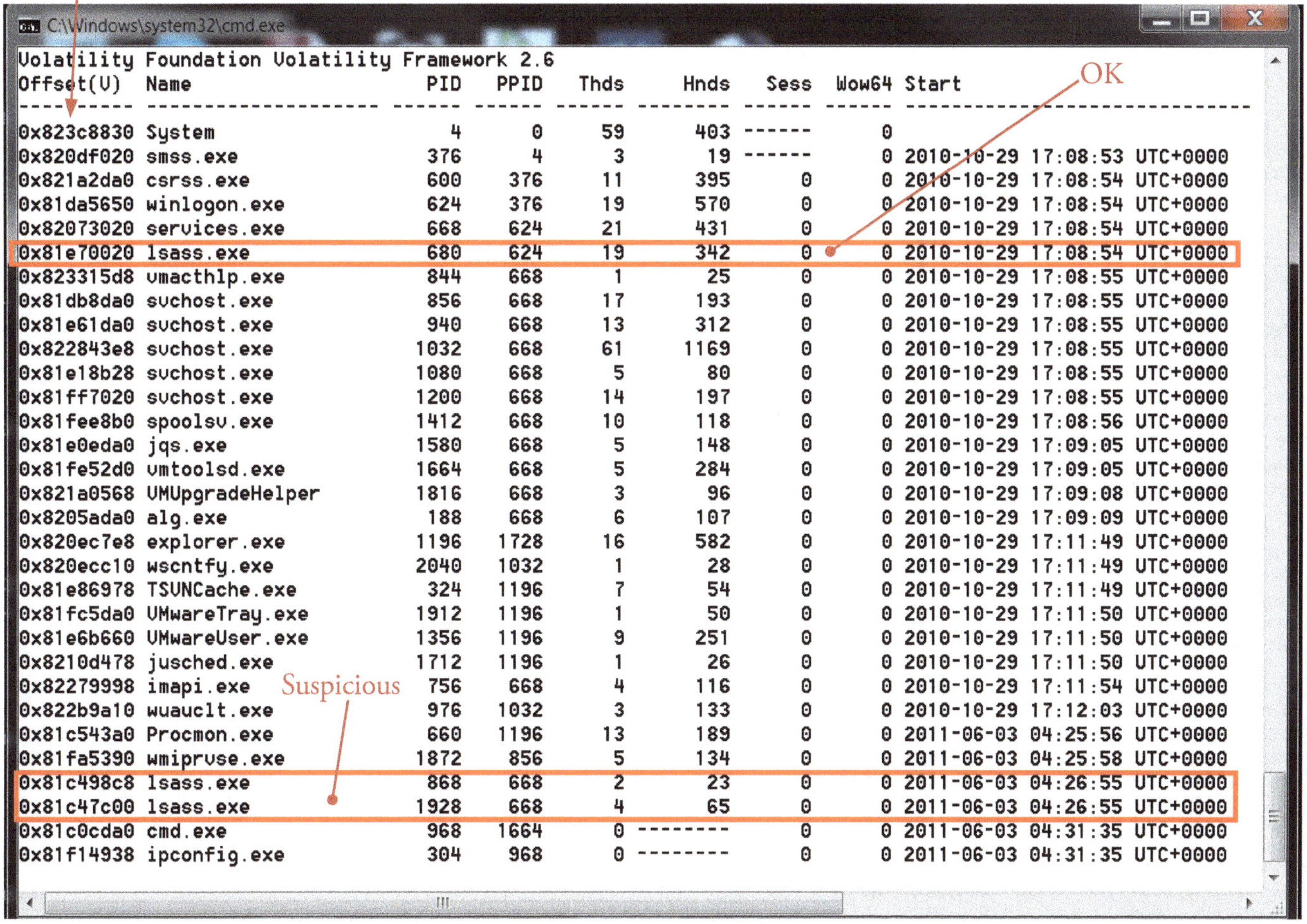

Information

lsass.exe:

This is a program that runs as a process that is responsible for enforcing the security policy on the system. It verifies users logging on to a Windows computer or server, handles password changes, and creates access tokens.

Hexadecimal address in RAM of start of process

```
C:\Windows\system32\cmd.exe

Volatility Foundation Volatility Framework 2.6
Offset(V)    Name                    PID    PPID   Thds   Hnds   Sess   Wow64  Start
---------- ---------------------- ------ ------ ------ ------ ------ ------ ----------------------------
0x823c8830 System                      4      0     59    403   ------      0
0x820df020 smss.exe                  376      4      3     19   ------      0 2010-10-29 17:08:53 UTC+0000
0x821a2da0 csrss.exe                 600    376     11    395        0      0 2010-10-29 17:08:54 UTC+0000
0x81da5650 winlogon.exe              624    376     19    570        0      0 2010-10-29 17:08:54 UTC+0000
0x82073020 services.exe              668    624     21    431        0      0 2010-10-29 17:08:54 UTC+0000
0x81e70020 lsass.exe                 680    624     19    342        0      0 2010-10-29 17:08:54 UTC+0000   OK
0x823315d8 vmacthlp.exe              844    668      1     25        0      0 2010-10-29 17:08:55 UTC+0000
0x81db8da0 svchost.exe               856    668     17    193        0      0 2010-10-29 17:08:55 UTC+0000
0x81e61da0 svchost.exe               940    668     13    312        0      0 2010-10-29 17:08:55 UTC+0000
0x822843e8 svchost.exe              1032    668     61   1169        0      0 2010-10-29 17:08:55 UTC+0000
0x81e18b28 svchost.exe              1080    668      5     80        0      0 2010-10-29 17:08:55 UTC+0000
0x81ff7020 svchost.exe              1200    668     14    197        0      0 2010-10-29 17:08:55 UTC+0000
0x81fee8b0 spoolsv.exe              1412    668     10    118        0      0 2010-10-29 17:08:56 UTC+0000
0x81e0eda0 jqs.exe                  1580    668      5    148        0      0 2010-10-29 17:09:05 UTC+0000
0x81fe52d0 vmtoolsd.exe             1664    668      5    284        0      0 2010-10-29 17:09:05 UTC+0000
0x821a0568 VMUpgradeHelper          1816    668      3     96        0      0 2010-10-29 17:09:08 UTC+0000
0x8205ada0 alg.exe                   188    668      6    107        0      0 2010-10-29 17:09:09 UTC+0000
0x820ec7e8 explorer.exe             1196   1728     16    582        0      0 2010-10-29 17:11:49 UTC+0000
0x820ecc10 wscntfy.exe              2040   1032      1     28        0      0 2010-10-29 17:11:49 UTC+0000
0x81e86978 TSVNCache.exe             324   1196      7     54        0      0 2010-10-29 17:11:49 UTC+0000
0x81fc5da0 VMwareTray.exe           1912   1196      1     50        0      0 2010-10-29 17:11:50 UTC+0000
0x81e6b660 VMwareUser.exe           1356   1196      9    251        0      0 2010-10-29 17:11:50 UTC+0000
0x8210d478 jusched.exe              1712   1196      1     26        0      0 2010-10-29 17:11:50 UTC+0000
0x82279998 imapi.exe                 756    668      4    116        0      0 2010-10-29 17:11:54 UTC+0000    Suspicious
0x822b9a10 wuauclt.exe               976   1032      3    133        0      0 2010-10-29 17:12:03 UTC+0000
0x81c543b0 Procmon.exe               660   1196     13    189        0      0 2011-06-03 04:25:56 UTC+0000
0x81fa5390 wmiprvse.exe             1872    856      5    134        0      0 2011-06-03 04:25:58 UTC+0000
0x81c498c8 lsass.exe                 868    668      2     23        0      0 2011-06-03 04:26:55 UTC+0000
0x81c47c00 lsass.exe                1928    668      4     65        0      0 2011-06-03 04:26:55 UTC+0000
0x81c0cda0 cmd.exe                   968   1664      0   ------      0      0 2011-06-03 04:31:35 UTC+0000
0x81f14938 ipconfig.exe              304    968      0   ------      0      0 2011-06-03 04:31:35 UTC+0000
```

Figure 6.2.2.1 A list of processes (instances of executing programs) in a Windows XP machine

6 Fundamentals of cyber security

Suspicion is raised further on examining the dynamic linked libraries used by the first of the suspect copies of lsass.exe. The list shown in *Figure 6.2.2.2* is not the list for the correct version of lsass.exe. When probed further, the malicious code shown in *Figure 6.2.2.3* is found. This code has the normal permissions associated with the correct lsass.exe of being able to execute and read but it also has a write permission which it shouldn't have. In fact, this computer has been infected with the Stuxnet malware (Stuxnet is a computer worm), a piece of malicious code designed to damage equipment called a centrifuge operated by the computer.

Key term

Malware:
Malicious computer software designed to do any of the following
- Alter in a harmful manner the way that your computer operates, e.g. reformats the hard drive on start up
- Enable information to be captured especially if it relates to security, e.g. passwords
- Take over your computer for purposes such as launching attacks on other computers or sending spam mail to other computers.

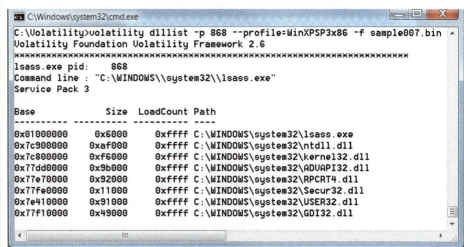

Figure 6.2.2.2 A list of dynamic linked libraries for the suspicious copy of lsass.exe

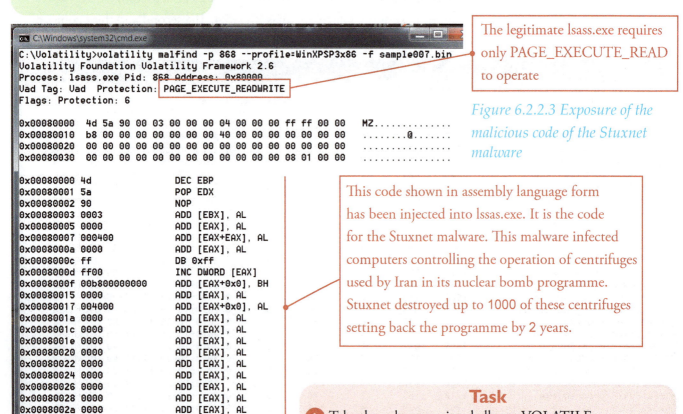

The legitimate lsass.exe requires only PAGE_EXECUTE_READ to operate

Figure 6.2.2.3 Exposure of the malicious code of the Stuxnet malware

This code shown in assembly language form has been injected into lssas.exe. It is the code for the Stuxnet malware. This malware infected computers controlling the operation of centrifuges used by Iran in its nuclear bomb programme. Stuxnet destroyed up to 1000 of these centrifuges setting back the programme by 2 years.

Task

1. Take the cyber security challenge VOLATILE SITUATIONS at https://www.cybergamesuk.com/. This game emulates the process of using open source software called Volatility to analyse a memory dump (copy of the contents of RAM) and find evidence of malware.

6.2.2 Malicious code

Virus

What is a virus?
A virus is a particular form of malware.

A virus is a self-replicating piece of software that, like a biological virus, attaches itself to another program, or in the case of macro viruses, to another file. The virus is only run and copied when the program it is attached to is run or the file it is attached to is opened.

If the program or file isn't accessed in any way, then the virus won't run and won't copy itself.

Program virus

In 1982 a virus labelled the Elk Cloner was written to attack the Apple II operating system. This virus ran whenever a computer was started from an infected floppy disk, and would infect with a copy of itself any other floppy disk put into the disk drive. This virus was attached to a program that ran every time the computer was booted from the infected floppy disk.

The Stuxnet malware was attached to a copy of the operating system program lssas.exe.

Viruses can have harmful effects, ranging from displaying irritating messages to stealing data or giving other users control over your computer.

For example, the virus Elk Cloner displayed a message every 50 times the computer was started.

Document virus

Document viruses do their damage via a macro attached to a document.

Figure 6.2.2.4 shows one way to create a macro in Visual Basic for Applications (VBA). The VBA code executes when the Word document containing this macro, Test2.docm, is opened in Microsoft Word. This results in a popup window appearing for 5 seconds on top of the opened Word document as shown in *Figure 6.2.2.5*.

> **Information**
>
> **Floppy disk:**
> A floppy disk is a removable storage device that is little used now. It is based on similar technology to magnetic disk storage technology.

> **Key term**
>
> **Virus:**
> A virus is a self-replicating piece of software that, like a biological virus, attaches itself to another program, or in the case of a macro virus, to another file. The virus is only run when the program it is attached to is run or the file it is attached to is opened.
> If the program or file isn't accessed in any way, then the virus won't run and won't copy itself.

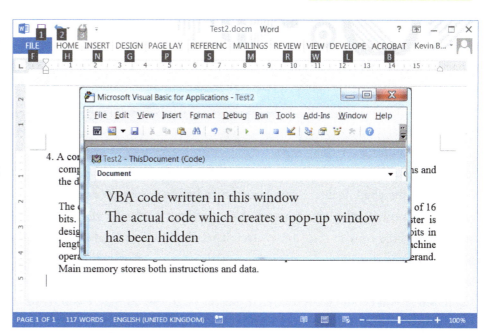

Figure 6.2.2.4 Shows a VBA coding window for creating code to embed in a Word document and which executes when the Word document is opened

VBA language statements would be written in the coding window shown in *Figure 6.2.2.4*.

Figure 6.2.2.5 PopUp window that appears on top of opened Word document Test2.docm

6 Fundamentals of cyber security

Email virus

This is illustrated by a Word document + VBA macro delivered by email as shown in *Figure 6.2.2.6*. The document Test2.docm attached to the email contains the VBA macro.

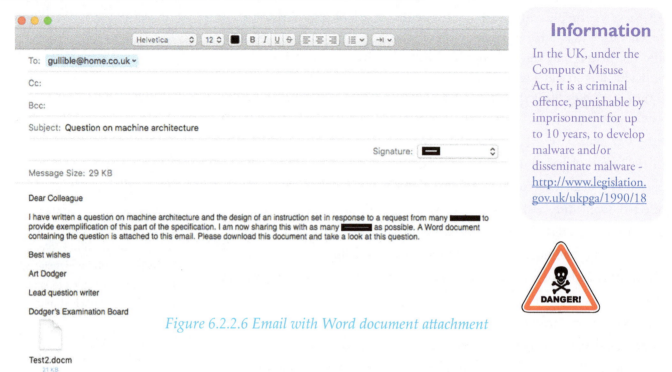

Figure 6.2.2.6 Email with Word document attachment

Information

In the UK, under the Computer Misuse Act, it is a criminal offence, punishable by imprisonment for up to 10 years, to develop malware and/or disseminate malware - http://www.legislation.gov.uk/ukpga/1990/18

The macro executes when document Test2.docm is opened unless the user of the document takes steps to prevent the macro running. Although this macro is relatively benign there are operating system commands it could run which have the potential to wreak havoc. The macro then becomes a virus, a piece of malicious code.

A macro virus author can program the macro to do almost anything that is possible with a PC.

For example, it can corrupt data, send files across the Internet, send a copy of itself by email to other email accounts and format hard drives. The punishment for writing and distributing viruses is prison for a very long time!

A macro virus can be written to attach itself to Microsoft Word via one or more Word's document templates, e.g. Normal.Dot thereby infecting every document subsequently opened in Word.

A macro virus can also be written to search the infected computer for files containing email addresses and then using these send a copy of itself to new recipients. Typically, such email viruses rely on people double-clicking on an attachment to distribute themselves automatically. Any attachment that you receive by email could carry a virus; and launching such an attachment could infect your computer.

One step that you could take is to disable macros or at least configure your computer to request confirmation before proceeding to open a document containing one of more macros.

Another is to use anti-virus software which scans a program/file for tell-tale signs of malicious code.

6.2.2 Malicious code

Questions

1. Which of the following statements are true.
   - A A computer virus is a form of software bug which can cause errors when executed.
   - B A computer virus does not need to be embedded in another program or document to spread or to wreak havoc in a computer system.
   - C A computer virus is a type of malware.
   - D A computer virus spreads when the software or document file it is attached to is transferred from one computer to another.
   - E A computer virus inserts a copy of itself into another program or document.

2. Explain why one needs to be careful when opening an email attachment.

3. It is believed that the Stuxnet malware infected the computers controlling the Uranium enrichment process when they were hooked-up to a Windows-based tablet computer for diagnostic purposes. Infection via the Internet was not possible since the computers were not connected to the Internet. What measure or measures could have been taken to reduce the likelihood of the computers becoming infected with a virus?

Trojan

A Trojan or Trojan horse is a program that pretends to be legitimate software, but actually carries hidden, harmful code.

A Trojan program claims to have one function (and may even carry out this function), e.g. it claims to be a game program, but it actually also does something harmful as well behind the scenes.

For example, Trojan horse software could be created by using a wrapper to bundle together legitimate software, a game, with two other files intended to do harm, into a single file, NoughtAndCrosses.exe, and to make this game of noughts and crosses available for download from a Web site, www.madeupdomainname.co.uk.

The three files could be

1. DodgyScript.vbs
2. OandXs.exe
3. SetUpTrojan.vbs

Files with extension .vbs are VBScript files. SetUpTrojan.vbs does what it says. It copies the malicious code file DodgyScript.vbs to the root directory of the C: drive. It inserts an entry into the computer's registry to ensure that the copy of DodgyScript at C:\ runs whenever the computer is started. The downloaded copies of DodgyScript and SetUpTrojan are then deleted from the download directory. Finally, it causes the game executable OandXs to run.

NoughtsAndCrosses.exe would be uploaded, say, to a directory games located within the Web site
www.madeupdomainname.co.uk.

The game + Trojan would be downloaded by clicking on the following download link
www.madeupdomainname.co.uk/games/NoughtsAndCrosses.exe

The next time that the computer starts, DodgyScript runs. This script may then download more malware, e.g. a keylogger.

Key term

Trojan:
A Trojan or Trojan horse is a program that pretends to be legitimate software, but actually carries hidden, harmful code. Once the Trojan is run, it adds a part of itself to the computer's startup routine. This part can then run when the computer is started up. A form of Trojan called a backdoor Trojan allows the person who sent the Trojan to run programs on the infected computer, access personal files, modify and upload files, track the user's keystrokes, or send out spam mail.

6 Fundamentals of cyber security

Alteration of the computer's Windows registry to allow DodgyScript to run whenever the computer is started requires that the user downloading the game + Trojan has admin rights.

Admin rights grant full access to all parts of the system.

Therefore, one strategy to prevent Trojan malware infecting a computer and potentially a network is **to remove admin rights from ordinary users**.

Possible vectors for a Trojan are

1. Email attachment
2. Link within the body of an email (email link)
3. Visiting a Web site (Web site drive-by) and downloading the Trojan.

The following can be used to protect against these three methods of attack

1. Use email filtering - blacklist of links to be avoided, emails with exe attachments blocked
2. Use up-to-date antivirus software to recognise the signature of the Trojan, if possible
3. Use Web filtering - keep a blacklist of Web sites to be avoided
4. User security awareness training -
    a. Don't click on email links without checking with the source that email is genuinely from a trusted source
    b. Don't download email attachments without checking with the source that email is genuinely from a trusted source
    c. Don't Web surf and click on download links, only download from trusted sites.

> **Information**
> **Malware vector:**
> A vector in computing, specifically when talking about malicious code such as viruses, trojans and adware, is the method that this code uses to propagate itself or infect a computer.

> **Information**
> Definition-based (or signature-based) antivirus compares the signatures (MD5 or SHA-1 hashes) of the files encountered to see if they match a list of known malware.
> Typically, when signature-based antivirus software encounters a signature match, the file is quarantined.
> Cyber criminals writing malware exploits such as Trojans know their malware may encounter antivirus software, so they frequently include malicious code that disables the antivirus software. In one highly specialized attack in May 2016, the presence of the antivirus software was used to actually install malicious code.
> https://www.digitalshadows.com

Questions

4 Which of the following statements are true.

A   A Trojan is a kind of virus.
B   A Trojan is a kind of malware.
C   A Trojan or Trojan horse is a program that pretends to be legitimate software, but actually carries hidden, harmful code.
D   Removing administrator rights from ordinary users can make it more difficult for a Trojan to infect computers.
E   A Trojan program claims to have one function but it actually also does something harmful as well behind the scenes.

5 State **three** measures other than user security awareness training that could be used to protect against downloading a Trojan.

6 State **three** things that users should avoid doing when using computers in order to minimise the chance of downloading a Trojan.

Spyware

Spyware is software installed in a computer to monitor the activities of its user and to report the gathered information to a third party, who may or may not have criminal intentions.

Spyware may be used, for example, to
- track the user's browsing activities
- log, using a keylogger, what is entered through the computer's keyboard
- obtain passwords using a piece of software called a password sniffer
- send collected data to a particular email address or server.

Tracking cookies may be used to store information about the user on their computer, and to send this information to advertisers or to third parties who may or may not have criminal intentions.

Spyware is a threat to a computer user's privacy but worse, if the spyware has been installed by cybercriminals then the computer's security may be breached. Sensitive information such as bank login details may be stolen and used to obtain money illegally from the computer user's bank account or used by a command and control server (C2) to take over the computer for the purposes of sending spam mail or engaging in a distributed denial of service attack.

Figure 6.2.2.7 shows an example in which spyware in the form of a keylogger is downloaded when an unsuspecting user clicks on the email link.

The user is taken to the bank's site Bank of Umo but only after a keylogger and trojan malware have been downloaded to the user's computer. Closer inspection of the web link reveals that the domain name used is bankofurno.com and not the genuine domain name bankofumo.com. The trojan software periodically or under command from a command and control server sends a log of keystrokes to the cybercriminal.

> **Key term**
>
> **Spyware:**
> Spyware is software that enables advertisers or cybercriminals to gather information without your permission.
> You may get spyware on your computer when you visit certain websites. A pop-up message may prompt you to download a software utility that you "need", e.g. a disk cleaner, or software may be downloaded automatically without your knowledge. Spyware may also be installed when you click on an email link.
> Spyware programs are not viruses. Cybercriminals often use a Trojan horse to install spyware.

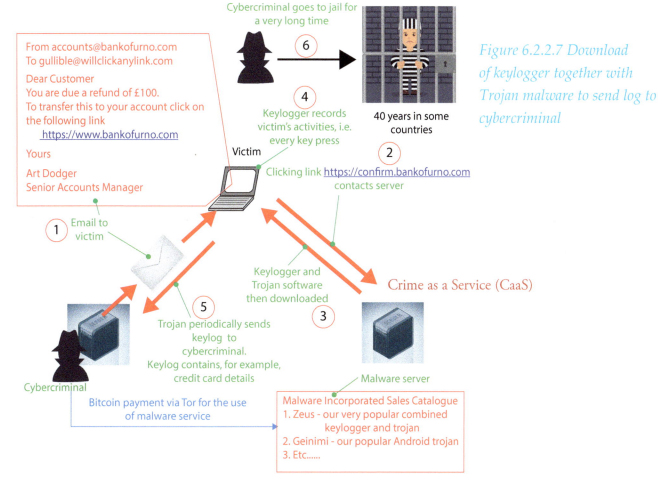

Figure 6.2.2.7 Download of keylogger together with Trojan malware to send log to cybercriminal

6 Fundamentals of cyber security

Spyware may be removed or prevented from infecting your computer with antispyware software, e.g. Spybot from www.safer-networking.org is one of several free antimalware and antispyware tool. Many antiviruses also include a antispyware tool.

If the spyware is delivered via a Trojan then the measures taken against Trojans also apply to spyware.

Question

7 Which of the following statements are true.

- A Spyware is a kind of virus.
- B Spyware is not a threat to a computer user's privacy.
- C Spyware may obtain passwords using a piece of software called a password sniffer
- D Spyware is software that enables advertisers or cybercriminals to gather information without your permission.
- E Spyware may take the form of a keylogger.

Task

2 Write an article for a student magazine on malware and the different types of malware: computer viruses, Trojans, and spyware. Your article should describe the similarities and differences between each and the measures that can be taken to reduce the risks posed by each of these.

In this chapter you have covered:

- The term 'malware'
- Describing what malware is and how it can be protected against
- The following forms of malware:
  - computer virus
  - Trojan
  - spyware.

6 Fundamentals of cyber security

6 Fundamentals of cyber security

Learning objectives:

- *Understand and be able to explain the following security measures:*
  - *biometric measures (particularly for mobile devices)*
  - *password systems*
  - *CAPTCHA (or similar)*
  - *using email confirmations to confirm a user's identity*
  - *automatic software updates.*

> **Key term**
>
> **Authentication:**
> The process or action of verifying the identity of a user or process.

> **Did you know?**
>
> The structure of vein patterns is unique amongst each and every individual. Scientific studies have shown that identical twins possess unique vein patterns as well.
>
> It is also very difficult to spoof a Vein Pattern Recognition device because a constant flow of blood is required in the veins for the raw images to be captured. However, vein pattern can change over the lifetime of an individual and therefore, re-registration will be needed.

> **Information**
>
> **Biometrics:**
> The term biometrics is derived from the Greek bio (life) and metric (measure).

6.3 Methods to detect and prevent cyber security threats

Biometric measures

Biometric authentication uses your body as your "password".

Instead of the "password" being something that you know, it is something **physical** and **unique** that you possess such as

- fingerprint pattern
- iris pattern
- retina pattern
- facial features
- voice pattern
- vein pattern of palm of hand.

The following technologies have been developed which exploit the above to **uniquely identify a user**:

- fingerprint scanner
- iris scanner
- retina scanner
- facial recognition
- voice recognition
- vein recognition.

Biometrics, however, are not fail-safe. For example, both fingerprint scanning and facial recognition systems have been fooled already.

Unfortunately, the consequences are more severe if a biometric system has been cracked because users can't change their fingerprint or facial features as they can a stolen password.

However, biometric authentication is still currently more secure than weak passwords.

Experts advise that the best approach is to use a combination of biometric technology and other security measures, such as a strong password (the first factor) in a two-factor authentication process which uses a PIN as the second factor.

Mobile devices are so numerous today that much attention is now devoted to securing them especially from hackers and the consequences of a device being lost or stolen. This is especially important given the rise of mobile phone apps such as Apple Pay, Android Pay, and Samsung Pay, that can make payments. Apple Pay, for example, uses fingerprint scanning to verify the identity of the user before allowing a transaction to proceed via the user's mobile phone.

Questions

1. State **two** biometric measures that could be used to verify the identity of a user of a mobile phone system.

Password systems

Passwords have already been covered in some depth in *Chapter 6.2 (page 293)*.

There are systems called **password managers** that manage passwords for users and ease the task of following these guidelines for passwords:

- passwords should be strong and unguessable
- a different password should be used for each system.

A typical password manager remembers your credentials (login name and password) and then offers to fill in these for you when logging in again to the corresponding online account or system, e.g. a website or an application. It therefore eases the burden of having to remember a different password for each system that you log into.

It may also include a password generator which can generate securely-long and random passwords for you.

Another way to ease the burden of remembering lots of passwords is to rely on a single password for all the online accounts or systems that you need to login to.

For example many systems allow you to use your Facebook or Google login credentials but now you are relying on your Facebook or Google account credentials remaining secure. If these credentials are hacked then all your sites where you have used your Facebook or Google credentials will also become insecure.

Also, linking two or more sites allows companies to collect more data, and more information about you which becomes a possible privacy issue for you. Some commentators advise caution because they say the main focus of a social network company is making a profit from your information, not protecting your privacy.

There's also a possibility that less scrupulous sites may do something else with your data that you didn't agree to, e.g. selling it on to another company that you would not wish to have access to any aspect of your online identity. Before using your existing social account to sign in to a third-party site, make sure you can trust the third party.

Questions

2. Which of the following statements are true of a typical password manager?
    - A   It remembers your credentials for each password-protected system that you log into.
    - B   It forces you to use the same password for all the systems that you log into.
    - C   It eliminates the need to use a password at all.
    - D   It offers to fill in your credentials for you when logging in again.
    - E   A typical password manager may include a password generator.

3. It is possible to rely on your Facebook or Google credentials as log in credentials for other websites.
   State **one** advantage and **one** disadvantage of doing this.

CAPTCHA

The term CAPTCHA (Completely Automated Public Turing Test To Tell Computers and Humans Apart) was coined in 2000 by Luis von Ahn[1] and others at Carnegie Mellon University for a technique that attempts to protect websites against Internet bots (or just bots).

A bot is a software application that runs automated tasks over the Internet, e.g. a bot that distorts the outcome of an online poll by voting automatically thousands or more times.

Luis von Ahn and his fellow workers created **an anti-bot program called a CAPTCHA which determined if a test, set by the program, is answered by a human or another computer program (a bot).**

Their CAPTCHA program generated an image comprised of several randomly selected and distorted characters as shown in *Figure 6.3.1*.

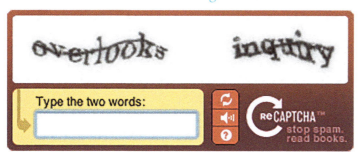

Figure 6.3.1 Example CAPTCHA test

In order to gain access to a CAPTCHA protected site, **users must prove that they are human and not a computer by correctly deciphering and retyping the characters.**

At the time that CAPTCHAs were introduced, computers could not process distorted images and text as well as humans could. Therefore, CAPTCHAs immediately proved effective at frustrating most automated attacks.

Eventually, though, hackers and spammers figured out ways to outsmart the technology by creating programs capable of reading and cracking CAPTCHAs. To counter this, the CAPTCHA technique was beefed up with monitoring software which analyses the user's entire engagement with the CAPTCHA - IP address, mouse movement, etc... - to differentiate between a human user and an abusive bot. This form of CAPTCHA has been renamed No-CAPTCHA.

Users now see a check box that humans just check and in most cases, they pass the test - *Figure 6.3.2*.

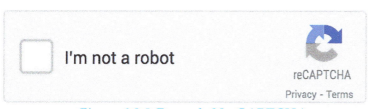

Figure 6.3.2 Example No-CAPTCHA

---

1 Luis von Ahn, Manuel Blum, Nicholas Hopper and John Langford

Key term

CAPTCHA:
A CAPTCHA is a program which attempts to determine if a test, set by the program, is answered by a human or another computer program. In its original form, the test required several randomly selected and distorted characters, generated by the program, to be deciphered and entered correctly. For success it relied on the fact that, at the time, computers/computer programs could not process distorted images and text as well as humans could.

Did you know?

Several years after introducing the world to CAPTCHA technology, von Ahn realized that, despite taking just a few seconds to type a CAPTCHA, humans were spending hundreds of thousands of hours each day typing in more than 100 million CAPTCHAs. CAPTCHAs were re-purposed as reCAPTCHA technology to use this time to decipher words tagged as unreadable in the digitizing of books and other printed material.
In just the first year after launching reCAPTCHA, humans correctly deciphered and transcribed more than **440** million words, roughly the equivalent of **17,600** books.

Information

Spammer:
A person or organization that sends irrelevant or unsolicited messages over the Internet, typically to large numbers of users, for the purposes of advertising, phishing, spreading malware, etc.

If the user engagement check can't confidently predict whether a user is a human or an abusive bot, it will prompt a more challenging CAPTCHA such as a test that shows the user a picture of a cat and asks for similar photos to be selected from a grid of photos as shown in *Figure 6.3.3*.

> ### CAPTCHAs
> ### Protect against spam and abuse
>
> Abusing online polls: If the result of an online poll is to be trusted then it must ensure that only humans can vote. CAPTCHAs force auto-polling hackers to type in CAPTCHAs by hand and thereby reduce the hackers' attempts to manipulate poll results.
>
> Abusing free email services: companies such as Yahoo offer free email services. CAPTCHAs are used to prevent a bot attack that signs up for thousands of email accounts every minute.
>
> Spam: CAPTCHAs are used against email spam: "I will only accept an email if I know there is a human behind the other computer."

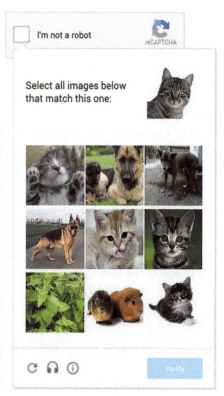

Figure 6.3.3 Example picture test CAPTCHA

Questions

4. Which of the following statements are true of the latest form of CAPTCHAs?

   A   A CAPTCHA can help to prevent tickets for a sporting event being bought thousands of time by a bot created for this purpose by ticket touts.

   B   A CAPTCHA can be used by a user as a direct replacement for a login password.

   C   CAPTCHAs can be used to detect viruses in downloaded files.

   D   CAPTCHAs can help to reduce the effects of automated voting in an online poll.

   E   A form of CAPTCHA can help to decipher words tagged as unreadable in the digitizing of books.

5. Many people post comments on blog websites in response to the websites' blog articles. Such articles can also attract bot-posted comments which advertise products. State **one** technique that could be used to thwart such bots and explain what it relies on to be successful.

6.3 Methods to detect and prevent cyber security threats

Using email confirmation to confirm a user's identity

Verifying identity is very important. For example, an account holder or user of an online account who cannot gain access to this account because they have forgotten their access password should be able to verify their identity to the system by some other means and then once verified be allowed to reset their password.

> **Key term**
>
> **Verification:**
> The process of establishing the truth, accuracy or validity of something.

One such method uses the account holder's email address to confirm their identity. This email address would have been supplied at the time that the account was set up.

The account holder clicks on a Forgot password link on the login page. The hyperlink takes the account holder to a page where they can enter their email address - *Figure 6.3.4*. The entered email address is checked against the email address recorded against this account. If matched then an email addressed to the account holder is sent which contains a password reset link - *Figure 6.3.5*.

Figure 6.3.4 Forgot your password?

An expiry date/time is usually applied to the password reset link so that it cannot be used after a certain time period. Other restrictions are also applied to this link such as

- it may only be used once
- it can no longer be used if superseded by a new link.

Figure 6.3.5 Email with password reset link

When a new user fills out an online registration form to apply to register an account, an email is often sent to the new user's supplied email address. This email can contain a link that the new user is required to click to complete registration and activate their account. Alternatively, it may contain a registration code that the user is then required to type into the registration page to confirm their identity. If this checks out then the user's account is activated.

> **Information**
>
> **Spambot:**
> A spambot is a computer program designed to assist in the sending of spam. Spambots usually create accounts and send spam messages with them.

Requiring a user to click a confirmation link in their email reduces the likelihood of spambots registering an account.

Questions

6. Explain how email may be used to confirm an account holder's identity when the account holder makes a request to reset their password.

Automatic software updates

Unpatched and/or outdated software is vulnerable to being exploited by malicious persons as described in detail in *Chapter 6.2 (page 298)*.

It is therefore important to check for software updates regularly and automatically so that vulnerabilities may be fixed as soon as patches or updates become available. You should select the install updates automatically option and not choose to install updates manually. It is very easy to forget to install updates or to delay applying updates leaving the system vulnerable.

In this chapter you have covered:

- The following security measures:
  - biometric measures (particularly for mobile devices)
  - password systems
  - CAPTCHA (or similar)
  - using email confirmations to confirm a user's identity
  - automatic software updates.

7 Relational databases and structured query language (SQL)

7 Relational databases and structured query language (SQL)

Learning objectives:

- *Explain the concept of a database*
- *Explain the concept of a relational database*
- *Understand the following database concepts:*
  - *table*
  - *record*
  - *field*
  - *primary key*
  - *foreign key*
- *Understand that the use of a relational database facilitates the elimination of data inconsistency and data redundancy.*

Key concept

Database:
A database is a collection of non-redundant, logically related data, and a description of this data, shareable between different application systems.

Non-redundant means no unnecessary duplication

7.1 Relational databases

What is a database?

In the early days of computerised data processing, a company's data was duplicated in separate files for the use of individual departments.

For example, the personnel department (now often called human resources) would hold details on name, address, qualifications, etc of each employee, while the payroll department would hold details of name, address and salary of each employee. Each department had its own set of programs (applications) to process the data in these files. This led to

- *duplicated data*, meaning wasted space
- *inconsistency problems*, where, for example, an address was updated on one file but not on another
- *the data was not shareable*: if one department needed data that was held by another, it was awkward to obtain it.

In an attempt to solve the above problems, the data from the various departments was centralised in a common pool so that *all applications had access to the same set of data*. For example, all the details of stock held by a builders merchant would be held in a database which was accessible by all applications using the data. The sales system would update quantities in stock, the marketing department would use the data to produce a catalogue, the reorder system would use it to decide what stock to reorder.

A **database**, therefore, is defined as **a collection of non-redundant data shareable between different application systems**.

What is a relational database?

In a **relational database**, the data is held as **a collection of tables**. *Figure 7.1.1* shows a snapshot of some data stored in two tables within a hospital relational database. Other tables within this database are not shown.

Field name/attribute (name)

PatientNo	Forename	Surname	Gender	DateOfBirth
1456	Fred	Smith	M	1/3/1970
1461	Mary	Berry	F	18/5/1965
1468	Abdul	Ali	M	11/10/1981
1472	Sui	Wang	F	27/11/1999

Record (row 1461 Mary Berry F 18/5/1965)

Field value or datum

WardId	WardName	WardType	NoOfBeds
1	Nightingale	Orthopaedic	30
2	Barnard	Cardiac	25
3	Seacole	Medical	35
4	Guttman	Geriatric	30

Table

Figure 7.1.1 Collection of tables - Patient table and Ward table - which belong to the hospital relational database

7 Relational databases and structured query language (SQL)

- The two tables in the hospital relational database are named **Patient** and **Ward**, respectively
- Each table consists of a number of rows
- Each row is called a **record**
- Each record has a number of fields and each field has a field value, e.g. '**Nightingale**'
- Each column of a table has a name, e.g. **PatientNo**, which is called a field name or attribute/attribute name or just field.

For example, in the table **Patient**, there is a record with the value '**Nightingale**' for field **WardType**.

> **Key concept**
> **Relational database:**
> A relational database is a collection of tables.

> **Key concept**
> **Record:**
> A record is composed of related pieces of information divided into named fields, e.g. all the information that a school holds about a particular student.

Questions

1. What is
   (a) a database?
   (b) a relational database?

2. For the table Patient, *Figure 7.1.1*, give one example of
   (a) a field name
   (b) a field value in the second record.

PatientNo	PatientName	WardName	WardType
1456	Smith	Nightingale	Orthopaedic
1461	Berry	Barnard	Cardiac
1468	Ali	Barnard	Cardiac
1472	Wang	Guttman	Geriatric
1478	Banderjee	Barnard	Cardiac
1483	Noggs	Nightingale	Orthopaedic
1497	Fadhil	Nightingale	Orthopaedic

Table 7.1.1 PatientWard table

3. (a) *Table 7.1.1* records patient information, patient no, patient name, which ward they are in and the ward type.
   In what way does this table contain redundant (unnecessary duplication) data?
   (b) Split this table into two separate tables, ensuring that each new table contains no redundant data (it may still contain some duplication) while preserving the link between patient and the ward that the patient is assigned to.
   (c) Do any of your new tables contain duplication and if so, is it necessary duplication?

Modelling a relationship between two tables

The relationship between patient and ward is modelled in a relational database by shared or common fields/attributes. *Figure 7.1.2* shows how this is done using field/attribute **WardId**.

Although the tables **Patient** and **Ward** contain multiple records for patient and ward, it is a convention to use the singular form to name the respective table.

The tables, in fact, record information about the entities patient and ward.

An entity is an object, person, place, relationship, concept, activity, event or thing of interest to an organisation and about which data is recorded.

WardId	WardName	WardType	NoOfBeds
1	Nightingale	Orthopaedic	30
2	Barnard	Cardiac	25
3	Seacole	Medical	35
4	Guttman	Geriatric	30

PatientNo	Forename	Surname	Gender	DateOfBirth	WardId
1456	Fred	Smith	M	1/3/1970	3
1461	Mary	Berry	F	18/5/1965	1
1468	Abdul	Ali	M	11/10/1981	3
1472	Sui	Wang	F	27/11/1999	1

> **Key concept**
> **Modelling relationships:**
> Relationships in a relational database are modelled by shared or common fields.

Figure 7.1.2 Tables Patient and Ward linked by a common field WardId

7.1 Relational databases

Entity relationship diagram (Beyond 8525 specification)

The relationships between entities are best represented diagrammatically in an **entity-relationship** diagram or **E-R diagram**. *Figure 7.1.3* shows the E-R diagram for the two tables **Ward** and **Patient**.

A ward is occupied by many patients (zero or more) and a patient is present in one ward at a time (at most one).

We say the relationship between the ward and patient entities is a **one-to-many**, symbol

A relationship is represented by a line drawn between two associated entities with a shape resembling a crow's foot drawn at the many end of the relationship as shown in *Figure 7.1.3*.

E-R diagraming is beyond AQA's 8525 specification but useful to know.

Figure 7.1.3 E-R diagram for the tables Patient and Ward

A relationship has a degree which may be one of the following:

- **one-to-one**
- **one-to-many**
- **many-to-one**
- **many-to-many**

Drawn as shown in *Figure 7.1.4*.

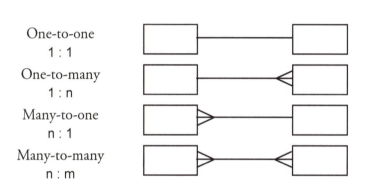

Figure 7.1.4 Diagrammatic representations of relationship degrees

Primary and foreign keys
Primary key

A **primary key is a field or minimum combination of fields which is unique for each record in a table.**

For example, **WardId** in the **Ward** table. A value for **WardId** of, say, **2**, identitifies one and only one record in the **Ward** table, i.e.

| 2 | Barnard | Cardiac | 25 |

The primary key for the **ExamResult** table shown in *Table 7.1.2* is a **composite primary key**, **StudentId**, **ExamCode**. Neither **StudentId** nor **ExamCode** alone is sufficient to guarantee uniqueness.

For example, **StudentId** value **1** identifies three records. **ExamCode** might seem promising as a primary key at first sight: **Phys1** and **Chem1** are unique in the table, but **Maths1** is definitely not as it identifies three records.

Foreign key

A **foreign key is a field/attribute in one table that is also the primary key of another table. It forms a link between the two tables via this shared or common field/attribute.**

For example, **WardId** has the role of primary key in the **Ward** table and foreign key in the **Patient** table shown in *Figure 7.1.2*.

Thus, in a relational database, relationships are modelled by the **foreign key mechanism**.

StudentId	ExamCode	Grade	Date
1	Phys1	A	June 2019
1	Chem1	C	June 2019
1	Maths1	B	June 2019
2	English1	D	June 2019
2	French1	B	June 2019
2	German1	C	June 2019
2	Maths1	B	June 2019
3	Sociology3	E	June 2019
3	Business2	A	June 2019
3	Maths1	C	June 2019

Table 7.1.2 ExamResult table

> **Key concept**
> **Primary key:**
> Attribute/field or combination of attributes/fields which uniquely identifies a single record in the table.
> **Composite primary key:**
> Minimal combination of fields that uniquely identifies a single record of the table.

7 Relational databases and structured query language (SQL)

Shorthand way of representing the structure of a table

It is rather cumbersome to show the structure of a table by drawing it as shown in Table 7.1.2 so a shorter representation is often used which omits the data/records. The shorthand representation of a table is called a **relation**.

> **Key concept**
> **Foreign key:**
> A foreign key is an attribute/field in one table which is also the primary key of another table. It forms a link between two tables via this attribute.

For example, the **Ward** and **Patient** tables shown in Figure 7.1.2 can be represented as follows

Primary key

Ward (<u>WardId</u>, WardName, WardType, NoOfBeds)

Foreign key

Patient (<u>PatientNo</u>, Forename, Surname, Gender, DateOfBirth, *WardId*)

Primary key

The primary key of each table is indicated by using an underline. The foreign key is indicated by italicising the field representing the foreign key.

Questions

4 The fields for each table shown in the E-R diagram in Figure 7.1.5 are as follows
Customer table: CustomerId, Name, Address
AuctionItem table: ItemId, AuctionPrice, PaidYN, CustomerId
CustomerId alone is unique in the Customer table and ItemId alone is unique in the AuctionItem table.
(a) Name a primary key for each table
(b)(i) Which table contains a foreign key?   (ii) Name this foreign key.

Figure 7.1.5 E-R diagram for the tables Customer and AuctionItem

5 Each GP (General Practitioner) is registered with one GP whereas a GP has many registered patients. This relationship is shown in the E-R diagram in Figure 7.1.6. Figure 7.1.7 shows the corresponding tables before the foreign key, modelling the relationship between the two tables, is added to one of the tables.
(a) State the primary key for each table.
(b)
  (i) Name the field to use as a foreign key
  (ii) Name the table it should be added to.

Figure 7.1.6 E-R diagram for the tables GP and Patient

GPId	GPSurname	GPForename	Gender
1	Bloggs	Arthur	M
2	Patel	Sami	F
3	Amari	Sarab	M
4	Oni	Ayomide	F

6 Represent in the shorthand way described above, the tables shown in Figure 7.1.7 without and then with the foreign key added.

PatientNo	Forename	Surname	Gender	DateOfBirth
1456	Fred	Smith	M	1/3/1970
1461	Mary	Berry	F	18/5/1965
1468	Abdul	Ali	M	11/10/1981
1472	Sui	Wang	F	27/11/1999

Figure 7.1.7 Tables GP and Patient with the foreign key not yet added

Link tables

A student is associated with zero or more subjects and a subject is associated with zero or more students. The table **Studies** shown as an entity in the E-R diagram in *Figure 7.1.8* provides the link that is needed between the tables **Student** and **Subject**.

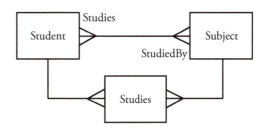

Figure 7.1.8 E-R diagram showing the relationships between the three entities Student, Subject and Studies

We ignore the many-to-many relationship when designing the corresponding relational database and just model the one-to-many relationships as shown in *Figure 7.1.9*.

Figure 7.1.9 E-R diagram showing the one-to-many relationship between Student and Studies and between Subject and Studies

Based on *Figure 7.1.9* the relational database thus consists of three tables described in shorthand form as

Subject (<u>SubjectId</u>, SubjectName)

Student (<u>StudentId</u>, Forename, Surname, Gender, DateOfBirth, Address)

Studies(<u>*StudentId, SubjectId*</u>)

TableName	Primary Key
Student	StudentId
Subject	SubjectId
Studies	StudentId, SubjectId

Table 7.1.3 Primary key for each table

The primary key for each table is shown in *Table 7.1.3*. Both **StudentId** and **SubjectId** in table **Studies** are foreign keys as well.

Question

7. A competition is made up of many events. Each event involves many teams and a team participates in many events. The entity-relationship diagram for this competition is shown in *Figure 7.1.10*.

   The tables for **Event** and **Team** are described in shorthand form as follows

   Event(<u>EventId</u>, EventDescription, Date, Time)

   Team(<u>TeamId</u>, TeamName, ContactTelNo)

   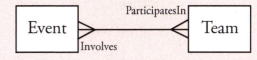

   Figure 7.1.10 E-R diagram showing the relationships between two entities Event and Team

   (a) Modify this entity-relationship diagram so that it uses a link entity and only one-to-many relationships.

   (b) State in shorthand form the table for the link entity.

7 Relational databases and structured query language (SQL)

Types of database

The two types of database considered by AQA's syllabus are
- Flat file databases - where data is stored in a single table
- Relational databases - where data is stored in multiple linked tables.

These are not the only types of database in use today.

Table 7.1.4 shows a single table database **CourseData** which if stored in a disk file would be classified as a **flat file database**. It is considered flat because it lacks structure other than being a collection of records made up of fields. The equivalent relational database is shown as an E-R diagram in *Figure 7.1.11* and in shorthand form in *Figure 7.1.12*.

StudentId	StudentName	Gender	CourseCode	CourseTitle	TeacherId	TeacherName
15898	Bond	M	AQA0643	A Level CS	1234	Mead
15898	Bond	M	UCL0675	A Level Maths	5678	Davies
15898	Bond	M	EDE0187	A Level Art	9123	Milsom
24298	Smith	F	UCL0675	A Level Maths	5678	Davies
24298	Smith	F	AQA0643	A Level CS	1234	Mead
24298	Smith	F	AQA0432	A Level ICT	1234	Mead
10598	Robert	M	EDE0187	A Level Art	9123	Milsom
10598	Robert	M	UOC0987	A Level French	4567	Crapper
10598	Robert	M	AQA0432	A Level ICT	1234	Mead
13497	Nixon	F	UOC0987	A Level French	4567	Crapper

Table 7.1.4 Single table database CourseData

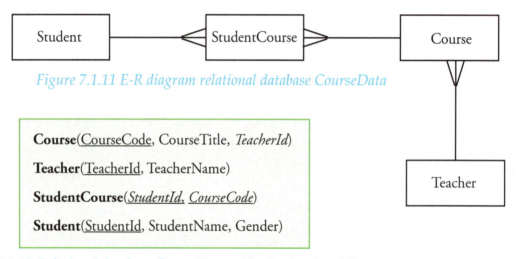

Figure 7.1.11 E-R diagram relational database CourseData

Course(<u>CourseCode</u>, CourseTitle, *TeacherId*)

Teacher(<u>TeacherId</u>, TeacherName)

StudentCourse(<u>*StudentId*</u>, <u>*CourseCode*</u>)

Student(<u>StudentId</u>, StudentName, Gender)

Figure 7.1.12 Relational database CourseData tables in shorthand form

The advantage of keeping all the information in one table (flat file), is that it is easier to set up. The disadvantages are that it is harder to manage and takes up more space because the same data is included multiple times, e.g. **CourseTitle** data in *Table 7.1.4* is stored unnecessarily several times. This can lead to inconsistencies in the data. For example, if the single table is edited because the course title changes from **A Level ICT** to **A Level IT**, it is possible that the second instance is not changed through oversight. **AQA0432** might now correspond to **A Level IT** in one record and still be **A Level ICT** in another. This is an **inconsistency**.

A relational database stores related information in separate tables - *Figure 7.1.13*. This means that individual pieces of information such as "course code has a given course title" is stored just once. There is now only one place where course title **A Level ICT** is stored, i.e. in the **Course** table. Any duplication which occurs is necessary and occurs where two tables need to be linked via a foreign key, e.g. **TeacherId** in **Course** table where teacher **Mead** teaches

7.1 Relational databases

both **A Level CS** and **A Level ICT**. Duplication which is necessary, as in the case of foreign key **TeacherId** in **Course** table shown in *Figure 7.1.13*, is **non-redundant duplication**.

Duplication which is unnecessary, such as **CourseTitle** data in the single table (flat file) shown in *Table 7.1.4*, is called **redundant duplication**.

CourseCode	CourseTitle	TeacherId
AQA0643	A Level CS	1234
UCL0675	A Level Maths	5678
EDE0187	A Level Art	9123
AQA0432	A Level ICT	1234
UOC0987	A Level French	4567

Course table

StudentId	StudentName	Gender
10598	Robert	M
13497	Nixon	F
15898	Bond	M
24298	Smith	F

Student table

Necessary duplication

TeacherId	TeacherName
1234	Mead
4567	Crapper
5678	Davies
9123	Milsom

Teacher table

StudentId	CourseCode
15898	AQA0643
15898	UCL0675
15898	EDE0187
24298	UCL0675
24298	AQA0643
24298	AQA0432
10598	EDE0187
10598	UOC0987
10598	AQA0432
13497	UOC0987

StudentCourse table

Figure 7.1.13 Relational database CourseData

Questions

8. What is a flat file database?

9. How does a relational database differ from a flat file database?

10. Explain what is meant by
    (a) data inconsistency
    (b) data redundancy

11. Explain how the use of a relational database facilititates the elimination of
    (a) data inconsistency
    (b) data redundancy

In this chapter you have covered:

- The concept of a database
- The concept of a relational database
- The following database concepts:
  - table
  - record
  - field
  - primary key
  - foreign key
- Understanding that the use of a relational database facilitates the elimination of data inconsistency and data redundancy.

7 Relational databases and structured query language (SQL)

7 Relational databases and structured query language (SQL)

Learning objectives:

- *Be able to use SQL to retrieve data from a relational database, using the commands*
  - *SELECT*
  - *FROM*
  - *WHERE*
  - *ORDER BY...ASC | DESC*

- *Be able to use SQL to insert data into a relational database using the command:*

  INSERT INTO table_name (column1, column2, ...) VALUES (value1, value2, ...)

- *Be able to use SQL to edit and delete data in a relational database using the commands:*

  UPDATE table_name SET column1 = value1, column2 = value2, ... WHERE condition

  DELETE FROM table_name WHERE condition.

7.2 Structured Query Language

Querying a database

The main purpose of storing data in a database is to enable applications to interrogate the database for information. This interrogation is called **querying the database**.

Structured Query Language (SQL)

Structured Query Language (SQL) can be used to query a database. It is a simplified programming language.

Retrieving data from a single table

Table 7.2.1 shows data for the **Student** table with structure

    Student (StudentId, StudentName, Gender)

The following query, expressed in SQL, will retrieve all of the data in the **Student** table

```
SELECT *
FROM Student;
```

The wildcard character * matches the attribute/field list

    StudentId, StudentName, Gender

StudentId	StudentName	Gender
1	Ames	M
2	Baloch	F
3	Cheng	F
4	Dodds	M
5	Groos	M
6	Smith	F

Table 7.2.1 Table Student

The ANSI/ISO SQL standard requires that a semicolon is used at the end of the SQL statement but some systems relax this requirement. When writing SQL the convention is to use upper case for the SQL commands.

If we wanted just the data for *StudentName* we would refine the query as follows

```
SELECT StudentName
FROM Student;
```

7 Relational databases and structured query language (SQL)

We could refine the search even further by adding a WHERE clause that applies a search condition as follows

```
SELECT StudentName
FROM Student
WHERE Gender = 'F';
```

The result set that would be returned when this query is applied to table **Student** would be as follows

Baloch

Cheng

Smith

because only these rows of the table match the search condition `Gender = 'F'`.

`Gender = 'F'` is actually called a predicate because it evaluates to either TRUE or FALSE.

If we also wanted the values of *StudentId* returned then the query would be

```
SELECT StudentId, StudentName
FROM Student
WHERE Gender = 'F';
```

Questions

1. Write an SQL query that returns the names of all students in *Table 7.2.1* who are male.

Retrieving data from multiple tables

Table 7.2.2 shows data in table form for the **Ward** table with structure

Ward (WardName, NurseInCharge, NoOfBeds)

WardName	NurseInCharge	NoOfBeds
Victoria	Sister Bunn	30
Aylesbury	Sister Moon	40

Table 7.2.2 Table Ward

Table 7.2.3 shows data in table form for the **Patient** table with structure

Patient (PatientId, Surname, *WardName*)

PatientId	Surname	WardName
1	Bond	Aylesbury
2	Smith	Victoria
3	Jones	Aylesbury
4	Biggs	Victoria

Table 7.2.3 Table Patient

The two tables are linked via a shared or common attribute *WardName*. The existence of an attribute common to both tables is not enough to join data from the corresponding tables correctly, as the following SQL query demonstrates

```
SELECT Ward.WardName, Ward.NurseInCharge,
       Patient.PatientId
FROM Ward, Patient;
```

The part of the query `Ward.WardName` references the *WardName* attribute in table **Ward** and the part `Patient.PatientId` references *PatientId* attribute in table **Patient**.

The `FROM Ward, Patient` part joins both relations without regard for the way that the data is actually linked via matching values of the shared attribute, *WardName*. The result set returned by the query is shown in *Table 7.2.4*.

Victoria	Sister Bunn	1
Victoria	Sister Bunn	2
Victoria	Sister Bunn	3
Victoria	Sister Bunn	4
Aylesbury	Sister Moon	1
Aylesbury	Sister Moon	2
Aylesbury	Sister Moon	3
Aylesbury	Sister Moon	4

Table 7.2.4 Result set ignoring relationship between Ward and Patient

When the search condition

```
WHERE Ward.WardName = Patient.WardName
```

is added to the SQL query, we are able to exclude values that are not linked by the attribute *WardName* and to include only those that are. This SQL query will return the result set that corresponds to the real world situation shown in Table 7.2.5.

```
SELECT Ward.WardName, Ward.NurseInCharge, Patient.PatientId
  FROM Ward, Patient
    WHERE Ward.WardName = Patient.WardName;
```

Aylesbury	Sister Moon	1
Victoria	Sister Bunn	2
Aylesbury	Sister Moon	3
Victoria	Sister Bunn	4

Table 7.2.5 Result set taking account of relationship between Ward and Patient

The two relations have been joined on their common attribute, *WardName*, i.e. where the value of *WardName* is the same in both tables.

Writing the query as follows would return the same result set because dropping the table name prefix before *NurseInCharge* and *PatientId* in the SELECT part of the SQL query is allowed where there is no ambiguity as to what is intended.

```
SELECT Ward.WardName , NurseInCharge, PatientId
  FROM Ward, Patient
    WHERE Ward.WardName = Patient.WardName;
```

> ### Questions
>
> 2. Write the SQL query that returns from Tables 7.2.2 and 7.2.3 the name of the nurse in charge of the ward, surnames of all patients in this ward and the ward name.

Ordering the result set returned by a query

We can order a result set returned by a query in ascending or descending order with the keyword ORDER BY qualified by one of the keywords ASC or DESC. If the qualifier is omitted then ASC is assumed. For example, we can place the result set returned in ascending order on *WardName* by the query opposite.

Table 7.2.6 shows the outcome of applying this query to the **Ward** and **Patient** tables.

```
SELECT Ward.WardName, NurseInCharge, PatientId
  FROM Ward, Patient
    WHERE Ward.WardName = Patient.WardName
      ORDER BY Ward.WardName ASC;
```

Aylesbury	Sister Moon	1
Aylesbury	Sister Moon	3
Victoria	Sister Bunn	2
Victoria	Sister Bunn	4

Table 7.2.6 Result set ordered on WardName in ascending alphabetic order

> ### Questions
>
> 3. Write the SQL query that returns the names of both nurses and their patients, from Tables 7.2.2 and 7.2.3, ordered in descending patient name order.

7 Relational databases and structured query language (SQL)

Relational or comparison operators for search condition

Table 7.2.7 shows comparison operators that may be used in SQL queries.

Table 7.2.8 shows the outcome of applying this query to the **Patient** table.

```
SELECT PatientId, Surname
   FROM Patient
      WHERE PatientId <> 2;
```

Comparison Operator	Description
=	Equal to
<	Less than
>	Greater than
<=	Less than or equal to
>=	Greater than or equal to
<>	Not equal to

Table 7.2.7 Comparison operators for SQL queries

1	Bond
3	Jones
4	Biggs

Table 7.2.8 Result set for PatientId <> 2

Table **Country** has the structure

Country (<u>Name</u>, Capital, Population, Area)

Table 7.2.9 shows some data for table **Country**.

The result set returned when the following SQL query

```
SELECT Name, Capital, Population
   FROM Country
      WHERE (Population < 7000000);
```

is applied to this **Country** table with attributes *Name, Capital, Population, Area* is shown below

El Salvador	San Salvador	5300000
Guyana	Georgetown	800000

Name	Capital	Population	Area
Argentina	Buenos Aires	32 300 003	2777815
Bolivia	La Paz	7 300 000	1098575
Brazil	Brasilia	150 400 000	8511196
Canada	Ottawa	26 500 000	9976147
Chile	Santiago	13 200 000	756943
Colombia	Bagota	33 000 000	1138907
Cuba	Havana	10 600 000	114524
Ecuador	Quito	10 600 000	455502
El Salvador	San Salvador	5 300 000	20865
Guyana	Georgetown	800 000	214969

Table 7.2.9 Table Country showing some values

Questions

4. Write the SQL query that returns the patient surnames from *Table 7.2.3*, for which the patient identifier is less than or equal to **3**. Order the result set in descending order of patient identifier (*PatientId* is the patient identifier).

5. What result set is returned when this SQL query is applied to the data in *Table 7.2.9*?

```
SELECT Capital, Population, Area
   FROM Country
      WHERE (Population > 32000000);
```

Deleting data in a single table

The **DELETE** statement is used to delete rows of a table.

```
DELETE FROM table_name
    WHERE some_column = some_value;
```

The WHERE clause specifies which row or rows should be deleted. If the WHERE clause is omitted, all rows will be deleted!

For example referencing *Table 7.2.9*,

```
DELETE FROM Country
    WHERE Capital = 'Brasilia';
```

deletes the row Brazil, Brasilia, 150400000, 8511196.

> **Questions**
>
> **6** Write the SQL statement to delete the row with BorrowerId 3 in the **Borrower** table shown in *Table 7.2.10*.
>
> **7** Write the SQL statement to delete the row(s) with Population > 15000000 in the **Country** table shown in *Table 7.2.9*.

BorrowerId	Surname	Initial
1	Smith	K
2	Barnes	W
3	Minns	M

Table 7.2.10 Table showing some values for the table Borrower

Inserting data into a single table

The **INSERT INTO** statement inserts a new row into a table. It is possible to write this statement in two forms.

The first form does not specify the column names where the data will be inserted, only their values:

```
INSERT INTO table_name
    VALUES (value1, value2, value3, ...);
```

The second form specifies both the column names and the values to be inserted:

```
INSERT INTO table_name (column1, column2, column3, ...)
    VALUES (value1, value2, value3, ...);
```

In the first form, a value of the correct data type must be supplied for every attribute of the table and the order of the supplied values must be the same as the corresponding columns in the table.

In the second form, a value for every specified column must be supplied and each value must match in data type the corresponding specified column, i.e. value1 corresponds to column1, value2 to column2, etc. The value `Null` will be inserted for any columns not referenced.

For example, for table **Ward**, *Table 7.2.2*, reproduced here

First form:

```
INSERT INTO Ward VALUES ('Gresham', 'Mr Oonga', 20);
```

WardName	NurseInCharge	NoOfBeds
Victoria	Sister Bunn	30
Aylesbury	Sister Moon	40

Table 7.2.2 Table Ward

This first form creates a new row in *Table 7.2.2* with values 'Gresham', 'Mr Oonga', 20

Second form:

```
INSERT INTO Ward (WardName, NurseInCharge) VALUES ('Savernake', 'Sister Teng');
```

This second form creates a new row in *Table 7.2.2* with values 'Savernake', 'Sister Teng', Null

7 Relational databases and structured query language (SQL)

Questions

8 Write the SQL statement to add a new row to the **Ward** table (*Table 7.2.2*) for ward 'Amersham', containing 25 beds. The nurse in charge is 'Sister Brody'.

9 Write the SQL statement to add a new row to the **Country** table (*Table 7.2.9*) for 'UK', 'London'.

Updating data in a single table

The **UPDATE** statement is used to update an existing row of a table.

```
UPDATE table_name
   SET column1 = value1, column2 = value2, ...
      WHERE some_column = some_value;
```

For example,

```
UPDATE Ward
   SET NurseInCharge = 'Mr Ali', NoOfBeds = 25
      WHERE WardName = 'Victoria';
```

Questions

10 Write the SQL statement to update the row of the **Country** table (*Table 7.2.9*) for 'UK' to add population 64100000, area 243610. Assume that an insert statement has inserted 'UK', 'London' already as in Q9.

SQL Tutorials

SQL tutorials are available at https://www.w3schools.com/sql/default.asp.

It is also possible to explore SQL locally by first installing a database engine and then a tool which supports the execution of SQL against a database accessed through the database engine.

SQLite is a self-contained, server-less, zero configuration, transactional SQL database engine. The code for SQLite is public domain and is thus free for use for any purpose, commercial or private. It can be obtained from http://www.sqlite.org/.

An easier route to using SQLite is to download DB Browser for SQLite from https://sqlitebrowser.org/. This application takes care of the installation of both the SQLite database engine and an interface for executing SQL - see *Figure 7.2.1*.

Figure 7.2.1 DB Browser for SQLite

After installing DB Browser for SQLite, launch the application. The user interface for DB Browser for SQLite is shown in *Figure 7.2.2*.

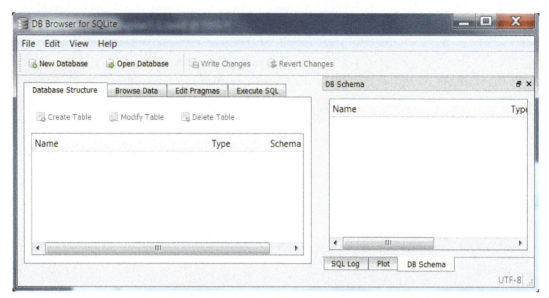

Figure 7.2.2 DB Browser for SQLite user interface

Download the **Hospital.db**, **Country.db**, **Library.db** and **School.db** databases from

www.educational-computing.co.uk/aqacs/gcsecs8525.html

Open **Hospital.db** database using the **Open Database** button. *Figure 7.2.3* shows that the opened database consists of two tables **Patient** and **Ward**.

The data stored in the **Ward** table is revealed by executing the SQL query

```
SELECT * FROM Ward;
```

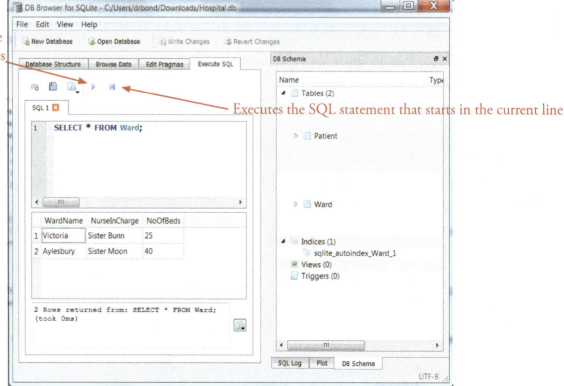

Figure 7.2.3 Execute SQL tab

7 Relational databases and structured query language (SQL)

Figure 7.2.4 shows the result of executing the SQL query

```
SELECT Ward.WardName, NurseInCharge, PatientId
  FROM Ward, Patient
    WHERE Ward.WardName = Patient.WardName
      ORDER BY Ward.WardName ASC;
```

Tasks

1. Try all the SQL examples in this chapter in DB Browser for SQLite.

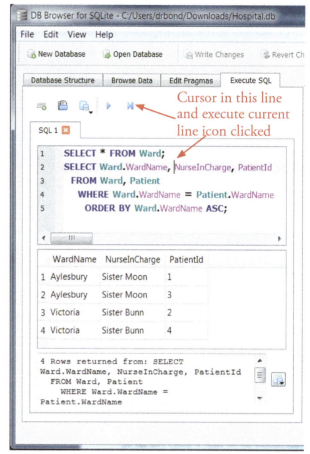

Figure 7.2.4 Querying Ward and Patient tables

In this chapter you have covered:

- How to use SQL to retrieve data from a relational database, using the commands
  - SELECT
  - FROM
  - WHERE
  - ORDER BY...ASC | DESC
- Using SQL to insert data into a relational database by using the command

  INSERT INTO *table_name*
  (column1, column2, ...)
  VALUES *(value1, value2, ...)*

- Using SQL to edit and delete data in a relational database by using the commands

  UPDATE *table_name*
  SET *column1 = value1,*
      column2 = value2, ...
  WHERE *condition*

  DELETE FROM *table_name*
  WHERE *condition*

8 Ethical, legal and environmental impacts of digital technology on wider society, including issues of privacy

Learning objectives:

- *Explain the current ethical, legal and environmental impacts and risks of digital technology on society. Where data privacy issues arise these should be considered.*

8 Ethical, legal and environmental impacts of digital technology on wider society, including issues of privacy

Ethical impacts of digital technology

What is ethics?

When a person 'thinks ethically' they are giving some thought to human action that has moral consequences for someone beyond themselves and their own desires and self-interest.

Digital technology has created new possibilities for human action but it has also raised new ethical questions, i.e. questions requiring new ethics with which to reason.

The European Data Protection Supervisor (EDPS), an independent institution of the EU, published a report in 2015 entitled

"Towards a New Digital Ethics"

(https://secure.edps.europa.eu/EDPSWEB/webdav/site/mySite/shared/Documents/Consultation/Opinions/2015/15-09-11_Data_Ethics_EN.pdf)

At its core is **the protection of human dignity and the fundamental rights to privacy and to the protection of personal data**.

The challenges facing legislators in the digital age

Laws have not kept pace with the development of digital technologies.

There is a general feeling that a person's privacy has shrunk in the global information society. There are something like five hundred companies that are able to track every move you make on the Internet, mining the raw material of the Web and selling it to marketers.

"Personal data are purchased, aggregated, analyzed, packaged, and sold by data brokers who operate, in the US at least, in secrecy – outside of statutory consumer protections and without consumers' knowledge, consent, or rights of privacy and due process" (*U.S. Committee on Commerce, Science, and Transportation, 2013*).

The nature of software, data, and information, and the degree and scale of control over software available to computer scientists and software engineers constrain what the lawyers and legislators can achieve when local laws run up against the global Internet.

"In today's digital environment, adherence to the law is not enough; we have to consider the ethical dimension of data processing."

(*Towards a New Digital Ethics*)

This is the case whether the right under scrutiny is any one of copyright, trademark, privacy, or freedom of expression. Can a law made in one country be successfully applied to the global Internet whose content, algorithms and access embed value judgments from different cultures, societies and legal systems?

Information

Hyperscale computing:

In computing, hyperscale is the ability of an architecture to scale appropriately and quickly in a cost-effective manner as increased demand is added to the system. Hyperscale computing is necessary in order to build a robust and scalable Cloud, and is often associated with the infrastructure required to run large distributed sites such as Facebook, Google, Microsoft Azure or Amazon AWS.

Key point

Having hyperscale ability enables many results to be extracted from individuals' personal data that would have remained unknown but for the scaling of the processing it makes possible, as well as the support for massive datasets of personal information it grants. The extracted information can be of benefit to society but it also has the potential for misuse if the processing is used for social or economic discrimination, unsolicited advertising, or reputational damage.

8 Ethical, legal and environmental impacts of digital

Information
The Web means the end of forgetting:
New York Times article by Jeffrey Rosen
http://www.nytimes.com/2010/07/25/magazine/25privacy-t2.html?pagewanted=all&_r=0

Key concept
Personal data:
Any information related to a natural person or "Data Subject", that can be used to directly or indirectly identify the person.
It now includes online identifiers, e.g. IP addresses, location data, and biometric/genetic data.

Questions for discussion
Topic: Practical obscurity

1. Practical obscurity is an important factor in the preservation of privacy. If the representation of information does not permit it to be easily queried, e.g. the information is on paper in a filing cabinet, then the extraction of important knowledge (usable information) is made more difficult.
Why does the ability to collect and process data on a mammoth scale in the way achieved by Google and other companies reduce practical obscurity?

2. "The average citizen has participated actively in their own surveillance when engaging with digital services and businesses". Explain why you agree or disagree with this statement.

3. In respect of the Internet, should the reach of the law for each of the following apply (i) globally or (ii) locally with each country deciding what law to apply?
(a) copyright (b) privacy (c) freedom of expression.

General Data Protection Regulation 2018

The EU's General Data Protection Regulation (GDPR) took effect on 25 May 2018, and affects not only EU-based organizations, but also possibly data controllers and processors around the world of data of EU data subjects. The UK has passed an Act of Parliament which implements the GDPR - Data Protection Act 2018. The fines for non-compliance per incident can be substantial (maximum € 20 million or 4% global annual turnover whichever is higher).

GDPR brings about widespread unification and standardisation of **data privacy** and **data security** requirements across all 28 member states. Its introduction has been prompted by the growth of use of Big Data, Cloud, and Internet Of Things (IoT) applications.

Entity:
The terms of the GDPR apply to anyone processing personal data except for individuals processing personal data for personal or household activities. This means that the GDPR applies to clubs or societies holding the names, contact details or other personal information about members.

The GDPR applies to
- Companies or entities with a seat of business or establishment in an EU member state and which process data in the context of their businesses regardless of where the actual processing takes place.
- Companies or entities with no establishment or physical presence in an EU member state which offer goods or services to individuals in the EU.
- Companies or entities with no establishment or physical presence in an EU member state which monitor the behaviour of individuals in the EU.

The GDPR offers an enhanced level of protection for data subjects:
- The definition of "Personal Data" now explicitly includes online identifiers, location data, and biometric/genetic data.
- Higher standards for privacy notices and for obtaining consent.
- Easier access to personal data by data subject.
- Enhanced right to request the erasure of their personal data.
- Right to object to processing now explicitly includes profiling.
- Right to transfer personal data to another organisation.

Key concept
Data subject:
A living person whose personal data is processed by a controller or processor.
Data Controller:
The person/entity who determines the purposes, conditions and means of the processing of personal data.
Data Processor:
The entity that processes data on behalf of the Data Controller.

Key concept
Information:
Data is how information is represented.

Before entering a website which gathers data personal to you, it must obtain your consent to do this, and to record and process this data. You have the right to opt-out.

Companies and entities must record that they have obtained your consent to gathering, recording and processing your personal data.

339

Ethical impacts of digital technology

Case studies for discussion

1 Consider the case of a large retail chain with establishments in member states of the EU. The retail chain collects personal data from customers in these member states. They also have an online website where they sell goods worldwide and they collect personal data in member states, and the US, Canada and Latin America. They move all their data processing activities to the Cloud. The data is stored on servers in the US and security for the data is managed from India.
Does the GDPR apply to this retail chain considering that the servers are not in the EU and the services are not managed in the EU and many data subjects whose data are collected are not in the EU?
The answer is yes because the company has an establishment in the EU and processes personal data. The main relevant factor is the seat of business. That is all that counts.

2 Where location data other than traffic data, relating to users or subscribers of public communications networks or publicly available electronic communications services can be processed, such data may only be processed when they are made anonymous, or with the consent of the users or subscribers to the extent and for the duration necessary for the provision of a value added service. The service provider must inform the users or subscribers, prior to obtaining their consent, of the type of location data other than traffic data which will be processed, of the purposes and duration of the processing and whether the data will be transmitted to a third party for the purpose of providing the value added service.

3 The GDPR states that the test for whether a person is "identifiable" depends upon "all the means reasonably likely to be used" to identify that person. This means that IP addresses of visitors to a website are personal data in certain circumstances.
IP addresses will be personal data in the hands of any party that can lawfully obtain sufficient additional data to link the information to a person's real world identity. On the other hand, IP addresses will not be personal data in the hands of a party that has no legal means of obtaining sufficient additional data to make such a link.

Questions for discussion

4 A company based in California, its only seat of business, operates servers and a subscription service for online multiuser gaming. It has members from everywhere in the world including the EU.
Does the GDPR apply to this company? Justify your answer.

5 A company based in Nevada, USA, its only seat of business, monitors the online behaviour of individuals in the EU so that it can create profiles of individuals to sell on to retail companies.
Does the GDPR apply to this company? Justify your answer.

6 Using your mobile phone you access an online game running on a company's servers but have noticed that wherever you are when playing this game, adverts pop up for retail stores in your current locality. You believe that this company is using your location data but you did not consent to this specific use of your location data when you consented for the company to process your personal data. Has this company broken the GDPR? Justify your answer.

7 Like many website operators, a company records the IP addresses of visitors of its websites.
(a) Will IP addresses qualify as personal data under the GDPR?
(b) If they do qualify then will the company be required to obtain consent in order to process such data from individuals visiting the company's websites?

8 Ethical, legal and environmental impacts of digital

Geolocation- tracking you and your location

Geolocation is the identification or estimation of the real-world geographic location of an object, such as a mobile phone, or Internet-connected computer.

Geolocation data collection can be categorised into three types according to how the data is collected:

1. **Voluntary geolocation data collection** - some people deliberately broadcast their geographic location by formally tagging their location and "checking in" at various places on social media sites using their GPS-enabled smartphones or by connecting to a Wi-Fi access point.

2. **Necessary geolocation data collection** - a mobile phone is constantly reporting its location to the nearest mobile base station. That is how the mobile phone network knows where the phone is located so that it can connect a call to the phone. The mobile phone company keeps records of where your mobile has been and where it is currently.

3. **Surreptitious geolocation data collection** - this is geolocation tracking without your knowledge or consent, e.g. StingRay which pretends to be a mobile base station by simulating its signal and thereby forcing each mobile phone in its area to disconnect from its service provider site (e.g. operated by Vodafone, EE, etc.) and establish a new connection with StingRay by which the mobile phone numbers and unique electronic serial identification numbers of each can be read and a target for surveillance identified. StingRay may then establish a connection with the mobile phone's provider and remain in the middle, listening and recording calls made from the connected mobile phones.

Tasks

1. Visit the following site and read about the use of StingRay equipment.
   http://www.bbc.co.uk/news/business-33076527

2. Visit the following site and view the video on Raytheon's Rapid Information Overlay Technology (RIOT) which uses only publicly available data from social media sites, Facebook, Instagram, etc to draw a detailed picture of a person based on where he or she goes: https://www.youtube.com/watch?v=fIIUVJ6PC1k

3. Optional: Visit the following site and view the video "Can You Track Me Now?"
   https://www.youtube.com/watch?v=NjuhdKUH6U4
   (Warning: This video is 1 hour 39 minutes long)

Society

A society of citizens is a society in which strangers can trust one another since everyone is bound by a common set of rules.

Trust can grow between strangers, because it does not depend upon family connections, tribal loyalty, or favours granted or earned.

Citizenship is the relation that arises between the state and the individual when each is fully accountable to the other:

- It consists of a web of reciprocal rights and duties upheld by a rule of law which stands higher than either party.
- The state enforces the law but it enforces it equally against itself and against the private citizen.
- The citizen has rights which the state is duty-bound to uphold.
- The citizen has duties which the state has a right to enforce e.g. when the state is threatened a citizen may be conscripted.

Ethical impacts of digital technology

It is generally accepted that we surrender certain freedoms in exchange for security provided by the state.

Citizens are supposed to have a clear conception of where their freedoms end because these rights and duties are defined and limited by law.

However, laws have not necessarily kept pace with the development of digital technologies whilst at the same time digital technologies have created new possibilities for human action such as state electronic mass surveillance of its citizens.

This has led to a general feeling that a person's privacy has shrunk in the global information society:

1. Citizens normally value their privacy and may not like it when governments or security services have too much access.
2. However, governments and security services often argue that they cannot keep their citizens safe from terrorism and other attacks unless they have access to private data.

Task

 Visit the site http://www.bbc.co.uk/news/technology-25085592 and answer the following questions:
   (a) What is *Prism*?
   (b) What is *Tempora*?
   (c) Why might Angry Birds and other mobile applications lead to a leakage of personal information?

Investigatory Powers Act 2016

In the light of concerns expressed by various quarters in society, especially following the Edward Snowden revelations, the Investigatory Powers Act 2000 was revised and replaced in 2016 by a new Act, the Investigatory Powers Act 2016. This new Act comprehensively sets out, and in limited respects, expands the electronic surveillance powers of the UK intelligence community and police whilst also improving the safeguards on the exercise of these powers.

This Act sets out the extent to which certain investigatory powers may be used **to interfere with privacy**.

The Act introduced new powers, and restated existing ones, for UK intelligence agencies and law enforcement to carry out targeted interception of communications, bulk collection of communications data, and bulk interception of communications.

The Secretary of State may, by retention notice, require a telecommunications operator to retain UK Internet users' "Internet connection records" for up to one year – which websites were visited, e.g. https://en.wikipedia.org, but not the particular pages and not the full browsing history. The retention notice warrant must be approved by a Judicial Commissioner.

It allows police, intelligence officers and other government department managers to see Internet connection records, as part of a targeted and filtered investigation, provided that a warrant has been granted for this purpose.

It permits the police and intelligence agencies to carry out targeted equipment interference, that is, hacking into computers or devices to access their data, and bulk equipment interference for national security matters related to foreign investigations covered by a warrant. A bulk interception warrant applies to the interception of overseas-related communications. A bulk acquisition warrant can be issued by the Secretary of State in the interests of national security or for the purpose of preventing or detecting serious crime.

Task

5 Visit the following site and view the video to get an overview of the implications of the Investigatory Powers Act 2016:

https://www.engadget.com/2016/12/20/investigatory-powers-act-explained/

What is meant by the double-lock for interception warrants?

Questions

8 The making of the law, as an activity, is itself governed by morality - what is right and what is wrong. There are three important moral considerations that must be taken into account in every decision the state makes:

- public welfare;
- individual rights;
- justice between individuals.

This question is about the Investigatory Powers Act.

(a) How does the Act target public welfare?

(b) The Act has the potential to interfere with the privacy of individuals. Explain.

(c) What safeguard(s) does the Act contain to protect the rights of individuals to privacy?

Wi-Fi hotspots

Wi-Fi hotspots can create data privacy issues because they are a means by which communications may be intercepted and data stolen.

Wi-Fi hotspots are wireless broadband networks which allow access to the Internet in various public spaces such as cafes, airports and public transport. They enable people to access their email and other network applications in public spaces. It's faster and more reliable than mobile broadband like 4G and avoids using some of a mobile phone's data allowance. But public Wi-Fi hotspots are not considered safe. For example, in 2016 a journalist wrote an article reporting that his email got intercepted by a hacker while using an airplane Wi-Fi - read the following article at http://securityaffairs.co/wordpress/44876/hacking/ournalist-hacked-on-plane.html.

For this reason, many people avoid using Wi-Fi hotspots or if they have to, don't communicate anything confidential such as bank account details or login details. Better still they use a Virtual Private Network (VPN) so that communications are encrypted or they use a messaging app such as WhatsApp®.

WhatsApp provides **end-to-end encryption** which means that messages are secure so only you and the person you're communicating with can read or listen to them, and nobody in between, not even WhatsApp (except for a security flaw that has been discovered recently - https://www.schneier.com/blog/archives/2017/01/whatsapp_securi.html)! End-to-end encryption relies on a temporary session key which is not saved so cannot be handed over to security services because once used it is destroyed.

Task

6 Read the article which is available on the following site:

https://www.theverge.com/2017/3/27/15070744/encryption-whatsapp-backdoor-uk-london-attacks

Give **one** argument for and **one** argument against a government being allowed to read end-to-end encrypted messages (the encryption key used must be saved somewhere if a government is to be able to decrypt a communication)?

Ethical impacts of digital technology

Wearable technologies

Wearables include anything strapped to or otherwise attached to the human body that
- Collect state, e.g. heart rate
- Communicate information, e.g. heart rate
- Or otherwise performs some type of control function on or around the individual, e.g. warn wearer heart rate too high.

Figure 8.1 shows an example containing two sensors and one actuator each with a controller and a low energy Bluetooth wireless interface called BLE.

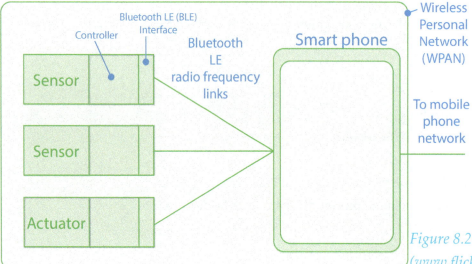

Figure 8.1 Wearable embedded system

Figure 8.2 Nike+ running watch and App (www.flickr.com/ivyfield/4762376623 CC BY 2.0)

These connect to a smart phone via Bluetooth forming a **Wireless Personal Network (WPAN)**.

The smart phone may then connect to the Internet via a mobile phone network then an Internet gateway in order to upload the data.

The Apple Watch, FitBit, Nike+ and others are well-known examples.

Figure 8.2 shows a Nike+ running watch with integrated sensors and the running app displaying data on an iPhone.

Wearable, networked sensors may detect heart rate, temperature, inertial acceleration (for example, to evaluate a runner's stride and tempo), location information (for calculating speed), and many others.

However, ethical concerns, from privacy to security, arise with the use of wearables such as who has access to a person's personal health data if the wearable(s) is used to monitor a person's health and communicated via a gateway such as Microsoft's Azure IoT hub? Who owns and controls it? Is it shared with third parties? Is it sold or loaned for marketing or advertising purposes?

8 Ethical, legal and environmental impacts of digital

Wearables may also be used by companies to track their employees' movements which again raises ethical concerns regarding how this information might be used.

One form of wearable, Google glass, prompted various sources to raise issues regarding the intrusion of privacy, and the etiquette and ethics of using the device in public and recording people without their permission. Google Glass displayed information in a smartphone-like hands-free format. Wearers communicated with the Internet via natural language voice commands. However, Google Glass also had a way to record everything going in front of the wearer. It turned out that very few people were willing to be recorded walking and talking because they considered it an invasion of their privacy. On January 15, 2015, Google announced that it would stop producing the Google Glass prototype but in July 2017 it announced that the Google Enterprise Edition would be released for use in the workplace as an assistive device.

Questions

9. Why might wearing Google Glass in a cinema prompt the management to request that you remove it or worse, leave the cinema?

10. A healthcare company which charges for its services provides each of its clients with a free wearable fitness tracker. Fitness data is sent from the clients' mobile phones via the Internet to the company's servers where the data is analysed.
    (a) State **one** concern that a client might have about how the personal health data obtained from the fitness tracker will be used by the healthcare company.
    (b) State **one** benefit that a client might receive from using the free wearable fitness tracker.

11. Current health care is doctor-centric. Society may have to get used to relying on a different model of health care in the future which raises ethical issues of access and privacy concerns regarding individuals' health data and how it is used.
    (a) One such model could involve the use of wearable technology.
    Suggest **three** uses of wearable technology connected to a smart phone that could assist individuals in monitoring and maintaining their health.
    (b) If this model is adopted, why might some individuals not be able to participate in such a programme of health care and therefore be disadvantaged?
    (c) Explain how the data collected by wearable technology could be communicated securely to individuals' doctors.
    (d) Give **two** reasons for society why in the future, a greater reliance on the use of wearable technology for healthcare might become necessary.

Internet of Things (IoT)

According to the IEEE[1], an Internet of Things (IoT) is a network that connects uniquely identifiable "things" to the Internet. The "things" have sensing/actuation, potential programmability capabilities, unique identification, information about the "thing" can be collected and the state of the "thing" can be changed from anywhere, anytime, by anything."

The "Things" in IoT are "Smart Things" which consist of
- Sensors (temperature, light, motion, moisture, etc).
- Displays.

Information

In 2012, Google filed a patent application for a device which receives the environment sounds heard at the same time with a conversation on a computer microphone or phone so that it could identify exactly what the user was doing and use this to make an advertisement highly adapted to the surrounding environment.

---

[1] IEEE - Institution of Electrical and Electronic Engineers

Ethical impacts of digital technology

- Actuators - a component responsible for moving or controlling a mechanism or system, e.g. opening or closing a valve.
- Computation (can run programs and logic).
- Communication interfaces (wired or wireless).

The IoT enables environmental monitoring of temperature, humidity, dew point, air quality and more.

The Internet of Things raises ethical questions such as "Who is the owner of the data retrieved by the sensors of the objects connected to the Internet of Things?" It is quite feasible for people to not know where their information ends up. The movement of individuals may be monitored without them being aware of it. How many people are aware that RFID tags are embedded in all sorts of objects from car tyres to goods purchased in shops? The data registered by the sensors can be sent in great quantities and in different ways through networks.

The information collected from a chip implanted with the person's consent (for medical purposes) might be used for purposes other than those for which consent has been obtained.

Computer based implants

Computer based implants include any sensor, controller, or communication device that is inserted and operated within the human body or an animal's body.

Information
Radio frequency identification (RFID):
Any method of identifying and tracking items using radio waves. Typically a reader (also called an interrogator) communicates with a transponder, which holds digital information in a microchip. Alternatively, a chipless RFID tag is used which just uses material to reflect back a portion of the radio waves beamed at them. People can be tracked by the RFID tag they have in their possession e.g. a bus pass, and those injected or implanted within human or animal skin.

Task

7. Visit the following site to see the world's smallest implantable computer:
https://www.eecs.umich.edu/eecs/about/articles/2015/Worlds-Smallest-Computer-Michigan-Micro-Mote.html

   Give **two** uses for this computer implanted within the body.

Information
Attempts are being made to control the wild pony population on Dartmoor using a medical implant that is injected under the skin of female ponies. The implant is designed to deliver a measured dose of a contraceptive.

Questions

12. Microchips are being developed containing a reservoir of a particular drug. These can be implanted under the skin and are designed to release 30 micrograms a day of the drug. The dosage may be altered by remote control, as well.
    Suggest **one** benefit and **one** danger from such a computer based implant.

13. Discuss benefits and dangers of using a computer based implant containing a person's complete medical record.

14. State **two** applications of computer based implants that have restored lost senses in human beings.

Information
1. Dick Cheney was US Secretary of Defense during Operation Desert Storm, the 1991 invasion of Iraq.
2. Dick Cheney has been fitted with a heart pacemaker, recently.
The pacemaker was specially adapted for Dick Cheney so that it would be resistant to hacking and disruption. This must be very reassuring to the rest of the population which has to make do with pacemakers that are vulnerable to hacking.

8 Ethical, legal and environmental impacts of digital

Issues around copyright of algorithms (not in AQA specification 8525)

The expression of an algorithm in a source code file (i.e. a program) can be copyrighted but the algorithm itself cannot be in many jurisdictions around the world because copyright cannot protect a concept, idea or fact. Every day stories covering the same news events appear in the nation's rival newspapers but because the words used in each case are different, there is no copyright infringement.

Copyright only protects the original expression of an idea while patent protects man-made, inventive and novel inventions based on ideas.

A famous patent is Google's search algorithm. Patent publication number US 6285999 B1 "Method for node ranking in a linked database, inventor Lawrence Page" was filed on July 6, 2001 by Lawrence Page - see www.google.com/patents/US6285999.

Copyright allows the rights holder to prevent unauthorised reproduction of particular pieces of source code that embody an algorithm. However, such rights do not pertain to the algorithm itself and so copyright itself does not prevent others creating other expressions of the same algorithm in some other form, such as a different source code file unless the algorithm is covered by a patent.

Most countries place some limits on the patenting of inventions involving software, but there is no one legal definition of a software patent. In Europe, "computer programs as such" are excluded from patentability, but despite this, the United Kingdom Intellectual Property Office (UKIPO) regularly grants patents to inventions that are partly or wholly implemented in software.

You must be careful not to violate copyright laws when using the work of others.

> **Information**
> The expression of an algorithm in a source code file can be copyrighted. However, to protect the expression of the algorithm it should be patented, provided it meets the criteria for a patent.

> **Information**
> **Proprietary software:**
> Only the original authors of proprietary software can legally copy, inspect, and alter that software. In order to use proprietary software, computer users must agree (usually by signing a license displayed the first time they run this software) that they will not do anything with the software that the software's authors have not expressly permitted. Microsoft Office and Adobe Photoshop are examples of proprietary software.
> **Open source software:**
> Open source software is software with source code that anyone can inspect, modify, and enhance.
> (Reproduced under Creative Commons licence CC BY-SA 4.0 from https://opensource.com)

Questions

15 Which of the following statements are true?
   A An algorithm can be copyrighted.
   B The expression of an algorithm in a source code file can be copyrighted.
   C An invention may be patented in the UK if partly or wholly implemented in software.
   D The expression of an algorithm in a source code file cannot be copyrighted.
   E An algorithm cannot be copyrighted.

Task

8 Read the article on open source software at https://opensource.com/resources/what-open-source

Questions

16 Some people prefer open source software to proprietary software whilst others prefer to use propriety software.
   State **one** reason for using open source software and **one** reason for using propriety software.

Theft of computer code (not in AQA specification 8525)

The theft of intellectual property is a crime. Software is intellectual property. The copying, use and distribution of software without permission is known as software piracy. Software piracy started to become an issue when the arrival of microcomputers in the late 1970s and early 1980s created a mass market, and software houses started to produce products that didn't require technical support to install and run.

Cracking and hacking (unauthorised access to a computer system) (not in AQA specification 8525)

Hacking and cracking are forms of Internet and computer related privacy and copyright breaches, usually malicious.

Cracking focuses on finding or making a back door in software, and exploiting it for malicious use or for an act which breaches copyright. For example, when installing software, the user is often required to enter a unique product key which came with the software. People who practise cracking try to find a way of subverting this protection. It might mean patching the software so that it will now accept a product key set by the cracker.

A hacker is someone that uses their extensive knowledge of software systems and computer code (or uses a tool provided by other hackers) for malicious purposes such as stealing passwords, creating a bot net, or in general committing acts that breach someone's privacy, without their knowledge, or consent. Broadly speaking, hacking is unauthorised access to a computer system.

More detail is covered in section 6, *Fundamentals of cyber security*, of this book.

> **Questions**
>
> Explain the difference between a *hacker* and a *cracker*.

Environmental impact

We live in an era where a multitude of devices are in use each day from servers to embedded systems, personal computers to smartphones.
All of these devices consumed natural resources when they were manufactured and create disposal problems which can impact on the environment when no longer required.

Manufacture

Manufacturing computer parts can result in direct and indirect damage to the environment from:

- the waste generated and the energy consumed in mining of raw materials needed to make the parts and their packaging
- the consumption of water needed during production of both parts and their packaging
- the power consumed to operate the factories of production
- the use of fossil fuel for transporting parts and their assemblies.

Greenhouse gas emissions result from the above activities which contribute to global warming.

Use

Energy is consumed when devices are in use and also when left unattended, switched on. Many systems include options for conserving power, but these only operate if the system is configured to use them when the system is on but inactive. In the UK in 2016 the annual cost of leaving devices on at work or home was estimated to be £120,000,000. Data centres are particularly high energy users. The Google data centre shown in *Figure 4.5.5.11, Chapter 4.5.5,* of some 100,000 commodity servers, consumes a total power of 40 MegaWatts. This is roughly the total power output of Coolkeeragh power station in Northern Island.

8 Ethical, legal and environmental impacts of digital

Heat generation, a by product of the use of technology, is also a problem for the environment. Whilst one computer alone may not seem to generate a lot of heat, the sheer volume of computers in use on this planet do. This heat doesn't disappear, it dissipates into the environment.

Disposal

One should always try to recycle components not only because computers contain precious or rare elements such as gold which can be reused but also because some components are toxic to the environment and some do not decompose readily resulting in the need for more landfill sites. The alternative of burning in an incinerator is harmful to the environment because it will result in the emission of greenhouse gases and the release of hazardous chemicals.

Environmental benefits

Whilst people should be concerned about the carbon footprint of digital technologies, some of this footprint can be offset against savings made elsewhere from changing the way things are done. These are listed below.

1. **Reduction in use of paper**

    Many items that traditionally were paper-based don't have to be any longer, electronic copies can now be stored and made available online, thus reducing the demand for paper. For example, consumers may now download electronic copies of books and read them on screen.

    Cloud storage has made it easier to collaborate online thus avoiding the need to work with multiple paper copies of a document.

    However, many people still prefer to read paper copies, but it is expected that this will change over time as the percentage of digital natives increases. When this is coupled with widespread, affordable, high speed Internet access it is expected that there will be less need for paper which should result in fewer trees being cut down, and less damage to the environment. Also, if less paper is needed there will be less of it to be disposed, and if disposal is by burning, less carbon emissions.

    Some schools and colleges have already adopted an e-book only policy further contributing to a reduction in the need for paper.

2. **Download versus supply in some storage media form**

    Software is downloaded nowadays instead of being supplied on storage media such as CD-ROM. This has led to a reduction in environmental costs incurred by the manufacturing, packaging and transportation of such storage media. Similarly, transactions are usually paid for online via electronic money, i.e. a credit or debit card, which avoids the need to use paper money or a paper cheque. Also downloading software avoids another source of carbon emissions which occurs when software goods have to be physically transported.

3. **Working from home**

    Cloud storage has created more opportunities to work from home as it is now possible to collaborate online on tasks and avoid journeys to and from the workplace via energy consuming and polluting forms of transport. This may be a model of working in the future for many people and from which much environmental benefit may be gained.

> **Information**
> **Carbon footprint:**
> The amount of carbon dioxide released into the atmosphere as a result of the activities of a particular individual, organization, or community.

> **Did you know?**
> **Medical prescriptions:**
> Many doctors' surgeries now send patient prescriptions to pharmacies electronically eliminating the need for paper prescriptions.

> **Information**
> **Digital native:**
> Someone who has grown up with digital technology.
> **Digital immigrant:**
> Someone who grew up before digital technology became prevalent.

Ethical impacts of digital technology

Smart systems

Smart or intelligent systems have the ability to make decisions on behalf of a user, reducing reliance on the need for human control. Smart home systems now allow users to automate many monitoring and control tasks based on initial settings plugged into an app. Software then makes decisions based upon external factors such as room temperature, the time of day, and the movement patterns and habits of the occupants of the house. Smarter control of heating and lighting systems can lead to energy savings which impact positively on the environment.

In conjunction with smart lighting, i.e. digitally controllable lighting, individual lights can be made to flash to warn an occupant of a central heating boiler fault that is causing the emission of harmful levels of carbon monoxide.

> ### Questions
>
> **18** Give **one** cause of the negative impact on the environment in each of the following:
> (a) the manufacture of digital technology devices.
> (b) the use of digital technology devices.
> (c) the disposal of digital technology devices.
>
> **19** Explain **three** different environmental benefits of the use of digital technology in particular ways.

Cyber security

See Section 6, *Fundamentals of cyber security*.

Cloud storage

See *Chapter 4.5.5*.

Autonomous vehicles

What is meant by autonomous vehicle?

The dictionary definition of autonomous is

Acting alone, independent, self-governing

Autonomous vehicles are **automated vehicles** with various degrees of control by "machine" where the machine consists of

- a range of sensors that sense the environment, e.g. other vehicles, and the behaviour of the vehicle, e.g. the vehicle's own speed
- actuators that physically carry out commands such as apply brakes
- processors that process sensor information, evaluate some or all aspects of the driving situation, make decisions that control the vehicle to a lesser or greater extent, e.g. take avoiding action; issue commands in the form of electronic signals to the actuators that carry out these decisions
- algorithms in the form of computer programs that execute in the processors to carry out the tasks of the previous bullet point.

Autonomous vehicles in the main rely on various levels of artificial intelligence.

The algorithms that are used are machine-learning algorithms.

Such algorithms are harder to test because they rely on statistical techniques.

Contrast this with autopilot software used in commercial aeroplanes which does not rely currently on machine-learning algorithms.

Autopilot software is considered provably safe because it relies on deterministic algorithms which lend themselves to proofs of correctness.

Machine-learning algorithms require massive amounts of training data to work properly, incorporating nearly every scenario the algorithm will encounter. And therein, lies the problem: the sheer number of "edge cases", i.e. unusual circumstances that autonomous cars have to handle. This is known as the **generalisation problem**.

8 Ethical, legal and environmental impacts of digital

> *Example 1 - Self-driving Uber car kills Arizona pedestrian*
>
> The death of Elaine Herzberg on March 18th 2018 was the first recorded case of a pedestrian fatality involving a self-driving (autonomous) car. Elaine was pushing a bicycle across a four-lane road in Tempe, Arizona, United States when she was struck by an Uber test vehicle, which was operating in self-drive mode with a human safety backup driver sitting in the driving seat.
>
> According to The National Traffic Safety Board (NTSB) which investigated the fatal crash, the software installed in Uber's vehicles to help it detect and classify other objects "did not include a consideration for jaywalking pedestrians". The software was only designed to detect pedestrians at known crossing points called crosswalks in the United States of America.
>
> Uber's vehicle detected Elaine's presence approximately 6 seconds before impact, but it failed to implement braking because it kept re-classifying her - alternating between vehicle, bicycle, and unknown object. Each time the automated driving system re-classified Elaine, it had to predict a new path for her. Unfortunately, while this was happening, the backup human driver was watching a streaming video on her mobile phone strictly against Uber's company policy. By the time that the software issued an auditory warning to the backup driver to take over, it was too late to avoid the collision.

Questions

20 Explain why *Example 1* above is an example of the *generalisation problem*.

Automated and fully-automated vehicle

The Society of Automobile Engineers has published a globally accepted taxonomy (detailed definitions) for six discrete and mutually exclusive levels of driving automation, ranging from no driving automation (level 0) to full driving automation (level 5). Central to this taxonomy are the respective roles of the (human) user and the driving automation system in relation to each other: — *The task of controlling the movement of the vehicle*

1. In **level 0** the driver performs the entire dynamic driving task, even when enhanced by active safety systems such as an anti-lock brake system, electronic stability control. These active safety systems provide **momentary intervention** but do not perform any part of the **Dynamic Driving Task (DDT)** on a **sustained basis**.

2. If the driving automation system performs subtasks of the DDT but not all then the system is classified as corresponding to **level 1 or 2**. e.g. adaptive cruise control, lane-keeping/lane-following assistance.

3. If the driving automation system performs the entire dynamic driving task then this is classified as corresponding to **levels 3, 4 and 5**.

Information

Levels 0-2:
In levels 0-2, the driver monitors the driving environment, the vehicle performance, and the driving automation system performance.

Adaptive cruise control: Maintains vehicle at a constant speed and at a constant distance from vehicle ahead.

Levels 0-2

In levels 0-2 driving automation, **the driver is expected to monitor the driving environment** and **the driver is expected to be receptive to evident vehicle system failures** and **not wait to be alerted**, e.g. a broken steering arm - the component that moves a front wheel in and out under steering wheel control.

Level 0

There is no automation. The driver performs all the DDT, i.e. driving tasks.

Levels 1-2

In levels 1-2 there is some driving automation. The driver performs the remainder of the DDT not performed by the driving automation system. **The driver is expected to be receptive to** and **react to evident driving automation system failures**, such as a failure in an adaptive cruise control system, **by resuming performance of the complete DDT**, i.e. the driver takes over control.

> **Information**
> Level 3 assumes that the driver is receptive to alerts or other indicators of a DDT performance-relevant system failure. Being receptive is not the same as monitoring. For example, a person can be alert to a fire alarm without necessarily monitoring the fire alarm.

The differences between the level 1 and level 2 are twofold:

1. The degree of control over the vehicle's movement
2. The degree of object and event detection and response.

Level 1 and 2 differences:

- Level 1 is labelled driver assistance because it has limited object and **external** event detection and response *(e.g. other vehicles, lane markings, traffic signs)*, and is limited to just one movement, either longitudinal or lateral, e.g. adaptive cruise control system (responds to external event of vehicle in front) or a lane-centering system (lateral vehicle motion control)
- Level 2 is labelled partial automation (but not self-driving) because it supports limited, but more than level 1, object and **external** event detection and response, whilst controlling both longitudinal (forward) and lateral (sideways) separation of the vehicle from other objects, e.g. both adaptive cruise control (maintaining safe separation from vehicle ahead) and lane-following/lane-keeping/lane-centering system.

Levels 3-5

In levels 3-5 **the Automated Driving System (ADS) monitors its own performance of the complete DDT**.

Level 3

In level 3 driving automation, **the driver must be receptive to a request from the Automated Driving System (ADS) to intervene and/or be receptive to an evident vehicle system failure**, e.g. a broken steering arm.

Levels 4-5

In levels 4-5 the ADS is responsible for handling any failures.
It should transition to a minimal risk condition by

- turning on the hazard lights
- manoeuvering the vehicle to the road shoulder and then parking it before automatically summoning emergency assistance.

> **Information**
> The fictional autonomous car KITT from the TV show *Knight Rider*, only achieved level 4 autonomy. Michael Knight was required on occasion to override KITT outside of KITT's autonomous region of operation.

This is called **DDT fallback** - the plan that is followed when a DDT performance-relevant system failure occurs. This means that while performing the DDT, the level 4 and 5 ADSs must monitor vehicle performance.
In summary, levels 4-5:

The difference between a **level 5 ADS** and a **level 4 ADS** is that the latter is **restricted by design to operate in a specific domain** (level 4 is said to be limited by **Operational Design Domain (ODD)**) whereas the former is not.

The ADS performs the entire DDT and **DDT fallback**, transitioning to a minimal risk condition **without any expectation that a user will respond to a request to intervene** (in level 3, ADS assumes that a DDT fallback-ready user is available to perform the DDT as required).

8 Ethical, legal and environmental impacts of digital

Level 4

Level 4 ADSs are limited by area/location i.e. geo-fenced; by speed (high or low); specific road types, e.g. motorways only; the presence or absence of certain road features such as lane markings, road side traffic barriers; lighting conditions, e.g. day time only, weather conditions; or parking only and others. This is what is meant by operating in a specific domain.

Level 5

Level 5 is designed to operate in an unrestricted domain:

> **A vehicle with a level 5 ADS should, once programmed with a destination, be capable of operating the vehicle throughout complete trips on public roads, regardless of the starting and end points or intervening road, traffic, and weather conditions.**

Table 8.1 shows the Society of Automotive Engineers (SAE) six levels of vehicle autonomy and the UK's Department of Transport (DOT) levels.

			Department for Transport levels		
			High automation		**Full automation**
SAE J3016 Levels 0 to 5 (globally adopted standard)			**DRIVER ATTENTION**		
Level 0	Level 1	Level 2	Level 3	Level 4	Level 5
No automation	**Automation provides driver assistance**	**Partial automation but not self-driving**	**Conditional automation**	**High automation**	**Full automation**
Manual control. The human performs all driving tasks (steering, accelerating, braking, etc). May have some control systems but these respond only to internal events, e.g. control of vehicle's speed by a cruise control system, and/OR are used only momentarily, e.g. anti-lock brakes, autonomous emergency braking.	The vehicle features an automated system which responds to external events, e.g an adaptive cruise control system which maintains vehicle's speed at a safe distance from vehicle ahead whilst driver controls steering. Alternatively, lateral positioning in a lane is maintained, i.e. lane centering, whilst the driver controls the brakes and acceleration. Automation assistance provides steering **OR** brake/acceleration support but not both at the same time.	The vehicle can perform multiple automated functionalities in tandem such as steering **AND** brake/acceleration - lane centering and adaptive cruise control **at the same time**. The human still monitors all tasks and can take control at any time. Tesla Autopilot and Cadillac (General Motors) Super Cruise systems both qualify as Level 2. Active parking/self-parking, e.g. Nissan's ProPILOT Assist's hand-free and foot-free operation.	Environmental detection capabilities. The vehicle can perform most driving tasks, but human override is still required.	The vehicle performs all driving tasks under specific circumstances. Geofencing is required. Human override is still an option.	The vehicle performs all driving tasks under all conditions. Zero human attention or interaction is required. Therefore, a driver does not need to be present.

Table 8.1 Six Levels of Vehicle Autonomy

Ethical impacts of digital technology

> **Example 2 - Fatal crash involving Tesla Autopilot Model S, March 1st 2019**
>
> A Tesla Model S with Autopilot was on a dual carriageway with Autopilot engaged when a white-sided articulated lorry crossed at a crossing point ahead of the Model S. Neither Autopilot nor the Model S driver registered the presence of the sidewise-on articulated lorry against a brightly lit sky, so the brake was not applied.
>
> Autopilot is a Tesla product that enables the Tesla car to steer, accelerate and brake automatically within its lane. Current Autopilot features require active driver supervision.
>
> Tesla state that
> - Autopilot is disabled by default;
> - when drivers activate Autopilot, they are required to acknowledge that the system is new technology and that it is "an assist feature that requires you to keep your hands on the wheel at all times", and that "you need to maintain control and responsibility for your vehicle" whilst using it;
> - everytime that Autopilot is engaged, the car reminds the driver to "Always keep your hands on the wheel. Be prepared to take over at any time."
>
> Tesla also state that
> - the system will make frequent checks to ensure that the driver's hands remain on the wheel;
> - visual and audible alerts will be made if hands-on is not detected and then the car will be gradually slowed until hands-on is detected again.
>
> This was the first known fatality in just over 130 million miles where Autopilot was activated. In contrast, there is a fatality every 94 million miles among all vehicles in the US and a fatality approximately every 60 million miles worldwide.

Questions

21 State the level of driving automation in the range level 0-5 for the Tesla Autopilot Model S described in *Example 2* above.

22 State using the range level 0 to level 5 which level of automation applies in each of the following

A The car can drive itself completely, but only within a well-mapped area.

B The car can drive itself on certain roads under certain conditions, but a driver is still needed and the driver must be receptive to a request to intervene from the Automated Driving System (ADS).

C The car manages both its speed and its steering on motorways but the driver must still pay attention to driving conditions at all times and decide to take over immediately if necessary.

D The car is kept at a safe distance from the car ahead whilst travelling in the slow lane on a motorway whilst the driver steers the car.

E The car can drive itself anytime, anywhere, under any conditions whilst the occupants of the car are passengers whose only role in the driving is to tell the car where to take them.

F The car's speed can be set and maintained autonomously but every other aspect of driving is done by the driver.

23 State **three** reasons why motorways are easier for autonomous driving systems than non-motorway roads.

8 Ethical, legal and environmental impacts of digital

Technology

Autonomous or self-driving vehicles must be able to "see" their environment in order to know where they can and cannot drive, detect other vehicles on the road, stop for pedestrians, and handle any unexpected circumstances they may encounter. For this purpose, autonomous cars use a range of sensors which may be classified as **active** or **passive**.

Active sensors send out energy in the form of a wave. The returned energy contains information about the objects that reflect this wave energy. Active sensors use high frequency radio waves in the form of radar, infrared light waves in the form of lidar and high frequency (beyond the audible range) sound waves in the form of ultrasonic waves.

Passive sensors simply take in information from the environment without emitting a wave, e.g. a stereo camera, infrared camera for seeing through fog and at night.

The range of sensors employed enable an autonomous car to have 360-degree vision, and thanks to lidar, radar, and ultrasonic sensors, the car can see through fog and in the dark.

Other very important sources of information used by autonomous cars are GPS, high definition maps, Vehicle-to-Vehicle (V2V) and Vehicle-to-Everything (V2X) communication.

High definition maps with a resolution of a centimetre provide an accurate, realistic representation of the road network, including lane structure, traffic signs, traffic lights, lane geometry and road furniture, e.g. lamp posts, crash barriers. Such maps reduce the amount of processing of sensor information that onboard computers in an autonomous vehicle have to do to navigate a safe route to a destination.

Vehicle-to-Vehicle and Vehicle-to-Everything communication enable sharing of more environmental information to enable autonomous vehicles to identify blindspots, avoid roadworks and traffic incidents, avoid collisions with pedestrians/cyclists, animals or other vehicles on the road, and interact electronically with street furniture. For example,

- Blindspot case: The lead vehicle in a convoy of three vehicles operating autonomously might slow abruptly on encountering a cyclist. The presence of the cyclist could be communicated in real time to the two vehicles behind which could also then slow their speed autonomously and drop back knowing now that there is a cyclist hidden from view by the lead car.

- Unexpected situation: Vehicle A switches lane suddenly in front of the path of vehicle B on a motorway. To avoid an accident, the sensors on both cars communicate with each other via V2V with the result that vehicle A speeds up and vehicle B brakes autonomously.

- "Telepathy": Vehicle A can inform vehicle B that it is considering changing lane before making the decision to do so.

- Optimising traffic flow: Vehicles can communicate with traffic lights to minimise wait times at junctions and optimise traffic flow.

- Turning on street lights: Vehicles can turn on street lights by communicating wirelessly with a controller mounted in each street light. When the vehicle is out of range, the controller can turn the light off thus saving energy.

- Driving abroad: If a self-driving car is taken to mainland Europe can it cope safely with the switch from driving on the left to driving on the right? Perhaps this is a case for geofencing and handing over to a human driver. Alternatively, if it is connected to its manufacturer via a 5G network, on recognising a change of country it could download the necessary software changes for driving on the right in a country with different signage, road customs, value system, etc in realtime.

A choice exists between a direct short-range wireless connection and a wireless network which supports far as well as near coverage, if vehicles are to be interconnected. Connecting to a wireless network supports vehicle-to-network, vehicle-to-cloud, vehicle-to-IoT (Internet of Things), in addition to vehicle-to-vehicle. Direct short-range wireless only supports vehicle-to-vehicle communication.

Any wireless network that supports V2V and V2X will need to be capable of relaying information sufficiently quickly to enable a decision to be made in a time that at least matches that of a human driver. To achieve on-all-the-time coverage and necessary speed of response nationally, car manufacturers will need to use Fifth Generation (5G) wireless networking. Current Fourth Generation (4G) wireless networking will not be fast enough.

Questions

24. List and describe **three** different technologies that a self-driving vehicle may use to accurately detect a hazard.

25. Explain why is it helpful to have pre-mapped the environment in which a self-driving car is to operate autonomously.

26. Describe **one** benefit that could follow if all road vehicles are self-driving and connected by a 5G wireless network.

Ethics

When an individual reaches a conclusion or decision as to the morally right course of action they often draw on a framework or set of principles to help their reasoning, e.g. our actions should do no harm. The framework or set of principles is called an ethical framework or just, ethics. When applied to particular cases, the framework can provide clear choices. Each ethical framework embodies the social norms and value system of the society which adopts it.

In the UK in 2018, more than 160,000 people were injured on the roads. Over 25,000 of these were seriously hurt. 1,784 people died[2]. The large majority of road traffic accidents are caused when a driver makes the wrong choice. By removing the driver from the decision-making process, autonomous vehicles hold out the possibility of removing the source of most errors and therefore of significantly improving safety. For this reason, **the mission of encouraging and facilitating the adoption of autonomous vehicles on the roads of the UK is a moral one**. Of course, autonomous vehicles may never attain a perfect safety record but the evidence to date is that their safety record is better than that of human drivers.

All driving involves risk. The technology within autonomous vehicles will use an "algorithm" that aims to minimise the risk of injury to the occupants of vehicles, pedestrians, cyclists, other road users as well as the risk of damage to property. This "algorithm" therefore must have an ethical component, as such it has been labelled the "moral algorithm".

Who should decide this "moral algorithm"?

Human drivers operate in the complex environment of the UK's road network and their driving decisions reflect the individual nature of each which ranges from risk-taker to risk-averse.

The "moral algorithm" will distribute risk among occupants of autonomous vehicles, pedestrians, cyclists, other road users, and property. How should this be done and by whom?

---

2   Department of Transport - Reported road casualties in Great Britain:2018 Annual report.

8 Ethical, legal and environmental impacts of digital

Task

 What is your answer to the ethical dilemma question posed in *Example 3*. Explain your answer.

Who do you think should decide on how the risk should be distributed? Explain your answer.

Example 3 – How should driving risk be distributed and by whom?

Example ethical dilemma:

Given no other option, should the autonomous vehicle (self-driving) harm several pedestrians by swerving, or sacrifice its own passengers to save a greater number of passers-by?

Who should decide on the distribution of risk embodied in the "moral algorithm":

Software engineers who will design and write the software, the vehicle manufacturer who is responsible in law for the autonomous vehicle or a public body regulator appointed by Government? Before answering this question you may like to consider the following statements:

- Software engineers should decide on the distribution of risk because they possess superior technical understanding and skill and therefore can make the right decision in all cases.
- The vehicle manufacturer should decide because they believe that liability in law won't ever arise since their vehicle will be safer than a reasonable human driver.
- A respected authority with legislative powers who can set the parameters for the "moral algorithm" in a way that will gain the trust of the public.

Task

 After reading *Example 4* do you think that the "moral algorithm" dilemma is really relevant? Explain your answer.

Example 4 – Is the moral algorithm really relevant?

1. Future autonomous vehicles should prioritise saving their own occupants in a no-win traffic situation, i.e. where someone is likely to die. If you know you can save at least one person, at least save that one, i.e. save the one in the car. The "moral algorithm" should therefore prioritize the safety of occupants of the vehicle over pedestrians.
2. A "moral algorithm" that takes the decision to run over the pedestrian in a no-win traffic situation would be unethical, unacceptable, and also illegal because for all these reasons, it is a decision in favour of one person and thus against another.
3. Neither programmers nor automated systems are entitled to weigh the value of human lives.
4. The "moral algorithm" dilemma situation can be completely avoided by, for example, implementing a risk-avoiding operating strategy in autonomous vehicles.
5. The ethical question of who to save won't be as relevant as people believe, today, because it will occur much less often in the future if autonomous vehicles are commonplace.
6. There are situations that human drivers, today, can't handle or which, from a physical stand point, are also unpreventable with both conventional and autonomous vehicles. However, autonomous vehicles will be far better than the average driver.
7. Autonomous vehicles won't drive into situations where the "moral algorithm" dilemma could happen and will drive away from potential situations where those decisions have to be made at all.
8. Human drivers don't make ethical decisions, they react on instinct and are either lucky or unlucky so why should we expect autonomous vehicles to do any better by employing a "moral algorithm".

Ethical impacts of digital technology

Question

 27 If a manufacturer offers different versions of its "moral algorithm", and a buyer knowingly chooses one of them, is the buyer to blame for the harmful consequences of the algorithm's decisions? Explain your answer.

The general consensus in the industry is that concerns over the so-called "moral algorithm" problem – where a vehicle is unable to avoid a collision and is asked to make a choice over which defined individuals it hits – are exaggerated, with most experts agreeing that autonomous vehicles would never be programmed to make such decisions.

However safety regulations would be needed for other "decisions", such as when it is permissible for an autonomous vehicle to break the rules of the road (see task 11), and how should a vehicle respond when interacting with other road users, e.g. at cross roads where who goes first is resolved by an accepted convention that the vehicle that starts to edge out, signals its driver's intention to go first to the other vehicle's driver.

Information

"The moral algorithm is a term that is good for tabloid newspapers. There is no such thing in the software that will tell the car to hit the 80-year old in order not to hit the group of kids."
Dr Heiko Schilling ("The Moral Algorithm", December 2016)

Questions

 28 A person of good judgement will know when to disregard the letter of the law in order to follow the spirit of the law, e.g. to briefly exceed the speed limit to get out of the way of an emergency vehicle flashing its blue lights. Read *Example 5*. Who do you think should set the confidence level of safety to be programmed into the software:

- Manufacturer
- Software designer
- An independent regulator appointed by Government?

100% confidence level means the car always operates safely
0% confidence level means the car never operates safely

Explain your reasoning.

29 Read the following article
https://www.theguardian.com/science/political-science/2018/apr/13/self-driving-car-companies-should-not-be-allowed-to-investigate-their-own-crashes

Explain why access to black box information from automated vehicles involved in crashes is important.

Example 5 - Following the letter of the law

Road traffic law is broken if a vehicle crosses a double white line in the centre of the road.
Double white lines in the centre of the road are there for a good reason: highway engineers have identified that this section of road is unsafe and for this reason want vehicles to stay on the left hand side of the road at all times.
A self-driving vehicle programmed to follow the letter of the law refuses to cross a double white line to avoid a drunken pedestrian who has stepped into the road, even though the vehicle knows that the other side of the road is empty of traffic.
Rarely will a self-driving vehicle be absolutely certain that crossing a double white line is safe but if the vehicle is reprogrammed to not always follow the letter of the law, then who decides what confidence level of safety to program into the software, e.g. 98%, and how this level must vary depending on what the vehicle is attempting to avoid, whether it is litter swept into its path by a breeze or a fallen pedestrian.

8 Ethical, legal and environmental impacts of digital

> **Task**
>
> 11. UK Autodrive is the largest of three UK consortia launched to support the introduction of self-driving vehicles in the UK. One of the cities chosen by UK Autodrive for their trials of self-driving vehicles was Milton Keynes in Buckinghamshire.
>
> Investigate the design of the road network of Milton Keynes to discover what makes it suitable for the trials of autonomous vehicles?

In summary, the main moral benefit of autonomous vehicles will be enhanced road safety. The degree to which this will be realised is in proportion to the degree to which

- autonomous vehicles dominate the road network
- the inter-connectedness (5G) of autonomous vehicles
- the support provided by the road network infrastructure, i.e. road networks designed to assist autonomous vehicles.

Legal

The **Automated and Electric Vehicles Act 2018** received Royal Assent on 19 July 2018.

The Act uses the term 'automated vehicles' (AVs) when referring to driverless cars.

According to the Bill,

> "a vehicle is 'driving itself' if it is operating in a mode in which it is not being controlled and does not need to be monitored by an individual."

Therefore, the Act applies only to levels 3-5 automated vehicles and excludes the current and near future semi-autonomous vehicles in which the driver is expected to be monitoring the vehicle whilst in AV mode, i.e. vehicles that operate at levels 1 and 2.

The exclusion of current and near future semi-autonomous vehcles from the scope of the Act means that accidents involving these vehicles may have to be resolved by the courts, in cases that may well require complex technical evidence and involve the manufacturer.

Under the Act an **insurer or owner** can be liable for the consequences of an accident caused by the actions of an AV at a time when it is not under the immediate physical control of a human being:

> "Where
>
> (a) an accident is caused by an automated vehicle when driving itself on a road or other public place in Great Britain,
>
> (b) the vehicle is insured at the time of the accident, and
>
> (c) an insured person or any other person suffers damage as a result of the accident, the **insurer is liable for that damage**."

Information

A driverless delivery lorry is being used alongside normal traffic on public roads in Sweden.

The large lorry, called a T-Pod, weighs 26 tonnes fully laden and transports goods between buildings on an industrial estate.

The vehicle is not entirely autonomous, as a remote operator monitors it from a control room while it works.

The lorry is limited to 5km/h while mixing with human-driven traffic and can make trips between only two locations on the industrial estate. Advanced communications systems have been placed along the route the lorry travels, so its remote human operator will never lose contact.

Information

A British driver pleaded guilty to dangerous driving after another driver took video of him sitting in the passenger seat, while his Tesla S 60 drove on its own with Autopilot. Autopilot is classified as level 2 automation.

The incident took place on the M1 near Hemel Hempstead on May 21st, 2017. Hertfordshire Police reported that the car was set to drive at 40mph, and that the driver had left the steering wheel and controls unattended, and that there was heavy traffic on the road at the time of the incident.

The driver was banned from driving for 18 months, fined £1,800, and ordered to carry out 10 days rehabilitation, and 100 hours of community service.

Ethical impacts of digital technology

'Damage' in this context can include death, personal injuries or damage to property, subject to certain specific limitations. This provision cannot be excluded by the terms of insurance policies.

The intention of the Act is for victims of accidents involving AVs to obtain compensation quickly and easily, without prolonging the process with complicated product liability claims against the AV technology manufacturers, or dealing with liability disputes between insurer and manufacturer.

> **Information**
>
> The Automated and Electric Vehicles Act 2018 Act amends the existing compulsory third party insurance framework by extending it to cover the use of automated vehicles.

The insurer remains free to pursue the manufacturer for any reimbursement or contribution if it can be established that the manufacturer is liable for the accident in question. Of course, manufacturers can claim a "state of the art" defence to escape liability by arguing that they could not have known about a particular danger or danger in their product at the time of making or selling it.

Liability may be limited, however, where the accident is caused by

- **modifications to software made by the injured party**, or with their knowledge, that are prohibited under the insurance policy, or
- **failure by the injured party to update safety critical software** when it becomes available. Software is 'safety critical' if it would be unsafe to use the vehicle without the updates being installed.

The criminal liability of Car vs Human

Where does liability reside when a road traffic offence is committed by an autonomous vehicle in which the vehicle is driving itself - levels 3-5. The human user(s) is not the 'driver' and therefore should not be liable for any offences which are committed while the car is in charge. This is the preliminary view of the UK Government which is proposing a manufacturer authorisation scheme for autonomous vehicles.

The Government proposes that manufacturers who gain authorisation for their vehicles would be liable for road traffic offences. These could include improvement notices, fines and where necessary suspension or withdrawal of approval.

Questions

30 Under the Automated and Electric Vehicles Act 2018 Act
  (a) Who can be liable in the first instance for the consequences of an accident caused by the actions of an automated vehicle (levels 3-5) at a time when it is not under the immediate physical control of a human being?
  (b) Who is liable in the case of an accident that is the direct result of a failure to update safety critical software:
   - The insured person who knows, or ought reasonably to know, that the software to be updated is safety-critical?
   - The insurer?
  (c) Who is liable in the case of an accident that is the direct result of software alterations made by the insured person, or with the insured person's knowledge, that were prohibited under the policy:
   - The insured person?
   - The insurer?

31 An insurer believes that the manufacturer of an automated vehicle that crashed in automated mode, injuring the insured "driver" and writing off the vehicle, is at fault because the vehicle hit a road barrier which it should have avoided. What defence might a manufacturer call upon to avoid product liability?

The General Data Protection Regulation (GDPR) 2018

The Internet of Things (IoT) can connect all types of devices to the Internet to share information and thereby augment their capabilities and understanding of their environment. Autonomous vehicles are connected for this very reason: to share information from their on-board sensors, as well as from smart phones of pedestrians and cyclists, traffic sensors, parking detectors, etc.

The GDPR has taken a stronger line on privacy than its predecessor, the Data Protection Act 1998, by tightening control and imposing greater accountability on organisations which collect, store and use personal data. For example, the rules on consent and privacy notices are much tighter.

Autonomous and connected vehicles thus present a problem because large amounts of data will be collected and communicated via V2V and V2X. For example, any journey to or from home in a connected vehicle will enable identification and tracking of individuals and so will involve collection and use of personal data. This data could potentially be used by any of the following:

- The car
- Insurers
- Other vehicles
- Traffic planners
- Infrastructure
- Police and other law enforcement agencies
- Commercial organisations

> **Information**
>
> **Connected vehicle**:
> A vehicle that connects to other vehicles and/or devices, networks and services outside the vehicle including the Internet, other vehicles, home, work office or infrastructure.
>
> **Internet of Things(IoT)**:
> The network of physical objects - vehicles and devices - embedded with electronics, sensors, software, and network connectivity that enables them to collect and exchange data.

In some cases, consent to use the data will be required, e.g. by a commercial organisation which has 'purchased' access to the data and wishes to send marketing to individuals in the vehicle such as "we've noticed that you are approaching a drive-through restaurant, would you like to get a meal as it is lunchtime?". In another case, insurers must obtain consent to profile the vehicle owner's driving in order to determine what to charge the owner for vehicle insurance. Anyone who has visited a website will recognise the all too common message:

> " We use cookies and similar methods to recognize /*Profiling* visitors and remember their preferences. We also use them to measure ad campaign effectiveness, *target ads* and analyze site traffic. To learn more about these methods, including how to disable them, view our Cookie Policy. By clicking 'accept,' you consent to the processing of your data by us and third parties using the above methods. You can always change your tracker preferences by visiting our Cookie Policy."

Imagine, if everytime the driver took a trip in their autonomous and connected vehicle, they had to spend the first ten minutes ticking or unticking consent boxes. This introduces the likelihood that regulators will have to legally mandate personal data sharing to reduce the inconvenience of consent-giving. But how much data should be shared?

GDPR requires that the organisation obtaining this consent also records this in order to prove that it has been given.

GDPR also states that any data collected must be used strictly for purposes which have been notified and consented to.

Autonomous car maunfacturers will be particularly exposed to GDPR because they will collect and process a lot of data to enable monitoring of the vehicles that they sell so that they can better understand how the vehicles perform.

Questions

32 Why does the General Data Protection Regulation 2018 present a problem for the operation of autonomous and connected vehicles on roads in the UK.

Cyber security of autonomous vehicles

Cyber attacks on connected, autonomous vehicles have the potential to threaten the safety and privacy of all road users. As the number of connections of these vehicles with the external environment and third parties increases so will the risks of cyber attacks. *Example 6* shows what was possible in 2016.

> **Example 6 - Potential for a cyber attack on an automotive system**
>
> In 2016, Hyundai had to update its Blue Link smartphone app to stop it releasing private data that could be used, potentially, to break into and steal people's cars. The smartphone app uses the Blue Link bluetooth connection to unlock the car and enable ignition. The vulnerable version of the smartphone app, in a separate process, used HTTP to transmit personal information such as username, password, PIN, GPS location records, encrypted with a fixed symmetric key, back to Hyundai. However, this encryption/decryption key could be extracted by a hacker from the smartphone app's code and used to decrypt the data, transmitted between smartphone app instance and Hyundai, to obtain the necessary information to break into the car. To get a copy of the data in the first place, a hacker eavesdrops on the app's network connections. Luckily, Hyundai became aware of the problem and fixed it before any cars could be stolen.

The modern car in 2020 has about 100 million lines of code (the Android operating system has 12 million). Unlike the code in a modern aircraft which has been designed from the top-down to a mathematically rigorous specification, and quality assured by proof that the code has the properties it ought to have, the code in the modern car has evolved in a bottom-up way as more and more features became available - see *Example 7*. Much of the code in the modern car is legacy code (code that is no longer supported) and some comes from open source libraries on the Internet. Connecting this code to a network increases the chances of a hacker finding an access point into a section of the code designed at a time when cyber security was not a threat.

> **Example 7 - Another potential for a cyber attack on an automotive system**
>
> Professor Phil Blythe, Professor of Intelligent Transport Systems, Newcastle University and Chief Scientific Adviser for the Department of Transport has stated
>
> *"We don't know every line of code that goes into each vehicle or why it's there."*

Questions

33 State **two** kinds of cyber security threat that autonomous and connected vehicles could be exposed to on UK roads?

34 Why should the owner of an autonomous and connected vehicle keep the vehicle's software up to date?

35 With the exception of new car manufacturers such as Tesla which have designed their autonomous and connected cars from the ground up, modern cars have evolved over time with software and hardware being bolted on to enable new features. Explain why the latter's approach to developing autonomous and connected cars might not be the most cyber attack resilient.

36 Give **two** reasons why a cyber attack on a modern passenger jet is less likely to succeed than a cyber attack on an autonomous and connected car?

Ethical impacts of digital technology

Environmental impact of autonomous vehicles

Autonomous vehicles have the potential for both positive and negative impacts on the environment. Significant effects either way depend upon whether autonomous vehicles become commonplace, and the greenness of the energy they consume. Even electric cars and hydrogen cars need recharging which consumes electrical energy directly or indirectly, respectively. The hydrogen that fills the "tanks" of hydrogen-powered cars is made before it goes into the car by splitting water, a process that consumes electrical energy.

Positive impact on the environment

Autonomous vehicles are able to drive closer to each other because their reaction times are faster than human drivers. This should raise the road capacity which means less congestion. Less congestion means shorter journey times and therefore lower energy consumption.

Vehicle-to-vehicle communication, vehicle-to-Cloud and vehicle-to-infrastructure enables
- braking and acceleration to be done in a smoother and more energy efficient manner
- an energy-optimal speed to be chosen for each section of a journey
- the most energy-saving route chosen in real time for the journey from A to B.

For example, traffic lights could be better coordinated at junctions to promote steadier flows of vehicles. These traffic lights which are part of the road infrastructure would need to be connected into the communication network shared with autonomous vehicles.

The accident statistics from public road trials conducted to date have demonstrated that autonomous vehicles are safer than human drivers. Manufacturers may decide when autonomous vehicles dominate the highways and are considerably safer than non-autonomous vehicles that they can dispense with many of the safety features currently needed in non-autonomous vehicles, e.g side-impact bars. If this is done then the weight of a vehicle can be reduced leading to a saving in the energy required to move the vehicle.

Negative impact on the environment

Autonomous vehicles should make travelling a lot easier and more convenient if the vehicle drives itself: "Let the car take the strain"!

However, this is likely to increase the number of miles travelled as car owners decide to make trips that they wouldn't have done otherwise. It might also encourage people to live further from work resulting in longer car journeys. Autonomous vehicles would enable people who are unable to drive for whatever reason to take to the road increasing the number of vehicles on the road or the number of journeys made. In areas such as city centres where unoccupied parking spaces are difficult to find and/or expensive, an owner of an autonomous vehicle might find that it is more convenient and cheaper to let the vehicle drive itself around and around instead of parking it. The net effect would then be that energy consumption might go up because more journeys are being taken overall. These journeys might also not be energy-efficient because the roads might become even more congested than they are currently.

Questions

37 State **two** reasons why autonomous vehicles could have a positive impact on the environment.

38 State **two** reasons why autonomous vehicles could have a negative effect on the environment.

In this chapter you have covered:
- The current ethical, legal and environmental impacts and risks of digital technology on society. Where data privacy issues arise these are considered.

Index

Symbols

! 76
[ ] 81
[] 101, 104
{ 57
} 57
& 76
&& 76
• 212
← 93, 127
↦ 92, 126, 365
'+' operator 110
< 74, 333
<= 74, 333
<> 74, 333
!= 63
= 74
== 74
> 74, 333
>= 74, 333
| 76
|| 76
≤ 74
≥ 74
⊕ 212
0x 160
32-bit IEEE 754 floating point 44
64-bit IEEE 754 floating point 44
\n 95
.NET Framework 111
symbol 160

A

abstraction 8, 11
access point 272
access rights 296
accumulator 220
active sensors 355
active verbs 51
actual parameter 51, 54, 127, 141
actuators 221, 346, 350
adaptive cruise control 351
addition 70
addresses 82
admin 295
administrator's account 295
admin rights 314
ADS 352
advantages of using subroutines 125
Adware 316
AIFF 190

algorithm 1, 2, 6, 13, 15, 16, 18, 19, 83, 88, 121, 142, 347, 350
algorithm for binary search 24
algorithm for linear search 22
ALU 247
Amazon Elastic Compute Cloud 282
Anaconda 83
analogue 187
analogue signal 188, 189
AND 76, 214, 238
AND logic gate 205
Angry Birds 342
ANSI 101
AnsiChar 41
antilock brake system 221
antivirus 307
anti-virus software 312
API 287
appending to a text file 98
application layer 286, 287
Application Programming Interface (API) 287
application programs 215
application software 215
AQA pseudo-code 149
archiving data 253
argument 55
Arithmetic and Logic Unit 228, 238
arithmetic expression 70
Arithmetic expression 70
Arithmetic operations 70
arithmetic operators 70
ARM Cortex 220
array 80, 81, 88, 131
array data structure 79
array index 81, 82
artificial intelligence 350
Asc function 111
ASC 332
ascending 332
ASCII 39, 94, 101, 111, 176, 177, 194
ASCII character set 176
ASCII code 92
assemble 226
assembler 221, 224
assembly language 219, 220, 222, 223
assembly language code 223
assembly language instruction 221
assembly language program 220
assignment operation 6
assignment operator 6 , 45
assignment statement 46, 57, 45

attribute 324
audio 189
audio file 190
audio processing 247
authentication 149, 283, 284, 317
authentication routine 150
authorisation 150, 283
Automated and Electric Vehicles Act 2018 359, 360
Automated Driving System (ADS) 352
automated vehicles 350, 359
automatic 322
automatic software updates 322
autonomous vehicles 350
Autopilot 359
autopilot software 350
AutoRun 297
Average search length 22
AV mode 359

B

B abbreviation for byte 165
backing store 229
backing up data 253
backup management 260
banking security device token 283
base 2 157, 160
base 10 157
base 10 system 157
base 16 158
bespoke software 216
Big Data 339
binary 157, 161, 162, 163
binary arithmetic 169
binary codes 219
binary data 254
binary numeral system 169
binary search 23, 24
binary shifts 173
binary to hexadecimal conversion 163
binding 128
biometric 339
biometric authentication 283, 317
biometric measures 317
BIOS 242
bit 165
Bit 38, 165
bit depth of bitmapped image 183
bitmap 182, 183, 184, 185, 247
bitmap image 182, 184, 186
bitmap image file size 184
Bitmap size 182
Bit pattern 38, 159, 220
Bits 254
black-box approach 300
black-box penetration testing 300
blagging 304

block 142
block-oriented storage device 253
Bluetooth 344
Bluetooth wireless interface 344
Blu-ray disc 254
Blu-ray optical disks 258
body of a procedure 142
body of a subroutine , 51
bool 41
Boolean 41
Boolean data type 40, 41
Boolean expressions 74, 76
Boolean flags 138
Boolean logic 201, 238
Boolean operands 76
Boolean operations 76
Boolean operators 76
boundary or extreme test data 152
boundary test data 153
branch (or jump) 4
bubble sort 16, 17, 31, 36
Bubble sort algorithm 28
bulk acquisition 342
bulk interception 342
bus 228, 237, 243
bus clock 240
bus network topology 268
Bus width 237, 238, 240
byte 101, 165
Byte quantities 166, 168

C

C# 56, 70, 76, 83, 89, 102, 106, 111, 112, 114, 116, 118, 127
cache 245
cache controller 245
cache memory 244
call by address 126
call by reference 126
call by Reference/Call by Address 127
call by value 126, 127
calling a procedure 52
calling statement 130
call a subroutine 51
CAPTCHA 319, 320
carriage return 94, 177
carrier of information 165
CATCH 147
CD-R 254
CD-ROM 254, 297
CD-RW 254
cell 79, 82
Central Processing Unit (CPU) 228, 232
C# function 131
char 41
character 92, 101, 178

character → character code 108
character code → character 111
character code form 179
character codes 177
character encoding 176
Char data type 110
CHAR_TO_CODE 110
chipset 237, 243
Chr 111
citizens 342
citizenship 341
clock frequency 242
clock multiplier 242
clock rate 248
clock speeds 247
Cloud 339
cloud storage 259, 260, 261
coaxial cable 268
CODE_TO_CHAR 111
coding tree 194
cohesion 135
cohesive 135
colour depth 183, 185
column 88, 324
combining principles 50, 69
command and control server 315
Comment 3, 67
common fields 324
communication interfaces 346
Compact Disc (CD) 252
comparing linear and binary search algorithms 26
comparison operators 333
compiled code 222
compiler 105, 222, 224
compiling 224
compilation and interpretation differences 225
component of the system 135
components 136, 143
composite data type 131
composite primary key 325
composition 131
compound sentence 136
compressed text 192
compressing text 194
compression 192
computer based implants 346
computer hardware 159
Computer Misuse Act 309, 312
computer network 263
computer program 159
computer virus 159
computer worm 310
concatenation 110
condition 60
conditional automation 353
condition-controlled 59

Conflicker worm 297
connected vehicle 361
connector 3
consent 339
console application 105
Console.WriteLine 105
Const 45
constant 44
constant declaration 44
construct 142
constructing a Huffman tree 197
contiguous 198
control 3
control character codes 94
control characters 94
control codes 177
control flow 125
control structure 142
control unit 228, 247
conversion error 153
cookie Policy 361
copper cable 268
copyright of algorithms 347
count-controlled 59
coupling 137, 140
CPU 228, 235, 242, 251
CPU clock frequency 242, 244
CPU performance 242
cracking 348
crow's foot 325
Current Instruction Register 239
cyber attack 362
cyber security 291
cyber security of autonomous vehicles 362
cyber warfare attack 300

D
DAT 189
data 39, 79, 92
database 323
data bus 242
data centre 348
data compression 192
Data Controller 339
datagrams 274, 288
data interface 138, 140, 141
Data Processor 339
Data Protection Act 1998 296, 361
data security 282
data structure 79, 80, 93
data subject 339
data type 38, 39, 40, 92
data type casting 111
data type interpretations 42
data types in some programming languages 41
data validation 145

datum 39, 93, 126, 166
DB Browser 335
DDoS 292
DDR 243
DDT 352
DDT fallback 352
debug 125, 137, 143, 223, 226
debugging 159
decimal 157
decimal to binary conversion 161
decimal to hexadecimal conversion 162
decision 3
decision flowchart element 4
decode phase 250
decomposition 7
def 54
default password 295
definite iteration , 59
DELETE 334
Deleting data 334
Delphi 70, 76, 83, 89, 112, 114, 115, 127
DESC 332
descending order 332
design 135
destination hardware address 289
deterministic algorithms 350
device drivers 221
Digital Audio Tapes 189
digital computer 230
digitally controllable lighting 350
digital signal 254
Digital Versatile Disc (DVD) 252
digitised image 181
digit key 92
direct access to registers 223
disciplined approach 142
disk block 252, 253
disk buffer , 76, 38, 44, 39, 40, 102, 178
disposal 349
Distributed denial-of-service 292
divide and conquer 33, 135
divide and conquer algorithm 33
division 70
DNS 292
DNS server 292
document virus 311
domain 292
Domain Name Service 292
Dotted decimal notation 276
double 41, 45
Do While 63
do while loop 65
download 349
DRAM 245, 255
driver assistance 353
Dropbox 261

duplicated data 323
duplication 328, 329
DVD+RW 254
DVD-R 254
DVD-RAM 254
DVD-ROM 254
DVD-RW 254
dynamic array 83
Dynamic Driving Task (DDT) 351
dynamic linked libraries 310

E
eavesdropping 269
edge cases 350
EDSAC 159, 219, 229
EDVAC 229
Edward Snowden 342
EEPROM 255
efficiency of algorithms 16
electrical signal 187
element 81, 87
email confirmation 321
email virus 312
embedded computer systems 222
embedded flash 255
embedded operating system 262
embedded system 221, 261, 262
Embedded system 261
encryption 150, 284
End Module 53
End Sub 53, 138
end-system 277
end-to-end encryption 343
end-to-end principle 275
engine management system 221
ENIAC computer 229
entity 324
entity relationship diagram 325
entry point 142
environmental benefits 349
environmental impact 348, 363
environmental information 166
equal to 74, 75
E-R diagram 325, 327
erroneous test data 153
error 137, 147
Ethernet 271, 289
Ethernet bus protocol 271
ethical concerns 344
ethical dilemma 357
ethical dimension of data processing 338
exception handling 146, 147
exceptions 95
executable binary codes 159, 220
Execute phase 250
execution times 18

existence check 147
exit point 142
expiry date 321
exponent 166
expressions 74
external hardware devices 70, 74, 76, 79, 92, 101, 121, 124, 135
extraction 82

F
facial features 317
facial recognition 317
factual information 166
False 76
Fetch-Execute cycle 250
Fetch phase 250
field 92, 324
field name 324
Fifth Generation (5G) 356
file 93
file access error 147
file handle 95, 97, 98
file handle variable 95
file mode 98
filename 93
file structure 95
File Transfer Protocol 279
fingerprint pattern 317
firewall 285
fixed-size coding scheme 193
flash-based solid state drives 255
flash memory 255, 261
flash ROM 236
flat file database 328
float 41, 44
floating point data type 40
floating point quotient 70
FloatToStr 117
float to string 116
flowchart 3, 119
flow of control 142
foreign key 325, 329
foreign key mechanism 325
for loop 59, 61, 67, 88
formal parameter 55, 126, 54, 126, 141
formal parameter of a subroutine 51
Fortran 222
Fourth Generation (4G) 356
frames 271
frequency/data pair 198
FROM 330
FTP 279
FTP client 279
FTP server 279
full automation 353
fully-automated vehicle 351

function 52, 54, 55, 125, 130, 131, 138, 141, 143
functional cohesion 136, 137
functional description 136
function call 82
function return 143
functions of an operating system 217

G
G abbreviation of Giga 166
gateway 344
GB abbreviation of Gigabyte 167
GDPR 296, 339, 361
General Data Protection Regulation 2018 339, 361
generalisation problem 350
general purpose application software 215
general purpose computer 221, 262
genetic data 339
geolocation 341
GET 288
GET / 278
Gi abbreviation of Gibi 168
GiB abbreviation of Gibibyte 160
gibi 168
GigaHertz 244
global variables 138, 143
good design 135
Google data centre 259
Google Drive 261
Google glass 345
Go To 142
gotoless programming 142
GPS 355
GPU 262
graphics controllers 243
graphics processor 262
grayscale bitmap 198
greater than 74, 75
greater than or equal to 74, 75

H
hacker 261, 291, 296
hacking 348
hand trace, hand-trace 48, 88
hand tracing, hand-tracing 15, 48
hard-coded 150
hardware 220
Hertz 189
hexadecimal 158, 159, 160, 164
hexadecimal as shorthand for binary 159
hexadecimal to binary conversion 162
Hierarchy chart 140, 141
high automation 353
high definition maps 355
higher coupling 138
high-level imperative programming languages 69
high-level language 219
High-level programming language 222

highly-cohesive 136
HLL programming 222, 223
host 276, 286
host computer 286
hostID 276
house-keeping 136
HTML 278
HTTP 278
HTTP application-layer protocol 287
HTTP GET 278
HTTP GET / 278
HTTP GET / request 278
HTTPS 278, 284
HTTPS application-layer protocol 287
Huffman code 195, 196
Huffman coding 193, 194
Huffman coding tree 194, 197
Huffman tree 195
hyperscale computing 338
Hypertext Markup Language 278

I

Identification 150, 283
identification check 150
identifier , 67
identity theft 301
If statement 49
image processing 247
image size 182
Image size 182
immutable 105
IN 127, 129, 141
inconsistencies in data 328
indefinite iteration 59, 62
Indentation 143
index 83, 104, 108
index range 110
infinite loop 62
Infinite loop 62
information 39, 165, 339
information = data + meaning 166
information types 166
infrared light waves 355
initialiser , 60
initialising variables 44
in line 125
inline 223
in line flow of control 124
in-memory sorting algorithm 36
inner for loop 66
IN-OUT 141
INOUT 127, 129, 130
IN-OUT parameter 141
INOUT parameter 126
IN parameter 126, 141
input 1, 3, 13

Inserting data 334
INSERT INTO 334
instructional information 166
instruction cycle 250
instruction set 220, 223
int 56
integer 41, 58
Integer data type 39
integer division 70, 71
integer division and integer remainder operators 72
integer division operator 71
integer quotient 70
integer remainder operators 72
integer to string 116
integrity checks 145
interface 129
internal buses 247
internal design of the components 143
internal structure of a processor/central processing unit 239
internet 266
Internet 266, 277
Internet connection records 342
Internet Message Access Protocol 280
Internet of Things (IoT) 221, 295, 339, 345, 361
Internet or IP (Internet Protocol) layer 286, 288
Internet Protocol 275
internetworked 266
interpreter 224
interpreter vs compiler 225, 226
INT_TO_STRING 116
invalid input 154
Investigatory Powers Act 2000 342
Investigatory Powers Act 2016 342
I/O controller 226, 232
IoT 295, 339, 346
IP address 276, 292
IP layer 288
IPv4 276
IPython 84
iris pattern 317
ISP 285
iterating 86, 88
iteration 46, 142
iteration statements 46
iterator 60

J

Java , 70, 76, 83, 89, 104, 106, 111, 114, 116, 57

K

k abbreviation for kilo 166
kB abbreviation for kilobyte 167
keyboard 92
keylogger 315
keyword 53
Ki abbreviation for kibi 168

KiB abbreviation for kibibyte 245
kibi 168
Kibibyte 245
kibi Ki 168
kilo k 168

L

L1 cache 245
L2 cache 245
L3 cache 246
LAN 265, 289
lane-keeping/lane-following assistance 351
language-defined subroutine 124
language keyword 44, 54
layered organisation 286
layers of software 215
least privilege principle 296
LEN 82, 88, 105
length checks 146
Length function 105
length of a string 105
Less Than 74
Less Than Or Equal To 74
Level 0 351, 353
Level 1 351, 353
Level 2 352, 353
Level 3 352, 353
Level 4 352, 353
Level 5 352, 353
Levels 3-5 automated vehicles 359
library of subroutines 125
lidar 355
lifetime 132l
linear search 21
line feed 177
line feed character 95
link layer , 289
link tables 327
list 83, 131
Local Area Network 265
local storage 261
local variable 132, 133, 135, 143
location 82, 126
lock frequency 243
logical shift left operation 172
logic circuit diagrams 207
logic errror 155
logic gate 201, 203
logic gate circuit 206
Logogram-based language 178
loop 46
loop body 46
loop control variable 61, 81, 86, 60, 105
loop flowchart 4
loop terminating condition 59
loose coupling 138

loosely coupled 135, 137, 143
loss of data 260
loss of privacy 260
low coupling 140
low-level language 219
low-level programming language 219

M

M abbreviation for mega 166
MAC address 277, 285, 289
MAC address filtering 285
machine code 219, 222, 223
machine code instruction 159, 220, 250
machine code language instruction 221
machine code language program 220
machine code program 250
machine dependent 223
machine instruction 159
machine learning 247
machine-learning algorithms 350
macro 311, 312
macro virus 312
magnetic core memory 233
magnetic disk 252
magnetic disk drives 257
Magnetic disks 258
magnetic hard disk drive (HDD) 252
magnetic storage 252, 258
magnetic tape 252, 253
Main() 53
main memory 228, 230, 232, 235, 251
malicious attachments 306
malicious code 292, 309, 310
malware 309, 310
malware vector 314
many-to-many 325
many-to-one 325
matplotlib 84
matrix 87
maximum search length 26
MB abbreviation for megabyte 167
meaningful identifier name 67, 68
meaningful identifiers 143
meaning of value 40
Mebibyte 245
mebi Mi 168
mega M 168
memory addresses 230
Memory Buffer Register 239
memory bus 243
memory cell 233
memory controller 243
memory footprint 222
memory location 160, 233
memory location 234
memory map 126

merge sort 16, 17, 35
merge sort algorithm 33, 34
messages 287
metadata 190
Mi abbreviation for mebi 168
MiB abbreviation for mebibytes 245
microchips 346
Microsoft's Azure IoT hub 344
misconfigured access rights 296
mnemonic 220
model 8
modelling data by variables 44
modelling relationships 324
modularisation 133
module 53, 135, 136, 137, 138, 140
moral algorithm 356, 357, 358
motherboard 240, 240
multi-level caches 245
multiple access medium 272
multiple-core CPU 248
multiple-cores 247
multiplication 70

N

NAND flash memory 257
nested for loop 66
nested iteration statements 66
nested selection statements 65
NetID 276
network adapter 271, 272
networking protocols , 286, 287
Network Interface Card (NIC) 271, 272, 289
Network or IP layer 288
network protocol 271
network security 282, 284
newline 95
newline character 94, 97
non-embedded system 262
non-redundant duplication 329
non-text files 94
non-volatile 93, 251, 255
non-volatile memory 236, 261
non-volatile storage 256
normal or typical test data 152
normal test data 153
NOT 76, 214
not equal to 74, 75
NOT logic gate 203, 204
number base 157
Numeric Python 83
numpy 83, 84

O

object code 224
OEM 101
offset 101, 102, 104, 107, 108
off-site backups 282

one-based string indexing 104
one-dimensional array 80, 82, 83, 86
OneDrive 261
one-to-many 325
one-to-one 325
ONE-to-ONE mapping 221
open source software 347
operand 76, 140
operating system 92, 262
operating system routines 223
Operating system software 216
operation 3, 140
Operational Design Domain (ODD) 352
operation code mnemonic 221
operator precedence 77
optical disc 254
optical storage 258
OR 76, 214, 238
Ord 110, 111
ordering a result set 332
ORDER BY 332
ordinal data type 60
ordinal number 104
OR gate 205
OR logic gate 205
oscillator 240
OUT 130, 130, 141
outdated code 298
outer for loop 66
out of date software 298
out of line 125
out of line block of code 124
out of line flow of control 124
OUT parameter 141
output 1, 13
OUTPUT 5, 93

P

packets 277
packet sniffing 269
packet switching 277
PAN 264, 265
Pan Area Network 265
parameter list 140
parameters 11
partial automation 353
Pascal 53, 70, 76, 83, 89, 112, 114, 115, 125, 127
Pascal/Delphi 116, 117
passive 355
passive sensors 355
password 294, 318
password check 150
password managers 318
password systems 318
patch 298
patches 322

patent 347
penetration test 299
penetration tester 299
penetration testing 299
pentester 299, 300
peripheral 232, 262
peripheral devices 232
Personal Area Network 264
personal data 338, 339
pharming 308
phishing 305
phishing attack 306
phishing email 305
phishing scams 307
physical bus network 268
physical phenomenon 166
picture element 181
pixel 159, 181, 184
platter 252
Position 110
POSITION 110
PowerShell 303
powers of 2 167
powers of 10 166
practical obscurity 339
predicate 331
presence check 146
pretexting 304
primary colour 183
primary key 325
primary storage 251
principles of structured programming 142
Prism 342
privacy 342, 344, 348
privacy notices 339
private 44
PRNG 121
procedure 52, 124, 125, 130, 138, 141, 53
procedure interface 54
procedure name 52
procedure name 54
procedures and functions 52
process 13, 286, 287, 309
process abstraction 10, 11
processing 13
processor 220, 226, 232, 243, 251
processor cores 247
processor family 223
profiling 339, 361
program 53
program block 124, 125, 143
program code 1
program crash 147
program source code 143
program statement 127
program structure 141

proofs of correctness 350
proprietary software 347
protocol software 286
protocol stack 286
pseudo 3, 6
pseudo-code 9, 13, 46, 47, 48, 49, 66, 67, 68, 73, 74, 81, 86, 87, 88, 91, 92, 93, 110, 111, 112, 114, 116, 119, 134, 146, 153, 155
pseudorandom number generator 121
pseudorandom numbers 121
public 44
public key cryptography 284
public Wi-Fi hotspots 343
punched paper tape 229
punch paper tape 220
pure binary representation 179
PyCharm 17
Python 43, 54, 70, 76, 83, 89, 94, 97, 112, 114, 116, 117, 127
Python object 128

Q

query 331
querying a database 330
quotient 73

R

radar 355
Radio frequency identification (RFID) 345, 346
RAM 38, 43, 93, 236, 232, 232
Random Access Memory 236
RANDOM_INT 123
randomizing the seed 121
random number generation 121
random numbers 121
random.seed 121
random sequence 121
range 61
range check 146
ransomware 292
Raptor 10
Raptor flowchart 12
readability 143
reading from a text file 94
read-write head 252
real/float and integer division 71
real number or float division 70
REAL_TO_STRING 116
record 91
record data structure 79
record type 93
reduction in use of paper 349
redundancy 192
redundant duplication 329
register 160, 238, 247

relation 326, 330
relational database 323, 324, 327
relational operators 74
relationship 324, 325
reliability 151
remainder 72, 73, 161
removable media 297
repeat loop 62, 63
repeat until 59
repetition 46
representational abstraction 8
request message 278
resolution 182
response message 278
Result 130
result set 331
retention notice 342
retina pattern 317
retina scanner 317
retrieving data from a single table 330
return expression 130
returning a result 130
RETURN mechanism 127
return statement 135
return type 56, 58
RFID tags 346
RIOT 341
risks of networking 264
RLE 198
program source code 143
role of a compiler 224
role of an assembler 224
role of an interpreter 225
ROM 236
router 277, 288
routine 10, 150
row 88, 324
Run Length Encoding (RLE) 198
RunningTotal 48

S

safety-critical system 36
sample 188
sample resolution 190
sampling rate 189
search condition 331
search length 22
secondary storage 93, 229, 251
secondary storage devices 101
sector 253
sector address 253
Secure Sockets Layer (SSL) 278
security 282, 344
SELECT 330, 332
SELECT * FROM 336
selection 50, 49

selection statement 65, 124
self-contained 133
self-contained block of instructions 50
self-describing identifiers 68
self-driving Uber car 351
semi-autonomous vehicles 359
sensors 221, 344, 345, 350
sequence 38, 49
sequence of instructions 51
sequence statements 49
SET 335
shifting bits 172
shift left 172
shift operation 172
shift right 172
shouldering 304
shoulder surfing 304
side-effect 127
simple calculator 140
Simple Mail Transfer Protocol 280
single character value 110
Slammer worm 298
slice 109
Small-Scale Experimental Machine 229
smart lighting 350
smart systems 350
social engineering 301, 303
social engineering threats 291
society of citizens 341
socket API 287
software 200, 200
software architecture 140, 143
software artefact 135
software classification 215
software modules 141
software patch 298
software system 136
software updates 298
solid state 258
Solid-state disk (SSD) 252, 256, 257
solid state storage 255
sorting 28
sorting algorithms 17, 28
sound 187, 189
sound file 159
sound file size 190
source code 224
source hardware address 289
spam 292
spambot 321
special control character 94, 97
special purpose applications software 216
spoofer 285
Spyder 83
spyware 315, 316
SQL 330

SQLite 335
SQL Tutorials 335
SRAM 245, 255
SSD 258
SSD drive 257
SSD storage 257
SSD vs other flash-based devices 258
SSL 278
star network topology 268
static 44, 56
static RAM 238
stealing credentials 305
stepwise refinement 143
stereo camera 355
StingRay equipment 341
storage location 220
storage service 259
stored program computer 229
stored program digital computer 159
storing 82
str 41
string 39, 41, 101, 105, 112, 114
string conversion error 154
string conversion operations 112
string-handling operations 101
string indexing 101, 105
string operations 101
string to float 114
STRING_TO_INT 112
string to integer 112
string value 101
string value 105
STRING_TO_REAL 114
strip() 95
strongly typed 43
strongly typed language 55
strong password 296
StrToFloat 115
struct 91
structure 91, 93
structured data type 131
structured design 135, 140, 142, 143
structured programming 135, 142, 143
Structured Query Language 330
structured result 55
STUXNET malware 292, 310, 311
Sub 53, 138
subroutine 10, 50, 51, 52, 119, 125, 127, 132, 134, 135, 137, 138, 143, 147
SUBROUTINE 126
subroutine call 127
subroutine interface 129, 135
subroutine name 51
subroutine parameter 126, 127, 129, 138, 143
subroutines 11, 124, 130, 135, 140
subset 108

substring 108
SUBSTRING 108
subtraction 70
successive division 162
surface address 253
symbolic name 44, 220
symbolic name for constant 44
syntax error 155
system bus 234
system bus 228, 237
system clock 240
system clock frequency 243
system programs 215
system software 215

T

T abbreviation for tera 166
tab 94
table 324
target ads 361
TB abbreviation for terabyte 167
TCP 273, 288
TCP/IP 290
TCP/IP model 286
TCP/IP protocol stack , 287
TCP/IP protocol suite 286
TCP/IP socket 288
TCP/IP stack 288
TCP segments 273, 288
TCP socket 279
tebi 168
Tempora 342
temporary session key 343
terminal 3
terminating condition , 46
Tesla Autopilot Model S 354
test case 152, 154, 155
test data 152
testing 151
test plan 152, 153, 155
test results 152
text 92, 93, 177
text editor 94
text file 94, 95, 177
theft of computer code 348
Ti abbreviation of tebi 168
time efficiency 19
time efficiency of an algorithm 19
timing 240
timing signals 240
top-down design 7
topology 268, 270
trace table 66, 83, 88
trace table 73
track 253
track address 253

tracking cookies 315
translator 222
Transmission Control Protocol (TCP) 273, 287
transport layer 287, 288
trap 147, 153, 154
trojan 313
trojan horse 292
trojan program 313
True 76
truth table 202, 203, 204, 205, 206
try catch 95
TRY CATCH ENDTRY 146, 147
TryParse 112
two-dimensional array 87, 88, 89
two-dimensional integer array 89
two-factor authentication 296, 317
two symbol code 38
type check 146
type of result returned 131

U

UDP (User Datagram Protocol) 274
ultrasonic waves 355
unauthorised access 282
unauthorized access 301
uncompressed text 192
unicode 41
Unicode 101, 111, 178
Unicode character 106
Unicode code point 178
uniform addressing scheme 277
United Kingdom Intellectual Property Office 347
unit of information 165
units of storage 166
unpatched 298, 322
UPDATE 335
updating data 335
USB flash drive 297
User Data Protocol (UDP) 287
USERINPUT 92
using local variables 133
UTF-8 94, 178
UTF-16 101, 178
utility programs 216

V

validate 145
validation 145
validation code 147
VALUES 334
variable 6, 43, 101, 130
variable declaration 43, 44
variable-size coding scheme 193
VBA 311
VB.Net 53
VB.NET 63, 70, 76, 89, 102, 106, 112, 114, 116, 117, 125, 127

VDU 177
vehicle-to-cloud 356
Vehicle-to-Everything (V2X) 355
vehicle-to-infrastructure 363
vehicle-to-IoT 356
vehicle-to-network 356
Vehicle-to-Vehicle (V2V) 355, 356
vein pattern 317
vein recognition 317
verification 321
video processing 247
virtualisation 259
virtual machine 224
virus 311
visibility 132, 56, 58
Visual Basic for Applications 311
Visual C# 2015 103
Visual Display Unit (VDU) 92, 182
Visual Studio 56
Visual Studio 2015 56
voice pattern 317
voice recognition 317
void 56
volatile 93, 251
volatile memory 236
volatile RAM 261, 262
von Neumann 231, 234
von Neumann architecture 228, 230

W

WAN 266
WAV 190
WAV audio file 190
waveform 187
weak passwords 293
wearables 344, 345
wearable technologies 344
WhatsApp 343
WHERE 331, 332
while 59
WHILE 10
while loop 62, 63, 83, 98
While loop 83
white-box penetration testing 300
whitespace 94, 95, 112, 114
whole number 163
Wide Area Network 266
Wi-Fi 272
Wi-Fi hotspots 343
Wi-Fi Protected Access 284
Wi-Fi Protected Access II 284
wildcard character * 330
Windows Registry 297
wired LAN 272
wired networks 267
wireless broadband networks 343
wireless LAN 272
wireless networks 267, 295
Wireless Personal Network 344
WLAN 272
working from home 349

Worm 297
worst-case complexity 36
WPA 284
WPA2 284
WPAN 344
write mode 97
writing to a text file 95

X

XOR 214, 238
XOR logic gate 205, 212

Y

Z

ZEROBASEDSTRINGS 104